Teach®
Yourself

Complete Writing for Children Course

Clémentine Beauvais

First published in Great Britain in 2014 by John Murray Learning. An Hachette UK company.

First published in US in 2014 by The McGraw-Hill Companies, Inc.

This edition published in 2014 by John Murray Learning

British Library Cataloguing in Publication Data: a catalogue record for this title is available from the British Library.

Library of Congress Catalog Card Number: on file.

Print ISBN 9781471804403

eBook ISBN 9781471804427

10 9 8 7 6 5 4 3 2 1

The publisher has used its best endeavours to ensure that any website addresses referred to in this book are correct and active at the time of going to press. However, the publisher and the author have no responsibility for the websites and can make no guarantee that a site will remain live or that the content will remain relevant, decent or appropriate.

The publisher has made every effort to mark as such all words which it believes to be trademarks. The publisher should also like to make it clear that the presence of a word in the book, whether marked or unmarked, in no way affects its legal status as a trademark.

Every reasonable effort has been made by the publisher to trace the copyright holders of material in this book. Any errors or omissions should be notified in writing to the publisher, who will endeavour to rectify the situation for any reprints and future editions.

Typeset by Cenveo® Publisher Services.

Printed and bound in Great Britain by CPI Group (UK) Ltd., Croydon, CR0 4YY.

John Murray Learning policy is to use papers that are natural, renewable and recyclable products and made from wood grown in sustainable forests. The logging and manufacturing processes are expected to conform to the environmental regulations of the country of origin.

John Murray Learning

338 Euston Road

London NW1 3BH

www.hodder.co.uk

Also available in ebook

Contents

About the author

Clémentine Beauvais is the author of 13 children's books in French and English, from picturebooks to Young Adult fiction. She also holds a PhD in Children's Literature from the University of Cambridge, where she is currently a junior research fellow, working on the sociology and philosophy of childhood. Her latest children's book in English is The Royal Babysitters *(Bloomsbury). Clémentine is an avid reader and critic of children's literature in French and English. She blogs about children's literature and academia on http://www.clementinebeauvais.com/eng and is on Twitter @ blueclementine. She frequently does school visits, writing workshops and book fairs both in the UK and in France. Clémentine also enjoys drawing, reading literature 'for adults', travelling, listening to podcasts and, like a good French person, all the strongest cheeses.*

Acknowledgements

I am extremely grateful to Lauren Davis, who has, by amusing twists of professional fate, accompanied me ever since I started writing children's books in English. This book is very much hers, and full of our conversations. Thank you, too, to Robert Anderson and to my agent, Kirsty McLachlan, for all their help and work on this volume.

The author and publisher would also like to express their thanks for generous permission to reprint the following illustrations:

Chapter 7: illustration by Sarah Horne

Chapter 10: illustration by Antoine Déprez, from Clémentine Beauvais, *La Louve* (Alice Editions, 2014).

Introduction

Many people, at some point in their lives, decide they want to write for children. This might be once they have their own children, or nieces and nephews. It might also happen if, suddenly enthralled by a film franchise drawn from a children's book, they suddenly 'realize' that they could just 'write something like that'. It might happen if they need money, and 'realize' they could potentially 'earn a lot by writing a few children's stories'.

For some people – very few of the above category – writing for children is about much more than writing *down* the stories that they make up on the spot for their own children. For those people, money, fame and film franchises don't matter as much as their desire to write something beautiful, something interesting, something intriguing that hundreds of children would treasure in the isolation of their rooms or in the back of a car during a long, long family road trip. Those aspiring children's writers imagine little children cherishing and loving these stories, just as they, the authors, cherished and loved the stories of their childhoods – *Little Women*, *Tom's Midnight Garden*, *A Little Princess*. Those were *good* stories, *real* stories for children, not like the trash we get these days – and so those people long to write similar, 'timeless classic' stories now.

And then there are some people (even fewer) who approach children's writing more realistically. They do have a genuine interest in writing for children, they do long for little readers to treasure and cherish their words ... but they've also read – and would like to read more – contemporary children's literature. Those aspiring writers want to position themselves within a resolutely *contemporary* strand of children's literature. They realize that we are in an age where children's literature is more exciting, transgressive and innovative than it ever was.

Those people are aware, albeit blurrily to start with, that a children's book is a collective work – a work in *tension*, pulled in sometimes opposite directions by author, editor, illustrator, marketing team, finance team, foreign rights team ... A work at the mercy of teachers, librarians, parents, booksellers, award bodies. They know, in short, that it's not going to be an easy ride, and that they should strive to learn as much as possible *both* about the art of children's literature *and* about the industry, if they want their dream to come true.

Given that you've picked up this book, you're probably in that third category already. You care about children and about children's literature; you want to write well, and you want your audience to be transformed by your words for the better. But you're not a hopeless romantic, a nostalgic, old-fashioned defender of the 'classics', who just wants to produce rewritings of *The Wind in the Willows*. You are a writer of your time, keen to give children stories that reflect their experiences. You want to write stories in tune with a type of literature which – as you probably already know, or can feel – is as audacious, varied and difficult as literature for adults. You are pragmatic, professional and forward-thinking: you want to know as much as possible about the cultural industry you'll be entering, and the people who will be helping you – or hindering you.

This book is for you. It treats children's literature both as an art form and as a career choice, and therefore it will address you as a professional artist. It assumes that you are ready to invest time and energy into writing children's books with the aim of getting them published. It will guide you in doing so, on several fronts, from the writing itself to the publishing process through to marketing and networking. It is a complete writing course because it addresses you as a *complete* professional artist, a contemporary one, with all the difficulties and frustrations that this career choice sometimes entails.

But why *children's* books?

But first: why would anyone want to write *children's books*?

As mentioned earlier, 'earning money' and 'rewriting the classics' aren't good reasons to write for children. 'Using it as a springboard to then upgrade to adult literature' is an even worse idea. But 'being adventurous' is a good reason. There are seemingly no genres that children's and Young Adult literature doesn't cover, no styles that it forbids, no themes that it fails to tackle. It is an immensely rich field, an imaginative author's dream playground, fervently hybrid – marrying visual and verbal elements, aesthetic and commercial imperatives, linear and fragmented storylines and characterization. Children's literature reflects artistic evolutions of its times: it is now an infinitely flexible, transgressive, plural and innovative art. Many authors 'for adults' have turned to children's literature, in fact, because they've realized that there are some stories they can't tell for an audience of adults; in the famous words of Philip Pullman, 'There are some themes, some subjects, too large for adult fiction; they can only be dealt with adequately in a children's book.' From Ted Hughes to Salman Rushdie, many prestigious authors have found themselves seduced by the idea of this different audience, which brings with it new demands and new possibilities.

That all sounds great, but of course children's literature is *also* a literature of constraints, and this book won't shy away from presenting them. Every time I go to an event in a bookshop that involves writers 'for adults', I ask them, during the Q&A session, if they've ever thought about writing for children. Many have, and many plan to; but others are (politely) adamant that it is out of the question. Among those, one reason frequently comes up: they don't want to be enslaved to the commercial imperatives of children's fiction.

And, indeed, children's and Young Adult fiction is a *commercial* art form, especially in the UK and the United States. *It must sell.* Such demands can feel hugely bothersome to some aspiring writers: if that's the case for you, maybe you shouldn't get into children's literature. Yes, children's literature is an amazing experimental platform, but it is also codified, supervised and verified by an army of market-savvy, pedagogically minded adults. Any children's book published now will have been edited not just for style and plot but also for its (supposed) suitability to current trends, and its (supposed) appropriateness for an audience of children of the (supposed) right age. Writing children's literature means you implicitly agree to expose yourself to remarks such as 'It's not commercial enough', and 'It's not suitable for children'. You may disagree with them with all your heart: I certainly do, most of the time. But this book's premise is that you would like to be a *published* children's author, so – better be warned – it will often nag you about market and pedagogy.

Why would anyone want to write children's literature in these conditions? Many children's writers enjoy balancing the freedom of expression, story and characterization that children's literature offers, while taking up the challenge of its limitations. It's a tightrope-walking exercise, a risky act – but one that makes many writers very excited. You will be writing not just for *one*, but for *two* implied addressees: 'the child', that elusive creature who generally will not stick with you unless you show them that you deeply care about their reading; and 'the mediators' or 'guardians', those busy adults whose good will you need to conquer for the book to be published in the first place. Every children's book in the world, by definition, has this *double address*. The first step in your writing career is to acknowledge that you are juggling with these different readerly categories at all times.

Children's literature is difficult to write. It requires genuine interest in children and children's books. It requires a generous mind, fine-tuned to the everyday reality of children's lives. It also requires strong writing skills: a solid sense of pace, impeccable characterization, perfect dialogue, a passion for action. It is in no way 'easier' than literature for adults. It should be written for its own sake. It is a cruel literature, too: its primary audience of children will let you know clearly enough whether they hate it or love it.

Reading children's books

If you want to write children's books, you must read children's books – *contemporary* ones, still warm from the printing presses. Fond memories of mushroom-smelling books from the seventies *don't count*. This is a much-repeated mantra of all creative writing courses, but it's absolutely true: you cannot hope to write good children's books without reading a vast number of the books produced by your future colleagues. In particular, you must read books in similar genres and writing styles, and for similar age ranges, as the ones you'd like to write. If you don't, you will inevitably end up reinventing the wheel. Only once you are fully familiar with a specific genre can you legitimately aspire to write in that genre.

How can you keep up to date with what's being published? There are many easy ways:

- On Twitter and Facebook (more on that much later in this book), follow children's publishers. They will post about their new books regularly.

- Still on social media, or more traditionally through good old RSS feeds, follow blogs that review children's and Young Adult books.

- Make a point of always reading the books that win major awards: the Carnegie, the Newbery, the Caldecott, Michael Printz, the Branford Boase, the Roald Dahl Funny Prize, the Waterstones, UKLA and Costa book awards. Sometimes the same book wins several of those.

- Go to your local bookshop and library often and ask, ask, ask. What's selling? What's good? What should I read now? It's the bookseller's and librarian's job to help you with that. These people are immensely knowledgeable; and making friends now could very well help in the future (we'll get to that in due course).

- Read the books which are mentioned throughout this volume. I've tried to pick a variety of exciting, interesting books, relatively recent, that any new author would benefit from reading.
- To avoid tut-tuts from your bank, don't buy all these books. Borrow them from public libraries[1] or from friends.

This keenness to discover, to learn, to *read*, will be invaluable to you as a future writer and will help your writing grow more mature. This reading experience will stratify into stronger structure, better characterization, more elegant writing. And you will be more likely to know what editors want, and what children like.

What children like? Really? Can anyone *ever* know that? In fact, wait a minute …

What's a child?

It might sound ludicrous, but we do need to define what 'a child' is when we think thoroughly about writing for children (this is me speaking with my academic mortarboard propped on my head now). There's no universal definition of 'the child'. This is because childhood is a socio-historical construct: it has no reality. Childhood isn't a 'thing' until society starts giving it attributes and separating it from adulthood. The existence of this separate category – of those people we call 'children' – is the condition for the existence of the category of literature we call 'children's literature'. The same goes, of course, for 'adolescence', and very recently for a new category, 'New Adult'. All these 'ages' have no biological basis: they're entirely made up by society. They therefore reflect attitudes, fears, beliefs and desires about what 'childhood' and 'adolescence' should mean, from people who have a vested interest in the constructs.

Every time we talk *about* children, every time we talk *to* them, we consciously and unconsciously transmit values and beliefs about what children should be like. Children's literature is made of those values and beliefs. Children's books are a vehicle for cultural and literary representations of childhood, whether conservative or transgressive. And the children who read children's literature will of course adopt and reject some of these representations, and in turn *perform* their own childhood with them or against them. 'A child' can only be loosely defined as a young person who, for a given amount of time, performs what is expected by a given society of the concept of 'childhood'.

This is very important to keep in mind as a children's author: you will be addressing a vast array of different individuals who are simply connected by the fact that, socially, politically, economically and culturally, they are categorized by 'us' *adults* as 'them' *children*. The differences that we attribute to this category of people, their specific traits – innocence, ignorance, purity, creativity, insight, energy, etc. – are constructed. By us. If you are a children's writer, then you are *by default* partaking in this differentiation of childhood from adulthood, and you are *by definition* contributing to a pool of representations of these differences (and, sometimes, similarities).

---

1 Authors and illustrators, by the way, receive a small amount of money every time you borrow a book from a public library.

This also means that you have to acknowledge – and make do with – editors, parents and teachers' expectations of what 'a good book for a child of X years old' might be. The editorial world is very strict, not just about what it sees as 'children', but also about supposed 'gender differences' and 'age differences'. There are conventions: child characters should be a year or two older than the intended audience; boys will not read books that are designed for girls and/or have girl main characters; some themes and writing styles should not be adopted until 'a certain age', etc.

These conventions can be irritating and, more importantly, they can have negative effects. You may profoundly disagree with the idea that some themes are 'not suitable for children', on the basis that such assertions make it sound like 'children' are one monolithic group. And goodness knows I'm on your side. But tough luck – such ideological dilemmas will be *ubiquitous* in your career as a children's writer. You'll have to react to them cleverly. Commercial imperatives govern the definition of what 'a child' is, in children's literature publishing terms. If you're brave enough to oppose them, be canny about it.

What's a children's book?

Just as many varied individuals are grouped under the label 'children' or 'teenagers', many different books are called 'children's books' ('Young Adult' literature is now also its own category, and this book covers it as well). Children's literature is an ever-changing body of texts, and I think the safest way of defining it for now is to say, like children's literature scholar Perry Nodelman, 'I happily accept the pragmatic definition that children's literature is the literature published as such'. Indeed, it is the publishing industry which regulates what we come to see as children's literature. Some books are reclaimed as children's books – for instance, Stephen Kelman's *Pigeon English*, after being published for adults, was published for teenagers. Other books progressively leave the 'canon' of children's literature: who, now, apart from adult scholars, really reads Isaac Watts's poetry for children?

This definition is important to you because the closest you can keep to current conceptions of children's literature, the better your chances of getting published. This doesn't mean forsaking all creativity and dignity, but simply being aware of trends. Young Adult literature is much racier now than it was 30 years ago; a book like Judy Blume's *Forever*, which achieved cult status in the 1980s, would probably not be published as such now. It's a literature in constant evolution: picturebooks are turning into apps, novels are becoming more graphic, and who knows where poetry for teenagers might take us in the next few years? Keep reading to keep up to date.

It's also a literature with its own body of criticism and theory. Many people read, review and study children's literature for a living; I am one of them. Reading the critical literature on children's literature can be a real eye-opener for writers, and I have tried to pepper this book with references to it. Often, reading scholarly articles and books about the type of children's literature you're trying to write can reveal how naive you might have been in thinking that your plot structure was original or your main character 'completely unique'. It can give you ideas about how to play with conventions and inscribe your story within the ancestry of its genre. Children's literature scholarship is generally highly accessible and even entertaining: I have provided a reading list of such writing in the reference list at the end of the book.

What kind of children's writer are you going to be?

You might have a clear idea already of the type of children's books you'd like to write, or you might be keeping your options open. This book is premised on the idea that you're happy to conjugate literary merit with commercial imperatives, but that you're not particularly interested in writing huge bestsellers (though, should it happen, all the better: feel free to send me a bar of sea-salt dark chocolate in the mail to thank me for my help). There are books out there that will teach you how to write a bestselling book. I'm more interested in sharing thoughts about what children's literature *is*, what different types of children's book there are, and how one can go about writing something that one cares deeply about, while being in tune with the demands of the market. I hope this book speaks to you whether you're intending to leave your day job for a writing career, to write educational books or literary fiction, to pen picturebooks or big fat Young Adult novels. I am assuming, above all, that you are interested in writing for children *both* as a viable career option *and* as an art form.

How can this book help?

Legitimate question. You might be wondering who I am and how on earth I ended up writing this book – couldn't they have got J.K. Rowling or someone? (I don't blame you – I would definitely buy J.K. Rowling's 'How to write children's books' book.) I'm a young author of over ten children's books and counting – in all different genres, for different ages, and in two different languages. I'm also an avid and methodical reader of literature, blogs, websites and articles about children's publishing, by authors, agents and editors, and of professional reviews. I'm a voracious reader of children's literature, for all ages and in all formats. Furthermore, I'm an academic in children's literature – I have a PhD in the field, and I work as a full-time researcher at the Children's Literature Research and Teaching Centre at the University of Cambridge.

All of those things put together constitute an answer to how this book might help you: I'm hoping I can lead you through children's literature from *multiple points of view*. As a children's writer, I'll share my experiences – including bad ones! – and, though no one can, I think, 'teach' anyone else to write, I hope I can help you pick a *voice*. As a both leisurely and professional reader of children's literature, I'll give you a sense of what good children's literature should entail – what to *aim* for. It doesn't necessarily mean *I* can *do* it; it means I can see *what's to be done*. And this book will be also full of insights into the workings of the industry, carried forward by the pragmatic view that you can't be a published children's writer if you don't have any information about how the publishing world functions. Finally, I'll be your cheerleader, motivating you relentlessly to *write*; as an active Internet user, blogger and Facebook and Twitter addict, I know some techniques to help you focus on your work. And as someone with a full-time job, I know how difficult it is to make time to write. It's the plurality of those viewpoints which makes, I think, the originality of this particular writing book.

This book is designed to function as a complete writing course. It will lead you through four main parts: 'Finding a voice', 'Finding a format', 'Finding a publisher' and 'Finding readers'. In other words, it will take you all the way from 'Once upon a time' to school visits. You don't have to read it in order, nor use every single chapter; you could focus on just the areas you're interested in, and the formats you intend to write in.

At the end of each chapter in the first two parts and some of the other two parts, you'll find a workshop. These workshops are designed to get you to *write*; to write something, *anything*, and reap the benefits of your reading. Often, when I read creative writing textbooks or blog posts, I feel excited and inspired. Having this exercise there can help you channel some of that excitement into something concrete. They're also meant to show how easy it is to write, a little bit, every day or so.

This book doesn't cover *everything*, of course. You won't find anything in this book on non-fiction for children; not only is it a field I don't know enough about, it's also so vast that it could constitute its own handbook. Children's theatre and screenwriting won't be tackled either, for the same reasons. There are guides to these, too: some are listed at the end of the book. Additionally, it's always worth having a look at the Internet. Spend time looking at blogs, websites, Twitter feeds; watch YouTube tutorials, listen to podcasts. Go to creative writing classes, if you can. Practising and training are the key words here: you're only a writer if you write, not if you think about writing.

Many people, especially published authors, will give you advice on the way. That's great, but remember, they all suffer from *survivorship bias*. *Survivorship bias* means that people who are in a place to give recommendations to others, and share their own experiences, are in this place mostly through many accidents of history and twists of fate. In retrospect, they construct a narrative of how they got here – but at the beginning, they were of course clueless as to what was going to happen. There's never just one way of getting published, of writing children's books, of finding a voice. This book celebrates the plurality of the ways. That's also why it doesn't spend too long talking about what established authors think about this process: you won't find hundreds of snippets of advice from writing superstars. Instead, I'll focus on what children's *literature* can tell us about writing for children, as it is often more revealing than what its authors have to say about it.

PART ONE
Finding a voice

1

Once upon a time ... and other beginnings

In the beginning was the word.

Well, that's the *optimistic* version of the story. Most often, in the beginning was the writer poring over a desperately pristine sheet of paper, empty Microsoft Word document, or the disciplined pale lines of a Moleskine notebook.

And the writer was thinking, 'How shall I begin my story? How shall those words which are in my mind find their way on to the snowy emptiness of yonder page? Ah! Wouldst that there existed cookie-cutter beginnings with which to seduce the muse into speaking to me!'

And then the writer remembered that he was writing for children, and said, 'Of course! I only need to write *once upon a time*, and all the rest will follow! Easy-peasy!'

So he did.

And no one saw that it was good.

Thankfully, there are ways of avoiding this tragic fate.

The first sentence

Arguably, it's possible to judge the quality of a book and its enduring success from how easily people remember its first sentence:

> 'In a hole in the ground there lived a Hobbit ...'

> 'Where's Papa going with that ax?'

> 'Here is Edward Bear, coming down the stairs now, bump bump bump, on the back of his head, behind Christopher Robin ...'

Those first sentences are intriguing: they trigger questions. What's a Hobbit? Where *is* Papa going? And what position can this Mr Edward Bear possibly have adopted to be coming down the stairs in this painful-sounding fashion? Notice a trend there, too: these first sentences aren't just intriguing, they have *hints of violence* to them. Whether quietly or overtly, they're saying to the reader, 'Look! The situation isn't quite right ...' Of course, first sentences don't always need to allude to underground monsters, head bumps or axe massacres, but it's quite a good way to attract the attention of the narrative-thirsty reader. Because what the reader wants from a first sentence is primarily this: *a problem that a narrative will solve.*

A good first sentence is one that contains both the *exposition* of a situation and the intrinsic *problem* with that situation: a problem which will constitute, hopefully, the main drive of the narrative. This is also why an ideal first sentence should have a third characteristic: it should 'sum up' the story in anticipation. It should contain *everything* that the book is going to be about.

No pressure, right?

An excellent example of this can be found in *A Monster Calls*, by Patrick Ness, of which the first sentence is:

> 'The monster showed up just after midnight. As they do.'

OK, that's two sentences – but it's the first line of the story, clearly distinct from the rest of the text on the page. The point is: those two sentences *on their own* can be read retrospectively as condensing the whole storyline and the whole feel of the story. The monster ('What monster?' Good question-raising here, Patrick Ness!) does indeed 'show up' after midnight throughout the whole story: that's the leitmotiv (the recurring motif) of the narrative. But the second sentence goes further than that. The sudden generalization – what? There's more than one monster? – leads us into a much more *real*, threatening, *plural* world of monsters which will become embodied by the young hero's mother's cancer. And the ineluctability of the sentence – *as they do*, as they *always* do, as they *cannot help but doing* – prefigures the tragic and ineluctable ending of the mother's death from cancer, a few minutes after midnight, on the very last page.[1]

So this is what you are expected to produce. Ready?

Not so fast. Breathe.

---

1 Yes, sorry, I should have said – this book contains countless spoilers which I won't bother warning you about.

Very few novels actually *began* with the sentence now printed on top of page 1. It's very rare that a writer nails the first sentence literally as s/he begins to write. This is because a story is much more often tickled open than cracked open. *Much* more often than not, you need to beat around the bush for a while. The story hasn't been told yet – there might be a thousand and one changes to it later on – so why trouble yourself with that first sentence *now*?

For now, make it quick, make it painless, and let it be absolutely erasable. It's very likely that it will be sacrificed later on. And the most important thing, really, is to *get writing* – get the second sentence on the page, and then the third, and then the fourth. Get the ball(pen) rolling; you'll come back to it later. In fact, even if you think it's genius already, *do* get back to it later. You might find that it doesn't really correspond to your conception of the book any more.

Key idea

What ends up as the first sentence of your story can be the very *last* you'll ever write in that book. In fact, it's *more likely* to be the case – very rarely does it remain unchanged from draft one to book form.

Who, what, where, when, why: the exposition scene

How's it going now? Are you comfortably tucked into the story, having left behind a few wobbly first sentences? Great. Now that you've started … Stop! Stop and think – what are you trying to achieve in these first few pages?

The automatic answer should be something like – 'set the scene', 'explain what's happening'. It seems like the logical thing to do – and it is – but there are several pitfalls to avoid when attempting to create what is known as the *exposition scene* (or expository scene).

The exposition scene, a term derived from classical theatre, should traditionally do what the first sentence does, but in a longer and more detailed form: namely, condense and anticipate the rest of the story. In classical theatre, the exposition scene tells the audience:

- who on earth all these characters in costume may be, repeating their names as many times as possible
- why they are all gathered here, and why some are looking gloomy while others are looking merry
- where this might be taking place, without or alongside the visual help given by the papier-mâché backdrop.
- when this masquerade is supposed to occur.

Of course, thank goodness, not all stories now follow this extremely codified pattern. It's much easier to think of counter-examples; *Harry Potter and the Philosopher's Stone* famously begins with an entire chapter set in the Muggle world, eleven years before the rest of the narrative, and makes it sound as if the Dursleys are the protagonists of the story. This creates an interesting diversion – raising subtle questions all along the way as to who this Harry Potter may be whose name is on the cover, and why the narrative is focusing on these remarkably unremarkable people who are not him.

A novel for children with an exemplary exposition scene is *Northern Lights*, by Philip Pullman. In the first chapter, we meet Lyra, our heroine, and her daemon – Pantalaimon. Her *what*? The first few scenes bring just enough answers, for now, to this question – Pullman subtly gives hints that it is a creature which is part of Lyra's 'soul' or 'person', and yet all seems quite normal. *Ergo*, this is taking place in another world. Lyra and Pantalaimon end up trespassing into a room they shouldn't have gone into – and spy on a group of adults, most of whom will be very important for the trilogy, who are discussing the main themes of the three books: the mysterious Dust; the North; experiments on children; and danger, danger everywhere …

Granted, such beginnings can seem a little heavy-going because the reader can have the uncomfortable impression of being, like Lyra, a spectator rather than an actor in this story. *This is why balance is needed.* A few golden rules apply, especially for children's literature:

- The characters, right from the beginning, must be *doing* something. They must not be passive spectators: they must not be 'explained' things by adults. Because the reader is likely to be more interested in child characters than adults, make sure child characters have interesting roles right from the start.

- Carefully evaluate what questions you need to raise now, and which ones you can leave for later. Don't overload your reader with random information which isn't needed here and now.

- This first scene must be as mobile, agile, nimble as possible. Avoid static description, genealogy and direct descriptions – 'Clara was a tomboyish sort of girl whose mother worked in finance and whose father was currently unemployed.' The hackneyed advice – show, don't tell – is perhaps nowhere more appropriate than at the beginning of a story.

In short: get on with it.

Static and latent plot elements

It can be helpful to ask yourself which elements of this beginning revolve around 'static' elements of the general plot, as opposed to 'latent' elements. What's the difference?

- **Static plot elements** are the ones that were already there when the story starts: they are, so to speak, 'past-bound', and they constitute the background of the story. They are *how things are.* They might include:
  - character names, backstories, relationships, personalities, tastes and dislikes at the beginning of the story
  - setting, both temporal and spatial
  - the social and political situation of that setting

- tone: the tone of your story might change later, but it is a 'static' element of the beginning which gives an idea of how things are.

- **Latent plot elements** are the ones that the story *truly* is concerned about. They are 'future-bound'; they constitute the fabric of your *plot*. At the beginning of your story, they will be present in *latency*, as *hints* of what is to come, as unfulfilled desires or antagonistic circumstances, as problems ready to strike. They are *how things will become.* They might include:
  - changes in the characters' situations, perhaps prefiguring changes in their personalities, in their course of action or choices, or in their relationships
  - what will happen to the setting – maybe we will never see it again
  - what's at stake, the new elements that come to disturb the story.

All of the above should be conveyed, intricately interlinked, ideally *at the same time*: namely, the reader should be able to get a grasp both of *what is* and of *what is to come*, in no particular order. Try not to resort to two pages of description of how 'everything was quiet in the little village of Laze-upon-Tranquillity', *before* going through to 'until the day when something unexpected happened'.

A good way of bringing latent plot elements into the static backdrop of the story is by giving hints to the reader that something isn't quite right. For instance, a young girl lives with her parents in a quiet suburban town. She has blue eyes, unlike either of her parents. Entirely possible, of course, but … and then immediately the 'static' relationship of this girl to her parents becomes veiled with doubt – what if they weren't her parents? That's a latent plot element woven into the static description of the girl.

Balancing these two types of plot element will make for a beginning that is delightfully open to the clever reader's anticipation of what's going to happen.

One thing I particularly like is the introduction, as early as the beginning, of a plot element, even tiny and discreet, which will have a huge influence on the climactic scene of the book. A character might, for instance, be given an inconspicuous birthday present which reveals itself to be what saves them all from the last big battle. Or, more prosaically, a character might remember in the very last pages of the book a random piece of advice which was given to her on the first page. This kind of detail, which can be, of course, back-engineered into a finished story, leaves the reader with the satisfying feeling of having read a well-plotted, well-prepared story.

Mirrors, dreams, flashbacks? Clichéd beginnings

In children's literature, some beginnings are better avoided. It's worth knowing about them early on, from a strategic perspective – many agents and publishers will look at this kind of beginning and form an idea of the writer as inexperienced and unsubtle. They might even reject the manuscript on account of 'Oh please, not that beginning again'. And before you start protesting that you *never* see such beginnings in published books – that's because they're generally *awful* beginnings. So they don't get published. And yet, again and again, agents and publishers receive submissions that begin with …

A DREAM

That's possibly the most frequent one, in many different versions. In one, the reader doesn't know it's all a dream – s/he thinks rather logically that s/he is being thrown into the story, until, two pages later, the treachery is revealed with a clichéd sentence of the kind – 'Arabella awoke in a sweat.' Sometimes the author is generous enough that s/he tells the reader it's a dream – for instance, by putting it all in italics. In both cases, the narrative of the dream is often of this kind:

> *Rustling trees and white moon, sliced in half by clouds. Arabella runs. Behind her, the sound of the beast's breathing. Breathing. Breathing. Twigs cracking under her feet. Where is Mom? Where's Zach? Night-time, silence, breathing, and then the crack of a whip and the cold, salty water …*
>
> *Arabella awoke in a sweat.*

This type of beginning makes it sound as if the author missed their lifetime vocation as a Hollywood film trailer editor. It's also extremely overdone and not very credible. If I ask you to tell me your latest nightmare, I doubt you'll resort to monosyllabic words, sentences with no verbs and random questions – you'd sound as if you were hallucinating.

Of course, sometimes it is perfectly valid to begin a novel with a dream – especially if the theme of the novel is dreams and dreaming: someone who sees the future in their dreams, say, or who can access another dimension through them. But, in this case, be quite honest with what kind of twist you're trying to give on the usual 'dream narrative'. Literature is peopled with absolutely exceptional dreamers – characters who can remember smells and flavours from dreams, and always awake with a start. How many times has that actually happened to you?

As for dreams that recapitulate episodes of the character's life – effectively functioning as flashbacks – they are even less believable, 99 per cent of the time. Yes, traumatic events do reappear in dreams, but it is strange (and shows very little knowledge of the way the mind works) to pretend that the character is reliving *exactly* what happened then. Avoid using dreams as a pretext to narrate 'what happened before' the story starts. There's always a better way.

MIRRORS

This device is extraordinarily common in submissions for young adult literature. It generally goes like this:

> *I'm late for school again, and rain is pummelling the window panes. One last look at the mirror before I go – yes, it's me, no doubt about that. Lila Mason, sixteen years old, your average dirty-blonde kid with green eyes, a bit shy, who doesn't make anyone go stark raving romantic. Nice enough, but with the upper lip a bit smaller than the lower lip.*

Not only are such beginnings extremely clichéd, they are also lazy. They allow you to unload on to the reader in one go what you should be spending the first chapter or so – and then much more – spinning out into subtle, sophisticated characterization.

The mirror scene is also extremely implausible – when do you ever look at yourself in the mirror and internally sum up every aspect of your personality and personal appearance in this way?

Finally, there's a lot to be said for adolescent fiction, specifically, which does not insist too much – or at least not too early – on physical appearance and physical description. The assumption in the mirror scene is that the young protagonists – and, by extension, the young readers – are quite self-obsessed, and need to identify with the character. The mirror seems to tell the reader – look, it's you! But in the guise of a shy, bookish, awkward character. Try to find more interesting ways of describing teenage angst.

PROLOGUES

There's nothing intrinsically wrong with prologues, and many extremely good books begin with them, but many agents and publishers admit that they do not like them very much and/or skip them. Purposes of prologues can vary. Ask yourself: why do I want my book to begin with a prologue?

- *To explain the background story before the actual story starts?* Avoid. You can and should integrate this kind of information later in the story.

- *To give the reader a feel for what's coming?* Why not? For instance, in the *Twilight* series, each book begins with a very short prologue, which features a snippet of the climactic scene in the novel. Such prologues, although a bit hackneyed, can be good if done well, and whet the appetite of the reader. But beware! After an exciting prologue, the first chapter can feel a bit flat …

- *To give an extract from a letter, a newspaper article, a news report, a phone conversation, about the story to come?* That can be very interesting.

The general rule seems to be that a prologue shouldn't be long at all. A page or two is enough; more and the reader will start wondering where the story is going, and lose patience.

One last tip: if you do have a prologue … don't call it 'prologue'. Just call it Chapter I. Psychologically, this can have a huge impact on the people reading it – and writing is about *strategy* as much as it is about style. If your book ends up getting picked up by a publisher, there will always be time to ask them if, just maybe, 'Chapter I' wouldn't work better as a 'Prologue'…

Long descriptions and long dialogues

Both should be avoided, for completely opposite reasons. Long descriptions – of a place, of a character, of a situation – can quickly become boring and didactic: telling the reader too much about the story to come is the best way of losing his or her interest. On the other side of the spectrum, a long dialogue, especially with little or no signposting and between many characters, can confuse and bewilder the reader.

Key idea

Avoiding such beginnings is easy, but of course it doesn't mean that your not-clichéd beginning will work. A general tip would be, once again – *get on with it.* Show us the action, show us what is at stake, show us why we would possibly want to spend the next 30, 120, 300, 800 pages with you and with your characters.

And remember: there will always be time to rewrite that beginning entirely.

Beginning *in medias res*

In medias res means 'in the middle of the thing'. So beginning *in medias res* simply means – *this is it, reader.* You're thrown into the story *now*. Deal with it.

Technically, of course, it's very difficult to point out where *in medias res* starts. Clearly, this doesn't happen, for instance, in Antoine de Saint-Exupéry's *The Little Prince*, where the story opens long before the narrator meets the otherworldly little boy – in fact, the first chapter is almost entirely devoted to the narrator's childhood and youth. But in other cases it is more difficult to establish. One could argue that Maurice Sendak's *Where the Wild Things Are* begins *in medias res*, since we're plunged directly into Max's mischief, which is what leads to his being sent to his room, which is what leads to his going to visit the Wild Things. But you can see from all the 'which is what leads' that I've had to deploy here that therefore it isn't really *in medias res*.

Interpretations can vary, but *in medias res* means, I think, 'as close as you can get to the first bout of action of the book without completely confusing the reader'. Hardly any set-up, no build-up, barely any description – the reader dives straight into the heart of the story, even if it means that backstory will need to be reintegrated later. A book that does this very well is *The Curious Incident of the Dog in the Night-time*, by Mark Haddon, which begins exactly where the title says it should: with the young autistic narrator looking straight at a dog, dead, on his neighbour's lawn, at '7 minutes past midnight', with a pitchfork sticking out of its body.

Professional readers of submitted manuscripts often tell you that *beginner writers almost always begin their stories too early*. Cut the first two chapters and you'll see where your story really starts. It might not be *in medias res* in the proper sense of the phrase, but it's still later than you think. The saying: 'arrive at the last minute and leave as soon as possible' isn't bad advice – especially for action-packed, hugely plot-driven stories.

Beginning *in medias res* is a less common device in literature for older readers, in which authors often spend a lot of time building up to the story. Teenage readers seem to have patience for this, and many Young Adult novels spend the first 50 pages or so only 'dropping hints' as to what is to come. Teri Terry's first novel, *Slated*, for instance, is narratively speaking extremely characteristic of this trend. The beginning of the story – the build-up, the descriptions of the characters and background, the hints as to what is to come – takes up almost 200 pages, in which curiosity is raised but action doesn't truly begin. This is the kind of beginning which can work well in a book series, since the reader and the author know that there will be more books in which to develop the narrative arc of the overall storyline.

For younger readers, however – in picturebooks and chapter books – the format of the book and the narrative expectations are completely different; it's relatively uncommon to have a long build-up. Take time to look analytically at books in the genre and age range that you're writing for: ask yourself if the beginning of the book you're reading is fast, drawn out, too long, too short, too action-packed, too description-heavy, confusing, or clear.

Don't forget that you can always go back to the beginning of your story – and in fact, you very much should – once you have finished writing the whole book. It often takes a few chapters to truly 'get' the tone of the whole story.

But really pay attention to it. Publishers and agents, most often, will read only the first tenth of a submission before deciding whether or not they want to continue. A dull 30 pages at the beginning of a novel, even followed by a splendid 200 pages, might mean that the book never hits the shelves – whereas in fact, an exciting, original beginning, even if the rest lacks the same energy, might trigger the agent or editor's request for important, but potentially fruitful, changes to the rest of the story.

Hooking the young reader: five tips

A young reader is different from an adult reader in perhaps only one respect: unless they have to read the book for school (and even then, arguably), they *will not keep reading if they don't like it.* Most of them don't care about the author's status, the cultural stigma associated with not reading such and such a book, or the social glory of having got to the end of that difficult one. They want to be entertained and learn new things and, if the beginning doesn't promise either, they'll put the book down. So how do you hook the young reader at the beginning of your book?

The best books for children, I think, do these five things:

1 Confirm genre expectations: the first chapter should roughly validate what the cover and back cover blurbs are talking about, and set up expectations that the rest of the story will, too.

2 But also unsettle: slight changes to the expected tone, storyline, characters, are ingredients for a different, original, interesting reading experience. The young reader longs to be taken out of his or her comfort zone.

3 Make the reader laugh or gasp – make the reader *react*: the best beginnings cause a physical reaction in the child reader. A child who's laughed already, or whose heartbeat has accelerated, in the span of the first chapter, is a child hooked to the story already. So it's worth packing a few more ha-ha- or oh!-inducing moments in these crucial first few pages.

4 Don't confuse the reader: although this is a debatable one (there are excellent books with incredibly confusing beginnings), it's easy to be put off by a complicated or befuddling beginning. This is partly because children are (wrongly) told by adults, very frequently, which books are below or above their imagined 'reading

level'. They'll thus get demotivated, or feel that a book 'isn't for them', if it isn't immediately comprehensible. Try to ease the entry of the child reader, of any age, into your book.

5 Play with language: dazzle the reader with wordplay, striking images or efficient dialogue immediately. This is a *book*: tell them it's going to do as much as it can with its main weapon: words. Make them savour the language you're giving to them – keep the clarity, but don't sacrifice style for explanatory purposes.

Workshop: writing an exposition scene

This workshop exercise doesn't need to be explained in great detail: I want you to write an exposition scene, in your chosen genre(s), format and age range, trying to integrate the advice given in this chapter. The term 'exposition scene' is deliberately left open: if you're writing a picturebook, it may be the first couple of pages; if you're writing a dark, urban Young Adult novel, it could be a whole chapter. Maybe you've already got one of those handy, in which case no homework for you today – you can skip directly to the 'review' part of the exercise.

Review

Now reread what you have written and evaluate yourself. How well, on a scale from 1 to 10, have you presented the following things?

'Static' elements:

- Main character   1 2 3 4 5 6 7 8 9 10
- Secondary characters   1 2 3 4 5 6 7 8 9 10
- Setting   1 2 3 4 5 6 7 8 9 10
- Time   1 2 3 4 5 6 7 8 9 10
- Tone   1 2 3 4 5 6 7 8 9 10
- Overall grade for 'static' plot elements   1 2 3 4 5 6 7 8 9 10

'Latent' plot elements:

- What's at stake   1 2 3 4 5 6 7 8 9 10
- Why it's important   1 2 3 4 5 6 7 8 9 10
- How the main character can deal with it   1 2 3 4 5 6 7 8 9 10
- How urgent the situation is   1 2 3 4 5 6 7 8 9 10
- Overall grade for 'latent' plot elements   1 2 3 4 5 6 7 8 9 10

Bonus: Have you been able to smuggle into the beginning a plot element which will be crucial at the very end of the story?

If possible, find someone who can read this beginning and ask them the following questions:

1 What do you think [main character] is like, as a person?
2 What do you think is going to happen?
3 What kind of a book is this? What genre? For which age range?
4 Were you bored at any point?
5 Was there anything that was particularly well done?

See whether their answers correspond to what you imagine your book to be like.

If you're not satisfied with what you've done, try to reintegrate details about the different areas which you feel aren't quite up to scratch. But *not too much.* It's extremely easy to spend ages on a beginning and somehow forget to write the rest of the story – or be discouraged by the time it will take, seeing as you've already spent weeks on just a dozen pages. It's perfectly normal to spend more time on the beginning of a book than on the middle bit and the end – generally, I find that the first third of the book is by far the hardest. But the more time you spend on it, the more likely it becomes that you'll abandon the book before getting to the end of that first third. So many books with superb beginnings are left bodiless in the bottom of a drawer because the initial passion and care have gone away. Don't let that happen to your story – don't lose momentum. *Keep writing* at all costs.

Where to next?

In this chapter you should have gained a bit of experience in writing beginnings, and had an overview of the things you shouldn't miss out. But there are two important aspects of beginnings – and, indeed, of whole stories – that deserve their own chapter: theme and thesis. In the next chapter you'll hear all about them, and why they should matter to your reflection about your book.

2

What's it about? Theme and thesis

'Oh, you're writing a children's book? *What's it about?*'

No matter how much you try to conceal the dark truth about why you've been hiding in your room for the past few months, somebody is bound to find out – and to ask you the dreaded question. So prepare for it, or else you're going to end up sounding like this:

> 'It's about, erm … a wolf … who lives in the forest … but he's, like, sad, 'cause he eats other animals so he doesn't have friends, you see. 'Cause, in fact, it's about friendship, mostly. But not in a mawkish way, in a good way. Well, you know what I mean.'

No, your inquisitive acquaintance doesn't know what you mean – and maybe you don't either … Because you clearly don't know what your *theme* is, and why it's different from your *thesis* and from your *story*.

Thankfully, it's not too difficult to understand.

Theme and thesis

- A **theme** is what you're talking *about*.
- A **thesis** is what you're *saying* about it

Both find themselves turned into a *story*.

Let's take a simplistic example: say one of the themes of your children's book is 'sibling rivalry'.

Your *thesis* is what your book will be *saying about* sibling rivalry. It could be saying: 'sibling rivalry is bad; brothers and sisters should try to get along'. Your story might be, as a result, that of a brother and a sister who hate each other at the beginning of the book, but after many adventures they learn to rely on each other and to enjoy each other's company.

Or your thesis could be: 'sibling rivalry is good and should be encouraged, because it helps siblings mature and be less dependent on one other'. Your story could be, for instance, about tween twin sisters who are very close to one another at the beginning, but gradually find that they need more space for their individualities to develop – and, at the end, manage to reach a healthy level of competitiveness and independence.

Bonus points if you've recognized the two children's books hidden in the previous paragraphs ... Anthony Browne's picturebook *The Tunnel* comes first, and then Jacqueline Wilson's teenage novel *Double Act*. Same theme. Different theses. (Very) different stories, using (very) different formats.

And, quite importantly, *very good books*. Yes, they may have a relatively clear-cut theme, and a thesis that's relatively easy to spell out – but that doesn't preclude subtlety and intelligence, nor stifle other aspects of the story. Bear this in mind if you're feeling reluctant about the theme-and-thesis approach ...

 Key idea

When writing your children's book, try to be clear about what its theme(s) and its thesis are. In the long term, this reflection will pay off.

SHOULD A CHILDREN'S BOOK BE EDUCATIONAL? QUESTIONING THE 'MESSAGE'

Theme and thesis are controversial matters. One temptation, when writing children's books, can be to find a theme with potential *educational value*. Children's bookshelves are full of books dealing with themes that are perceived as particularly 'relevant to children' by adult authors and publishers. First day of school, first kiss, first adolescent rebellion – there are so many first times, so many new discoveries in a child's or a teenager's life, that it seems logical to want to 'teach' the child reader how to approach them.

There's no intrinsic problem with that. Children's literature, many scholars agree, is didactic by definition: it's a type of literature written *by* adults *for* children. Therefore it *always* introduces children to a culture and a society. Whether the adult author is aware of it or not, s/he is transmitting values, beliefs, fears and knowledge when writing. In other words, the author is *educating* the child reader.

So every children's book has a 'message', that is to say a *thesis*, however implicit it can be, and whether you like it or not. Many writers *don't* like it – they'd be inclined to say, as Ernest Hemingway apparently did, 'When I need to send a message, I go to the post office!' Wise. But, for children's literature at least, wrong. Every children's book is educational to an extent, and there's no such thing as a 'neutral' theme, or a book without a 'message'.

So how can you make sure that you don't write a dogmatic children's book that sounds more like a textbook of (what you think is) 'good' behaviour than an engaging story? Have a think about how closed or open-ended your thesis is. Do you want to teach children that it's absolutely always wrong to steal, or that there's a possibility for some ethical ambivalence in certain cases? Your story, in the former case, risks ending up prescriptive and boring, while the latter will challenge the reader to think about moral dilemmas. And perhaps, in the process, you'll 'teach' more about the imperfections of society than about categorical, inflexible obligations.

Common themes

Children's literature, depending on the age of the targeted readership and the format of the book, has some recurrent themes – some of them clichéd and overdone, some of them so profound that their richness will never be exhausted.

Regardless of age group, here are examples of classic themes that can be tackled in an infinite number of ways through children's literature:

DEATH

From fairy tales to Young Adult literature, death – the deaths of animals, grandparents, parents, and even children – is omnipresent in children's literature.

And yes, even in picturebooks. John Burningham *Granpa* is a perfect example of a sensitive, ambivalent way of presenting death in a picturebook. At the end of the quiet, tender story – which presents a little girl's relationship with her grandfather through dialogue – the last page of the book shows us that Granpa is *simply not there any more*. This leaves a large degree of freedom to the child reader, who can decide whether they want to interpret this as the grandfather's death, or wait until they can cope with this explanation in another reading. Mourning is, of course, another common theme – intricately linked to death.

LOVE AND FRIENDSHIP

This is a very frequent theme in children's literature, with never-ending possibilities. Children and teenagers are constantly negotiating their place in society, with and among others – and their literature reflects that.

When opting for such a theme, try to steer away from easy, benign, straightforward portrayals of relationships. Give credit to the complexities of *togetherness* in childhood and adolescence – try to remember how joyful-but-painful, ambiguous and contradictory your feelings towards other children were when you were a child yourself. There's no such thing as an easy reconciliation between friends; and it's very rare to find eternal love at 16 … Be truthful and honest with your audience. Philip Pullman broke many hearts with the ending of his trilogy, *His Dark Materials*; but his decision to separate the young couple was arguably the most courageous aspect of the trilogy's *thesis* on the *theme* of love. That *thesis* is that at 13 or 14 years old, one can fall passionately in love; but one can't commit to the other person for their whole lives, because there's still so much to discover outside of that relationship. Bittersweet – but beautifully respectful of the audience's emotional intelligence.

PLACE AND SPACE

Whether we're just talking about nature – animals, plants, the countryside, and the place of the human on earth – or about the social environment, children's books can deal very cleverly with the concepts of space and place. Children and teenagers are people who, by definition, don't own any land – they're roamers, vagabonds, borrowers of *adult* space. What they do with that space, how they view it, use it and transform it, is up to you to invent. Look at the first stanza of A.A. Milne's famous poem 'The Wrong House':

> *I went into a house, and it wasn't a house,*
> *It has big steps and a great big hall;*
> *But it hasn't got a garden,*
> *A garden,*
> *A garden,*
> *It isn't like a house at all.*

Theme and thesis, anyone? Well, the poem is 'about' a child's sense of place; 'about' a child's judgement of what a house should be. And the *thesis* is that this judgement differs from the (bourgeois) adult ideals of what a house is, because – in a highly romantic fashion – the child is perceived to be closer to nature than the adults. To him, it's the garden that grants *houseness* to the house, not the 'big steps' of what we imagine to be an impressive Edwardian staircase.

From the same theme, you also get, for instance, a whole range of ecological books that encourage the child reader to recycle and love the planet. Not exactly a very open-ended thesis, for most of them … Or you can end up with high-fantasy novels in which humans, elves, wizards and other creatures must all negotiate their territories and fight against the forces of nature.

SCHOOL LIFE

School stories are immensely popular, especially for chapter books and 'tween' literature; even in Young Adult literature, day-to-day life in high school is often depicted. We'll get back to it in detail in a later chapter. School life has many aspects: learning, of course, but also relationships with other students and with teachers. What do you want to spotlight? Bullying, as in R.J. Palacio's moving teenage novel *Wonder*? A child's first day at school, as in Lauren Child's hilarious picturebook in the *Charlie and Lola* series, *I Am Too Absolutely Small for School*? We'll talk about the school story in more depth later; suffice it to say here that it's a well-trodden path and you could do worse than picking it – as long as you've got an original *thesis* to do it justice.

FAMILY, AND ADULT AUTHORITY

Children and teenagers are still under the authority of their parents. Well, in theory … Children's literature is an ideal medium to talk both about the joys of family life and about current issues, such as the breakdown of the family. Anne Fine's *Mrs Doubtfire* does just that: it's a teenage novel about divorce, but also about family love, with a solid dose of humour. Jacqueline Wilson, throughout her whole writing career, has closely followed the evolution of the family and of sometimes wobbly parental authorities, and her books can be read as a reflection of that evolution since the 1990s. Their *thesis*, quite often, is that the children of such families are resourceful and responsible, and can take over from the weakened parents. They become more authoritative in the process, but they are still loving and protective of their family.

Those all-encompassing themes can be developed for any targeted readership (including adults!). But there are, evidently, other themes which are strongly age-related. However much I'd love to see what they'd look like, I wouldn't encourage you to invest all your time and energy in a Young Adult novel on potty-training or a picturebook on knife crime.

'Taboo' themes?

Are there themes we can't tackle in children's literature? Well, there are certainly themes that will make it very *difficult*, if not *impossible* for you to sell your *debut* work, whatever the thesis is. Publishers, especially in children's literature and especially if you're a complete unknown, are keen to make sure that they can promote, market and sell your book. And some themes are simply *that* much more difficult to promote, market and sell than usual ones, which adds to the publisher's difficulties when you're also a debut author with no following or notoriety. These themes include:

- **handicap and grave illness:** whether it's a child or an adult character who's gravely ill or handicapped, this theme is likely to put off many traditional publishers
- **depression:** this particular mental illness is a hard sell
- **drugs, rape, prostitution, incest:** even in Young Adult literature, which, as we shall see, can be extremely dark and violent, a debut novel that tackles those themes frontally or revolves around them would need to be truly exceptional to convince a publisher to gamble on you. This is partly because your book might end up banned, notably in the United States
- **religion:** a slippery theme, whether your *thesis* is critical or supportive of it. Ask yourself whether religion could be an aspect of your story, or a secondary theme, rather than its central theme.

But, of course, there are always counter-examples – the main point is, 'simply', to write an exceptional book. Patrick Ness's *A Monster Calls* is the award-winning, heartbreaking tale of a boy dealing with his mum's cancer and death. Michael Rosen's picturebook *Sad Book*, illustrated by Quentin Blake, describes his depression after his son's death. Melvin Burgess's *Junk* rocked the adolescent literature world with its representation of hard-drug addiction in teenagers.

Key idea

Children's literature is a powerful experimental platform. There may be 'taboo' themes – but only until someone finds the words to tell them right.

Spinning the theme into ideas

At this point, you'd be forgiven for exclaiming – 'but surely *theme* isn't truly what comes first!' What does seem to happen most often is that the plot or the central character springs to mind before everything else. It's more natural for writers to have plot ideas or a character's voice popping into their heads; it seems artificial to derive them painstakingly from a chosen theme and thesis. You might think it's strangely cerebral to think about theme and thesis before thinking about the where, when and who of your story.

You might also think that you're above writing books that are 'about' something, or that have a clear-cut thesis. You might be huffing and puffing reading these lines right now – you're writing high-quality literature, theme-less, thesis-less, just art for art's sake, thank you very much. You might be thinking, too, that most good books are 'about' lots of things at the same time; that a work of art would lack richness and depth if it were only 'about' one thing.

All of that is true. But firstly, remember you're a debut author, trying to seduce a busy, well-oiled publishing industry that will want to be able to label your book as a '10–12 school story' or as a 'picturebook on divorce', however much you protest that it's far more complex and multifaceted than that. That's the pragmatic reply.

But there's another, more literary reply. Even if your idea for a story or character seems to arrive fully formed in your mind, think about it more closely and you'll see that it already contains elements of theme and thesis, whether you like it or not. We all have our little obsessions – mine are time and adult authority – and these little obsessions find themselves distilled in the books we write. Theme and thesis are *always already there*, permeating plot and characters. And yes, there may be several themes at the same time, or one main theme and then secondary themes. And no, your thesis doesn't need to be boringly clear-cut: that's OK, ethical ambivalence is good; psychological complexity is good.

But identifying your theme, secondary themes and thesis, however multifarious and complex, will help you spin a story that's coherent, intelligent and subtle. How come? Because theme and thesis are the conceptual basis of your story. They'll give it meaning, significance, importance and a sense of continuity. If done well, they'll offer your young reader that lovely, intense feeling that the book *speaks to them* beyond the singular events in the story.

OK, but how does that happen concretely?

The challenge is to try to turn themes and theses into plot elements, vocabulary, character traits, events and symbols, which will translate into a story. Here are some tips on how to achieve that trickling-down of theme and thesis into text:

- **Think about lexical fields:** brainstorm a small dictionary of words and expressions, linked to your theme(s), which you can sprinkle throughout your story, to allow for both linguistic variation and thematic continuity.

- **Make the most of imagery and symbols:** in that form, you can discreetly weave the thread of your theme and thesis into descriptions, dialogues and characterization. Avoid clichéd imagery – winter to symbolize old age, storms to connote anger, bespectacled characters to evoke intelligence. Try to think creatively, magically – this is children's literature, not your usual boring adult book …

  Shaun Tan's *The Red Tree*, for instance, is a picturebook partly 'about' depression, for which the thesis is that there's always hope in the darkest times. A single blood-red leaf appears on every single page of the picturebook. The leaf is mentioned nowhere in the text, but it is visibly *there*, scintillating against the sepia colour scheme of the pictures. This single red leaf symbolizes the whole thesis of the book.

- **Strategize your uses of dialogue:** dialogue is a good way of keeping track of the theme and thesis, while remaining subtle about it. During dialogues, your narrator isn't burdened with the task of spelling out to the reader what the book is 'about'. Your *characters*, instead, can organize that debate, grab on to your thematic thread, expose different points of view and plot future action in much more complex, lively and multiform ways than a singular narrative voice could have achieved on its own.

- **Optimize your beginnings and endings:** the exposition scene, as discussed earlier, should give hints of theme and thesis. As for your ending, which we'll talk about in depth later, it should tie up – or leave purposefully open – what you set out to talk about in the book. Endings, as a text's last impression, have a powerful hold on the reader. They shouldn't be just about fireworks, emotional closure and quickly filling up plot holes: they are your opportunity to confer a lasting sense of meaning to the text.

Workshop: theme-to-story brainstorm

For this workshop exercise, I'm going to put you in the apparently absurd position of having to write a story on a set theme.

Well, not quite absurd. Because as a debut author, at the moment, there's just you and your book idea and you're free to do whatever you want – enjoy! But once you start getting published and stacking awards and medals all over your fireplace (move over, ghastly china dogs, scented candles and wedding pictures), it wouldn't be out of the ordinary if your editor said to you over lunch – 'Oh, I could really do with a fun, gripping chapter book series on friendship. It would also have secondary themes like jealousy, loss, competition, and a bit of romance … Would you be interested in doing that?'

And then you'll say, 'But of course! I am terrific at turning themes into story – for, dearest editor, all those years ago, I did a workshop exercise in a book on writing children's fiction that asked me to do precisely that!'

Then she'll immediately write you a big cheque and you'll get started, unafraid of having to go from theme to story, and knowing exactly how to lend it coherence and continuity.

I'd like you to write a two- to five-page story for early readers about moving house. I've given you the theme, not the thesis, nor any secondary themes. You are entirely free to say whatever you want on the matter; to have any number of human or non-human characters, and any number of secondary themes and plotlines; to set it in the past, in the future, or here and now.

Review

Without rereading your work, try to sum up the following in one sentence:

> This story's primary theme is 'moving house', and the secondary themes
> are _____. The story's thesis is that _____.

If you haven't managed it, why not? If you feel that your thesis is deep, intricate and not easily 'sum-up-able', try to articulate that complexity to a degree. If you can't, try to resist arguing that it's too subtle for words, and ask yourself how to address that.

Now reread your work once, and rate your text out of 10 according to whether you think your theme and thesis are present in:

- the exposition scene   1 2 3 4 5 6 7 8 9 10
- dialogues   1 2 3 4 5 6 7 8 9 10
- descriptions   1 2 3 4 5 6 7 8 9 10
- characterization   1 2 3 4 5 6 7 8 9 10
- imagery   1 2 3 4 5 6 7 8 9 10
- the ending.   1 2 3 4 5 6 7 8 9 10

If some passages are less satisfactory, try to rewrite or rephrase them.

Now read your work again. This time, circle the words and expressions which relate to the main theme of the story. How many *different* words and expressions can you find?

How would you rate, out of 10, the richness
and originality of this vocabulary?   1 2 3 4 5 6 7 8 9 10

Locate passages where the same words are repeated, or where you feel the vocabulary and imagery aren't quite as evocative as you would like. Try to rephrase these passages.

Now try to understand your thesis. As objectively as possible, which of the following adjectives best apply to your thesis? (You can select several.)

ambivalent	☐
controversial	☐
closed to interpretation	☐
open to interpretation	☐
original	☐
comforting	☐
conservative	☐
revolutionary	☐
pedagogical	☐
authoritative	☐
liberating	☐

Are you happy with defining your thesis as such, or do you think you would like to modify it? If you're unhappy with it, try to reflect on what happened in the process of writing to make you lose track of your thesis. How could you rephrase and edit the story to make it more faithful to your wishes?

Now reread the whole story one last time, thinking of the child reader, and rate your writing in response to the following statements:

- The theme is presented clearly throughout the story.

  1 2 3 4 5 6 7 8 9 10

- There are several secondary themes.

  1 2 3 4 5 6 7 8 9 10

- The thesis appears clearly throughout the story.

  1 2 3 4 5 6 7 8 9 10

- The story leaves the reader space for questioning and nuancing the thesis.

  1 2 3 4 5 6 7 8 9 10

- The theme does not overshadow character development and plot conflict.

  1 2 3 4 5 6 7 8 9 10

- The thesis does not stifle different character voices and opinions.

  1 2 3 4 5 6 7 8 9 10

Where to next?

Maybe you're now feeling liberated – it's OK to write 'about' something! It's OK to have a 'message', as long as it's interesting and complex! And it's OK not to wait for the muse: it's OK to write, like a mercenary, quite a good little story from just one little imposed theme. But for an even better, even bigger story to develop from an even better, even bigger range of themes and ideas, you now need to focus on structure – on the skeleton of your future book. The next chapter takes you to a building site.

3

Crafting a plot and sticking to it

At least 50 per cent of the people reading this now will be thinking: 'I can skip this part. I don't plan. I'm a seat-of-the-pantser, an improviser, a risk-taker, I don't do synopses. I follow my intuition to wherever it takes me.'

If that's what you think, you're in good company. Famously, Stephen King says in *On Writing* (a must-read), that he never writes a synopsis, never plans anything – he just *writes.* I can't explain how toxic this revelation has been for 'planners'. My (non-writer) cousin derisively told me one day, when I explained how much plotting I do, that I clearly wasn't doing things right, since that's not how Stephen King does it.

But Stephen King never says one shouldn't plan. He says *he* doesn't plan. And the next, less palatable thing he says, which people tend to lose sight of, is that he *edits like crazy*. That's the harsh truth: a story isn't going to magically structure itself as you write it if you haven't synopsized anything at all. At some point in the process, a structure will have to emerge. And if it's not *before* you write, it will be *after*.

Planning doesn't matter so much at the level of a stand-alone book, because there will always be time to edit, both alone and with the editor. But at the level of a whole series, it's absolutely indispensable. It took J.K. Rowling many years to plan the monstrous seven books of the *Harry Potter* series. *Harry Potter* remains, it's fair to say, one of the best-planned children's series ever written. The number of plot holes is minuscule. Resonances from book one to book seven are phenomenally well prepared. Thank goodness she'd planned it all before the books became a hit, because it would have been a disaster if it'd turned out she had no idea what was going to happen. Meanwhile, the screenwriters of *Lost* ... well, I'll let you be the judge of how much of a plane crash it can be when such things aren't thought through from the beginning.

It can't hurt to practise planning and synopsizing, even if you eventually reject the idea. For years I resisted the thought that I needed to plan – I liked to think of myself as a free-flowing spirit – but now, for me it is much easier to write with a neat little synopsis.

Character-led, story-led – or both?

One possible objection to the totalitarian writer of these lines: 'But *my* stories are character-led!' is the implication that not everyone writes detective novels or mysteries or adventure novels that need to have rigorous and coherent narrative arcs. 'Character-led' stories (whatever that means) can just be improvised, following the muse's murmur, because structure doesn't matter at all when describing a fictional character's psychological development.

But 'character-led' stories, or let's say psychological dramas, absolutely need to lean on strong narrative structures. The fact that most of the development happens 'in the mind' doesn't mean that it should be entirely 'discovery-written'. On the contrary – your story is much more likely to be incomprehensible, boring and impossible to edit if it is composed of unstructured internal ramblings. A badly structured story arc will still be mechanically easier to fix.

Teenage novels are especially likely to have 'psychological' or character-led storylines. You may want to write about a young girl coming to terms with the death of a friend, or about a young boy standing up to bullying. Every new development of these characters' personalities and relationships will need to be grafted upon solid narrative scaffolding. It cannot exist in a vacuum, for its own sake.

 Key idea

Whether your story is 'abstract' and psychological, or a very 'concrete' whirlwind of action and adventure, synopsizing is useful. All stories require pacing and structure – that is, preparation.

The home-and-away pattern in children's literature

In children's literature, and to a very large extent in Young Adult literature too, there is a traditional story arc which you will, intuitively, almost always return to: the home-and-away pattern.

It does exactly what its name indicates. Hansel and Gretel are sent away from home, kill the witch and go back home (having somehow forgiven their parents) with lots of cash. Max leaves home, tames the monsters, and goes back home to find his supper still hot. Alice falls through a rabbit hole in the quiet garden, runs around Wonderland for a bit, and is sucked back up to waking life when the situation gets a bit tricky (please don't do that).

The home-and-away pattern, inherited from traditional fairy and folk tales and, before that, from legends and myths, carries ideological assumptions about children's literature: namely, the idea that the child, 'in order to grow up', must solve a conflict away from the comfort of the family nest, and then fly back to it to confirm that s/he has both evolved personally and improved society. This prodigal child has shown that they can survive in adverse conditions, but adventures are sandwiched between two comfortable slices of home.

There's nothing wrong with this story arc, which creeps up in many adult books, films and series – think of *Family Guy*, where every story is about restoring the status quo disturbed in the first few minutes of the episode. It can be unexciting if the only thing at stake is to set things back to what they used to be. But it can be very interesting if the endpoint is *not quite* similar to the beginning: if the situation has been improved and transformed by the child character, and if s/he has developed intriguingly in the process.

Children's literature scholar Maria Nikolajeva has theorized that this home-and-away pattern lends the children's book a 'carnivalesque' feel. The carnivalesque is a literary concept Nikolajeva draws from Russian thinker Mikhail Bakhtin, who was himself inspired by what happened in medieval carnivals. For one day only, the rich and the poor, women and men, adults and children would swap costumes and roles. For Nikolajeva, children's literature, especially with home-and-away patterns, *temporarily* allows children to live exciting, 'adult' adventures, to be stronger and more powerful than adults, to change the adult world. But all these adventures take place in the safe knowledge that home will be there before and after the carnivalesque rise to power of the children: that the traditional order will be restored. However, this traditional order will always retain within itself the possibility of further transgression, since it's happened before …

This traditional story arc requires a number of features, which can be found in very different stories, as shown in the following table.

	Hansel and Gretel	Where the Wild Things Are	Tintin: The Castafiore Emerald	The Hunger Games, Book 1
Home: beginning situation	Live with parents, who are poor	Lives with at least a mother, wreaks havoc	Live in Marlinspike Hall, enjoy the countryside	Lives in District 9
Home: problem arises	Parents are too poor to take care of them; decide to abandon them	Mother sends Max to bedroom	Several different groups of people come to 'invade' Marlinspike	Nominates herself to represent the District in the Hunger Games
'Away': lives adventures	Go to the witch's house and kill her	Tames the wild things	Get the people out	Wins the Hunger Games
Back home	With money and riches	To find the supper still hot	To the quiet, drama-free Marlinspike	Having changed people's perceptions of the Games; more battles ahead

Let's focus on *The Castafiore Emerald*, which is a particularly interesting example of the home-and-away pattern. In case you're not familiar with this (brilliant) *Tintin* book, here's a brief summary: Tintin and his friend Captain Haddock are enjoying a nice summer in Marlinspike Hall, Haddock's manor. But suddenly everything starts going wrong. A group of gypsies settle on the domain. A crazy neighbour and his whole family keep invading the place. And, worst of all, the ear-splitting diva, Bianca Castafiore, comes along with her tribe of helpers and paparazzi, and her emerald jewel is stolen. The whole story physically takes place at Marlinspike Hall – at 'home' – but it is precisely *not-home* any more: Tintin and Haddock are constantly engaged in trying to gain back their home, namely, to get everyone out. During this 'adventure', the home is constantly threatened, physically and symbolically: the staircase breaks, people and animals keep walking in, nothing seems to *work*.

So in the home-and-away pattern, there doesn't need to be a *literal* away-ness at the centre of the story. The breaking-up of the home, or the 'unrecognizable home' (the 'uncanny' feeling you get in stories like Neil Gaiman's *Coraline)*, can constitute this 'away' moment – until the 'real' home is restored at the end.

Traditional plot arcs, between clichés and reinventions

I can hear some of you mumbling in your beards that you don't want to follow any patterns, thank you very much. But can you avoid following them? A fascinating fact about narrative is that an overwhelming majority of books and films 'inadvertently' follow very well-trodden paths of traditional narratives. This is well explained by Christopher Booker in his comprehensive book *The Seven Basic Plots*, but it has been theorized before, in the field of anthropology, by Joseph Campbell – in his famous book *The Hero with a Thousand Faces*.

Campbell's theory – he was a historian of religion and folklore, not a literary critic – is that there are narrative patterns which are common to almost all ancient stories, religious or legendary, told throughout the world. He wasn't making a claim about literature or film, but many people since then have theorized that all the stories we 'spontaneously' tell follow roughly the same lines – probably because they've been culturally imprinted on us, though some people would argue that there's something 'natural' about them.

So it doesn't mean you have to do it on purpose. Few people do, apart from George Lucas who famously used Campbell's book to write *Star Wars*. But it does mean that it's useful to be aware of the 'monomyth' (that's what Campbell calls the archetypal plot of the hero's journey), if only so as not to resort to plot devices and encounters which have been done countless times before.

Campbell's book is extremely dense and complex – no beach reading – but let's simplify his monomyth to the following elements:

1 **Hello hero:** Our future hero, let's call him Harry, Eragon or Katniss (though the 'authentic' monomyth is very much masculine), lives a quiet life somewhere, but either has always felt that there was something strange about him/her (maybe s/he isn't actually the child of her/his parents) or proves him/herself particularly adept at certain tasks.

2 **Ring-ring:** the hero is suddenly 'called'. Whether it's a giant knocking on the door or a selection for a TV show, the hero is selected to take part in an adventure possibly resulting in him/her getting bruised or dying. The hero might not be too keen at first, but ultimately s/he is swayed, and goes.

3 **Your father wanted you to have this:** the hero is given something – a sword, a cloak of invisibility, a piece of jewellery – which has magical or symbolic properties and will help him/her in the quest.

4 **Mind the gap!:** the hero is invited to cross a threshold to a 'magical' world – which (we'll get back to that) doesn't need to be magical – and is whooshed away to …

5 **A series of adventures:** after a period of initiation, this is the time for trials, tribulations, emotions, defeats and victories. This part is almost endlessly stretchable. Campbell notes that it often comprises a number of events such as being tempted, obtaining help from various people, going down to hell and back again, setting things straight with one's dad, and finally getting to 'the boon', the big object of the quest which will reconcile the two worlds and prevent nasty things from happening to everyone.

6 **Return of the grumpy teen:** just as the hero is starting to enjoy her/his successes, s/he has to go back to where s/he started. S/he is understandably a bit miffed at this. But it is necessary, the narrative tells us, because the victories must make him/her the king or queen of the two worlds and save his or her little friends who aren't lucky enough to be as good at magic spells or archery.

Campbell sums it up as follows:

> *A hero ventures forth from the world of common day into a region of supernatural wonder: fabulous forces are there encountered and a decisive victory is won: the hero comes back from this mysterious adventure with the power to bestow boons on his fellow man.*

The monomyth is a useful tool. The fact that it is so omnipresent, generally speaking, in bestsellers of all genres does show that there is something about it that works, that resonates. But it is also immensely boring. We've all encountered both children's and adult books that studiously follow the monomyth and make us want to pick our nails with the corners of the pages while lazily looking out of the window instead of reading them.

 Key idea

Use the monomyth if you like. But transgress. Adorn it. Kill it. Pick and choose. Drown it in its own wealth of clichés. Be cleverer than it. And please, don't think of saying of your hero that he is 'The Chosen One' unless you're writing a parody.

Another important thing to bear in mind is that the monomyth isn't just for adventure stories or fantasy. The world that the hero goes to can be simply another part of the real world – in the case of *The Hunger Games*, for instance, Katniss steps into the world of reality TV.

And finally: the monomyth, despite its concrete stages of trials, temptations, tribulations and treasons, recapitulates psychological moments of development in the hero and his helpers. There's no point in writing a story full of such adventures if we cannot feel the hero's tale of *maturation*. Children's literature is by definition characterized as *Bildungsroman*, as the Germans would have it: as a tale of growth, of getting to know one's place in the adult world. That's what your child readers are actually interested in, not just in the exact way of defeating a draffin (a dragon-griffin hybrid), though that's quite exciting too, in its own way.

Secondary plotlines

Secondary plotlines are one of my favourite things as a reader and as a writer. They give stories density and depth, and are deliciously multi-purpose. They can be used for characterization, but also as red herrings, and – my favourite thing – they can be innocuously *there* the whole time until it is suddenly revealed that they contained a key ingredient of the main plot.

Someone who does this to perfection is J.K. Rowling. Each *Harry Potter* book is a masterclass in secondary plotlines, with their various uses, more or less dramatic. Here's a sample from *Harry Potter and the Prisoner of Azkaban*, which beautifully fuses unobtrusive secondary plotlines into a grand finale:

1 There is a recurrent worry about Ron's rat, Scabbers, who keeps running away and being injured and scared. This is all attributed to the arrival of Hermione's cat, Crookshanks – until the very end, when we discover that Scabbers was a wizard-turned-rat, who was terrified by the escape of the good wizard Sirius Black whom he was responsible for throwing into jail. Scabbers's metamorphosis into Peter Pettigrew will precipitate the return of Voldemort.

2 Hermione's behaviour is strange and she tends to forget things – or seems to disappear. Ron and Harry don't pay much attention to it. Only at the end, in the final chapters, will Harry discover that she had been using a Time-Turner to go to several classes at the same time – and this object will be indispensable to saving Sirius Black.

3 Buckbeak, the ferocious hippogriff, has his own secondary plotline: he injures Draco Malfoy and is unfairly condemned to death. His liberation, at the end, by Hermione and Harry, will allow them to take to the skies to save Sirius from one of the towers of Hogwarts.

4 One of the teachers, Remus Lupin, seems to have a strange illness, and his 'biggest fear' is apparently just a silver ball. Only Hermione has guessed that he is in fact a werewolf, and this discovery will be of crucial importance, once again, in the final scenes of the book.

5 Harry's gradual apprenticeship with Lupin leads to him being able to master the Patronus spell, which chases the terrifying Dementors away. At the very end, he uses this spell to dispel the Dementors ready to suck the soul out of Sirius – and discovers that his Patronus has taken the shape of his father's, who was the fourth of the Marauders.

6 The what? The Marauders, of course – Lupin, James Potter, Sirius and Peter Pettigrew – who were, all that time, the creators of the map that Harry had been given by Ron's brothers, and had been using to get in and out of Hogwarts …

Secondary plotlines are, in this series, impeccably and impressively arranged. Their uses are not solely narrative: they are also essential for characterization, and smoothly lead to indispensable flashbacks which help Harry and others understand their past.

Secondary plotlines, I think, are one of the more difficult aspects of planning and plotting, but the good news is that they can often be reintegrated afterwards – precisely because they only need to pop up here and there. Here are a few tips for planning them:

• Think about 'giving' secondary characters plotlines of their own. One of your main character's sidekicks, for instance, could be discreetly doing something on the side which is ultimately revealed to be important. For instance, in *Scam on the Cam*, the third book in my *Sesame Seade* series, Toby's fascination for frogs – which annoys Sesame and her friend Gemma no end – actually leads to a vital clue being revealed at the end.

• Try to 'expel' crucial plot elements towards the 'margins' of the story. If your character absolutely needs a certain object to complete his or her quest, the temptation is to make him or her aware of this very early on, and focus on his or her efforts to get it. But what if the character *doesn't know* that s/he needs this object? And what if this object is unobtrusively presented, here and there, until the revelation that it was always in plain sight?

• Use every mode of narration you can exploit. Snippets from newspapers, a radio programme the main character lazily listens to, a conversation overheard in the street … all of these can be cobbled together by the intelligent reader to understand that they form a secondary plotline.

• Make mental notes, or, better, write down notes to yourself as to when and where you can best slot in these secondary plotlines. It's unsubtle to have a conversation between your main character and her friend starting with 'By the way, Annie, did you know that an old man has just moved into the house next to mine? He looks extremely weird!' and leave it at that – the reader will probably guess that something is happening. But only a committed, clever reader will know that something's on if, just as she leaves her house, Annie's friend takes in the general scenery, and notices 'children playing baseball in the street, as usual – and pretty badly, as usual. She smiled as the ball hit a removal van discharging furniture into the house next door – that poor kid would have to apologize to the cranky old man who was supervising the whole operation.'

Secondary plotlines that have crucial narrative importance are particularly effective in stories in which the reader isn't expecting any sort of big revelation – because it means that they're not wondering whether such and such a clue will be relevant or important. 'Psychological' stories, which might not depend on final twists, can benefit a lot from secondary plotlines which bring in new information or density to their main storyline.

Key idea

Secondary plotlines add depth and density to your plot. It's worth knowing how to use them – and a good place to start is by beginning to notice how other people use them.

The postmodern plot for children

'Postmodern' is a weird word to use in relation to children's literature, but it is increasingly frequent these days – especially in relation to picture books, as we'll see when we get there. A work of art defined as 'postmodern' is one where some of these features appear:

• A lack of clear chronology; mixture of temporalities, temporal inconsistencies

• Metafiction (the work of art plays with the fact that it is a work of art)

• Intertextuality or intervisuality (the work of art makes obvious references to other works of art)

• A mixture of genres, styles, tones, narrative modes

• Difficulty in finding a clear meaning or in fully 'understanding' what the text is getting at.

If you're scratching your head wondering what kind of children's book that could be: there are dozens of these wonderful, 'radical' children's books, as scholar Kimberley Reynolds calls them, from picturebooks to Young Adult novels. Let's take the example of Anthony Browne's picturebooks – *Willy's Pictures* or *Voices in the Park*. You will see how Browne plays, in the former, with references to 'high' art mixed with his own reinterpretation of the paintings. In the latter, he has a field day – or should we say a park day? – with interlinked plots and voices: four people, the same day, telling the same story … but not quite.

Postmodern literature for children recognizes the multiplicity of experiences, the temporal confusion we often experience, the impossibility sometimes of making sense of situations in a reassuringly solid way. How do you make a plot out of elements that are so wilfully perplexing?

Well, firstly – you absolutely *have to plot*. Literature that aims at being nonsensical, ambiguous and befuddling must be extremely well structured, or else your readers will have the strange and boring impression that they've stumbled into someone's LSD-induced dreams. Don't get lost in:

- **multiple temporalities:** flashbacks and flash forwards are great, but the main storyline must keep the reader's attention
- **endless wordplay:** make sure that the reader is still aware that there's a story in this puntastic book, and that the wordplay isn't completely impenetrable
- **references:** don't show off your whole literary and artistic culture in just one book. Remember that all these open windows may remain firmly shut for your readers: does the story still work without knowledge of the referred-to texts?

Dave Shelton's Branford-Boase-award-winning novel *A Boy and a Bear in a Boat* is a great example of a postmodern book for children with still a very clear storyline – quite literally, a boy and a bear in (several sorts of) boats, drifting on the ocean and encountering all kinds of monsters, storms and other problems. But it is postmodern because the reader must work hard against their own desire to know what on earth (or rather, on sea) is going on. We don't know why the boy went into the boat with the bear. We don't know when this is taking place or – even less – where. There is no satisfactory happy ending – or is there? All of this plays with – and frustrates – our usual expectations of narrative. But this playing around remains firmly anchored within a storyline which makes sense, is easy to follow and brings more opportunities for questions.

If you're going to write a relatively postmodern children's book, keep in mind that, although such books are probably more likely to win awards and be internationally respected than more formulaic fiction, they're also more difficult to pitch. It could make sense, from a career perspective, to start pitching to agents and editors with slightly more traditional narrative forms and then, once you're 'in the place', to take out the Postmodern Book which will transform our assumptions about children's narratives for ever.

Cliffhangers: keeping the reader hooked

Cliffhangers, in comics and in films, are moments when the main character is literally or symbolically hanging off a cliff when the episode finishes. In serialized comics or webcomics in particular, it isn't uncommon to find, at the end of the page, a panel in which the character is put in a very tricky situation – which will be solved next week. This recipe is used, of course, abundantly in TV series.

When you're writing your synopsis, make the most of the moments at the end of your chapters, or towards the comfy middle of the story, when you can strategically introduce cliffhangers. These are, famously, those moments that simply require the reader to keep reading; try as they may, they will not be able to put the book down. They are generally of the following type:

- The character has been engaged in some kind of extenuating action, and you leave them 'hanging' there without telling the reader what happens next (until they turn the page).

- The character is relieved: she's won something or found success in one aspect of the plot, and she now thinks all is well in the world. But suddenly she realizes something … or a new plot element is introduced … and it changes *everything* …

- The character has decided to do something very important for the plot that sounds extremely exciting. But before you show the reader what that is, you're going to have a whole chapter of Something Else (flashback, flash-forward, other scene, etc.).

Of course, there can be many other types of cliffhanger. Try to see where you can include scenes like these; they speed up the pace and keep the reader hooked. Generally, a good place to start is by identifying the times when your story takes a new turn: a new element is revealed, your character makes an important decision, or the villain suddenly returns from the dead. These are strategic places which you shouldn't waste on lukewarm dialogue, and which you should work on pushing towards the end of chapters. Many people think: 'Oh, I'll read just another chapter and then turn off the light and sleep.' You don't want them to turn off the light – *ever.* Well, not until they've finished your book, at least.

Cliffhangers can be overused and hackneyed, so don't do it all the time. In particular, avoid cliffhangers that are completely meaningless. The reader will feel cheated if the menacing 'knock knock' at the door was actually a woodpecker (unless you're doing it for comic effect), and won't 'believe' in the next cliffhanger. ('Oh, it's probably just another bird. I'll turn the light off and continue reading tomorrow.' Failure.)

Other ways of spicing up the plot

Tip a few of these into your plot and let it simmer for a while …

- **Red herrings:** the character, the place, the object, the theme, the word your reader will think is all-important to the story – and will keep an eye on the whole time-but then discovers that you've discreetly assigned that role to something else. 'Distracting' your readers doesn't just mean entertaining them – it means tricking them and cheating them and playing with them. And they'll love you even more for it – which is great, isn't it?

- **Tragic irony:** easily inserted a posteriori (but why not gain time and do it now, at synopsis stage?), tragic irony is traditionally reserved for sad or difficult plots or subplots, or for characters whose fate is harsh in some way. The point of tragic irony is to include a trail of hints, puns, clues of what is going to befall a character – but making it sound as if they're great things at the time. For instance, in a teenage novel where a very popular girl ends up disgraced and falling into a fountain during prom night, there could be scenes throughout the novel where water is alluded to whenever she's around. It can range from her pushing a rival into the fountain first (less subtle) to her being alluded to as the fount of all gossip (puntastic) through to her voice being described as crystalline and fast-flowing (relatively impenetrable). These clues are 'ironic' because, at the time, they seem to confirm the character's superiority. Tragic irony is a technique inherited from classical tragedy.

- **Foreshadowing:** foreshadowing works like tragic irony, except that it doesn't have the negative connotations and is much more wide-ranging – it actually includes red herrings, which are a form of foreshadowing. Foreshadowing is all about giving discreet signs of major plot events (even plot resolutions) or character development, in such a way that only the most attentive readers will pick them up – or readers who are reading the book for the second time. Foreshadowing is very easy to get wrong – in which case you end up with *telegraphing*, which is when your attempt at foreshadowing is so bad that your reader immediately understands what it's all about. This is the kind of mistake that will easily be picked up on by your beta readers (see Chapter 16).

- **Ellipses:** Ellipses are moments when the narrator suddenly 'forgets' to tell part of the story. This could cause, for instance, a jump forward in time, and it's only later on that we will find out what happened in that 'invisible' segment of the narrative. For example, a character could be in a very tricky situation at the end of a chapter, and the reader might expect the next chapter to follow directly from that scene, but … no! wait a minute, the next chapter starts the day after! What happened that night? How's the main character still alive? Has something changed in the story? Maybe the hero did something that night that you don't want your reader to know quite yet. And you can be fairly sure that this secret will keep them reading. Ellipses, as you can see, work very well with cliffhangers.

  The interesting thing with ellipses is that they can be used for first-person narratives as well as third-person narratives, so feel free to experiment. There is no reason why the 'I' of your story should tell your reader everything. In fact, it makes it much more exciting if they don't (but more on that later).

All of these devices share one overarching aim: *to keep the reader hooked.* While there's no reason to expect that your reader should read a 600-page teenage novel in one sitting, it's important to ensure that the thought of free-time-with-your-book will occupy their heads all day while they revise for their exams. This is why the synopsis stage is so important: it is the moment when you're going to put in place a solid structure on to which to pin their nascent addiction for your words.

How to write a synopsis

But how do you write a synopsis? How do you even start?

People have different ways of doing it. Some use flashcards that they can swap around and organize in different ways, each of them symbolizing a chapter or scene. Others do the same thing on computer programs. Others draw spider diagrams. There's no big universal recipe (when is there ever one?). But I find it quite useful, whatever medium you choose, to begin by writing down a few sentences with all the main information that you want to convey in the book. Write down the main storyline, but also the secondary plotlines you can think of at that point. Write them very factually and with no concern for anything but the basic plot; the development of the characters' personalities that you want to achieve; potential references and symbolism.

Then try to spin this by writing, chapter by chapter – or section by section – what happens in the story. Begin with just a few words or sentences by chapter, and see how it feels – you might want to add more information or take some out. Trust your intuition – if you feel you're stifling improvisation and creativity, don't tell your future-writing-self *everything*. Write down things like 'Find way of getting Arabella out of burning room' instead of 'Plant fire extinguisher in Chapter 2 to use in Chapter 5'.

I've made writing a synopsis sound very academic and rigorous, but it's a bit messier than that. In fact, writing a synopsis is quite like assembling IKEA furniture.

1 It requires fitting together lots of bits and bobs that you had lying around in different places and had no idea what went where, before you read …

2 … the instructions – also known as: your jotted-down notes on a tiny Moleskine that must have made sense some time in the faraway past but don't any more. Therefore you're going to follow the most understandable ones, but for the rest …

3 … improvise. Especially as that tool that screws something into place on Step 3 doesn't work at all for Step 9, unless you sort of hold it at a different angle and help it fit with an old kitchen knife …

4 … Ouch! Erm, what the hell are all those random pieces that fit nowhere?

5 … and why the hell has that flimsy thing on Step 6 completely gone loose all of a sudden?

6 … Dammit, it's bigger than I thought.

7 … Except that part, which is surprisingly short – I'm sure that's not what I had in mind …

8 … I know – what if I started with the last steps and then worked my way backwards? YES, it works!

9 … Nope, it doesn't. Ah, wait, now it sort of does: it's a bit wobbly, but let's say it's fine …

10 … except that I somehow need to move that piece I've already used in Step 21 back to Step 4.

11 … *huge racket signalling the heavy collapse of something studded with metal*

12 … That's it, I'll never be able to salvage it. Why, why? Why am I so useless? What basic motor skills do I lack? What part of my brain has stopped working? I knew I wasn't ever made to do this; I knew it was too complicated for me. I'm such a fraud. O cruel object, I had such grand designs for you … such wonderful ideas of how to decorate you, how to make you mine, how to get people to like you! It's all gone now, gone! I'm going to chuck you in the bin! *kicks it furiously*

13 *clunky noise* Oh, what's that piece?

14 Could it be the one that was missing from Step 3 …?

15 YES! IT WORKS!

16 IT WORKS! Look at it! Look! Look! I've done it! DONE DONE DONE! Ta-dah!

17 Can now go and sleep. The work is done, my friends.

18 Except the whole place is in a huge mess. Will deal with it tomorrow.

19 Next day: damn. The work is not actually done. I now need to put things in it, and on it, and decorate it, and make it mine. This is just the … *gulp*… beginning.

20 God. The whole structure'd better not crumble down on me the minute I try to put a tiny little thing on it. Let's see … *Huge racket*

21 Put the kettle on.

Workshop: building a synopsis

We're almost done with this chapter. I'm now going to ask you – guess what? – to build a synopsis for your book. If you're halfway through your book already, try to write a synopsis for another one rather than the one you're writing; but if you're only a few pages in, then why not try to synopsize the whole thing?

So I'll let you write your synopsis the way you prefer – flashcards, computerized, Moleskine, Scrivener, Post-it notes stuck all over your windows.

And now have a look at it and …

Review

Pacing and rhythm

Reread your synopsis. What constitutes, would you say, the *build-up* to the main action? How much of it *is* the main action? And how much of it is about winding down towards the end?

How do those three moments balance one an other out? Is there one that seems too long – typically, the beginning – and one that might be too short – typically, the ending?

Have you added elements that speed up or slow down the pace, such as cliffhangers and ellipses? Evaluate how well placed they are – are they strategic or just gimmicky?

Main plotline

From your synopsis, rate, out of ten, how clearly these elements appear:

- General thrust of the story (what is at stake)   1 2 3 4 5 6 7 8 9 10
- How the main character is involved in it   1 2 3 4 5 6 7 8 9 10
- How difficult it will be to achieve it   1 2 3 4 5 6 7 8 9 10
- How original this struggle will be (variation from the basic pattern/monomyth)   1 2 3 4 5 6 7 8 9 10

Secondary plotlines

How many secondary plotlines do you have? Are they purely entertaining, 'decorative'? Or are they important for the main storyline? If the former, see how you can make them interlink with the main storyline, as opposed to just existing in parallel.

Special effects

How well have you prepared your reader for the ending of the story? Rate out of ten the potential success of these effects, if you use them:

- Planting of clues   [1] [2] [3] [4] [5] [6] [7] [8] [9] [10]
- Red herrings   [1] [2] [3] [4] [5] [6] [7] [8] [9] [10]
- Foreshadowing   [1] [2] [3] [4] [5] [6] [7] [8] [9] [10]

And last but not least, try to answer the following questions honestly:

1 Do you still want to write this story?

2 If not – why? Has the synopsis taken some of the 'mystery' out of the writing process?

3 Do you feel more confident now about writing this story?

4 If not – why? Has the synopsis got 'too much' in it to remain manageable?

Try to rewrite the synopsis according to your needs and the needs of the story. Then decide how you want to use it. Some people 'write over' their synopsis: it's always there on the page, and they erase it as they write chapter after chapter. Other people – such as me – keep the synopsis in a separate document, and only refer to it when needed. Once again, there are no right or wrong answers.

Where to next?

In this chapter you will have learned the type of effort that you might want to put into the writing of a synopsis before beginning to write. There are basic plots and basic plotlines but, perhaps more importantly, there are special effects that you can use and twist and play with to give your story momentum and keep the reader interested.

In the next chapter we're going to go further into the technicalities of the telling, rather than the structuring. These technicalities – tense and perspective – are essential to get right in order to captivate the reader and serve the synopsis you've now so painstakingly written.

4

Perspective and tense: who speaks, and when?

Is it necessary to have a whole chapter on perspective and tense? Well, obviously, I believe so – and will, I hope, persuade you that a great deal of reflection should be devoted to these two aspects of your future text. You don't want to be in that terrible situation when you're halfway through the book, you've just switched on the kettle for cup of tea number four of the morning, and suddenly it dawns on you …

'My book doesn't work using that perspective.'

In fact, right now, as I type these lines on a grisly grey morning (of May, it being Britain), I am procrastinating (and have been for the past two weeks) rewriting a book proposal in another perspective. The first-person narrative *didn't work*. The editor wants it in third person. Easy, right?

It's torture. Rewriting a book in another narrative perspective is actually one of the hardest things you could have to do, because everything that constituted the atmosphere and tone of the book has to be modified. If first and third person were that easily interchangeable, there wouldn't be such intense anxiety when you realize that the one you've chosen doesn't work.

Tense is also strikingly important because the tense you use will modify the experience that the reader has of very many things in the narrative, including the all-important trust in the narrative voice, and distance from the events. A story told retrospectively in the first-person pronoun will send a very different message from the same story told in the present tense with a third-person internal narrator.

Children's books these days – especially Young Adult – will happily try to convince you that all stories should be 'I, in the present tense'. Don't believe them. All these decisions aren't self-evident, but they are essential. So let's dive into their subtleties.

Internal, external, omniscient: all about the narrator

Hello, academia! It has been a while. Here are definitions from literary criticism that can help us see more clearly what a narrator *does*.

- To begin with, **what is a narrator?** You've probably got a fairly good inkling, but perhaps you're not sure about the difference between narrator and narrative voice or perspective. A narrator is the fictional persona created by the author to tell the story. This persona can remain unnamed and as discreet as possible – as is the case for many third-person narratives – or it can be named and very much visible – when it's also one of the characters acting within the story, as in first-person narratives. Regardless, there's *always* a narrator in any story, including picturebooks.

- **The narrative voice and tone** are characteristics of the narrator's speech. The narrator may be sarcastic, tender, joyful, deadpan: anything that real and fictive characters can be. It may be extremely bland, too, which sometimes can be useful for strategic reasons.

- **The narrative perspective** corresponds to where this narrator is placed, and therefore announces whence the story comes.

- The narrator can be **intradiegetic** or **extradiegetic, homodiegetic** or **heterodiegetic**. I won't overload you with jargon, but the existence of that jargon is justified: we've had to categorize the many ways in which a narrator can be present or absent from the story it is telling. The *diegesis* is, roughly speaking, the story; so an intradiegetic narrator is 'inside' the story, and an extradiegetic narrator is 'outside' the story. A homodiegetic narrator is 'itself' in the story (i.e. first person), a heterodiegetic narrator is 'different' from the story (i.e. third person). There can be, therefore, at least four different basic combinations making up the narrative voice, which I'll simplify as follows:

  - A narrator who is also a character in the story and tells it in the first person: for instance, Georgia Nicolson in *Angus, Thongs and Full-frontal Snogging*, by Louise Rennison, who writes her own teenage diary.

  - A narrator who is not a character in the story and tells it in the third person: for instance, the narrator in *The Jolly Postman*, by the Ahlbergs.

  - A narrator who is not a character in the story and tells it in the first person: for instance, the narrator in *A Series of Unfortunate Events*, by Lemony Snicket, where the narrator says 'I', but describes events happening to other characters.

  - A narrator who is a character in the story and tells it in the third person: this one is more contentious but, roughly speaking, it defines those narrative voices that are in the third person but intensely focused on one character and his or her emotional and psychological life, 'following' him or her only – for instance, the narrator in *Harry Potter*.

First-person narrators who are also characters in the story may or may not be telling their own story. For instance, two of my French Young Adult novels have a first-person narrator who follows all the events, but doesn't actively take part in them; other characters are the 'stars' of the show. A first-person narrator who tells their own story (as happens most frequently) is called an autodiegetic narrator.

There are many subtleties with narrative perspectives, but let's simplify. Here are places 'where' the narrator can be:

- **Inside the head of one character:** whether in the first or third person, the internal narrator has access to thoughts and feelings of this privileged character.
- **Inside the head of several characters:** this type of narrator, either pluri-internal or omniscient ('who knows everything'), can dive in and out of all or some heads.
- **Outside the head of any character, or with only restricted access:** the external narrator, generally in the third person, has much more distance from the internal lives of the characters and can only describe events.

All these decisions have crucial effects. An internal narrator will shorten the distance between reader and character, giving access to more psychological information than an external narrator; therefore the reader may have to work less hard to derive this information from the character's behaviour and actions. This is why, perhaps, such narrative viewpoints are often privileged in children's literature: there may be an expectation that children aren't able to understand psychological states unless they are clearly stated. This is, of course, highly debatable.

There are trends in narrative voices. Omniscient narrators have fallen out of fashion, but they used to be very common. As for entirely external narrators with little access to the characters' inner lives, they are relatively rare and quite difficult to get right. They are, however, found in picturebooks.

Key idea

If you feel your book isn't working right now, it could be because the voice isn't right. There are many different combinations for narrative voices to emerge, so try to see if another could work better.

Each genre and format will be tied to a number of narrative expectations, but don't feel that you have to follow them all. Yes, it is common for adventure stories to be told through an internal third-person narrator, while much Young Adult fiction these days has a first-person narrator, but there's no reason to abide by these conventions. Actually, there are many reasons, in children's and Young Adult literature, to be cautious with first-person narratives.

Me, myself and I: the omnipresent first-person

First-person autodiegetic narratives are legion in children's and teenage literature of all genres. Towards the 1970s the trend started spreading, perhaps following a psychologizing trend in adult literature which had been going on for much longer.

Literature for children and teenagers really centred on the self – on the lived experiences, thoughts and emotions of the young protagonists, on their inner lives.

But the first-person pronoun isn't a neutral choice and shouldn't be seen as a choice by default. First-person narratives are, by definition, very close to the main character – the narrator and the main character conflate – and therefore it can be difficult to allow the young reader to remain critical towards the character's actions; to ensure that s/he isn't tricked into adopting one omnipotent point of view.

First-person narratives can be quite totalitarian if badly used – many cheap, 'emo', pathos-ridden teenage books rely on easy responses from readers, because after spending so much time 'inside' the head of a character, it can be hard to adopt a sophisticated readerly attitude towards this character – to remember that this character might be wrong, or excessive, or simply 'not-them'.

Ask yourself why you want to write in the first person: is it because you feel it will make identification easier in the reader? Is it because you feel it will make the description of psychological states a bit less tricky? If this is the case, it might be worth reconsidering that choice. Or is it because you want to do something interesting with that first-person voice, because the narrative *is* this first-person voice, and you want the reader to play and interact with it? If this is the case, that's probably the winning decision.

There are wonderful examples of exceptional first-person narratives in children's literature. Jeff Kinney's *Diary of a Wimpy Kid* is a world-famous, bestselling series of 'novels in cartoons' in which the distinctive voice of the 'wimpy' narrator is truly the star of the show. The first-person narrative allows for the narrator to be at different times witty and self-deprecating, which the young reader delights in.

Amazing things that can be done with the first-person pronoun include double first-person narratives, or even more. *The Lottie Project*, by Jacqueline Wilson, cleverly works in that way: the narrator, Charlie, is both the autodiegetic narrator of her own story, and, in alternating chapters, the author of a first-person narrative of the life of her alter ego, a Victorian chambermaid named Lottie. This beautiful Chinese-box treatment of first-person narratives shows the reader what can 'hide' behind a first-person narrative. The first-person narrator doesn't say *everything*; the reader can remain critical towards the two stories.

Third-person narratives

The third-person pronoun used to be the most evident choice when writing a book – any book – for children. It's interesting to think of the reasons for that – maybe adults didn't feel they could get 'inside the head' of a child, to speak the 'I' of the child character. And yet, even very early on, third-person narratives for children forayed into the heads of child characters, accessing their psychological states and feelings. The Countess of Ségur, France's most famous classic writer for children, who wrote in the late nineteenth century and is still widely read, used the third-person pronoun almost exclusively. But she also provided a lot of information about what was going on in the heads of the children.

The third-person narrative, when it is very close to the thoughts and feelings of just one character, can be basically indistinguishable from a first-person narrative. However, the third-person pronoun can be used for more significant reasons. Once again, distance is crucial, especially if your story has a very tricky theme. Do you want the reader to be plunged directly into your character's head, or do you want them to be able to experience critical distance from it – to be reminded that they are *not* the main character? Dissolving identification is sometimes good, and the third-person pronoun can help.

For instance, Sita Brahmachari's teenage novel *Kite Spirit* has a young protagonist, Kite, who is grieving the loss of her best friend Dawn, who has committed suicide. Teenage suicide is an extremely difficult theme – it's crucial not to glamorize or romanticize it. It's also a very sombre theme which could make for an unbearably dark narrative. Cleverly, Brahmachari uses the third-person pronoun to create some distance between the reader and the distressed Kite. Although the prologue and some small parts of the novel are written in the first person, the rest of it is 'she'. See how she describes the burial of Kite's friend:

> *Kite peered down into the deep hole that had been dug where now a murky pool of water was forming. Jimmy followed Kite's gaze into the hole and as he did two great tears rolled down his face and dropped into the filthy mud puddle. Jimmy and Hazel clung together, holding each other up. Hazel's face was still blank, as if her kind, lively spirit had flown out of her. Kite recognized something of how she herself felt mirrored in Hazel's eyes.*
>
> Brahmachari, 2013, p. 53

Brahmachari's use of the third person is very shrewd. She shows the reader not just Kite but other people who are mourning Dawn (here, her parents), and she shows them, not through Kite's eyes, but independently. There are several perspective shifts in this extract. The narrator, who in the first sentence conflates with Kite, peels away from this viewpoint, 'leaving her', so to speak, to look into the hole. It then focuses on Dawn's parents. It's only in the last sentence that the narrator 'reintegrates' Kite's mind, explaining how she feels once again, but even this happens in relation to *other* people – Hazel, in this case. Brahmachari takes great care to distance us and herself from the potentially claustrophobic, narcissistic focus on Kite which a first-person pronoun could have produced.

The third-person pronoun can also be a strategic plot device. It allows you to:

- pop in and out of the main storyline to mention other secondary storylines
- temporarily abandon your main character (ellipsis!) and let him or her 'have their little secrets'
- tell the reader something the character doesn't know.

The third-person narrator is also a good way of introducing humour, even if your characters are completely humourless. Additionally, it allows the narrative voice to have a higher register of language and a more nourished vocabulary than the age of your protagonists would allow. The narrator can be extremely literary even as your characters are five or seven years old; as it is telling the story, it can do whatever it likes. A first-person narrative needs to have a more realistic 'voice', closer to what the protagonists would be expected to utter.

Other types of narrative

How about narratives in 'you' and 'we'? They're perfectly possible and appear regularly in children's books. The Young Adult novel *Stolen*, by Lucy Christopher, is written entirely in the second-person pronoun 'you', and in the past tense. Distinctively, this 'you' is the kidnapper of the heroine, Gemma: she's writing him a letter. The use of this pronoun is extremely important. Firstly, it tells the reader that Gemma has left her kidnapper; she is writing 'from the future', so the question is never whether she will get away from him, but how, and what happened. Secondly, the second-person pronoun creates a claustrophobic atmosphere perfectly in tune with the story: this is a tale, the narrative voice says, of 'me and you', and no one else. Thirdly, the effect it has on the reader is unsettling, because it is indirectly addressing the reader *as* Gemma's kidnapper.

The use of the second-person pronoun is, of course, even more common in picturebooks. *Don't Let the Pigeon Drive the Bus!*, by Mo Willems, directly addresses the reader, telling them not to let that pigeon be in charge of anything. *A Book*, by Hervé Tullet, is written in the imperative voice: press here, turn the page, etc. In my own *Sesame Seade* books, and in many humorous series for young readers, the narrator sporadically breaks into questions – 'Don't you think?' or 'You see?', which give a sense of communication with the reader. This 'you' is a different 'you' from the one in *Stolen*; it is unmistakably the reader who is addressed, not another character in the story.

The collective pronoun 'we' has also been used in children's literature. E. Nesbit's novel *The Treasure Seekers*, for instance, is told as a collective 'we' encompassing all of the Bastable children, though the shrewd reader recognizes that one of them in particular might be 'writing the story down'. In *Cheaper by the Dozen*, by Frank and Ernestine Galbraith, the collective 'we' is impeccably respected, and stands for the 12 Galbraith children.

Key idea

Relatively unusual viewpoints need to be justified; they must make narrative sense, not just be gimmicky.

The tradition of the past tense

Let's turn to tenses now, starting with the past tense. The past is the 'traditional' way of telling a story; 'Once upon a time' sets one up for a tale of a distant past. However, even in old stories there are moments in the present tense, or even in the future. The irruption of the present tense accelerates the action or highlights a particularly intense moment of the story, and the future tense can project the reader far, far away from the story being told, into its long-term consequences.

The past tense is a crucial device for the narrative distance I've been going on about. This tense sends a clear indication to your reader that the story is over and the narrator knows what's happened. This allows you to drop hints about the ending, and to detach the narrative voice from the character voice. The past tense thus isn't just a default choice; it has narrative purposes. If your main character dies at the end of the story and the story is in the first person, you might want to revise your decision to tell the whole thing in the past tense.

I won't get into too much detail about the past tense as it is the one, I think, that beginner writers are most likely to know best … and most likely to discard, in favour of the snazzy, sexy, kinky present tense. Let's have a look at the temptations of that tense, then, and the potential benefits and issues of its (mis)use.

The temptation of the present tense

At an event I attended in Cambridge a while ago, Philip Pullman talked about Philippa Pearce, and mentioned her relationship to time and temporality. He made an offhand comment about how she stuck to the past tense – not like those contemporary novels which all seem written in the present. The audience latched on to this passing sentence to such an extent that all the questions after the talk revolved around it. Many questioners, who, it must be said, were quite old, argued that the omnipresence of the present tense in contemporary texts for children could only mean one thing – children and teenagers are taught to 'live in the present', to receive 'instant gratification', to 'forget about their roots' and to 'have no patience'.

This position is, of course, absurd (and not at all what Pullman meant). There's no *intrinsic* link between a narrative in the present tense and 'living in the present', just as narratives in the past tense don't make anyone more old-fashioned or more ancestry-obsessed.

However, it is true that the present tense is too often used thoughtlessly, automatically, just to follow trends, particularly in Young Adult literature. It's such a powerful tense that it would really benefit from not being misused, from not being generalized too much. Here are some examples of narratives in which it can be used meaningfully:

- **Action-packed, life-endangering stories** where the outcome for the main character is uncertain; the present tense casts doubt over whether they will survive

- **Diaries, chronicles and 'live' accounts:** these particular stories modes should of course be written by mimicking what they would be like in real life – that is, day-to-day narratives.

- **Narratives where the present tense is linked to the very themes and values of the story:** this is the case, for instance, for the Young Adult series *Slated*, by Teri Terry. In these novels, the young heroine, Kyla, has been 'slated' – her memory has been erased after she allegedly committed a crime, and she quite literally lives in the present. The novel uses the present tense to reinforce the fact that she has no past.

When writing in the present tense, you might find it difficult to do things that are easy and feel 'normal' in the past tense. One of them is foreshadowing – although it is entirely possible to do foreshadowing in present-tense narratives, it is difficult to do it *well* and the result can be quite jarring – mostly because it suddenly causes the reader to ask uncomfortable questions. So do they *know* what is going to happen?

For instance, a sentence like this:

> *I told her I didn't know, which was true at the time.*

is relatively unobtrusive within a narrative because, although it gives a slight hint that 1. the character *will* know more later on, and 2. might choose to lie about it, it doesn't really distract from the flow of the general story. Try it in the present tense:

> *I tell her I don't know, which is true right now.*

This sentence is much more confusing for the reader because the 'right now' indicates the possibility of a future in which the character might know and lie, and yet the present tense seems to contradict the idea that the character would be able to project himself that far with certainty.

When little occurrences like this happen, the reader generally realizes that this is what we might call a *false* present tense: a narrative tense which seemingly presents events as they happen, but which actually recalls them as such. With such a device, foreshadowing is possible. It is quite a different use of the present tense from a 'true' present tense, which 'pretends' that neither characters nor narrator have any knowledge whatsoever of what will happen next.

So remain aware of what your present tense is doing, and where your narrator is. Are you going for a false present tense? In which case, why not use the past? Are your characters and narrator 'discovering' the story as they go along ('true' present tense)? All this needs to be sorted out.

 ## Key idea

The tense of a story has important consequences for the story itself; there's no easy disconnecting of the two. Having to change the tense of a whole story is not just a matter of modifying the endings of the verbs.

Mixing tenses and/or viewpoints

These days, it's very common – especially in Young Adult literature – to mix tenses and viewpoints. This device used to be avant-garde but has now fallen into the mainstream, and people are used to reading texts which alternate between past, present and even future, and 'I', 'you', 'he' and 'she' or even 'we'. Some books – once again, especially Young Adult – 'help' the reader shift viewpoints by using different fonts, or splitting the different perspectives into tidy chapters, or suddenly switching to italics when a different 'voice' arrives. This device can, I personally think, become corny and should be used sparsely, but many editors would beg to differ – they sometimes think teenagers can't cope with the difficulty, and insist on typographical eccentricities. As always with writing, it's up to you, up until the point when it isn't up to you any more.

Mixing viewpoints is a particularly good strategy in two prominent cases:

1 You have a complex, fragmented plot, in which different people have to do different things independently of one another.

2 You have quite a simple, linear plot, but the main interest of your story resides in showcasing the variety of personalities and reactions of your characters.

In the first instance, different perspectives will help you build the plot, retain suspense and create expectations and surprise. In the second instance, different perspectives contribute to psychological depth and richness.

The first case is best exemplified by contemporary TV series: *Lost*, *24* and so on are textbook cases of the endless possibilities of mixing viewpoints in order to deconstruct (and then reconstruct!) a complicated plot. It works particularly well for action-packed stories, political drama, fantasy and some crime stories. Philip Pullman's *His Dark Materials* trilogy thus becomes increasingly choral, because many characters have important parts to play and they are playing them in completely different worlds.

The second reason to mix viewpoints is 'quieter': it can add psychological interest. The same question or theme can be explored from the various perspectives of different characters who will have different things to say about it. This device can prop up a story to the extent that the plotline itself becomes secondary. A good example of this is R.J. Palacio's *Wonder*. We first meet Auggie Pullman speaking in the first-person pronoun, and understand that he was born disfigured. We follow him as he goes to high school for the first time, under the vacillating glances of all his schoolmates. But then the viewpoint shifts; we 'jump' from head to head – from Auggie's sister to her boyfriend, to Auggie's 'best friend', to Auggie's 'enemy' – and we learn different things in the process about what it feels like to live with Auggie, to go to school with him, and also to have things in one's life that have nothing to do with Auggie. The young boy who is the centre of gravity of the text is sometimes displaced to leave room for other concerns – as, indeed, is the case in real life.

This choral dimension of mixed viewpoints allows for 'breathing space', particularly in Young Adult books which would otherwise feel quite claustrophobic and centred on the same heavy topic. But there are some cases where 'simple' mixed viewpoints (typically s/he stories, where only a couple of characters alternate) can have the opposite effect: that of closing down on to one main storyline, only seen from two different angles.

Mixing tenses is somewhat rarer, in children's and Young Adult fiction, than mixing viewpoints, but the same rule applies: it must have narrative or psychological interest. In the instance when a whole story is told in the present tense, incursions into the past (flashbacks) or into the future (flash-forwards) can logically be told in the past or the future. But this always needs to be connected to what you're trying to achieve in the first place.

The unreliable narrator

Ah, the unreliable narrator – the Holy Grail of postmodern narration (though it existed long before the twentieth century). The unreliable narrator – generally a first-person narrator, though not always – is a device which, if used well, can have staggering effects on the reader and lead them to question not just the story but also the very concept of fiction. Unreliable narrators can indeed be very metafictional, namely, raise questions about the process of writing and the nature of the 'suspension of disbelief, a term that Coleridge coined as the main psychological process at work when we open a book or (though Coleridge wasn't much of a cinema-goer) watch a film.

The unreliable narrator is a narrator who doesn't *quite* tell the reader everything that s/he *could*. That narrator wilfully retains information, or even lies, or 'forgets' to say something crucial, or hints at that something in a way that may or may not attract the attention of some or all readers. In other words, the reader who encounters an unreliable narrator should realize that s/he can't count on that narrator to tell the whole story. Everything will be a struggle: the reader must wrestle with whatever the unreliable narrator grants him or her, and recompose and interpret the story from the fragmentary information s/he is given.

Sometimes a story quickly lets us guess that its narrator is unreliable and that we'll have to make do with that. Mark Haddon's Young Adult novel *The Curious Incident of the Dog in the Night-time* plays on the fact that its narrator and main character, Christopher, is autistic – he has Asperger's syndrome – and that his vision of the world will be unreliable. This interferes even with the format of the book: since Christopher is often more visual and mathematical than verbal, he doesn't tell the story as a more 'usual' narrator would. He chooses to number the chapters using prime numbers rather than cardinal numbers. The reader is led to understand, after Christopher explains why he likes prime numbers, that this book is truly Christopher's creation, on which he exerts his control: he wants the story to be told his way, and that means the reader had better be clever if s/he wants the full picture.

Christopher gives clues, however, as to how the reader may better understand his condition and therefore decipher the story 'through' his 'unreliable' eyes. He tells the reader that he finds people 'confusing' (p.19), because 'people do a lot of talking without using any words', and 'often talk using metaphors' (ibid.). The idea is to warn the reader that Christopher will have a very literal understanding of the world, and that he will find it difficult to analyse other people's reactions to events. This will arm the reader with useful knowledge for interpreting the story.

Sometimes the reader faced with an unreliable narrator will have to rely on previous knowledge and experience to 'fight' it and gain access to the story. This is the case even in picturebooks. The so-called 'postmodern picturebook' (a term for complex, fragmentary, multifaceted contemporary picturebooks) is often characterized by an unreliable narrator. Let's take *The True Story of the Three Little Pigs*, by Jon Scieszka and Lane Smith. In this hilarious and profound picturebook, the Big Bad Wolf (or Alexander T. Wolf, as he prefers to be known) takes his own defence and explains what 'really' happens. It's unfair, he claims – 'nobody knows the real story, because nobody has heard my side of the story'. And on he goes, arguing that it was all really a very big mistake ...

The young reader who will doubtless have heard the 'other side' of the story will recognize moments where both 'versions' match, and s/he will also be alert to differences between the two. The interplay between words and images, as we'll see in the chapter on picturebooks, is of course a central dimension of the success of this ironic, unreliable tale.

Children's literature can offer readers their first encounters with unreliability in story-telling. It's a radical device which calls into question more things – parental reliability, the concept of fiction, and the power of pictures to 'lie' as well as tell the truth …

Workshop: the same scene … from different angles

The idea of this workshop exercise is to narrate the same scene from different angles. I'll leave you free to decide whether these different angles are temporal or character-led; in other words, you can choose to tell this scene 'as it is lived', 'as it is remembered', and 'as it is anticipated', or you can choose to tell it as it was lived by different characters at the same time, or you can mix the two: one character lives it, the other one remembers it, and the last one has long hoped for it … The idea is to help you gain narrative fluency with different tenses or viewpoints, and also to show you, possibly, that the first one you pick – perhaps more intuitively – isn't necessarily the most exciting one or the 'best' for the particular purpose. You may have much more fun when you go past 'obvious' narrative viewpoint and tense and try something new.

I'll give you a choice of three famous scenes. Pick one, and match it to any genre of children's or Young Adult literature:

1 Cinderella losing her shoe at the ball
2 John Fitzgerald Kennedy being assassinated
3 Moses opening up the Red Sea.

Explore this scene from at least three different angles, and play around with style and tone.

Review

Now, without rereading your work, try to finish the following sentences for each viewpoint:

The main narrative advantage of this viewpoint is _____

_____.

It also adds to the psychological depth of the scene because _____

_____.

It is incomplete and 'needs' the other two viewpoints because _____

_____.

This is the 'rational' aspect of your reflective process: try to think as an editor would here. The editor would want to know *why* you're using this particular viewpoint, *how* it adds depth to your work, and finally *why* it needs other, presumably complementary viewpoints. If you find that you're struggling with one of those sentences, it could be that the viewpoint you chose is gratuitous, or so 'full', so complete, that it does not interplay nicely with the others.

Now reread your work. The main dangers of multiple angles (whether temporal or character-led) are repetitions and redundancies. As objectively as possible, rate yourself (from 1 to 10) on the following:

- I haven't repeated the same elements without some degree of constructive variation. 1 2 3 4 5 6 7 8 9 10
- I haven't dwelled on exactly the same elements every time. 1 2 3 4 5 6 7 8 9 10
- Each perspective has focused on some elements which other perspectives haven't. 1 2 3 4 5 6 7 8 9 10
- The reader learns something new with each new perspective. 1 2 3 4 5 6 7 8 9 10
- The overall interpretation of the scene is enriched by the triple outlook on it. 1 2 3 4 5 6 7 8 9 10

Try to address issues. Have you talked too much about one aspect of the scene, to the detriment of other, potentially interesting, aspects? Have you retold the same story without enough variation to make it exciting? Try to diversify your viewpoints by making your different characters, or your different perspectives, focus on various objects which the other perspectives don't allow for.

But, most of all, have fun. This is a great creative exercise because it truly allows you to play with style, tone, genre, and as a prompt it might even lead to something greater.

Where to next?

We've talked a lot so far about 'characters' as if it were possible to take that concept for granted. Obviously, it isn't. The next chapter focuses on characters as crucial units of your story. And of course, when talking about children's literature, we can't talk about characters as we would if we were talking about stories for adults. We'll see how psychological depth and richness can arise from animal characters as well as human ones, and how child and adult characters should differ (and also not differ) to enrich the fabric of your text and avoid caricature.

5

Children, adults, animals, monsters: characters in children's literature

Hardly had the editor pushed the button for floor 12 than the author started talking to her.

'So I have this great idea for a great book. It rests on a great trio of great characters. First there's a rabbit called Robert Rabbit, and he's got a friend called Catriona Cat, and they're both really scared of the mean Felicia Fox, and they live on a farm where …'

The editor looked right and left. There was no escape. She wondered for a moment whether she could open the vent on the ceiling of the lift but, even then, where would she go? She was trapped. The author carried on:

'…and they get some help from Roland Rooster and Ryan Raven …'

DING! The lift stopped and the doors slid open to let someone in. 'If you'll excuse me,' said the editor, 'this is my floor.'

'This is only floor 3,' remarked the author. 'I thought you were going all the way to the top?'

'I've just remembered I had something urgent to do on this floor,' said the editor.

'But this is a car park,' said the author.

'Bye, then!' said the editor.

'Call me!' said the author.

'Sure,' the editor replied, and she took off her high heels and ran away at rocket speed.

For your 'elevator pitch' to work, you need to show immediately that you've got good characters. Not just a good story – good characters that lead your story. That means: not characters that you got straight out of a Beatrix Potter story. Not characters that smell so strongly of cardboard that you could stick them under a wobbly chest of drawers. Not characters which have a big 'recycled' sign on their faces.

Good characters, then. Great characters, even. And you're writing for children and young adults, and that means that you have no excuse: characters are one of the central things which children's books do so much more richly than literature for adults.

Main characters, from heroes to antiheroes

Often, on editors' and agents' 'wish lists', you'll find that they ask for 'strong character-led stories'. The idea behind such a request is that the book should have not just an exhilarating plot, but also depend on the personality and actions of one or more central characters. This is particularly important if the editor wants a series: the main attraction of a series, as we'll see later, is the familiarity-and-change dynamic, and main characters are a dominant force in this dynamic.

In all books, from picturebooks to Young Adult novels, a strong main character is a necessity. Characters are entry-points into the story. Many years after reading a book, you might not remember all the details of the plot, but you fondly remember the strong heroine, or the swoon-inducing hero, or the funny little brother, or the irascible teacher.

It all begins with the main character, and there's a wide variety of ways in which this main character can be given shape and strength. Generally, the main character isn't the most difficult one: many authors find that s/he springs to mind at the same time as the story, or even before. People speak of 'a voice' that suddenly occurs to them. Authors become lyrical at this point, saying mystically that they 'don't know' where the main character comes from. Sarah Crossan, author of Carnegie-shortlisted *The Weight of Water*, says that it's only after writing the first 'chapter' (/poem) of the novel that she 'discovered' that her young heroine was a Polish immigrant.

The problem with this reliance on 'inspiration' is that it can lead to stock main characters as easily as it can lead to genius characters. When you think you've got your main character, try to analyse it according to where it might stand in relation to these admittedly crude 'categories' of main characters.

- **The hero:** the typical main character of epic and fantasy literature. Think Eragon, Harry, Luke Skywalker and the knights of old mediaeval tales. The hero is superlatively gifted and (as discussed in Chapter 3) is characterized by his quest as much as he is by any personality traits. He is loyal, he is right, sometimes righteous. He has dark sides, which he struggles against once in a while, and wins.

- **The heroine:** the female version of the hero, still in epic or fantasy, more recent and arguably more complex. Characters like Meg Murry of Madeleine L'Engle's *A Wrinkle in Time*, Lyra Belacqua of Philip Pullman's *His Dark Materials*, Lettie Peppercorn of Sam Gayton's *The Snow Merchant*, are, like heroes, taken on a quest, led to achieve great things, and feisty and strong, but also sensitive and troubled by doubts.

- **The 'kick-ass' Young Adult heroine:** a very typical, recently emerged type of main female character. Heroines like Katniss Everdeen in Suzanne Collins's *The Hunger Games*, Jenna Strong (the name says it all) in Emma Pass's *Acid*, or Page Mulroney in Samantha Shannon's *The Bone Season* are extremely strong, defiant, enterprising heroines, very active, with a bit of a killer instinct, animated by a sense of revenge or involved in dark deeds.

- **The funnies:** girl or boy, nerd or dork or wimpy kids, the funny hero or heroine is often a winner in fiction for young readers. There are countless examples, from Astrid Lindgren's Pippi Longstocking to (my own favourite) Anthony Buckeridge's Jennings and Darbishire, in classic children's literature, and, of course, Richmal Crompton's

Just William, Babette Cole's *Princess Smartypants*, and nowadays Greg the Wimpy Kid and Louise Rennison's Georgia Nicolson. Pretty much all the books that win the Roald Dahl Funny Prize have a funny hero or heroine. They can have very different personalities: some are funny because they're strong and sarcastic, others because they're weak and pitiful.

- **The antihero:** many of the 'funnies' are antiheroes – the Wimpy Kid definitely is – but the antihero or antiheroine can be very different from that, too. It can be a character who appears faulty, an unlikely protagonist, but turns out to be heroic, either in reaction to something or because s/he is looking for something. Christopher, in *The Curious Incident of the Dog in the Night-time*, is an example of an antihero. So is Hannah, in Anthony Browne's picturebook *Gorilla*, who is weak and sad until her toy gorilla becomes transformed.

From über-powerful, strong, relatively 'simple' hero to antihero, there's plenty of personality scope for your protagonist. And your protagonist is also likely to change over the course of your story or series. So leave space for openings, for subtlety in characterization.

Once you have a clearer idea of what your protagonist is going to be like, and once you've decided which perspective to use, it can be a good idea to decide what voice you're going to give him or her. A funny character leading a deadpan first-person narrative isn't the same thing as a character who is funny because the third-person narrator gently mocks him or her. Voice and main character are almost impossible to separate, because so much of what you give away through characterization is a question of form rather than content.

How do you get to *know* your main character? Many authors have 'character sheets', which can look a little bit like this. I have used, for this particular sheet, two very different characters: Jo March of Louisa May Alcott's *Little Women*, and Todd Hewitt of Patrick Ness's *The Knife of Never Letting Go*.

Character	Strengths	Weaknesses	Physical characteristics	Characteristics of voice	Object of quest
Jo March	Strong, leading Creative Funny Rebellious Independent Intelligent	Irascible Easily frustrated Impulsive	Beautiful hair 'Plain' to her, but beautiful to others Imposing	'Complicated' words Speaks a lot Imperatives Questions	Gaining independence while supporting her family Writing
Todd Hewitt	Loyal Emotional Intuitive Righteous Kind	Inexperienced Not very intelligent Easily perturbed	Unremarkable Increasingly manly	Inaccurate spelling and grammar Exclamations Questions Internal monologue	Understanding what happened to the village Running away

From these sheets, some characteristics emerge that are not just linked to the characters but constitute part of plot and style. For instance, while Jo March is the leader of her own story, which is very much a 'quest' type of story, Todd Hewitt often responds to events. These two different kinds of plot (active and reactive) require different kinds of main characters.

But character sheets aren't indispensable, especially for main characters. I know that many writers recommend having very detailed sheets, with 'full backstories' of each character (J.K. Rowling contributed to the myth by saying she'd written the entire biographies of most of the characters in *Harry Potter*). When I see that, I think – yeah, sure. You've got the whole backstory of the hero's mum, even though she only appears at the beginning and at the end of the story and doesn't say much more than 'Put your coat on' and 'Have you had a nice day?'? I'm caricaturing this a bit, but the point is that there's a moment when you have to stop worrying about whether the characters are as close as possible to real people and start wondering whether they're doing a good job in your story.

Another problem, if you begin to consider your characters as real people, is the 'amorous author' syndrome. When you're published, you'll meet a lot of amorous authors. They're the most annoying people on this side of the galaxy. They're purely and simply in love with their characters – they'd like to marry the swoon-worthy gallant they created, they're 'best friends' with their protagonist, they 'just adore' the dog. They're bizarre. Don't become one of those. Cultivate distance. Your characters might confuse you into thinking they're real, because they're people in your story, but they're just literary creations.

Now give that main character some friends. And enemies.

Secondary characters, from friends to foes

'IMMEDIATE' SECONDARY CHARACTERS

What I would call 'immediate' secondary characters are, in my experience, the trickiest to get right. The protagonist's sidekicks, in particular, or his or her close friends, are very difficult because they can't outshine the protagonist, and as a result it's hard to give them a strong, engaging personality.

And yet in children's literature it's absolutely indispensable to give your main character at least one person with whom to interact regularly. Duos, trios and quartets of characters are legion in children's books: Harry has Ron and Hermione; Pippi Longstocking has Tommy and Annika; Tintin has Snowy and Captain Haddock. Writing a children's book with a lonely hero isn't a good strategy; children like stories of friendship as well as adventure.

But those damned sidekicks! I'll dive for a moment into personal experience here. I was aware that I had to give my heroine, Sesame Seade, two friends to help her solve her mysteries. But though her voice was extremely strong and assertive, theirs weren't. They seemed to be there just to show the reader how clever Sesame was; but it felt bizarre, in the first draft, that they had any kind of relationship with her, since she didn't seem to care too much about them. Plus, they had apparently the same personality; there was no clear difference between Toby and Gemma.

The Toby and Gemma duo had to be rewritten entirely, once with my agent and then again, when I had a contract, with my editor. I was asked a lot of questions:

1 Why are Gemma and Toby friends with Sesame? Why do they like her?

2 What does Sesame get from her friendship with them? Why does she like and need them?

3 What are Gemma's and Toby's personality traits? How can they contribute to the stories?

Gradually, I started to see that I'd been very lazy in characterizing Sesame's sidekicks. Taken as I was by the overpowering 'voice' of the protagonist, I hadn't noticed that her friends weren't fleshed out. Gemma became her intelligent, righteous, quite posh friend, who can actually reply to Sesame as an equal. Toby became the dreamy, slightly show-off-ish friend, knowledgeable, and constantly arguing with Gemma. They developed credible personalities, and became helpers to Sesame as well as friends. I took care to give them their own side-stories, so that they were never there just to support the main act.

The problem, of course, is that you risk falling into caricature with immediate secondary characters like that: it's tempting to go for Laurel and Hardy, the nerd and the goofy, the posh and the wild kid, and so on. But think about it this way: couples of friends are often quite different from each other and their differences are often what motivates their friendship. Try to see how they can be constructed, not in isolation, but constantly in conversation with each other.

Giving them distinctive features can help. I characterized Gemma as 'wearing pearl earrings', which became the symbol for her being both posh and well liked by adults; but it has narrative importance. We'll talk about all these details later when addressing characterization.

REMOTE SECONDARY CHARACTERS, FROM HELPERS TO INDIFFERENT

You will have to people your world with many different characters, and some of them will inevitably be only remotely connected to the main plot (which shouldn't mean, of course, that they're not useful). Your protagonist might have parents, teachers or adult carers who must be there in the story but are not hugely important. Your protagonist might also have a cohort of schoolmates, some of whom s/he can interact with, but most of whom might just be there in the background.

Such characters can fulfil an incredible variety of narrative functions, so think carefully about them. To avoid bland descriptions and unexciting dialogue with secondary characters of that kind, see whether they can help in one or more of the following ways:

• **Inadvertently giving information that will be crucial to the plot,** whether or not the main character understands it as such immediately

• **'Blocking' the protagonist,** making it more difficult for him or her to succeed, whether or not it's voluntary (adults are particularly good for this)

• **Providing comic relief** – this is a very important strategy: an external character, bringing with him or her new events, can temporarily distract the reader (and yourself!) from a fast-going or quite dark story

- **World-building:** secondary characters, in their variety and disparity, give texture to the world you're trying to create. Through them we discover (or are reminded) that not everything revolves around the main character: there is a world beyond him or her, and it 'feels real'.

So this cohort of 'necessary' characters – at school, at home, in the street, in your intergalactic spaceship – can (and should) also have roles to play in the plot.

ENEMIES AND ARCH-ENEMIES

Depending on what type of children's book you're writing, the enemies can be scary or mundane, but it's likely that there's often going to be at least one antagonistic character in most stories. It's entirely possible, of course, that your antagonist might not be a character but a tornado, a wolf, or even the main character him- or herself.

To create your own villains, think of the different villains, enemies and arch-enemies of children's literature. The first to spring to mind are probably Sauron, Voldemort, the Big Bad Wolf and so on. But actually, even in those stories, there are other, secondary enemies, or less obvious enemies who still antagonize and block the main character. Gollum and Malfoy are not as bad as the arch-enemies in the books, but they still hinder the main characters' paths. Of course, many Young Adult novels will have antagonists who are just normal teenagers but a bit obnoxious – like the annoying Lindsay of *Angus, Thongs and Full-frontal Snogging*.

To give texture and depth to your villains, think of them, as you would your main characters, as complete individuals. They might be funny sometimes; they might also be pitiful. They might have reasons, in their twisted minds, to act as they do. They might also not realize that they are antagonists: this is the case, for instance, with adult characters who act simply to 'protect' the children in the stories, unaware that their actions will have the effect of slowing down the protagonists' quest.

When working on the characterization of the villains or the antagonists, it's worth bearing in mind that such characters are perhaps the easiest to caricature or to get 'wrong'. Ask yourself at all times whether you've seen a villain like this one before, and whether you're not just falling into a common pattern.

Characterization, direct and indirect

Characterization defines the process whereby a reader gets to know and understand a character. One essential rule about characterization is: don't make it simple. Just as there are many ways to get to know someone – by asking them questions, by hearing their voice, by seeing where they live, by reading their Facebook statuses, by listening to what other people say of them – there's an infinity of ways to get to know a character, and 'just letting the narrator tell you' is not a good strategy.

Broadly speaking, there are two types of characterization, which very often intersect:

1 **Direct characterization**

Robbie was the kind of nice kid in the neighbourhood you'd be happy to play with on Sundays if you got bored, but that you easily forgot to ask over if you were having fun with friends. He was short and funny-looking with his shock of brown hair. He liked boats and airplanes. He was quite a serious kid and his parents made him work hard on his schoolwork; that's probably why he was sort of shy and thoughtful a lot of the time.

Here, the narrator (maybe another child, or maybe a third-person narrator) directly describes Robbie, physically and psychologically, and although Robbie might reveal himself as entirely different from that, for now the picture is quite clear in the reader's mind, and they don't have to do much work to understand what Robbie's like.

2 Indirect characterization

I first met Robbie because his model airplane had landed in my garden. He turned up at the door muttering something about whether he could please get it back because he'd received it for Christmas and his parents would tell him off if he'd lost it. My mum laughed and said, 'Of course, Robbie, go pick up your plane.' Robbie came back with the plane, and before he could leave I asked him if he wanted to play with me for the rest of the afternoon. His face lit up like he'd never heard of such a thing before. It was the first of many a Sunday with Robbie. When he invited me to his place the next week, I got to know his parents, and his dishevelled dog, Obi-Wan, and his tidy little room with too much space for textbooks and not enough for toys. The kids in the neighbourhood seemed to think he was nice, but a bit transparent – a bit invisible.

Here the narrator doesn't directly describe Robbie, and yet the reader gets a clear idea of what kind of child he is. His shyness is expressed through his 'muttering', and through the lack of punctuation and quotation marks, which conveys that he speaks fast and in a low voice as if he's afraid to be there. His dog's name, which he presumably chose, evokes a quite nerdy taste for *Star Wars*, and the description of the bedroom says something about his education, which fits with what we know about him: he has strict parents, and is serious and well read. The narrator ends with a description of what other people say about Robbie; this is a common device of indirect characterization, as it allows for a complex picture of the character to be given: not just how he is perceived by the narrator or by himself, but also by others.

Indirect characterization is generally seen as more 'mature' and sophisticated than direct characterization. This is partly because it's objectively more difficult, and requires more skill, to build a whole world, style and tone *around* a character – almost, so to speak, not touching the character, and yet giving a strong sense of what s/he may be like. Indirect characterization could be seen as 'negative' characterization: you're describing the space that surrounds the character, but you refrain from direct comments on what s/he is like.

Of course, direct characterization should not be rejected outright. You're perfectly free to describe your characters; in fact, it's hard to think how you couldn't. There are some secondary characters which you may need for such a brief amount of time that they will have to be introduced with direct description. But try to see how the more complex characters – and especially the main character – can be painted impressionistically, by little touches, rather than by colouring in predefined contours.

If you're writing picturebooks, it's almost a deadly sin to go into direct characterization. Why start saying that 'Robbie was a brown-haired boy who lived in a big house' when it's very clear from the picture that this is the case? Obviously, the different formats and genres you choose call for different ways of describing the protagonists.

You'll have heard the advice 'Show, don't tell'. Characterization is one of those areas for which this motto absolutely applies. Try to work on that by thinking *outside* the character. Rather than asking yourself, 'What's the character like?', ask yourself 'How does the character influence his environment? How does the character speak? What do other people think of him? How does he dress?' and see how this can give interesting clues to his personality.

 Key idea

'Bathing' the reader in the character's aura, rather than giving the reader a pre-cooked, solid vision of the character, is the best way to elicit understanding, affection and empathy with him or her.

While we're on this topic …

Identification or empathy?

One thing you'll surely hear all the time regarding children's literature is this: 'The reader must identify with the characters.' And you've probably accepted this as fact: children 'need' to 'identify', they must be able to 'project themselves into' the character, to 'put themselves in her shoes'. It's generally seen as a sign of a good children's book if the child 'identifies'.

And yet the term 'identification' is highly problematic and children's literature academics don't like it very much. Identification is a weird process. We don't ask adults whether they 'identify' with Humbert Humbert, the nymphet fetishist of Nabokov's *Lolita*. And yet it's a great book and a great character. But you don't *identify* with him; that's not the point. So why ask children to do so?

'Identifying' with a character is the mark of an immature, unsophisticated and, above all, quite narcissistic reading. It means that the reader can't extract themselves from the subject position of the character: that you're forcing them to 'see themselves' in the book. Asking them to identify elicits an easy but problematic response: they'll lack critical distance to assess the character.

So how can you get your readers to empathize without necessarily always agreeing with your main character to the point of identification? Here are a few tips:

- **Give your character flaws.** Let them be objectively wrong sometimes, and yet still loveable. We don't think our friends are right all the time, and yet we respond to their pain and joys even if we don't think they did the right thing. A good example of this can be found in Louise Rennison's *Angus, Thongs and Full-frontal Snogging* series. The heroine, Georgia, is outrageous in many ways – excessive, obnoxious, sometimes completely lacking common sense, and quite selfish. But because she's so full of life and so much fun, we can empathize with her even when she's 100-per-cent responsible for the mess she's found herself in.

- **Play with language to create distance between the character and the reader.** Texts that trigger blind identification do so because they're in first-person pronoun and there's little space out of that subject position for the reader to relocate. If you're working with that narrative viewpoint, you'll have to think precisely about your use of language. Using modulators can help. Modulators are words and phrases like 'might', 'could', 'perhaps', 'one could say' and so on; they indicate a lack of certainty, or at least a question, on the narrator's part. Sprinkling some of them into your manuscript strategically can introduce hesitation, doubt or even just a trace of 'not-quite-right', which can suddenly loosen the leash you're holding the reader with.

- **Use irony, hyperbole, sarcasm and wit.** Exaggerations and humour are often a good way, even in a first-person narrative, of 'bypassing' the main character and winking to the reader above the narrator's head: you're saying, look, s/he's being silly, ignorant or simply wrong. And it doesn't need to deactivate empathy completely. In fact, the more delusional a character appears – the more ignorant of their flaws, or the happier with what s/he perceives as good but that we perceive as bad – the more we have to adjust to this vision and respond with empathy towards the character. This is, by the way, why narratives about serial killers or 'mad' people can be so strangely disturbing: to their excesses and absurdities we respond with feelings of care and tenderness mingled with repulsion and horror. This kind of unease can be the mark of a great book.

Look at this passage from Anthony McGowan's *Henry Tumour*, when the hero, Hector, starts daydreaming:

> *Small brains*, you see, *crocodiles. A guy came to our school once, talking about them. He had a skin and a skull.* I mean, *belonging to a crocodile. Of course the man had a skin and a skull too, or he'd have looked pretty stupid, not to mention dead. We all filed up to feel them. The crocodile's bits and bobs, that is. There was a tiny little hole at the back of the skull. The man said it was the brain cavity. A snug fit for your thumb. Or something else. In fact I had a little fantasy while he was talking to the class, in which I was left in charge of the thing, and I got horny and as no one was around (in the fantasy, maybe a fire alarm or something), I gave it a quickie, but then the man and the class all came in again, and I turned round with my knob in this crocodile skull, wearing it like a Gothic codpiece.*
>
> McGowan 2006, p. 10 (my emphasis)

Hector's hesitations (marked through modulators I emphasized by plain type), rambling, relatively poor humour and teenage obsession with sex makes his 'little fantasy' impossible to *identify* with – crudely speaking, we're not sexually aroused by it – but we're definitely amused. In terms of characterization, McGowan manages here to tell us all that matters about Hector (he's imaginative, very desperate sexually, and quite funny), without forcing us to adopt his perspective all the time: we still have the option to find him disgusting or pathetic.

Adult and child characters

One crucial difference between children's literature and literature for adults is the attention you have to pay to age. Let's get the first big question out of the way: Can I write a children's book with an adult protagonist?

Of course you can. Can you get it published? I wouldn't be so optimistic.

It may be unfortunate, but children's books with adult main characters are extremely rare. The only exception to this rule, which we will discuss later in detail, is books with animal characters, who tend to be ageless rather than, purely speaking, 'adult'. But writing a children's book that features children only as secondary characters is extremely risky. Paradoxically, the only format where it's likely to be OK is picturebooks. But I wouldn't recommend trying to write a middle-grade or Young Adult novel with adult protagonists.

A children's book 'should' have as its main character a child who is as old, or older, than the upper age of the intended audience for the book. This is because – once again, I don't necessarily endorse this! – publishers believe that child readers love reading about slightly older children, and will not want to read about younger children. According to this vague rule of thumb, therefore, you would have an 8 or 9-year-old protagonist for the 6–8 range, and a 16 or 17-year-old protagonist for the 14–16 range.

Of course, there are major exceptions to this rule, and of course you may be writing a book where the protagonist is 7 years old at the beginning and 16 by the end. Don't let this rule break everything. But it's essential, though authors don't generally like to admit they do this, to think about the age of your intended audience, because you can bet the publisher will, and must, if they're going to sell your book.

So how can you gauge the age of your intended audience? Again, it's all about reading, reading, reading, reading. Read all the children's books you can get your hands on. Chances are, your perception of an 8 year-old is much cuter and twee-er than what actual 8-year-olds are like now. Read (good) books that are generally given to primary-school kids (ask a bookseller). Are you writing something that is at roughly the same level of language, of humour, of plot, of characterization, of theme? Don't think it's shameful to ponder this kind of thing. It doesn't make you a bad person to think about your audience's age just because J.K. Rowling says she never does. Think of it as part of your career-building as a children's author: you're not writing in the ether, you're writing for an audience that can be accessed only through publishers.

Other characters around the protagonist can be of varying ages, of course, and it can be great to show how your protagonist interacts with younger children, with older children, with teenagers and, of course, with adults and with old people. All these differences in age can lead to fascinating characterization and plot devices. But when we get to adults – whether parents, teachers or random passers-by – it's important to get them right.

Adult characters, crudely speaking, can be said to fall into two categories: protectors and antagonists. Albus Dumbledore is a typical father figure: helper, carer, protector; the Dursleys are typical antagonists: cold, angry, useless, mean. The former helps Harry along the way; the latter block his project in any way they can (sometimes even without realizing). Both, however, play a crucial role in his adventures.

But, of course, adult characters – especially parents and teachers – often have these two characteristics. Because adults in charge are protective, they can sometimes block the protagonist's project out of worry or authority. The protagonist can then decide to follow their orders or to bypass them; or perhaps s/he has little choice in the matter. As a result, quite often, in children's literature, you'll find that the adult–child relationships are characterized by one or more of the following:

• The child is blocked by one or more adults from doing something. Some of her quest involves finding a way of disobeying the adults.

• Some adults don't want the child to carry on with her quest; some do. The child is helped by some adults and thwarted by others.

• The child is led to negotiate conditions of her project or quest with adults.

What is at stake here is an important constant of children's literature, well explored by children's literature theorists. In children's literature, there's a persistent tension between the adult impulse to let the child roam free and do their thing, and the adult tendency to control the child and exert their authority. In other words, in most children's books, children have to fight against adults constantly to acquire some freedom for their actions to take place.

Try to think of your adult protagonists' motivations as well as the children's. Why would they *not* want the child protagonist to act in this way? Are they being excessive or unfair, thus justifying the child's disobedience? Will they evolve in some way, perhaps recognizing later that the child was cannier than them? Character evolution of *adults* can be extremely interesting in children's books.

Adults also provide priceless comic relief. Think of children's literature as a transgressive, subversive literature. The powerless and the vulnerable are always delighted to laugh at authority figures. Presenting adults under a not-very-good-light is always a winner. Children winning against them, even in the smallest sense, are winners at life. The best scenes of humour in children's literature – *Pippi Longstocking*, *Jennings*, *Just William* – are scenes of children finding adults ridiculous in one way or another.

Should you get rid of adults entirely? You might have heard that 'getting rid of the parents' is the number-one 'rule' of children's literature. Personally, I think it's wrong; it's one possible device, but it is a great shame to turn it into an axiom. Children are forced to live among adults, whether they like it or not. You might feel that you'll appeal to their most private fantasies if you get rid of the tall humans entirely, but it's more difficult, more exciting and, I think, more honest to try to orchestrate this living-together of adults and children in a meaningful way.

Anthropomorphic and animal characters

Another essential aspect of characterization in children's literature that differs radically from literature destined for adults is anthropomorphic creatures and animals. Since *Animal Farm*, by George Orwell, adult literature hasn't often gone very far into animal tales and animalistic characters. But in children's literature – especially for younger readers – animal characters are everywhere. How do they work, and how can you tell whether you 'need' animals or humans?

There are many types of animal in children's books:

THE 'NORMAL' ANIMAL, FROM PET TO WILD BEAST

I'm calling it 'normal' in the sense that it is an actual animal with realistic characteristics, but it takes part in some way in the plot. This animal can be important or not; it can help humans, or thwart them. In Anthony Browne's wonderful picturebook *Zoo*, the animals at the zoo are essential to the story but they remain realistic; it is what they *evoke*, by their body language and the way they are caged, that truly creates the story. An extreme example of the importance of 'normal', realistic animals is the pony story. In such books, the animal is at the heart of all concerns; it is perceived as a 'friend', the protagonists may 'confide' in it, but it remains an animal.

THE 'TOY' ANIMAL

What I call a 'toy' animal is a quasi-realistic animal, alive but sitting at the crossroads between cuddly toy, pet, comfort blanket and friend. This is the case, for instance, with Snowy, Tintin's dog: cuddly and faithful, it sometimes speaks (though it is unclear whether Tintin understands him), and he accompanies Tintin everywhere. It is even clearer, of course, in stories where animals are actually cuddly toys, such as *Winnie the Pooh*, *The Velveteen Rabbit* and many other children's books. The 'toy' pet can be seen as a 'child's child', so to speak, granting the child protagonist and the child reader a sense of domination while letting that 'toy' possess some human characteristics, some of which are childlike.

THE ANTHROPOMORPHIC ANIMAL

Entirely anthropomorphic animals, who can speak, walk, dress and have adventures (with or without humans next to them) are extremely common in children's literature, especially in comics and picturebooks. They can be aware of their identity as animals, or not; there can be a hierarchy between different animals. The big advantage of such characters is the lesser importance of age; it's difficult to tell how old Babar is or whether Snoopy is a child.

Another huge advantage of anthropomorphic animals is that they allow for 'difficult' themes to be developed in a softer, fable-like way. This is the case, for instance, with *Duck, Death and the Tulip*, by Wolf Erlbruch; the duck-protagonist's death is less violent than if it were a child character.

Of course, anthropomorphic animals can also make for funny stories, preserving some aspects of humanity while exaggerating the 'animal' side of the characters. As always with animal characters, it's a game between alienation and recognition: the animal is not-quite-human.

THE ANIMAL IN FABLES OR ALLEGORIES

In fables and allegories, character traits attributed to anthropomorphic animals generally add up to a 'moral' or 'message'. This is evident in the popular picturebook series *Click, Clack, Moo! Cows That Type*, by Betsy Lewin and Doreen Cronin, which present in allegorical form the struggles of workers' unions against CEOs, in the guise of a microcosm (the farmyard) that symbolizes the working world. Be careful, however, with fable animal characters; *Click, Clack, Moo!* was criticized precisely because it represents workers as cows and hens … yep, even with the best intentions in the world, representing humans as animals isn't a neutral thing to do.

MONSTERS

Where do animals stop and where do monsters begin? Children's literature is full of monsters and weird creatures, more or less anthropomorphic. They belong to a different domain and are more dangerous, more unpredictable. Like animals, monsters condense traits of humanity but at their most excessive: anger, sadness, violence or hilarity. Monsters, like dragons and unicorns, can help the hero on his quest, or kill him; some monsters are impossible to tame, others are very much tameable – see *Where the Wild Things Are* – but remain unpredictable – '"Oh please don't go! We'll eat you up – we love you so!"' They symbolize the most hidden aspects of the child's psyche. And the adult's, of course …

In Young Adult literature, monsters and hybrid creatures are very frequent, perhaps because writers feel that teenagers recognize themselves in the not-quite-human aspects of the monster or animal. Werewolves and animorphs can translate the profound anguish of adolescence into literature.

THE ANIMAL STORY: IN THE ANIMAL'S HEAD

Many children's books tell the story from the point of view of the animal, literally giving a voice to these silent beings. This is the case, famously, for Anna Sewell's *Black Beauty*, which describes and denounces the treatment of horses in Victorian England. Michael Morpurgo, in *War Horse*, offers the same kind of committed text. The animal can be used as a sensitive, permeable, perhaps more naive and yet more knowledgeable viewpoint on a troubled world.

This (in many ways quite crude) classification might help you decide when and how to use animal characters in your story. Ask yourself whether you're using them because everyone else seems to be doing so, or because there's some really interesting characteristic of animality you're trying to tease out.

Stock characters and how to avoid them

In children's literature, as in all other types of genre fiction, stock characters are a constant risk. One easy way to remedy this is – *read*! If you recognize your character in all the books for the age range you're writing for, it's not a good sign. But, broadly speaking, here are a few stock characters to avoid. I'm not saying that they don't 'work': you might object that you see all of them in bestsellers. I'm just saying that they are uninteresting from a literary perspective, and that any self-respecting author should strive to go beyond them.

THE 'MARY SUE'

'Mary Sue' is the derogatory name given to heroines, generally of Young Adult literature, whose characterization relies on an easy response from daydreaming girl readers. Typically, these heroines are shy, solitary, bookish, lack self-confidence, and describe themselves as plain and uninteresting. However, the story reveals that they attract the interest of improbably handsome and popular boys, one of whom is the Dark and Tenebrous Boy (see below). They all see something in her that she isn't aware of. I'll stop here; the essential thing is that the Mary Sue is designed to appeal to shy, bookish girls who lack confidence, too, and who might through the book entertain the fantasy of being secretly irresistible to everyone. These characters are quite insulting for young readers, and they're also extremely boring. Avoid them.

THE DARK AND TENEBROUS BOY

He is generally the love interest of the Mary Sue, as well as of a whole clique of girls (whom he doesn't care about). He has a secret, or even two or three, and is characterized by Mystery and Anguish. He's tough on the outside but extremely romantic on the inside, and he is impossibly faithful, strong, protective, courageous and fair. He has some violence in him, too; he's often jealous, exclusive and possessive, but these flaws are passed off as evidence of love. You get the picture; such male protagonists are stock characters to be avoided at all costs if you don't want to fall into the trap of bad romance novels.

THE TRAUMATIZED VILLAIN

This is the arch-enemy who 'had a good reason' for becoming a horrible bloodthirsty killer. The reason is to be found in childhood or adolescence and involved some kind of trauma – their friend or parent was killed, or equivalent. We find this out just before the villain is killed or vanquished, and it adds a little bit to our understanding of their motivations, but frankly not very much. Such 'explanations' are always a bit puzzling: what are we supposed to think? 'Oh, now I get it!'? It's especially cringe-worthy when it all relies on a pseudo-Freudian conflict with a dead father, or equivalent. Avoid this *deus ex machina*.

THE PROTAGONIST WHO IS A TREE

For some reason, countless manuscripts for young readers by aspiring authors involve protagonists who are trees, water drops, seeds, clouds and other inanimate objects. I'm not saying it can't be done right: it has in the past and probably will be in the future; but as a general rule of thumb, avoid these 'characters'. It's very difficult to interest anyone in the story of the passing of the seasons over a great oak. I am not exaggerating when I say that almost a third of the manuscripts I rejected when I worked at the 'slushpile' of a British publisher were manuscripts about all kinds of inanimate objects or plants.

THE MAGIC PARENT

What I call 'magic parent' is the idealized, dreamed-of parent that the child protagonist (generally orphaned or half-orphaned) longs for and looks for during his or her quest.

It can be the mother or the father, but it's always a perfect parent, always unfairly treated in some way, and always relatively boring. If you're going to have parents in your story, treat them like any other human character: give them interesting flaws and texture and don't make them the object of your main character's fantasies; they've gone past the Oedipal stage by now.

THE COOL, FUNNY, CLEVER RACIAL FRIEND

We'll discuss questions of race, class and gender at some other stage, but there's always the temptation to give your main character (the white middle-class kid) a whole battalion of United Colours of Benetton friends. There's the Chinese Miss Know-it-all, the hilarious Pakistani pal, the cool Caribbean slammer. Or not. You don't need to compensate for your WASP protagonist by hammering it into the head of the reader that you're not a racist. Supporting casts of 'ethnic' friends are the best way of showing that you don't think very much of them.

How to know your characters while letting them surprise you

One funny aspect of the writing process is that, as many writers say rather mystically, 'the characters take over'. This isn't necessarily a good thing. I don't believe in muses and gods of inspiration, so I tend to interpret the idea of a 'character taking over' as simply a failure to plan for something more complex to happen. But, of course, some degree of freedom must be retained; of course, you must be open to the joyful possibility that your characters might 'surprise' you. This can happen, as you certainly know if you've written before, at any turn of a sentence, in a dialogue, *anywhere*. You write a few lines of conversation and suddenly someone says something that seemingly comes from nowhere and doesn't quite fit with the rest of the story. You wonder why s/he's suddenly come up with that. And then there are two options:

1 You 'listen' to the character and modify the course of the conversation, the chapter, or even the ending of the book to conform to that unexpected statement.

2 You tell your character to shut up by deleting the incriminating line, and rewriting a more reasonable one in its place.

Whatever you decide to do, the most important thing, I think, is that it has to be a rational and unsystematic decision. You have to get rid of mystical feelings ('The character is speaking to me!' 'My unconscious has all the answers!') and instead assess the situation: why did *I* (not the character: the character isn't a person, nor your Socratic daemon, nor a muse, nor 'your unconscious') spontaneously write that? Did I feel, somehow, that the story I'd planned wasn't quite on the right track? Or am I just making it even more difficult for myself to finish the book?

Yes, because, of course, your character 'surprising you' can mean more than one thing. It's not any 'truer' if it's spontaneous and unexpected. It can simply be a downright waste of time. Writers are 'inspired' sometimes, but sometimes they're just looking for a way of procrastinating even more, or even failing to finish their own books. I've seen that happen to quite a few people, who back themselves into corners because they 'listened' to their characters too much (understand: 'unconsciously agreed with themselves that the book was going nowhere'). So retain control over your creation. Demystify 'character agency': it's not a thing. You're the creator; they are just beings of language.

On the other end of the spectrum, there's the controlled, rational, plan-obsessed writer. There's nothing that sticks out as odd or unexpected in their characterization: all the characters, even when they're being humorous or distressed, are giving a sense of dutiful obedience. That writer, you can tell, has got so many 'character sheets' that they will not allow anyone to step out of the tidy boxes. They know what each character should be doing and when, and that's the end of the story.

Of course, this extreme isn't the right one either, and that's why I'd personally advise against obsessive-compulsive character-sheet writing. I don't think it's necessary to have the backstories of everyone written down, nor their tastes and distastes or faults and qualities. I think you're clever enough to retain a lot of that in your head, and thereby keep it flowing, malleable and free. Characterization will adjust according to what you're writing. Some characters will evolve by small degrees. Others will remain more or less what you wanted them to be like at the beginning. If you've frozen all their characteristics on paper from day 1, you won't leave yourself enough leeway to stay open to changes. And think about it this way: *you* are constantly evolving as you're writing; why would your day 1 reasoning be the same as on day 150? New ideas emerge all the time; the story takes shape in both expected and unexpected ways. Follow your synopsis and follow your characterization only to the extent that it doesn't clash with the person you're slowly becoming.

Workshop: characters from one sentence

This workshop exercise will be a little bit freer than the ones before. Write a few pages – of any genre and medium that you feel comfortable with – laying the emphasis on characterization: indirect, direct, through dialogue, description and so on. The idea is to get you to flesh out one or more characters in a short amount of time; give yourself no more than 30–45 minutes.

The only prompt is the following sentence, from Simone de Beauvoir's *Memoirs of a Dutiful Daughter*, which you are welcome to interpret figuratively or literally:

'It doesn't take much for a child to turn into a monkey.'

Review

Now reread what you've just written and try to evaluate the following aspects of your work as objectively as possible:

1 How much of your characterization is direct characterization, and how much indirect?

2 Could you turn some of the direct characterization into indirect characterization?

3 Is/are your character/s coherent? If you had them speak, does their tone correspond to how they are presented? If you had them act, are their actions in tune with their speech and their descriptions?

4 In terms of indirect characterization, how many different devices did you use? You can use the following list: Metonymous setting – Description of actions – Speech – Description by other characters – Activities – Clothes – Family situation – Conversation – Thoughts – Other …

5 How exciting, original, new and interesting are your characters? Do they correspond to common categories of characters? How do they differ from them?

6 How well did you incorporate the prompt within your writing? Did it enrich characterization? Did you take advantage of all the possibilities that writing for children offers?

Based on your observations, try to modify your text so that the characterization is as rich as it can be, and the characters as original and fresh as possible.

Where to next?

Now that you've got your plot and your characterization sorted, we'll focus a little bit more on language – though, of course, language was never absent from your work. Children's literature, unlike what many people think, is one of the best opportunities for a writer to be creative with language. We'll cover this in the next chapter.

6

Playing with language

'So what does your wife do?'

'She's a writer.'

'Ah? Great! Anything I'd have heard of?'

'I don't know – do you read much children's literature?'

'Oh, right, she's a *children's* writer!'

Translation: 'Oh, so she's *not actually* a writer!'

Many people think that, because children's literature is intended primarily for, well, children, it's not *really* writing: it's crafting a good story; it's finding funny plot elements; it's creating characters kids might like; but it's not writing. There's no style, there's no complexity: the language must be transparent and simple because the story's what matters.

There's no such thing as a 'difficult word': respecting the child reader

Let's get things straight: *there's no such thing as a 'difficult word'*. A word is only 'difficult' until one knows what it means. Then it's easy. There are no 'difficult' words, only words one knows, and words one doesn't know. In the case of children, they are constantly learning new words: that is what being a child entails. Every day, they have to hear, understand and assimilate new words. If they don't hear the word 'cantankerous' from you first, they'll hear it from someone else. It's no big deal. They can cope with it.

So if you catch yourself trying to turn 'abandon' into 'give up', 'unkempt' into 'messy' or 'cavernous' into 'big', give yourself a symbolic slap on the hand (or a real one) and keep the 'difficult word'. There's *really* no need to cater to an imaginary audience of illiterate ninnies; enough people are doing that already. Children will understand. The same goes for longish sentences, sophisticated turns of phrase and interesting syntax. Don't 'simplify' all that.

You might object that, if an editor ever picks up your book, they will ruthlessly cross out all the complicated adverbs and bizarre phrases you've put in it. This is partly true – and it's exactly why you shouldn't censor your own work to start with. They might get rid of some 'big' words, indeed – so the more you've slipped in, the more there will be left once the culling is done.

Anyway, you may find editors more receptive than you think. I was terrified that my editor at Hodder – a relatively commercial publisher – would cut many of the funny but quite 'complicated' words and phrases in my manuscript. She didn't. She made me rewrite some sentences for legibility and fluidity, but never once asked whether 'children would understand' this or that. I respected her all the more for that.

 Key idea

> Don't ask yourself whether children will understand. Ask yourself whether *readers* will understand, within the context of the sentence and the book, what a word or sentence means. If readers in general can cope, children will cope.

Once you become a published children's writer, please, *please*, don't let anyone say that writing for children means simplifying and clarifying language, and using 'simple words'. Expostulate with them that they should relinquish their obsolete preconceptions.

Imagery, metaphors and similes

A good place to start analysing the language of children's literature is with metaphors and similes. These can help create exciting, fresh, bubbly imagery. The difference between metaphor and simile is simple. Imagine you have a (human!) character called Peter. Here are two things you could say about him:

- **Metaphor:** 'Peter is a lion.'
- **Simile:** 'Peter is like a lion' (or 'Peter is as brave as a lion').

The metaphor assumes that the reader will understand that Peter isn't *actually* a lion, but possesses characteristics of the fearsome animal. The simile is more straightforward: you are telling the reader, in the former case, that Peter is not actually a lion but *comparable* to a lion; in the latter case, you're telling the reader exactly why Peter is comparable to a lion.

Metaphors are arguably more sophisticated than similes, because the reader has to do more work. Their effect is often more striking. But both can be interesting and fun, as long as they're not corny. Many common phrases rely on metaphor or simile: 'She's a shrinking violet', 'He sticks out like a sore thumb' and so forth. Tacky similes, especially in descriptions (and particularly of girls), are to be avoided at all costs:

- 'Her eyes were as green as emeralds / blue as sapphires / black as obsidian, etc.' Gemstone-like eyes make for ludicrously corny imagery.
- 'Her hair was like champagne / honey / warm chocolate, etc.' Hair and foodstuff, for some reason, have long been associated – and overdone.
- 'Her skin was white and fragile like silk / porcelain/ snow/ toilet paper, etc.' Enough with the fragility and whiteness compared to all kinds of fabric and ceramics.

You get the idea. If it's a metaphor or simile you feel you've heard somewhere else, don't use it – unless, of course, you're trying to parody it. Avoid comparing girls to flowers, jewels, birds or precious fabrics. You're not Hans Christian Andersen; we're almost a fifth of the way into the twenty-first century.

It's difficult to say exactly how to find nice, funny, interesting, moving similes and metaphors. Some of them helpfully just pop into your head. Others require a bit of work. Here's my technique.

When you find yourself describing someone or something, try to think of the 'logical' adjectives that spring to mind. Then ask yourself what these adjectives are, in turn, associated with. You've thus gone two steps away from the original object. For instance: an armchair can be:

comfortable, cosy, warm, soft, deep, comforting (*immediate response*)

and then you can jump from those adjectives to other, associated ones:

plump, chubby, motherly, grandmotherly; like a yawning mouth, like a chocolate muffin, like a sleepy grizzly bear.

The idea is to latch on to the adjectives you spontaneously thought of and let them take you to other adjectives or similes in a free association of ideas. And marvel at the imaginative possibilities. Julian Sedgwick, in *The Black Dragon*, wrote, 'Coming into view are two small islands – furry green caterpillars crawling on the surface of the water' (p. 280). Isn't that a lovely metaphor? You can *see* them, those fluffy green islands which appear to shimmer like caterpillars on the flat sea.

With children's literature you can be very wacky. 'Lily Barnett left the house at noon. The sun like a happy yellow dog licked her face as she opened the door.' Everyone understands immediately what that means – and rejoices, because it's such a cheerful, funny, sunny simile. Children's literature, if you take the time to look, is full of these lovely images. Perhaps because it takes itself less seriously than literature for adults, it is also more daring and adventurous in its metaphors and similes.

Just don't overdo it; the same similes or metaphors can get old, even if they felt so fresh the first time, if reiterated too often. Try not to recycle the same images. There are so many others you could invent.

ALLITERATION AND ASSONANCE, AND WHEN TO KNOW IT'S TOO MUCH

Another good thing you can definitely have too much of is alliteration – as well as its alter ego, assonance. Alliteration is the repetition, in close sequence, of the same consonant or group of consonants; assonance is the repetition of vowel sounds. For instance, Julia Donaldson's famous Gruffalo is described as such:

> *He has terrible tusks, and terrible claws,*
> *And terrible teeth in his terrible jaws*

That's a clear example of alliteration in [t]. He's then described as having 'knobbly knees', and 'turned-out toes', and 'purple prickles'. These alliterations lend energy to the poem and assist memorization. But, of course, poetry for children isn't the only genre in which alliteration or assonance is permissible. One of Chris Priestley's scary stories in *Uncle Montague's Tales of Terror* begins as follows:

> *The garden was enclosed on all sides by a high stone wall that was splashed and speckled with yellow, grey and cream-white lichen ... Set between two fiercely spiked shrubs was a scratched and weathered, arched, bottle-green door with a heavy wrought-iron hoop to lift the hatch that held it shut.*
>
> Priestley 2007, p. 23

Try reading this out loud. You might struggle to do so, or find your mouth full of saliva pretty quickly. The alliterations in [sh], [ch], [s], [k], [r] make you stumble and stutter; it conveys an impression of wildness, danger and also claustrophobia. You feel halted by those stones and plants hindering your walk and your words. Added to that, the very short (monosyllabic) words at the end force you to slow down because they're difficult to pronounce in quick succession. You can just feel the weight of that hoop in your mouth ...

Children's literature relies very much on oral – and aural – pleasure. Think of your works read out loud. Think of the children munching on your words. Alliteration is an excellent way of conveying atmosphere and retaining the attention of the readers or listeners. I use it often, especially in book titles – *Sleuth on Skates*, *Gargoyles Gone AWOL*, and even in the name of my heroine – Sesame Seade. It's a very common device.

However, a mistake often made, I think, by beginner writers, is alliteration frenzy, particularly in picturebooks and poetry books. Sometimes their books look as if no two words following one another could ever start with different sounds. It can become tacky quite quickly. Better resort to the Chris Priestley option: discreet, multiple alliterative sounds, all entangled, rather than the 'easy' option of word duets starting with the same letter.

Metre and rhythm

Linked to alliteration and assonance are other ways of playing with the plasticity, the texture, of language. Metre, rhythm and rhyme are not limited to poetry. Of course, generally, we only tend to talk of iambic pentameters, dactylic tetrameters and all their jargonny little friends when analysing poetry. But, evidently, everyday language has its own rhythm and metre, its own stresses, its own emphasized syllables. And rhyme exists in verse as well, of course – perhaps not as evidently as in poetry, but just as powerfully sometimes.

Just to go back to basics:

The common ballad metre is the most often found in nursery rhymes and in children's poetry:

> Mary *had* a *little lamb*
> Its fleece was white as snow

It is formed of an iambic tetrameter (four beats, all falling on the second syllable – *Mary* here is missing her 'head', so to speak!) followed by an iambic trimeter (three beats, all falling on the second syllable). The iambic trimeters tend to rhyme together; not the tetrameters. Many children's poems follow the ballad form, even if they don't look as if they do. For example, look at the poem 'Busy', by A.A. Milne:

> I *think* I *am* a *Muf*fin *Man*. I *haven't got* a *bell*,
> I *haven't got* the *muf*fin *things* that *muf*fin *people sell*.

Each line is formed of seven beats, easily 'splittable' into one iambic tetrameter and one iambic trimeter. If you've ever tried to write poetry for children, you will doubtless find that you return to this metre very often, because it's so common.

There are many metric variations. To sum up very simply: the iamb goes *taDAM taDAM*, the trochee goes *TAdam TAdam*, the anapaest *tadaDAM tadaDAM*, the spondee *TA-DAM, TA-DAM*, the dactyl *TAdadam*.

These forms translate to specific rhythmical patterns in literature, whether in prose or in poetry, and being able to spot them in your prose will help you make it more grabbing, more interesting, more readable. Readers, especially young readers, are sensitive to the internal rhythm of texts. Feel the stresses and emphases of your words. They are what makes reading like this exhilarating – this is from Philippa Pearce's *Tom's Midnight Garden*:

> *The hall of the big house was not mean nor was it ugly, but it was unwelcoming. Here it lay at the heart of the house ... and the heart of the house was empty – cold – dead. ... Tom heard the only sound that went on: the tick, and then tick, and then tick, of a grandfather's clock.*
>
> Pearce 2008/1956, p. 5

Listen to the precise, beautiful anapaest of 'Here it *lay* at the *heart* of the *house*', echoed later by 'and then *tick*, and then *tick*, and then *tick*, of a *grand*father's *clock*'. This is a story of time, a story about timings that are just a little off-centre. The anapaest, which seems always to be running ahead of itself, perfectly conveys this impression. You will probably also have noticed the alliterations in [h], [t] and [k]. And the heavy 'empty – cold – dead', a placid spondee, prefigures the slow, boring moments of the days that Tom will spend with his uncle and aunt.

Rhythm and metre are essential aspects of language. Learning to play with them will give richness and texture to your descriptions and enliven your dialogues. It will also help you weave together your theme and your thesis, as we saw in Chapter 2, by having them trickle down to the very fabric of the story: language.

Delicious words

There are things you can do to add complexity, lushness and beauty to your language as you are writing and before you write – even as you are thinking of writing. What I call 'delicious words' or 'scintillating words' are words that I find, for some reason – often difficult to explain, and highly personal – *different* in some way: particularly beautiful, particularly gross, particularly sticky or glutinous; in any case, interesting. When I come across one of these words, I note it down in a notebook – I'm by no means a notebook fetishist, by the way; noting it down on your phone is perfectly acceptable. I end up with a list of great words that I cherry-pick, for one story or another, and place at strategic moments.

They can be complicated words like 'coruscating', 'hieratic', 'odalisque', which add mystery to the text. They can be funny, bizarre words like 'smorgasbord', 'bedazzle', 'grotto', which add texture and grab the reader's attention. They can be words that I simply find stand out from the crowd: 'slithering', 'squidgy', 'butterbean'. Whatever you choose, these words that you particularly like will be important to your writing. You will build up to them; you will place them where no one can miss them: they will shine. Try to think of them as little beacons in your book: they should attract the reader's eye, the better to propel it towards the next one, maintaining the momentum of the writing and ensuring that the fascinated reader can't put the story down. Don't drown them in the middle of an action scene; try to fit them at the beginning or end of chapters, in long descriptions, or in important dialogues.

This will force you to slow down as you write. Many books that are described as 'sloppy' are books that were written too fast, perhaps in a bout of inspiration, and not really sustained by attention to detail. Be controlled, precise: words are, after all, your tools. You can't just pick the first one that springs to mind. Just as you don't screw all screws with just one universal screwdriver, you don't describe all cats in the same way, and you don't speak to your brother in the same way all the time. Take your time to select the best words for the scene you're writing. It's being constructed before your eyes; it deserves your attention and patience. Think of your delicious words; would one fit here or there? Try to evaluate whether your first impulse to use a certain word is justified; couldn't there be a better way to express what you want to say?

Key idea

There shouldn't be any difference between children's fiction and 'literary' fiction for adults. Both of them should rely on the finest craft, on the most patient assembling of sentences. Don't get carried away by your own plot and by the exhilarating feeling of being almost done.

On having a notebook, and not throwing things away

I mentioned having a notebook earlier, and I'll expand a bit on what you can draw from carrying a small one around at all times. Personally, I've yielded to peer pressure and generally use small Moleskines. But any notebook will do; or indeed, as I said earlier, a mobile phone or tablet.

I'm by no means a notebook idolater, and I certainly wouldn't say that 'all writers should carry a notebook'. But I do find it useful for the following reasons:

- **Diary:** I write a diary, generally every day, of what's happening in my life but also of what progress I've made on my various projects. It propels me to work more and helps me sum up my own thoughts on how well they're going. I can also easily trace the emergence (and, sometimes, the discarding) of my literary projects.

- **Delicious words:** as mentioned earlier, I do note down words I like or that suddenly strike me as interesting.

- **Similes and metaphors:** if I suddenly think of an interesting simile or metaphor, down it goes in the notebook. You can be sure that you're going to forget it if you don't write it down.

- **Interesting facts I hear and names that could end up in one of the books:** you hear funny, interesting facts every day. A lot of them get lost because, past the first few minutes of enjoyment, you just forget them. Noting them down will help you retain the information. It will also help you think about ways in which it could end up in a book project.

- **Trying out dialogues, pre-writing scenes, working on snippets:** if I'm in a waiting room or on a train with not much to do, I sketch out a future scene or write down a piece of dialogue, or just discovery-write on random topics. These 'verbal doodles', very much like sketches for visual artists, help me prepare for actual writing.

The notebook is, I think, at its most useful when it's used as a repository for words, ideas, expressions and writing exercises. I don't do character dossiers or complex synopses in a notebook. But, particularly for working on language, I find it a very useful format.

Workshop: from banal to beautiful

For this workshop exercise, please excavate from your drawers, hard drive or notebooks an old piece of writing – no longer than three to four pages – which you discarded for some reason; perhaps because it was just an exercise, or perhaps because you never really liked it or it didn't fit anywhere. Pieces of work from the previous workshop exercises are also perfectly acceptable. It should preferably be something that you haven't looked at in a while.

The point of this exercise is to transform this piece of work from lacklustre and banal to splendid and powerful. No pressure.

To begin with, take a pen – red preferably for the symbolism, but any colour will do – and circle or underline the passages which you feel don't quite work. Pay particular attention to similes and metaphors (or lack thereof!); to the use of imagery; to the common, uninteresting words in descriptions or dialogue.

Once you've done this, ask yourself how you could modify that text, diving into the language, to make it truly different. This word that sprang to mind immediately – could there be a better one? Use a thesaurus if necessary. This adjective you glued unthinkingly to this noun – can you find another one? Use the strategy developed earlier: take it one step further. That turn of phrase that doesn't have an edge to it – could you use rhythm to make it more energetic? This adjective plus noun couple – could it benefit from alliteration?

Review

Once you've gone through your work, reread it entirely and assess whether your changes have had an interesting impact. Perhaps you'll find you've made too many; adjust as necessary. Then type up (or write down) the full version, and read it again as it is now, all 'clean' and improved. How would you rate the extent of your corrections?

Of course, this forensic work is artificial; you won't often get the opportunity to work in such depth on a text so short. But that's precisely why you should take full advantage of it; it's by giving yourself time to have this attention to detail that you will develop good reflexes while writing and while editing, and gradually your language will become more sophisticated and more rigorous.

Where to next?

Next, we'll dive into a very specific type of writing for children which, of course, you will have encountered – and might even be thinking of doing: series. Series require their own plotting, their own language, their own narrative strategies and their own characterization – we'll see which ones in the next chapter.

7

Stand-alone or series?

'I'm going to write a stand-alone,' said the children's writer. 'None of that series nonsense for me! I'm a *serious* writer.'

A year and a half later, in the editor's office:

'We just loved your book. It's amazing. And Carmilla Grant is such a wonderful character. We're looking forward to her adventures in the next book! So, shall we sign this four-book deal?'

'What?' stuttered the writer. 'But it's not a series!'

'Well, it *could* be!'

'But it's not!'

'It is now. Just sign on the dotted line. Here's 20K.'

The writer groaned, signed and mumbled, 'Next time, I'll write a real stand-alone. The heroine dies at the end.'

'Oh,' shrugged the editor, 'that would still be OK. We'd contract you for a prequel.'

In children's publishing, everyone is constantly thinking about series. Series, series, series. And chocolate. Editors think about chocolate quite a lot as well.

Most genre and commercial fiction is dominated by series. Detective novels, fantasy, science fiction, comic fiction – there's only romance, really, which tends to be stand-alone, because we'd be hugely bored if we had to pore over the happy marriage of the two protagonists once the chase is over. Children's literature is no exception. Publishers are unanimously and constantly on the hunt for good children's series, of any genre and for all age ranges.

This shouldn't mean at all that you mustn't write a stand-alone book. There are plenty of them, and they tend to be the ones that win prestigious awards, and they tend to be more literary. But you should also consider writing series; in fact, your editor and/or agent will probably be nudging you in that direction one day or another.

And once you know all this, get ready to write (and to be called, all the time, relentlessly, exhaustingly, 'the next J.K. Rowling' by your friends and family).

The stand-alone children's book, and the 'stand-alone with series potential'

A stand-alone children's book is fairly straightforward: it's a picturebook, novella or novel that is self-contained, that has 'nothing else to say': it has a story arc, character development, and a theme and a thesis, and when it's over, it's over.

But there are bastard varieties of stand-alone books. One of them is the stand-alone with additional material online (we'll talk about that later). Another is the 'stand-alone with series potential'.

What does that mean? Quite simply that you're leaving open to the appreciation of the agent and editor whether or not it should be the first in a series. In other words, the book can work on its own, but it could also be followed by more books. This is very advantageous when looking for a publisher, and a good strategy to ponder. Think about it: if you've decided already that you're going to write a four-book series, and have planned the whole synopsis over four books, then the editor has no choice but to contract you for four books. Which means big money and a big deal, but also much more risk on the editor's part, so they might pass it entirely.

Whereas if you have one coherent book that potentially could lead to a whole series, the editor contracting you can discuss with you how many books they want to start with. It could be two or three, or even just that one with an option on the next one. That way, it's much less risky for them and they're more likely to take you on. Not to mention that you might be more open to discussing potential sequels with them, and therefore they're retaining some control over the process.

I know I'm making it sound as if all the power should be in the editor's hands but, by strategizing it in that way, you're also retaining some control over the process. You don't have to sell the publisher the next ten books, even if they really want them. You can try them for two or three, and then taunt them with the next few books. It's also your call, not just theirs.

So how do you write a 'stand-alone with series potential'? You have to make sure that it contains the following ingredients:

- A self-contained plot, which begins and ends satisfactorily within just that book. There may be still questions that are raised, but not too many. There can be hints of more, but not too many.

- A lead character (or two or three) who is interesting and appealing enough that they could live more adventures past this particular one; they haven't exhausted their possibilities. In other words, they took part in this adventure for a reason but they could find other reasons to have more adventures. And, preferably, they don't get killed at the end of the first book, though Malorie Blackman did that at the end of *Noughts and Crosses*.

- A setting, secondary characters, a time and a situation that all allow for potential further adventures to take place.

- A 'tone' or style, with recurring phrases or elements, that distinguishes the book and could constitute a 'style brand' for the rest of the series.

A good example of a stand-alone with series potential is the first *Pippi Longstocking* book, by Astrid Lindgren. It works perfectly on its own, but we have a reckless, strong heroine, two secondary characters, a little town, a whole cast of adult characters, and a recognizable overall 'tone', all of which it is possible to 'reinvest' in further books.

Don't worry, for now, about making it 'too' stand-alone. If you get a contract for several books, you will have time to insert potential leads in the first book that make it clearer that it's now part of a series. But don't scare the editors away by making it so much of a 'first in a series' book that they won't want to take a chance on you.

Different types of series

EPISODIC SERIES

Typical of fiction for younger readers, books in episodic series have recurring characters, settings, tone and type of story, but the plots are fairly disconnected from one another. This gives them the great advantage of being readable in any order.

More rigorously, I should say that most episodic series are only really 'quasi-episodic', in the sense that the reader would generally benefit from starting with the first book or the first few. This is the case, for instance, with the *Mildred Hubble* series by Jill Murphy, where the first book sets the stage (stand-alone with series potential!) and explains who the main characters are. Similarly, it's not absolutely indispensable to begin Anthony Horowitz's *Groosham Grange* series with the first one, but it's highly advisable – because many important elements of further plots have been explained there.

It's very likely, if you begin to write an episodic series, that the first book will do a lot more exposition than the next ones. In my *Sesame Seade* series, for instance, I spend a little while explaining in the first book, *Sleuth on Skates*, why the heroine is living in a college, what her parents are doing, who her best friends are, and so on. In the next book, so as not to bore to tears the readers who've read the first one, I scatter semi-expository notes here and there, but I mostly trust that new readers will understand what it's about. They would, however, gain a more complete appreciation of the series if they started with the first one.

Generally speaking, books in episodic series should stand on their own, and it should be possible to read them in any order. This is of strategic use to publishers and booksellers: it means that whichever book in the series is currently in stock at a bookshop, someone may buy it even though they haven't bought the first few. In fact, when I expressed surprise that the *Sesame* books didn't have numbers written on them, my editor immediately replied that it was absolutely on purpose: you don't want to put off someone from buying it because 'Number 3' is the only one on the shelf, if they (mistakenly) think you can't start the series in the middle.

Of course, episodic series can comprise evolutions: new characters can arrive, others can leave and die. Captain Haddock, for instance, only appears a quarter of the way through the *Tintin* series. And yet if I hadn't told you that, and you haven't read *The Crab with the Golden Claws* where he is first introduced, maybe you would never have noticed – or never wondered whence he ever came. There's no need to reiterate, in each book, what happened in the previous one. But giving hints can help ease the reader into a series s/he's picked up 'in the middle'.

SERIES WITH AN OVERARCHING STORY ARC

More common in literature for older readers, and particularly common in Young Adult literature, series with overarching story arcs are generally defined by the number of books they are composed of. Trilogies (3), tetralogies (4) and heptalogies (7) are, for no clear reason, the most common numbers, but there are also duologies (2), pentalogies (5), hexalogies (6) … and octologies (8) and ennealogies (9), and … please don't write more than that.

This way of talking about them ('Pullman's *His Dark Materials* trilogy') accentuates the notion that they constitute a self-contained story and should be read in order. In fact, not reading them in order would constitute a problem akin to – but not quite the same as! – beginning a book a third of the way through it.

Such series should be (but are not always) entirely planned from the beginning as one story. The *Twilight* tetralogy, famously, wasn't; the first book was a stand-alone with some series potential, but the others were not planned. Meyer's desperate efforts to tie up loose ends in the last book ended, in my opinion, in one of the biggest narrative disasters in literary history. Coherence throughout must be maintained, and it is helpful if you know as much as possible of 'what happens next', both for pitching the series and for yourself.

I said earlier that it wasn't *exactly* the same thing to start reading such a series halfway through as to start reading a single book halfway through. This is because, of course, each book should be as complete as it can be while staying incomplete on its own, *and* contain in itself an overarching story arc with, probably, the classic plot structure (call–action–return) and psychological development that you would expect for just one book.

In other words, it would be absurd to plan a trilogy by setting up Book 1 as the Calling, Book 2 as the Action and Book 3 as the Return. Many series, unfortunately, do this, spending an inordinate amount of time in the first book presenting characters and setting up the Call, and then giving place to a second book yawningly full of battles and journeys, and finally using up most of Book 3 to wind down.

Rather, each book in a series should be planned so as to have its own purpose, while simultaneously serving the purpose of the overall series. It's very hard to achieve, and the bigger the series, the harder it is. Maybe beginning authors should avoid starting with a series – it's hard enough learning how to pace a story, develop characters and craft tone over just one book. But many do, and some successfully.

The biggest advantage of this type of series for publishers is the addiction that a well-crafted series can lead to in the audience, and therefore the endless ramifications that a successful series can have. The need to know what happens next, or the need to relive the latest opus in a series, leads to ferocious consumption by readers of extra material, films and derived products, and can create buzz on the Internet, sustained by theories, hypotheses, and fan art and fan fiction. I've briefly mentioned films, and of course one of the most hoped-for benefits of this type of writing is the acquisition of film rights and the creation of a franchise around a series. This happens very rarely, if we consider the ratio of published series to the number of actual film productions drawn from them.

THEMATIC SERIES

Books in thematic series are visually united by 'paratextual features' – that is to say, elements of cover design, pitch, presentation and so on that mark them out as all belonging to the same series. Conceptually, they are also united by their dealing with the same themes and/or motifs. But individual stories can be quite different from one another and have no recurring characters or settings. For instance, the *Goosebumps* books, by R.L. Stine, are visibly part of the same series, but the only common point between the different stories is that they are scary and generally, though not always, rely on magical or fantastic elements. Despite their (relative) variety, *Goosebumps* books are created to address young readers' specific and recognizable desires for scary fiction. Some *Goosebumps* books are themselves duologies or trilogies with an overarching storyline; they could be called sub-series (e.g. *The Curse of the Mummy's Tomb* and *Return of the Mummy*).

Similarly, the *Mr Men* picturebooks are unified by the premise that each of them describes a character type, and does so with the same old felt-tip and geometrical type of illustration. The books are not interdependent; they are not really episodic, though some characters invite themselves into other characters' stories. Paratextually, though, they are eminently recognizable as part of a series, to the extent that aligning *Mr Men* books in order gives rise to a drawing on the conjoined spines.

Very often, such series are at least partly pseudonymous. Writing one or several books in the series under another name is a lucrative option for writers. Many professional children's writers spend some of their time working on such contracts. There's little space for innovation and originality, and the book generally comes with a script that 'simply' needs to be written down, but this type of work is well paid and arguably less difficult – though more challenging than one would think! – than penning more 'literary' fiction for children.

Having written two children's books as part of a series under a pseudonym, I can testify that there's something exhilarating about the constraints of this type of writing. Every interstitial space of potential freedom can be exploited, and there's something transgressive in getting sophisticated vocabulary and interesting characterization 'accepted' by the editor in those very formulaic series. Writing such series, under a pseudonym or not, is generally not an entry-point option for children's writers, but it can be considered a little bit further along the way; opportunities can arise when having lunch with an editor, or over drinks at a book launch.

 Key idea

Series can be episodic, thematic or with an overarching storyline; think of what kind of series yours is going to be, and study the market to see where it would be positioned.

Series strategies: between repetition and change

Episodic series fiction was long neglected by children's literature critics because it used to be considered uninteresting, formulaic and unoriginal. But in fact it is a fascinating and demanding type of writing, and wildly popular with children and teenagers. Analysing series fiction in a seminal study, children's literature scholar Victor Watson theorizes that such works rely on a feeling of *friendliness* towards the characters by the reader. The young reader must feel, when 'tucking into' a new book in a series, the feeling of comfort that one gets when returning to a 'room full of friends'. I'm sure that everyone can identify with this feeling, and it's probably already bringing back memories for you – of favourite, heart-warming books from series, read and reread in bed or in the bath.

However, there's a fine balance between cultivating this feeling of familiarity and introducing enough variation to make the different books worth while. When a series becomes samey, the audience drops out. Each book in a series must therefore introduce elements of defamiliarization as well as keep up the familiarity and attachment that it has constructed in other respects. Deciding which elements will become alien and which will remain identical should be the object of strategic narrative reflection.

Should you, for instance, add a new …

… MAIN CHARACTER?

The Famous Five wouldn't be Five if a Sixth Famous One suddenly turned up in one episode. Worse, it would make it difficult for readers to read the books in any order – why would Mandy be there in one book and not in the next? And being able to read the books in any order is, as we've said, a major selling point of episodic series fiction.

Remember, you're addressing children, who, albeit endlessly fascinating creatures of profound intelligence and insight, might not be familiar with the publishing practices associated with series fiction. Unlike you, they might not realize that a character might have appeared in a book they have never read. Especially with younger readers, you must give them the time to develop their readerly practices.

... VILLAIN?

A new villain is an entirely different matter. Unless your whole series is based around a conflict between a specific hero/ine and a specific villain – think *A Series of Unfortunate Events*, by Lemony Snicket – villains are not necessarily tied to episodic series. Superhero comics rarely present the same villain from book to book – in fact, the newness of the villain is frequently the most interesting aspect of each *Spiderman* book, for instance. Every *Spiderman* story, after all, follows more or less the same story structure: a new menace weighs upon the city; Spiderman is introduced to the villain once; he defeats him; he meets him or her again, and is defeated; he gets very depressed or incapacitated; the menace now becomes worse, and he has to make a choice between the people he loves and the people of the city. He then defeats the villain. This is a gross simplification, of course; but this is to show that the defamiliarization element, in general, does not come from the plot itself but from the particular challenges that each particular villain presents.

... SETTING?

This is a tricky one. Setting is often, in series fiction, almost as important as characters. Unless the series is premised on a constant change of setting from book to book – we could imagine a series about an air pilot's child, for instance – it's difficult to evaluate whether the defamiliarization created by a change of scenery wouldn't alienate your readership. Personally, as a child, I was upset by the only Anthony Buckeridge *Jennings* story that takes place away from Linbury School – in *Jennings at Large*.

... PERSONALITY OR PHYSICAL TRAIT?

Can your main character suddenly become permanently disabled by a worse-than-usual encounter with a villain? Can he or she, having endured something more painful than normal, become disillusioned, sad, pessimistic? Such major changes to the protagonist of your series can be fascinating, but they will always be a major risk – your protagonist, very often, *is* your series, and having a protagonist so changed that s/he feels 'new' is almost akin to introducing a new series. Maybe this would be a strategic move at a later stage, if and when the series begins to ask for a radical change. And it is, perhaps, more appropriate for teenage than children's literature.

... DEATH OR BIRTH?

Kill your protagonist, and the series is dead, right? Well ... as Conan Doyle famously experienced, there might always be people who'll ask you to unkill him. However, in general, killing off one's protagonist is a firm sign that you don't want to continue a book series. In children's literature, a symbolic way of killing off your protagonist is, of course, simply to let him or her grow up. Child characters can remain heroes of their own series only if they're carefully kept prepubescent or pre-adult. Theatrically announce that your hero has grown his first facial hair, and that's it – your series has ended.

Other deaths can be a dramatic move for your series. Killing the protagonist's parents, close friends, mascot pet or teacher can add tragic tension to one book, but over the course of a whole episodic series we get back to the issues discussed above – of adding (or, in this case, removing) main characters, and of modifying irremediably the personality of your protagonist.

Illustration, paratext, epitext and peritext

For children's series, it's generally expected that the same illustrator will be used for all the books. This gives the series a recognizable visual identity and, depending on the number of illustrations for each book, it will also contribute to the dynamic of recognition and defamiliarization that I've just developed. You shouldn't worry about finding an illustrator when you're planning to write a series – the publisher will do that if and when they take on your project.

As soon as the publisher approaches an illustrator for your book, they will ask him or her to draw sketches of the main characters, the setting, and any particularly important element of your series. Here are examples of sketches for my own character, Sesame Seade, by the illustrator Sarah Horne:

© Sarah Horne

These sketches are tremendously important: if the illustrator is going to give life to your protagonist, for not just one but a potentially endless series of books, the graphic identity of the character is essential. Interestingly, the way the illustrator 'sees' your character and his or her setting might also make you reconsider some aspects of the stories. In my Sesame books, for instance, one of the 'familiar' elements is the presence of wild animals. But maybe I wouldn't have developed this element so much if I hadn't realized how amazingly Sarah draws wild animals.

Coherence in the illustration is generally paralleled by coherence in the paratext, epitext and peritext. These are the elements of the book that are not directly part of the story but contribute to the general reading experience: cover, endpapers, potential websites, Twitter accounts and more. For an author to become a 'brand', the publisher already wants these elements to be coherent from book to book, even if they're stand-alones. But for a series, it's absolutely crucial. The design of each book, including its paratextual features, must echo the design of the previous book – with just enough defamiliarization. For instance, the endpapers of the Sesame books are all different animals, but these animals are shown doing quirky or crazy things.

The paratext in each book will also refer to the other books in the series, so as to trigger the readers' desire to read the other books. Other peritextual features might strengthen the series' 'branding', and cultivate attachment – online, in particular, it is common to see blogs about characters from series. Alex T. Smith thus has a blog 'written by' his hugely successful character Claude.

Your publisher will be extremely careful about all those details when they snap up your series. From colour scheme to online presence through to derived products if you're lucky (or not …), you'll feel a push towards coherence which you might sometimes interpret as a desire for sameness. Or just safety.

Key idea

Nothing prevents you from spicing up the series or making it evolve, but it will have to be approved by the editorial team who, by then, will know your series perhaps even better than you do …

Characters and characterization in series fiction

Perhaps one key aspect of series fiction to get right – not that it isn't important in other works – is characterization. If you're going to give children a bunch of character-friends to hang out with for three, four or eighteen books, the characters had better be interesting, funny, friendly, ingenious, quirky and full of surprises. In the case of character-led series fiction, which is the most frequent type of series, it's essential to think not just of one central attractive character but of many.

This is difficult because series fiction can become dominated by the voice, evolution, thoughts and actions of just one central character, and this character can become not just dominant but domineering. While the protagonist, who might even give the series his or her name, is essential – and if you don't get that right, you won't get anything right – secondary characters are indispensable to help the protagonist carry the series forward.

In series fiction for children, the characterization of primary and secondary characters has to rely on the dynamic, described above, of *repetition* and *change*. In other words, characters must be, in their voices, attitudes, decisions and thoughts, predictable to a degree: they must elicit friendly recognition, or even the comfort of sustained unfriendliness, in the child who has read several books in the series. But they must also have it in them to act differently when required, and to evolve from book to book. This works for both episodic series and overarching storyline series. For instance, you might have a secondary character who evolves in the following way:

- **Book 1:** Bertie is a shy, quiet little boy, who tags along with the superhero because he is in awe of him. But at the end of the first book, he finds the answer, thanks to his love of animals, to an important question which will help the superhero beat the villain.

- **Book 2:** Bertie is now more confident. He knows that his side interests, such as animals, can be important in his friend's quest. He teaches his superhero friend to ride a horse, and this will be important for the current plot. But at the last minute he refuses to let the superhero go away with the horse because he is worried about the animal getting hurt. The superhero has to go by his own means.

- **Book 3:** Bertie, who is being shunned by the superhero for his decision, spends most of the first part of the book away from centre-stage. It is understood that he has found a girlfriend who shares his interests. But this girlfriend, unbeknown to him, is attempting to obtain information from Bertie about the superhero. Having discovered this, he has to make a choice between his crush and his friend.

Bertie, in those (admittedly rather hackneyed) subplots, is never the main character and never fully in the spotlight; and yet, if the characterization works, he should be absolutely essential to the series. He will surprise the reader in the first book by being suddenly inventive, and in the second book by apparently abandoning his friend. By the third book, the reader will have learned to see him as someone who could be good *or* bad for the work of the superhero. Therefore the choice he will make will not have a straightforward answer, which will increase the psychological tension.

Series fiction is a handy way of honing your skill at characterization, both of secondary and of primary characters, precisely because it gives you so much space and time to do so. A character can become fleshed out in not just one book but several. He can work his way out of a background of secondary figures and emerge as an important player in the game. Simultaneously, the main character must constantly reinvent herself so that the series can continue to function, and the interplay between her and the secondary characters will fuel her quests.

Familiarity thus doesn't mean that the characters are static: the characters can't always respond in the same, preprogrammed way. But they must remain coherent throughout the series, and their unpredictable responses must link back to what they are like as *people*. We must be able to feel which traits of their personality are consistent and which are still in development, still ready to take an unexpected turn.

Inclusivity and exclusivity

What I particularly love about series is that, after a while, you're potentially talking to two audiences at the same time: firstly, the first-time readers, who have just picked up the book at random, and secondly, the long-time readers, who have read and reread several books in the series and have been waiting for the latest one to come out. Because you are talking to these two very different readers, you need to put in something satisfying for both – different 'gifts' that will give them both the feeling that their reading is valued.

The long-time readers will relish a feeling of exclusivity. They have stuck with you all this time: they deserve to feel that you are talking to them over the heads of the philistines who don't know the series as well as they do. Play with that superiority: give these readers echoes and resonances, allusions to the other books in the series, hints that they know more than the average reader. For instance, if in another episode of the series there was a villainess who had a number of striking characteristics – a coarse voice and bright turquoise hair – introduce her again in a new episode with only, at the beginning, a *hint* of these characteristics – not naming her immediately, but simply alluding to the person's 'coarse voice' on the other end of the phone line. Thanks to their thorough knowledge of the series, the long-time reader will guess who it is, and when confirmation occurs they will love to know that they were one of the happy few who already *knew*. This is quite an unsubtle hint, of course – there are many more ways of orchestrating echoes between different books to give that temporary sense of exclusivity to those who have already read some of your books.

But careful! The first-time reader will relish, on the other hand, a feeling of inclusivity. Jumping into a series can be a destabilizing experience if you don't start at the beginning – and, as I said before, you must expect that for an episodic series people will *not* start at the beginning. So help your first-time readers. You need to tell them who these characters are – not just in the first book, but in *all* the books. Short introductory sentences will do – but they need to be there, and they can't be boring. Avoid the 'in the last episode, this happened, and now these characters X, Y and Z are in this situation' type of recap. Your imagination will need to work hard to make these introductions creative, funny and *inclusive*. Don't make your first-time readers feel, especially at the start of the book, that they're missing out on crucial information.

This can be done in brief but not very interesting brushstrokes. 'Just as the bell rang, Maya, sporting her usual red glasses and untied tie, jumped out of her dad's taxi and ran towards the school.' A bit of information is being conveyed here that might be important – Maya's quirkiness and dishevelled look, her dad's job, and that she's probably often late. Long-time readers might know all this, but the first-time reader will thank you for not starting the scene directly with an undescribed Maya talking to the protagonist.

It can also be done more subtly, by avoiding description and integrating character traits into the main storyline. Maya doesn't need to be described as 'sporting her usual red glasses'; those red glasses can be mentioned, later on, as 'sliding down her nose' as the children run to catch the thief. Dialogues are also a good way to convey new information while recapitulating old facts about the characters and the setting. But avoid making your characters tell too much of their own life in an unbelievable fashion, clearly for the benefit of the reader ('As you know,' said Maya, 'my dad is a taxi driver …').

There's a difficult balance to strike here. Repeat too much from the previous book and you will bore the long-time reader. But don't say anything and the first-time reader will have no chance of ever getting involved in the series. The latter is, arguably, worse than the former; always ask yourself if all the crucial plot points, jokes and character traits would be understandable if you'd just picked a book in the middle of the series.

Key idea

Seduce the repeat reader with echoes from other books; secure the first-time reader with facts about this one.

Bonus: metafictional fun

In the *Sesame* books, I included short sentences here and there to refer to the existence of other books: 'You would know this if you had read the previous volume of my adventures …' This strategy both augments readerly exclusivity ('I have!') and allows first-time readers to realize, just in case they hadn't, that there are indeed other books in the series and that they should join the club. Of course, this only works with a specific (that is, cocky) type of narrative voice …

Workshop: writing a series proposal

For this workshop I'd like to focus on episodic series rather than series with an overarching storyline – partly because we'll discuss those again when talking about Young Adult literature. I'd like you to write a mock proposal for a 'stand-alone with series potential' for an episodic series for children or teenagers; picture-book series are, of course, acceptable too. This proposal will be the kind that an editor would expect, though they would probably also want to see a sample of writing – if not of a whole book, at least of the first few chapters. We'll get back to how to write a book proposal in Part Three.

Your series proposal should include the following:

- One or two sentences about the series, including the name of the main character(s) and what's at stake. I need to get a sense of why this could make a good episodic series – e.g. don't just tell me that little Leo is the son of an airline pilot and travels all around the world; tell me also that, in every different country, a new murder mystery occurs.
- Give me a sense of what the first book is about – see 'Writing a synopsis' in Chapter 5 for help. I want to know who the characters are, where the action takes place, what happens, and the ending. It doesn't need to be a fully fledged synopsis, but I want an overarching storyline with all the important elements in place.

- Finally, write a brief synopsis (one paragraph) of two other books in the same series, negotiating the difficult balance between familiarity and surprise.

Review

This exercise is closer to planning than to writing. In real life, you'd probably want to 'warm up' by drafting a chapter or two of the series before diving into synopses. But leave the writing alone for a little bit, and then reread your proposal, donning the hat of an editor (generally a panda hat, or a woolly multi-coloured hat with pompoms; editors are usually young, female and quirky).

Now try to evaluate your work.

- How appealing is your pitch? Can you see the appeal of such a series ever declining? If so, why? Which variations on that theme could you find?
- The first book: how well does it fulfil the following criteria on a scale from 1 to 10?
  - It functions as a stand-alone. | 1 | 2 | 3 | 4 | 5 | 6 | 7 | 8 | 9 | 10 |
  - It calls for further books. | 1 | 2 | 3 | 4 | 5 | 6 | 7 | 8 | 9 | 10 |
  - It introduces all the main characters. | 1 | 2 | 3 | 4 | 5 | 6 | 7 | 8 | 9 | 10 |
  - It establishes the protagonist. | 1 | 2 | 3 | 4 | 5 | 6 | 7 | 8 | 9 | 10 |
- The next two books: how well do they fulfil the following criteria?
  - They function on their own. | 1 | 2 | 3 | 4 | 5 | 6 | 7 | 8 | 9 | 10 |
  - They strengthen the protagonist. | 1 | 2 | 3 | 4 | 5 | 6 | 7 | 8 | 9 | 10 |
  - They introduce change. | 1 | 2 | 3 | 4 | 5 | 6 | 7 | 8 | 9 | 10 |
  - They preserve and strengthen familiarity. | 1 | 2 | 3 | 4 | 5 | 6 | 7 | 8 | 9 | 10 |

If you're happy with what your proposal is doing at this stage, try to think – that's the fun part – about paratextual and illustration decisions that could help the books function as a series. You wouldn't be expected to take charge of that in a traditional publishing setting, but thinking about it might very well prompt new ideas.

Where to next?

Whether for a stand-alone or a series, where do you get your ideas from? This question might remain unanswered for ever (though it will be the most commonly asked question you'll get), but there's another question in there: how do you make sure your ideas, if they involve things in the real world, are actually sound? The next chapter turns to research, a difficult but necessary part of fiction writing.

8

Research

'Did you write your book today?'

'No, I did some research.'

'Research? On what?'

'The love life of killer whales.'

'?...?'

'My story will be about killer whales who fall in love.'

'I ... see. Actually, I don't. It's a fictional story, right?'

'Yeah, I suppose. Well, in the sense that it isn't autobiographical.'

'So why are you *researching* it?'

Why, indeed, should fiction writers research their stories before and during writing? Of course, if you were a non-fiction writer, it would be a truth universally acknowledged that your books should 'reflect reality', or at least have explicit links to it. You would be expected, in writing *A Child's Guide to Nuclear Warfare*, to become well informed about the splitting of atoms in the confection of such weaponry. But none of that seems to be expected from the writer of the comedic children's series *Neon Yello (Almost) Destroys the World (Again)*, because it is assumed that there's no need to go into detail about how exactly young Neon is attempting to achieve this disastrous feat.

As I'm sure you could predict from my sarcastic tone, I believe that this is a mistake. Authors of fiction, even wacky or fantasy fiction, need to do their research. Doing research on the main elements of the plot is as much part of a writer's job as making sure that said plot holds together properly.

So open your *Encyclopaedia Britannica*, or, for the most 2.0. of you, the latest version of Encarta …

What needs researching, and what doesn't?

Not everything in a story needs the strong backup of evidence-based facts. But from trivial and quick to essential and tiresome, research takes many forms, at different stages of the book's development:

FACT-CHECKING

Many things can be checked in one click. Demonizing Wikipedia is all very well, but when you need to check that a Corolla is indeed a Toyota and not a Nissan so that your character doesn't accidentally end up hijacking a non-existent car, it's very helpful.

Fact-checking of this kind is easily done. But it relies on your having identified where small mistakes might occur in your text – and that's tricky. Small mistakes are annoyingly innocuous. The closest I got to a very embarrassing small mistake of that kind was a throwaway comment, in a historical children's novel, about the child King Louis XIV living in Versailles. Of course, King Louis XIV is associated with Versailles, but that's because he had it built. So when he was a child … that's right, Versailles didn't exist. It took the razor-sharp eye of the publisher's summer intern to spot the mistake, in the very last stages of editing. Embarrassing, but it could have been worse – at least it hadn't been published yet.

So do check your facts, even when they appear small or not a matter for any misunderstanding. Your main character has just stopped under 'flowery apple trees': is it the right season for those to be in bloom? Your antagonist is watching the Olympic Games: have you mentioned the year in which the story is set? If so, is it the right year for the Games to take place? There's a mother duck with her ducklings; I hope you're not describing her as green-headed, since only male mallards are …

These details can of course be fact-checked *after writing*. In fact, I wouldn't recommend doing it as you write – it can make you lose momentum. When you feel something might need checking, make a note to yourself to do so (highlight the word or sentence in yellow on the manuscript, for instance) and get back to it later. There's no rush, unless it's really bugging you.

DETAILS WITH IMPORTANT CONSEQUENCES FOR THE PLOT

Beyond those anecdotal facts, others require your full attention because they have a direct impact on the story. The type of revolver your antagonist is using might not matter, *unless* you need to know how many bullets it can shoot, how easily, and how fast. That's the difference between your main character having time to escape and not having time to escape. It's also important to know how long the King's Cross to Leicester Square commute normally takes, because that determines exactly how long the conversation between your love-struck main characters can actually last. Such things must be checked before your writing can go on. They're details, but important details.

Such details, again, could if unnoticed ruin your carefully structured plot, the little devils. If at the end of a long, convoluted, sophisticated spy story culminating at the top of Notre-Dame after a terrifyingly steep climb, your reader can simply say, 'Why didn't they just take the stairs that lead there?', you've got a problem. Sometimes those things can be fixed a posteriori (stating at the beginning of the story that 'Notre-Dame was being restored and all access to stairs was blocked for visitors') but … yes, it can sound very clumsy.

Key idea

If you're relying on any fact, however small, for the plot to function, fact-check and double-check that fact.

But, of course, you might not need to care that those aspects don't quite correspond to reality. It doesn't matter, you could say, that in the real world you can't (yet) play the Wii on a transatlantic flight; you can in *my* book. And that's perfectly fine: artistic licence is absolutely acceptable in those cases. For other elements, however, your editor might oppose your decision, and you may prefer to tweak the plot to accommodate reality. When I wrote *Scam on the Cam,* it was essential to me to say that there was somehow no drug testing at all on the Oxford–Cambridge Boat Race, or else the drugged team would have been spotted from the beginning. I asked a friend of mine, who is on the team, and, O miracle!, he told me there was no drug testing on the race. I was surprised, but hugely relieved. I often wondered, afterwards, what I would have done if he'd said, 'Are you crazy? Of course we get drug-tested.' To be honest, I would probably have gone with the original idea, and pretended that 'in this world, rowers just don't get drug-tested'. But I would have felt uneasy about it – I much prefer it this way, with this real aspect of the Boat Race corresponding to the story.

However, I've also felt free to disregard many aspects of 'reality'. The rowers of the real university team wouldn't let in three children from a nearby school to have a look around the boat house. Frog-skin poison probably wouldn't have vomit-inducing effects. Such things didn't matter to me too much, because I see them as incorporated within the willing suspension of disbelief – the 'pact' that you make with the reader. They belong to the more whimsical realm of the story, the part where animals are almost human and people find weird ways of poisoning one another. Readers and editor may disagree with your choices, however, so be prepared to defend them.

RESEARCH ABOUT PSYCHOLOGICAL AND SOCIAL STATES

This type of research is possibly the most sensitive and the most important to get right. It refers to the facts that you must check before beginning to write about mental or psychological conditions that you don't have, and also social and cultural positions that are not your own. You might want to write about a working-class white boy who becomes suicidal after he discovers he's gay, but from your position as a fifty-five-year-old, upper-middle-class heterosexual woman, it doesn't come without ideological issues. I'm not saying it can't be done, of course, but it needs to be thoroughly researched. Go on blogs and forums where people like your main character might interact. Read articles about teenage suicide, and scientific research on the psychological state of working-class youth.

Similarly, you might feel insecure or uncomfortable talking about, say, a family going through the grief of having lost a child, especially if it hasn't happened to you personally. Read testimonies on websites, talk to people from associations, try to garner a sense of the emotions, fears and desires that arise in these occasions. This will also help you become aware that real people are undergoing what you're making your fictional characters undergo: in other words, you can't just use this event as a plot device. You need to do it responsibly, sensitively. This is your story, but not just. It's happened to other people, to real people, and they have the right to see it represented correctly.

Most authors thoroughly research the mental states of the type of people they're talking about. At the end of *Kite Spirit*, Sita Brahmachari explains how she got in touch with networks of parents who lost teenagers to suicide. Marcus Sedgwick also talks about his meetings with a school of blind children before he wrote *She Is Not Invisible*. John Green never hid the fact that he had partly based *The Fault in Our Stars* on his conversations with a terminally ill young girl with cancer, Esther Grace Earl – whose own book was published posthumously as *This Star Won't Go Out*.

RESEARCH ABOUT SPECIFIC PLACES OR TIMES

If your story takes place in the Tudor era, don't think you're going to get away with wishy-washy historical knowledge. Children's writers, like writers 'for adults', are held accountable for all the mistakes they make. The same applies if your story is set in Japan. You can, of course, write about Japan without having been there yourself (after all, no one expects you to have been to the Tudor era), but research, research, research. The devil is in the details: is it indeed likely that your heroine would have had hot chocolate at that time in history?

But what if your novel is a fantasy novel, or steampunk, or dystopian? Surely you can then use your imagination, and facts don't need to be checked all the time. Well, again, it's up to how much artistic licence you can get away with, and how clearly you signpost the events that are absolutely invented. For instance, you're completely free to write a novel about Julius Caesar, but with the great man turning out to be a giant extra-terrestrial tortoise in human shape; that's fine. That fact will probably be carefully signposted. Does that mean, however, that you shouldn't care about what this reptilian emperor eats? A tomato salad seems appropriate, but … tomatoes were brought back from South America hundreds of years after Caesar's realm. They didn't exist in Europe. It is up to you to say:

1 **'Doesn't matter:** this is a funny story with no respect for historical accuracy.' OK, then make it so.

2 **'It does matter:** Julius Caesar's actual tortoise identity should be the only thing departing from historical accuracy.' Then do your research.

It's generally a question of signposting, and this signposting can be explicit or implicit. A comical story such as *Asterix* (which is, actually, uncannily accurate in many respects) can be allowed to deviate from historical fact. Here, it's the generic identity of the book that singles it out as 'probably historically inaccurate'. Within some stories, there will be elements of fact and elements of pure fiction, and the writer might have to tell you which is which. In fact, sometimes, they really *should*; it's partly because Dan Brown keeps mum about which parts of the *Da Vinci Code* stem from his wild imagination and which are 'accurate' that there is so much speculation – and so much controversy – around the book.

Some historical periods and some geographical places are more sensitive than others. Venice and Paris are fair game – they've been romanticized so much, you can just use them as your infinitely flexible playground; go for it. And have fun with prehistoric times. But really, *really* be careful with historical and/or geographical facts when writing about:

• any of the twentieth-century genocides

• the colonial era

• Australia's 'stolen generation' or equivalent crimes perpetrated on indigenous people of the Americas, for instance.

• the First World War, especially the trenches

• the 9/11 Attacks

• seemingly 'exotic' places such as Africa, South America, Asia – they are particularly likely to crystallize 'orientalist', romanticized visions that smack of racism or neocolonialism.

For these, don't just set your story there in the hope that it will make for good plot twists. You can't write about them without engaging with them as painful topics for many people, and you can't engage with them as such without researching them.

Key idea

To write fiction that is respectful about different cultures, geographical places and historical times, read widely about them and let the voices be heard through your voice.

Research planning and methodology: a few tips from academia

You might now be thinking, dammit – I'd planned this great children's story set during the Second World War, and now I have to research so much stuff – I'm not sure that I can be bothered ... Where do I start? Where do I stop? How will I know what will be useful, and what won't be?

This is a perfectly normal reaction: tackling a new field of research is daunting and stressful. You might also feel illegitimate, as if you're going to walk into someone else's garden and trample their lovingly grown fruit and vegetables. Keep distance from these anxieties by *planning* your research.

Here are a few tips, borrowed directly from academic practice. The main idea is to go from the general to the particular, and to do so methodically. I know it's very tempting to hop from Wikipedia to various random websites and do plenty of cutting and pasting into a Word document you probably won't open again, but trust me, methodical research is much more productive, more energy-efficient, more rewarding and less time-consuming.

Let's assume your book is set during the Second World War, in France. Your two protagonists are French teenagers who are hoping to join the Resistance. In order to research this rather hot topic, you will go through the following stages:

1 MAPPING THE FIELD: 'SHORT INTRODUCTIONS'

This step is about getting a *broad idea* of what's been written about the *thing* you're hoping to research, and what the current debates are.

The best way to do this is to head to your local library, and seek out – either by yourself or by asking librarians, whose job it is, happily, to help you with such tasks – general introductions to the field. Countless 'short introductions', 'companions' and 'handbooks' to the Second World War exist. Look for those addressed to undergraduates, as they are generally very clear and delineate current debates.

Read several of them and take notes (more on that later). At the end of such books, you will always find bibliographies of relevant secondary texts. Some of them will be yet more general works, but many will be more specific: some of them might focus, for instance, solely on the French Resistance.

2 GETTING INTO DETAIL: MORE SPECIFIC BOOKS

These more specific books will delve into the particulars of what you're interested in.

Read those books on the Resistance, and you will learn more about the motivations and modes of functioning of the various movements within it. You will probably have access to maps, too – scan some of those, or take pictures – which will show you the places where the *maquisards* hid. The *who*? These books will teach you important specific vocabulary about your research project.

You might then find, in those more specific books, references to academic or newspaper articles, or other books, which zoom even more on to your main interest: teenagers taking part in the Resistance. These are the pieces of writing you should be heading for next.

3 GETTING CLOSER: TEXTS ABOUT YOUR MAIN INTEREST

From your local library, you should have access to a number of these academic articles. If not, I'm afraid a day trip to the British Library could be necessary, unless you have a nice academic friend who could log in for you and download articles.

You might also have access to old newspaper articles online or in archives. And you might want to read, say, biographies or autobiographies of now-old people who joined the Resistance as teenagers. Your knowledge will become much more specific and also much more individualistic: from a big, scary, political and social event, your research has now zoomed on to the lives of human beings.

4 GETTING THE DETAILS RIGHT

Once you've got the information you need to be able to talk about this era and the people who 'made' it, you will probably find yourself assailed by a flow of smaller questions: What did they *eat*? How did they sleep? And what did their families think about all that?

Such questions – which will keep emerging – will require yet more research as you go along and you will be in a much more comfortable position to tackle them, because you will have a clearer sense of the field and will know where to look for answers.

> ## Key idea
>
>
> The usual mistake with research is to waste precious time looking for details without first getting a sense of the bigger picture. Instead, always go from the general to the particular.

I've only mentioned texts, but of course there are countless types of discourse that can compose your research, including videos, audio recordings, photographs, artworks, music, and day- or week-long trips to the places you will be writing about. Research will gradually make you feel completely comfortable with your topic, bathed in it; it will stimulate your creativity.

How to take notes

Quite a few of my undergraduate students don't take notes efficiently. They either write down page after page after page of notes (or worse, copy/paste, barely reading the text, into a document), or just take a few notes per book. They often pick up only on very general notions, such as 'The Second World War was the second armed conflict of the twentieth century for France, and this was a difficult time' (Smith & Dawson 2012,

p. 3). When you ask them what Smith and Dawson's argument is throughout their book, they don't know – they jumped to the easily reusable general quote, and didn't take anything else into account.

To take notes fruitfully, you need to know at all stages *what you're looking for*. As a writer, like a student writing an essay, you already have an idea of what you're looking for. Your 'research question', in this case, for instance, might be 'What were the experiences of teenagers joining the French Resistance during the Second World War?'

Knowing this, at all different stages of your research, take notes only on those facts or notions that are precise enough to require being written down. These could be:

- **A general outline of the Second World War:** why it started, when and how, and how many countries were central to the conflict. There's no need to note down entire sentences for that; phrase it in your own words. This will also help you begin to articulate these historical events in your own voice.

- **Dates of major events:** you might want to draw a chronology of the German occupation of France.

- **Statistics:** how many dead? How many Resistants? According to whom? Interesting statistics and data will help to give you a sense of proportion. Is it realistic that your hero should have five friends who join the Resistance, or are you exaggerating the movement?

- **Names:** of famous people, of newspapers, of places and so on.

You don't need to write down full quotations – contrary to academics, I wouldn't recommend copying out full sentences from the books you read. They will sound, well, academic; and might end up in your book as dry, pedagogical sentences, even when rephrased in your own words. Make your note-taking process transformative: try to see and speak these facts as if they were already yours, woven into your story.

As you take notes, keep your writer's mind alert. Maybe images will come to you, maybe feelings … These snippets of thoughts and emotions, note them down, too, put them on the page, so that they continue to exist alongside the drier stuff. They'll be useful later when you're trying to reorganize your thoughts. If, inspired by a book or article, you feel like writing a scene, a dialogue, a paragraph, by all means do it – do it *now*.

These rather anarchic pieces of writing may or may not end up in the finished work, but they will continue to orient your research and help your project develop. They will begin the creative process, even as the general structure is being slowly put together. So listen to yourself *as a writer* as you research; if inspiration comes – strongly aided, of course, by your reading – then respond to its calling.

Finally, 'take notes' that are pictures, old interviews, videos, pieces of music; create a private Pinterest board if it helps (we'll talk about this later) or a real one, on corkboard. Download songs and music into a playlist and listen to it while writing, or before. Surround yourself with all these 'notes', and make them part of your writing environment.

Knowing when to stop

At some point, researching a book becomes a convenient procrastination strategy. This is when you've got to stop. Many writers accumulate pages and pages of notes, gather hundreds of pictures, watch hours of videos, and … never write the book. Because, so to speak, all has been said; their story has been swallowed up by those of others.

Or maybe they just can't start the story: it's too scary now, too big a deal; after spending so much time researching it, how could any beginning, any middle, any end do? They decide to leave it aside for a week, for two weeks, and never pick it up again. Of course, they've learned a lot in the process, and maybe some of their research will find its way into future works but, in the meantime, of the promised book there is no sign.

Or maybe they do start the book, and it's going OK, but they're always stopping to fact-check compulsively every little detail, and the next thing you know they're tweeting or updating their blog with funny things about their research, and the book takes ages to write – if it ever gets written at all – because research has become their legitimate-sounding way of procrastinating.

To avoid this, one strategy is to start writing – even timidly, even sporadically – as you start researching. Once your synopsis is more or less in place, go for it, not worrying for now about incoherence. Get the first third of the work done. Split your time between research and writing. And as I mentioned earlier, take 'creative' notes as well as informative ones.

Another strategy is to limit yourself to, say, three weeks of research – and then tell yourself 'I'm done!' Then force yourself just to write. Of course, as all academics know, research is never done; but more can be undertaken at a later stage and reincorporated within the work. It's sometimes helpful just to shut down the noise of all these references and books clamouring for attention, and simply make do with what you've got so far.

Whatever you do, think about your story all the time when researching; think about how your characters would react if faced with the events depicted in such a book, think about what how they would feel about such a politician's decision, picture them walking in the shade of those buildings and those trees in the black-and-white photographs. Make your research an organic part of your creative and reflective process for your book.

Strange encounters of the third kind: reality and fiction

The moon, by her comparative proximity, and the constantly varying appearances produced by her several phases, has always occupied a considerable share of the attention of the inhabitants of the earth.

From the time of Thales of Miletus, in the fifth century BC, down to that of Copernicus in the fifteenth and Tycho Brahe in the sixteenth century AD, observations have been from time to time carried on with more or less correctness, until in the present day the altitudes of the lunar mountains have been determined with exactitude. Galileo explained the phenomena of the lunar light produced during certain of her phases by the existence of mountains, to which he assigned a mean altitude of 27,000 feet. After him Hevelius, an astronomer of Dantzic, reduced the highest elevations to 15,000 feet; but the calculations of Riccioli brought them up again to 21,000 feet.

Yes ... bit of a mouthful, isn't it? This (tiny) portion of a (very long) chapter almost entirely devoted to such prose is drawn from a children's novel by the famously fact-obsessed Jules Verne, *From the Earth to the Moon* (Chapter 5). First published in 1865, this book would of course never be published as such now if it were written by a contemporary author. You may find it sad, but for today's readers there is something quite unfriendly about this avalanche of dates, numbers and names with no story on the horizon.

The alchemy between fact and fiction must work – in other words, your reader must get the correct dose of necessary facts drawn from your research, while still focusing, *at all times*, on *your* story. It's quite difficult to achieve, because of the temptation to slot in some facts every time you mention a new character or place. And it can become very cumbersome: 'They'd reached the Eiffel Tower, which had been built in 1889. It was supposed to be destroyed after the 1889 World's Fair, but it wasn't. Emma was glad it hadn't been destroyed: she liked its metallic lattice structure, towering at 324 metres.'

Of course, such information might be important for your book: maybe it's the first time Emma comes to Paris, and a very important scene is going to happen at the top of the Eiffel Tower at the end. But find more subtle ways of making those facts clear to the reader:

> *Emma gazed up at the tower. From where she stood it looked thin and fragile, just lacy metal in the wind. She remembered her grandmother laughing when she told the tale of when it was built. She was barely a child then, it was the last decade of the century, 'and that great big metal thing was being built, and they promised us they'd destroy it afterwards!' They hadn't. The Paris World's Fair had gone, and the tower had stayed. It was so high its pointy head was capped with clouds; Emma blinked in the sun.*

It's not the most perfect paragraph, but it works fine; no need for numbers and dates – allusions are enough; and so as not to make it sound as if the narrator is telling you everything, Emma's memories of her grandmother come in to play a small part. It's livelier, warmer and just as informative.

This is just one way of integrating important research elements into your story without making it sound as if you're suddenly giving a short lecture. Dialogues are good for conveying such facts, too. Be careful, however, not to get into long dialogues chock-full of details that the characters should have known long ago. But dialogues can be used cleverly to give information about ways of life, values and beliefs of the times and places you're writing about. A strong argument between a father and a mother in a story set in the 1950s, overheard by the main child character, can give away just as much about the female condition in that era as any book on the history of gender relations.

Err on the side of caution: reread each dialogue and paragraph, asking yourself honestly whether you are being more pedagogical than creative, more didactic than imaginative.

On the other hand, you do want your story to be understood, so some facts will be necessary. A tip: it's always better to *delete* facts from your story. Your editor will probably want to *keep* all the informative stuff – children's literature is, unfortunately or not (you're the judge), a very pedagogical form of writing still. Let your editor tell you where more factual information is needed; in the meantime, keep it discreet.

Workshop: the marriage of fact and fiction

This workshop is slightly artificial, but useful. I'm going to give you a list of facts, and I would like you to integrate them seamlessly, without sounding doctrinal or educational, within a few short paragraphs and/or dialogue of a work of children's fiction. You are welcome not to use numbers, but do make your imagination work so that you give a *sense* of those numbers.

Here are the facts:

- There are elephants in Asia and in Africa. The elephant in this story is an Asian elephant.
- Such elephants are a bit taller than eight foot.
- The one in this story, like many Asian elephants, is used by humans to carry wood through forests.
- They are in danger from poachers who are looking for ivory from their tusks.
- They eat 100 kilograms of plants per day and drink 100 litres of water.

How do you make such facts clear but discreet within your own writing? Have a go.

Review

Now reread your work and, attempting to remain objective, rate yourself on a scale of 1 to 10 according to the following criteria:

- Fluidity of reading: do the facts stand out from the fiction, or are the two well interwoven?   1 2 3 4 5 6 7 8 9 10
- How well did you 'convert' the numbers into reading-friendly comparisons?   1 2 3 4 5 6 7 8 9 10
- If you used dialogue, does it feel and sound natural?   1 2 3 4 5 6 7 8 9 10
- Did you describe other aspects of the elephant in question that made it clear that it was *this* elephant, not just 'a representative of its species'? Does it have sufficient personality?   1 2 3 4 5 6 7 8 9 10
- Is tension, emotion, curiosity or tenderness maintained throughout the scene?   1 2 3 4 5 6 7 8 9 10

As if you were sandpapering out the flaws on a wooden sculpture, try to smoothe the 'facts' so that they are as integrated as possible into the story. Of course, this is quite an artificial situation; in 'real' writing life, you'll have more space to squeeze in those facts and you will make them more immediately relevant. But this short exercise should have helped you gain canniness in doing so on a smaller and more concentrated scale.

Where to next?

We're almost done with this first big part about finding your voice. By now, you should be thinking about writing as an activity you might want to spend a lot more time on – and not just because there's so much of this massive book left to read. But how do you begin to write consistently enough to be a writer? The next chapter tackles the difficult problems of routine, procrastination, enthusiasm and discouragement.

9

Writing, writing, writing, writing

As a writer, whether published or not, the one question you get asked even more often than 'Where do you get your ideas from?' is 'How do you find the time?'

People are mystified. How, how, *how* do you find the time? Where is all that time you seem to have that they don't? You can see them thinking:

Option 1: she has too much time on her hands or else she wouldn't have any time to write.

Option 2: she's a workaholic with no social life.

The right answer to this question is 'I don't *find* time to write; I *make* time to write.' (You're welcome.)

People generally don't realize how much time they could make in a day, even one that involves a full-time job and a bunch of kids. (I have to admit I don't have experience in the latter matter, but I have many prolific writer friends who are also equipped with a non-negligible number of smaller humans.) There's always, always more time than you think.

If your best friend turned up at the door right now with pizza and a DVD of your favourite film, and said, 'Got two hours to spend with me?' – wouldn't you make the time for it?

If your sister phoned you in tears, having just broken up with her long-time boyfriend, and asked you, 'Have you got a minute to talk to me?' (and you know it means an hour) – wouldn't you make the time for it?

If you got a puppy, and it needed to be trained for a year, and walked every day for an hour so that it didn't bark at night, bite the neighbours and poo on your carpet – wouldn't you make the time for it?

Why wouldn't *writing* be your best friend complete with pizza and DVD? Why wouldn't *writing* be your weeping sister? Why wouldn't *writing* be a puppy threatening to bark, bite and poo?

Do you have the time to read about all that? Gosh, how do you find that time?

Keeping to a schedule

Personally, I *don't* keep to a schedule – not in any rigorous definition of the word 'schedule'; certainly not as many authors do. This is partly because I have a full-time job, as you probably do, and it's difficult to stick to an unbending daily schedule when the job gets in the way. People like J.K. Rowling and Philip Pullman, if they want, can write from exactly 7.15 to 11.45 every morning, take a one-hour walk, have lunch, do another hour from 2.10 to 3.10, and then attend to other job requirements such as school visits, interviews, talks, checking proofs and replying to fan mail. I can't. And I don't think you can, either.

There's huge pressure among writers, professional or not, to stick to a daily schedule. Blog after blog, you'll find similar requests: write 500 words a day. Write 1,000 words a day. Write in the morning, from five to seven, before the kids are awake. Write in the evening, from eleven to midnight, after the kids are asleep. Write when you're driving, by talking into a Dictaphone; write on your commute, by typing on your Blackberry. Some people do that, it's true; I know a few. But I think the pressure is mostly unhealthy, and guilt-trips would-be writers into thinking that they should get less sleep.

This ubiquitous request, though, does make would-be writers realize that writing is a job which requires regular practice, and which can be triggered by regular practice. This is in opposition to the common misconception that writing is some mystical process which occurs only following flashes of inspiration. Stephen King famously says that amateurs wait for the muse, while real writers just get up and go to work. There's a lot of truth in that statement.

But there's also a lot of truth in the fact that not all days are the same; that, generally speaking, we tend to have more time at weekends and on holidays; that some days are just already too full. Some days we're also tired, ill, grumpy, not in the mood. Writing one thousand words every day ('and just one thousand!' some people will say – 'not one more!') is an excellent idea in theory. But there's no point in producing a thousand bad words every Monday morning because you're stressed by the weekly meeting with your boss, and stopping exactly at one thousand excellent words on Sunday afternoon when you're alone in the house and the kids are away for three hours playing rugby. There's something worryingly obsessive-compulsive about blogs emitting orders to would-be writers about time management.

As a result, writers often feel unreasonably guilty for not writing. This guilt crops up even in titles of blogs and podcasts about writing – see the very popular 'I Should Be Writing' and 'Writing Excuses' podcasts. But seriously, be kind to yourself. It's not *that* important. It's not as if you're not doing your job as a firefighter and dozens are dying while you twiddle your thumbs. It's just writing.

Key idea

If you genuinely want to write, you do need to write regularly. But find and set your own rhythm.

Write, maybe not every day, but perhaps two or three times a week. Or once a week, but seriously and keenly, for a relatively long time. Word targets can be good and bad; writing a thousand words can feel good, but if you have to delete them all tomorrow because they were sloppy, there's not much point. Tell yourself you're going to work every Tuesday, Thursday and Sunday, because these are the easiest days for you. It doesn't have to be 'from five to six' or 'one thousand words only'. If one Tuesday you feel like writing over lunchtime, and produce five hundred excellent words, don't force another tired five hundred words out at the 'scheduled time'. Don't listen to the muse, but do listen to yourself.

There's one thing that will magically make you work, though: deadlines. Once you get a book contract, you'll suddenly be keener to work. Funny, that. Maybe it's the advance money in the bank that you don't really want to have to pay back; maybe it's the feeling that yes, this *is* a real job. For this very book, which is due, at the time of writing, in six months, I'm writing one *good* thousand words a day – that's the plan. But often I write more. I make time for it. Because of this book, I still haven't watched the three episodes of *Sherlock*, Season 3. Oh the sacrifices I make.

The perils of online procrastination

Kids take time, pets take time, ensuring that your spouse still has some interest in remaining with you for ever despite time passing and the cute new colleague at work takes time. But there's another thing that takes time: the Internet.

Writers, it seems to me from my Twitter and Facebook accounts, are particularly vulnerable to online procrastination. As we shall discuss in the later part of this book, having an 'online presence' is now a requirement in the English-speaking publishing world. And, unless you genuinely hate the Internet, it's very hard not to get sucked into it, and spend an astronomical amount of time reading blogs, updating yours, tweeting, retweeting, checking Facebook, sending emails, reviewing a book on GoodReads, and I'm not even talking about Pinterest, Tumblr, YouTube and other websites.

Writers, above all, love saying that they're writing. The 'hashtag' #amwriting, which is very common on Twitter, accompanies snippets of information about what you're writing and the silly-funny-cute things that happen in the process. The interesting paradox, of course, is that you're not writing if you're tweeting #amwriting. You're tweeting.

It's not completely surprising that writers should often fall prey to such problems, because writing is a lonely business, and one for which the finished product takes a long time to be born. So being online and stating that you're writing gives reality to the writing process; it validates it. It makes it briefly tangible, credible, to the hundreds of people who follow you (often with little other interest than whether you might retweet their self-promoting tweets).

On the other hand, online 'procrastination' can be hugely interesting, motivational, enriching, essential. We'll get to the good aspects of that in the later chapter on the Internet; for now we're focusing on *closing down* the Internet.

Yes, closing it down. If you feel that you can't write five hundred words without immediately tweeting '500 words! going well #amwriting'; if you feel that every tea break is also an opportunity to check your email, Facebook and Google News, and lengthen said tea break by 20 minutes – then you need to shut down the Internet entirely. And turning off the Wi-Fi button isn't enough – you can just flick it on again.

One of the best things you can do for your writing career is downloading an Internet-blocking software. I use Cold Turkey, which is free and works with Windows. The equivalent for Mac users is ironically named Self Control. There are many others, for which you sometimes have to pay.

I set Cold Turkey to block all websites that pose a threat to my writing: Facebook, YouTube, Twitter, my two email addresses and so on. But I keep it open for all the rest, which still allows me to do research or check facts. I would not have been able to write most of my books or do most of my academic work without it. Don't listen to those who say snarkily that once upon a time people would write poetry in the trenches with bombs whizzing over their heads, and it's ridiculous to have to block an Internet connection for which you pay good money every month. If they're able to focus without it, well done to them. If you're not, do yourself a favour and take the temptation away entirely.

Writer's block and the anxiety of the white page

You've ~~found~~ made time to write, and the Internet isn't dragging you to it with its superglue-coated tentacles. But suddenly you realize you can't write a thing. The page is there, alluringly white, but … Why can't you bring yourself to *write*? Gracious heavens, it must be writer's block!

Most writers don't actually believe in writer's block. At least, not as it is generally conceived – a genuine impossibility to write *anything* at all. Writing *badly*, yes – that happens. But not being able to write anything is most often considered by writers to be laziness, except in cases when you have other, very pressing things on your mind – mourning or attending to a very ill person is *not* a good time for writing.

My say on the matter doesn't differ much from what you will read on most writer blogs. Beginning to write is the most efficient way to remedy 'writer's block'. Just as you sometimes really don't feel hungry until you start eating delicious food, you sometimes really don't feel like writing until the first few sentences are on the page. Remember, those first few sentences are eminently deletable. They're not being tattooed on anyone's skin (not yet, at least). Write a couple of bad sentences, a couple of bad paragraphs. Don't worry about their badness. At some point, on those flat phrases, an interesting little bump will emerge, followed by another, and the increasingly grubby surface will give your imagination a thousand places to grab on to, and climb.

NaNoWriMo-ing your way to a finished book

If you've already begun to burrow your way through the writerly blogosphere and Twittersphere, you've doubtlessly heard of NaNoWriMo. This initiative, launched in 1999 by a San Francisco writer, Chris Baty, is now so popular that it's virtually impossible to open your TweetDeck in November without spotting a #nanowrimo somewhere. This 'National Novel Writing Month' (very much international these days) runs between the first and the last day of November each year. Writers of all genres, in all formats and for all audiences set themselves a monthly goal – traditionally 50,000 words, but this target is often adapted by individual authors to their own needs and desires – divided into more or less manageable daily goals.

The aim of the exercise is to get writing and keep writing, at a fast pace and with little concern for ongoing editing, for 30 days solid. The Internet adds extra thrill to the enterprise: you can tweet your daily word count, write blog posts about how difficult or easy you are finding it, and publicly delight in the progress you're making on your heretofore unwritten manuscript. The advantages are clear: at the end of the month, you should have a significant number of words written – whether enough to constitute a whole novel or not, you will be on your way. Furthermore, you will have discovered that, in fact, it *is* possible to write every day; it may be fast, unpolished prose, but you are getting your story down on paper.

NaNoWriMo boasts a number of published novels – that is to say, novels started during a NaNoWriMo month, which is very different from saying 'novels written in a month and barely edited'. Such novels went through, of course, the same strenuous editing process – and perhaps even more so, since they were written so fast – as their bookshelf peers. Therefore, at the end of NaNoWriMo, even if you do have a 'finished' piece in terms of word count, you obviously should not rush to send it to agents or publishers. They are as aware as you are that thousands of people throughout the world are sprinting through manuscript writing, and they will be highly suspicious of any manuscript that lands in their inbox at 00.01 in the morning on 1 December. Take time to rework it for many, many weeks – we'll talk about this process in the last part of this book – before sending it off.

NaNoWriMo, of course, does not have to take place in November. It is a challenge you could give yourself at any time of the year, on your own or shared with a number of other writing friends. It could last for less than a month, or much longer. In fact, erm … It's a challenge published writers, once they have deadlines, just have to give themselves all the time. I have 20 days left to write two-thirds of my latest children's novel, for instance. Fake NaNoWriMo, here I come …

The difficult second third: how to keep going

NaNoWriMo also has the advantage of forcing you to speed through the 'difficult second third'. Yes, there are different stages in the writing of a work of fiction. They vary according to different people, but from talking to other writers I think we tend to agree that, while the beginning of a story is generally quite easy – spurred by the impression of a higher mission for the world – and the ending is generally not too bad either – fuelled by the desire for it to end and be called a new book-baby – the part of the story which constitutes roughly the second third is the most difficult to write.

This is, I think, for several reasons:

- It's the meat of the nut, the centrepiece of the story. It needs to be carefully thought through: it requires a lot of effort.
- In order to fulfil the different aspects of the plot, it tends to be composed of many different types of scene – contrary to the expository scenes and to the ending, which are more homogeneous.
- But most prominently, it is a *dangerous* space, because it is the part where you're most likely to abandon the book altogether.

Yes – abandon it. Come on – don't tell me you haven't got a dozen unfinished manuscripts lying around somewhere. That story you fell so much in love with, that story you thought you were going to see through to the end, and which is now forever just a head with no body attached? When I do school visits, I often tell the kids it's like falling in love. First you think the person is the most beautiful in the whole world. There's no way you can't *not* be with this story/person. It's the most bestest ever – everyone will want to steal it! (a very common fear among writers). So you start writing the story/going out with the person. And then something happens. You start noticing the wobbly structure/dandruff. The slightly unbelievable secondary plotline/tendency not to iron his shirts. And you increasingly think – that story/person I loved so much – is it possible I was *wrong*?

The difficult second third is the moment when you have to make the decision to rethink your relationship with your story and decide whether it's worth investing the required time to finish it. Push through, and turn your flaming passion into long-lasting trust and tenderness. If you decide that it was just a crush, a nice one-night stand with no future, then let it go, and look for a new love.

> ## Key idea
>
> Don't finish a story you don't believe in any more. But do think about it carefully. Don't let it drag and abandon it out of laziness: make a conscious decision to do so.

Help! My story is taking over!

The opposite situation to writer's block is 'writer's blah'. Writer's blah is what happens when you're very, very passionate about what you're writing – so passionate, in fact, that you're writing pages, pages and pages of slimy, mushy, smelly logorrhoea (logorrhoea = diarrhoea of language – not nice). Rereading all that the next day, week or month, you will bang your head on the keyboard at random in the hope that it will produce slightly more interesting writing. You will think of those fervent hours of typing and realize they were wasted, and that you will need to rewrite most of what came out of them.

This is why many writer bloggers rightly insist that writing, writing, writing is not enough: you need to make sure you're writing *well*. Writing well means keeping in control. Keeping in control means dominating your emotions when you write. Of course, a degree of spontaneity is necessary and healthy, but stories are very good at seducing you into grand moments of lyricism, endless descriptions, overlong dialogues, lazy choices of verbs and adjectives. This is the moment when the story takes over, and it can lead to major problems on several different levels:

- **Structure:** You might diverge from the original outline. Depending on whether you're a planner or a 'seat-of-the-pantser', this can have rather bad or even worse outcomes. It might be OK to venture slightly off-limits, and to add an episode or two that were not supposed to be there. But suddenly killing off your protagonist's love interest in a moment of caffeine-fuelled rage at two in the morning cannot be passed off as an inspired, spontaneous move. Be careful not to get sidetracked into alluring alternative plotlines which you will have to delete entirely and rewrite in six months.

- **Language:** when the story takes over, language is rarely at its best. Again, many writers might disagree with this, and argue that their most luminescent images, their most coruscating turns of phrase, are born of a trance-like state over which they have no control. And perhaps it's true for some. But it's also convenient to remember only those flashes of inspiration rather than the weeks of editing that were then necessary to chisel down the lyrical, sloppy sentences to their ultimate gem-like appearance. If you're a fast writer (as I am), you might want to slow down and take a breath once in a while. Review the past five or six sentences you've written. Look for tell-tale typos, missing words, misuses of verbs and adjectives, wobbly syntax. If there are some, it probably means you could do with some *rallentando* and a camomile tea. Hold your horses – it's not a race. The words aren't just the tools you tell your story with; they *are* your story, the *substance* of it. They deserve your full attention and care, not your maniacal brutality.

- **Characters:** a commonly heard 'complaint' (read: 'humblebrag') of writers is that 'characters are taking over'. This remark is, I think, intended to showcase, again, the *inspired* nature of the writer's work: 'I don't know what happened there; the characters *decided* to do this.' And, indeed, sometimes it does feel that that is what is happening. You might think: 'Hey, why are you falling in love with this random secondary character, Main Character?' Don't immediately think, 'Oh well, it must be meant to be. Let's follow that lead.' The character might have 'decided' to fall in love with another character than the one you intended, but so what? She's not a real person. She is *yours*. She is under your responsibility, and if she's taking over, it means you're not in control any more. Characters are obnoxiously fond of freedom, but they can create chaos if they're not whipped into line. You're the whipper; whip. Ask yourself if the character's 'decision' can be integrated with the story and how well, and whether it truly makes sense. It's not a sign from God, or your unconscious, or your dead great-grandmother if a character is 'taking over': it's a normal and quite common event in the course of storytelling, which needs to be understood and processed rationally.

So don't get carried away. Especially if, like me, you're allergic to editing, don't give your future self good reasons to hate your present self. Take a deep breath, take a walk. Work through it independently. Remember that you're the creator – you're the flesh-and-blood person, in front of the metal-and-plastic computer or spiral-bound notebook. As for *them*, don't listen to them too much. They're just people of paper in a world of words.

Managing several projects at the same time

Once you start writing professionally, you're likely to have to juggle different projects at the same time, and at different stages of production. Here's an example, based on what I'm currently doing:

- Writing a non-fiction book (this very one!), due in six months.
- Writing a Young Adult book in French (first three chapters written), due in four months.
- Writing a children's book in English (writing not started, synopsis finished), due in three months.
- Editing a children's book in English (second round of edits), due next week.
- Editing a picturebook in French (last round of edits), due in two days.
- Writing a picturebook in English (at idea stage, not written yet), no deadline.
- Presenting a proposal for a Young Adult series in English (at idea stage, not written yet), no deadline – but preferably within a month.

This is in addition to my full-time academic job, as well as, of course, to the other things you have to do as a writer, which we'll talk about later (school visits, updating your blog, replying to professional emails, etc.). As you can see, the difficulty of this writerly multitasking is that all of these projects are very different and also at various stages of development. Some are urgent; some don't even have a deadline. Some don't seem that urgent (like this book) because the deadline is in a long time – and yet they are so long that they do need attention *now*.

So how do you manage all this at the same time?

I borrow my technique from the incredibly prolific French writer René Goscinny, who used to write wildly popular children's and comic series – such as *Asterix*, *Young Nicholas* and *Iznogoud*. Goscinny had so many projects to work on at the same time (and he was constantly making up new ones) that he would set an alarm to ring every hour and a half. Whenever the alarm rang, he stopped working on one project and switched to another – no matter how 'inspired' he felt about the first one, no matter how motivated he was to start the second one. With an hour and a half of work on each project a day, the projects evolved together, slowly but surely.

Obviously, I'm not advocating this rather military treatment of writing. But whenever I feel overwhelmed, I do roughly that. In order to see all the projects progressing well, it's better to do a little bit of each regularly rather than spend a week on one, then a week on another. Every day, I try to work a little bit on each of my projects. It doesn't need to take long – no more than an hour a day, for instance, for the French Young Adult novel; no more than half an hour of edits. The lowest-priority projects (the ones with no deadlines) can be pushed out of the daily schedule if other, more pressing matters arise. Juggling with commitments becomes much easier when you start considering them as slowly advancing projects rather than feeling you have to be entirely committed to them for a whole day.

Practising this will also help you cut down the amount of mental preparation you need to 'get into' a project. You actually don't need the amount of time you think. You open the document and you get started. You close it again when it's time, even if you're in the middle of something, and you don't need half an hour to recover from the creative trance. You get on with things. It's a very liberating process.

Finally, you might discover that managing several projects at the same time gives rise to what I call 'productive procrastination': when you really don't want to work on project A, you'll find yourself compensating by working on project B (which you might have previously neglected). And then project C will emerge, but you won't feel like working on it – so you'll compensate by working on project A. Ultimately, they all get done. I thought I was the only one thinking that, but of course I wasn't – I was amused to read recently a book by John Perry which exposed exactly this theory: *The Art of Procrastination*. Procrastination is indeed an art: you need to practise effective procrastination, so that tasks get done rather than postponed for ever.

Workshop: unblocking the story

This workshop exercise might not be relevant to you right now, but it might be one day – and then you can come back to it. That day is the dreaded day when you find yourself blocked, uninspired, demotivated – when the story you fell in love with is no longer the seductive creature it once was. You're thinking of sneakily cheating on it with another story. You're at the dreaded stage where it must flow again, or be put aside.

Take the last couple of pages of the blocked story. They might be made up of a description, of a dialogue, of an action scene. Don't reread them; just chuck them in the bin.

Then go back to what is now the last page. What you wrote afterwards, and is now all crunched-up in the recycling basket, is probably still fresh in your mind, but it's not fresh to the extent that you can still remember it by heart. Try to push it away from your memory. Get back to your outline: what are you trying to achieve now? What were you trying to get to next? This might be an unexciting moment in the plot, or a difficult passage to write because of complex character emotions; why aren't you motivated to write it?

Having thought constructively about your own reluctance to write and about what will happen once you've pushed through this stage of the writing, sit down and write again, from what is now the last page. The next couple of pages or so will help you get into the flow of writing, since you already wrote them once in the past; but they will be somewhat different, too – more goal-oriented, more focused, more thoughtful. You will know where you're going.

Keep writing for another hour or so, trying to remain fuelled by the energy of the first two rewritten pages.

Review

The first question to ask is:

- Did you enjoy writing this? Do you feel it unlocked the story, or just created an extra few pages of blah? Are you still demotivated about the story?

Reread what you have written. Now fish the two crumpled-up pages from the recycling bin and read them again, too.

- How different are the two versions? Which one is best?
- What can you salvage from the first version and reintegrate into the second version?
- Has the second version got more energy, more intensity? It is more purposeful, more future-bound?

It should be. This exercise should have allowed you to write in a relatively constrained state at the beginning, before allowing you to roam more freely afterwards; it should have helped unblock the story.

But if you still don't like the story, if there's something that prevents you from writing the rest, if the writing process is made up of starts and stops that are draining you of energy and motivation, you will need to think about the work in more depth, and perhaps accept that it's not you, it's *it*: the story is just not working.

Let's not end this part on a pessimistic note. For each dead story, another seven spring forth; it's like a young and sprightly hydra, this writing business. And in children's literature, we're lucky enough that a dead story in one format might be a very lively story in another. We've got a huge playground – no, a whole attraction park, really – of different formats, genres and types of writing to play around with. And that's what the next part of this book is about. Now that you've, with any luck, found your voice, let's find you a format.

PART TWO
Finding a format

10

Picturebooks: for the love of words and pictures

The evening has been full of good anecdotes, good wine and good cheese. It's almost midnight, plates of apple crumble-cum-vanilla ice cream have been licked clean, the guests have reclined back into their seats. Yes, it's been a nice evening, with your partner, your best friend and her new boyfriend – four contented smiles in the smoky light of the electric chandeliers.

It's time for the Usual Question:

Best Friend: So what are you writing now?

You: Hmm, I've been writing a picturebook.

Best Friend's New Boyfriend: What do you mean, 'You've been writing a picturebook'? How long can it possibly take to write a picturebook?

Best Friend: [*awkward laugh*] Don't joke, darling, apparently it's not as easy as we tend to think.

Best Friend's New Boyfriend: Oh *pur-lease*. Give me a pen and I'll write a picturebook right now on this napkin. 'Gary was a tree who was really unhappy because he got cold in the winter …'

Best Friend: [*awkwarder laugh*] Ha-ha. Right, it's time to go, my love.

Best Friend's New Boyfriend: Hey, seriously – I think I've got a really good idea, actually. Listen to this – then Gary gets the spider to knit him a coat … You know what? We could ask your sister to do the drawings. She sort of draws, right? She doodles. [*To you:*] When we've finished writing the picturebook, can we send it to you so you can give it to your publisher?

You get the gist.

When I was working on the slush piles of both British and French publishers, the most terrible submissions by far were picturebooks. Children's literature in general attracts enough deluded people who think they can write; but these people are over-represented in the production of 'picturebooks'. These are people who can't be bothered to write long books, so they'd rather write short ones, and they believe that their neighbour/ niece/ wife draws *amazingly well*, so she can illustrate the story. There must be a special place in Hell for these people to be burned on a stake fuelled by their own 'creations'.

This chapter will show you how not to become one of these people (though by buying this book you have already signalled that you aren't).

What a picturebook is, and is not

You'll notice I've been writing 'picturebook' as one word rather than as the perhaps more usual picture-book or picture book. This is a convention among most children's literature critics and theorists. It denotes the fact that in a (good) picturebook, words and pictures should be inseparable. There can be no picturebook text that does not *require* pictures – not just 'benefit from' pictures, but really *need* them, organically. The story in a picturebook cannot be complete without the pictures; it grows from the interaction between words and images.

Let me bombard you with a few definitions of picturebooks by picturebook theorists (yes, picturebook theory is a very well-developed field of study):

- For Barbara Bader, picturebooks are 'text, illustrations, total design; an item of manufacture and a commercial product; a social, cultural, historical document; and foremost an experience for a child. As an art form it hinges on the interdependence of pictures and words, on the simultaneous display of two facing pages, and on the drama of the turning page' (1976, p. 1).

- Maria Nikolajeva: 'The unique nature of picturebooks as a medium and an art form is based on the combination of two levels of communication, the verbal and the visual' (2003, p. 37).

- Judith Graham: 'So interwoven with the text are the pictures that to give the text alone would be like giving a performance of a concerto without an orchestra' (1990, p. 17).

- Jane Doonan: 'The pictures may elaborate, amplify, extend, and complement the words. Or the pictures may appear to contradict or "deviate" in feeling from what the words imply' (1993, p. 18).

Congratulations, you're now a long way ahead of most would-be picturebook writers. Too many people think picturebooks are essentially very short stories which, in the near future, someone will be happy to illustrate. So they write things like:

> *'Damian was a blond boy with blue eyes who lived with his mum and dad in a little house near a river. He had a cat, a dog and a little yellow duck.'*

And the kind of illustration they're imagining to go with this text (if they go to the trouble of imagining it at all) shows a blond boy with blue eyes near an older man and woman, a cat, a dog and a little yellow duck in front of a little house by a river.

This is a very basic case of what a picturebook is *not*. In a picturebook, the words normally shouldn't say what the pictures already show. There's no point; it is a redundancy, a redundancy just as shocking as if you wrote a novel starting with the sentence 'Damian was a blond boy whose hair was blond'.

Instead, this is what happens in a good picturebook, such as Anthony Browne's *Piggybook*, in which a father and his two sons, chauvinistic pigs all three, are left in a rather sorry state after their wife and mum decides to leave the house. In short, they are turned into pigs. But in the first spread that shows in the pictures the transformed Piggotts, no mention is made of this in words. Rather, throughout the picturebook, Browne lets the reader marvel at the delightful tension between words and images – the text doesn't appear to *notice* what the pictures are so blatantly showing.

This treatment of word–picture interaction, typical of Browne, gives rise to a subtle, magical-realist story, the crux of which cannot quite be articulated by language. Is it a metaphor? Is it the 'truth'?

Key idea

Young readers are captivated by what is unsaid in picturebooks. Leave them that space of freedom.

The gap

That space of freedom, by the way, is termed the 'readerly gap' or simply 'gap' by picturebook scholars. It's the core of the format. Morag Styles and Victor Watson (1996, p. 2) say: 'Central to the picturebook is the notion of the readerly gap – that imaginative space that lies hidden somewhere between the words and the pictures.' A 'gap' is born every time the verbal narrator doesn't say something that the visual narrator shows, and vice versa.

How should this inform the way you write a picturebook? Well, since words don't work without pictures, and vice versa, you have to think about what text *and* pictures are doing, at the same time and inseparably. It's not enough just to write the words. Imagine you're writing a film script: you can't just write what is being said by the characters on screen. For the story to work, you'll have to tell the filming team what happens in between ('Sally gets out of the car, turns left into the garage, flicks on the light'). It's exactly the same with picturebook writing, where you might have a page that looks like this:

SPREAD 5. (TEXT)

[In the kitchen. Mr Piggott & sons are pigs (dressed in normal human clothes). Washing up crockery. Everything dirty. Pig heads appearing everywhere].

This text between brackets will serve both as instructions to the illustrator and as an indication to the publisher of what's going on in the story. You cannot do without this – let me reiterate that if your story functions just as words, with no need for any description of what happens in the pictures, then it's *not* a picturebook. It will be, perhaps, an illustrated text.

The good news is that you have a million ways of making this word–picture interaction exhilarating, fascinating, hilarious, beautiful and earth-shattering. And this is how.

Different types of word–picture interactions

I have hinted at this before, but if you really want to know about children's literature, writing for children and the art of children's books, you could do much worse than take a look at children's literature criticism and theory. This is nowhere truer, perhaps, than with picturebook theory. Your indispensable bible here is *How Picturebooks Work*, by Maria Nikolajeva and Carole Scott, which is probably the best book about how to write picturebooks that you could possibly read – if you read it with your author hat on.

Here are some of the different types of word–picture interactions Nikolajeva and Scott analyse:

1 RELATION OF COMPLEMENTARITY OR ENHANCEMENT

This is the most basic type of word–picture interaction: pictures and words show different things, once in a while covering the same ground. Such interaction can be more or less complex, from pictures that are mostly illustrative to pictures that are so sophisticated that they significantly enhance the textual material.

2 RELATION OF COUNTERPOINT

This is when text and pictures deliberately keep key information in only one element or the other. The – example above, from *Piggybook*, shows what happens when a crucial element of the plot is contained solely in the picture. The reader has to work hard to gather the different elements, as if two different narrators were fighting against each other …

3 RELATION OF CONTRADICTION

In this extreme form of 'fight' between two narrators, the text and the pictures seem to completely disagree about the story. In Jan Pienkowski's famous pop-up picturebook *Haunted House*, the reader/viewer is taken on a 'quiet visit' of a very strange house. Each new room is filled, in the pictures, with monsters and ghosts of all shapes and sizes – but the narrative voice, who, we are led to understand, is our host, doesn't seem quite aware that the house doesn't much correspond to his descriptions… In the bathroom, for instance, a giant pop-up monster with tentacles, as well as an alligator, very much contradict the host's assertion that 'No, I don't have many visitors.'

The whole book is premised on a 'quiet visit' of the house by the reader, but clearly our host isn't quite aware (or is he?) that the house doesn't much correspond to his description …

These different types of relations (here very simplified; do refer back to Nikolajeva and Scott's book!) can really open up possibilities for your storytelling. Think hard about it – the best and most sophisticated picturebooks are the ones where much reflection has gone into orchestrating the 'concerto' of words and pictures.

Thinking in pictures

It might be very difficult, at first, to think 'in pictures'. As a writer, and not necessarily, I assume, an illustrator, you might not be a very visual person. In fact, many picturebook scholars would claim that as *adults*, we are by default not very visual. We tend to lose, after childhood, our ability to decrypt images, to understand the world as a canvas. It's normal – humans are verbal creatures above all. Talking, reading, writing – language *in words* calibrates our lives. We don't need pictures to get by as much as we did as children and pre-readers. Words are now for us what pictures used to be.

But illustrators, photographers, painters, designers and, to a more mercenary extent, anyone who works in advertising, will be extremely sensitive to the pictorial and the visual, and very aware of how pictures work. They know about visual composition, colour, angles. It's not easy to learn all of these tricks, to switch to a visual understanding of your writing. Most writers say that they 'visualize' what they're writing, but a lot of the visualization, let's be honest, is probably quite lazy. When you say you can 'see' your characters, your settings and so on, I'm willing to bet you can see them only from the front, rather frozen, Sim-like. You're probably not thinking of the orientation of the light falling on to their faces; of their posture in relation to the rest of the scene; of the fact that a different angle would make them look more threatening. I doubt that you've got a mental picture which, were it ever transferred to canvas in oils, would look like a Vermeer.

And, of course, this doesn't matter at all in a novel, but it does for a picturebook. In order to think in pictures and think with pictures, you need to know about important conventions of Western visual composition – at least enough to give the illustrator and the picturebook editor indications that you've thought about the picturebook's pictures and are, therefore, a professional picturebook writer.

Here are some of these conventions:

LEFT-TO-RIGHT ORIENTATION

Just like the words on this page, pictures are conventionally 'read' from left to right. This means that there's a temporal dimension to the composition of an illustration. We will automatically read a movement as 'faster' if it is going from the left to the right than vice versa.

This has many interesting consequences:

- A window will appear to be broken more violently (even, perhaps, more noisily!) by a baseball if the window is positioned to the right of the young batter than if it is positioned to his left.

- A neutral-faced character looking to the left of a picture will appear more longing, nostalgic and thoughtful (because she is looking into the past) than the same character looking to the right of a picture, who will appear more hopeful, forward-thinking, or at least contemplating what she is going to do next (because she is looking into the future).

- A picture where characters are walking or running towards the left will perceptibly require more visual effort on the part of the reader – and this can be used in many ways for storytelling purposes.
- Time will pass from left to right.

ANGLE

The angle at which a scene is 'shot' greatly influences the mood of a picture. Representing a scared character at the top of a very high diving board, you can choose, for instance, to show him from the bottom, with the reader looking up towards him – which will make him appear small and scared – or from the top, looking down towards the swimming-pool – which will make the distance appear huge, and scare the *reader*. Your choice depends on whether the message you want to convey is 'Bob is really scared', or 'Bob really has a reason to be scared'.

Play around with angles in your head. Look at the same scene from the side, from the top, from the bottom. Break it up into small frames from different angles. How does the mood change? What impact does it have on the story?

An interesting angle in picturebooks, to use sparingly perhaps, is known as 'subjective camera'. This is when the character is not visible in the picture, but it is understood that the reader sees what the character is seeing.

PAGE ORIENTATION AND FORMAT

As the writer of the picturebook, you should think about the orientation of the book and its format. There are different types of page orientation. Two facing pages in a picturebook are called a *spread*; these two open pages are also called a *double(-page) spread*.

The number of pages in a picturebook needs to be divisible by four. This is essential when writing a picturebook storyboard: don't feel you can write a random number of pages; you need to stick to the required number. The norm is 12 double spreads (24 pages), though there's space for negotiation.

The right-hand page of a double spread is called the *recto*, while the left-hand page is the *verso*.

You probably know the difference between *landscape* – where the page is longer horizontally than vertically – and *portrait* – the opposite. This difference has important implications for a picturebooks. Picturebooks in landscape have very wide double spreads; this can be used to convey long durations (because it takes longer to read them from left to right), for instance.

A great French picturebook, *Plouf!* by Philippe Corentin, uses the landscape format but requires the book to be held vertically, and read from top to bottom across this format. The space on the page is used to convey the up-and-down movements of the characters, which constitute the core of the picturebook's story.

Some picturebooks have square pages; those are generally characteristic of picturebooks for very young readers, or for the mass market (e.g. the *Mr Men* series).

Some picturebooks have paper engineering – from lift-the-flap books to amazing pop-ups – and these of course need to be taken into account as you write the text.

The 'drama of the turning page', as Barbara Bader put it, is crucial. Whatever you can do to keep the suspense going by placing new elements as a new page is turned – do it. Surprise the reader by accelerating the pace or slowing it down.

THE GUTTER

That's the name of the fold down the middle of the picturebook's double spreads. The illustrator will be careful that nothing too important happens 'in' the gutter or near it, or it might disappear in the crack for ever. The gutter can be used as a 'natural' line of separation between texts and pictures, as is the case for instance at the beginning of *Where the Wild Things Are*.

BLEED

A picture is said to 'bleed' if it is not bound, on one side or more, by a frame. In other words, it goes all the way to the edge of the page. The effect of a picture that bleeds is visual 'totality'. *Where the Wild Things Are* plays with bleed: at the beginning, pictures are confined to a small space on the white pages, until they come to bleed over the whole double spread in the famous 'Wild Rumpus' scene, making the words disappear entirely.

ENDPAPERS

These are the two double spreads at the beginning and the end of a picturebook. They're not directly a part of the story, but in sophisticated picturebooks many endpapers contribute to or enhance the story. For instance, the endpapers in Anthony Browne's *Piggybook* are covered with flying pigs. 'Pigs may fly …' Do these pigs question the whole 'message' of the picturebook – that one day women might be liberated from household chores and chauvinistic males? If you know what you'd like your endpapers to be like, tell your editor.

> ## Key idea
>
>
> These words aren't just jargon. Using this vocabulary when describing your picturebook will make it easier for everyone to understand what you mean, and it will make your writing more professional and worthy of attention.

The relationship with the illustrator

Picturebook illustrators are *artists*; they're not just there to draw what you tell them. Thinking in pictures doesn't mean you have to do the illustrator's job; they've got years of training, experience and knowledge about what it takes to draw a good picture. They might laugh at your idea to show the villain from a low angle, and rightly inform you that it's a cliché. Or they might tell you that, in this context, the villain should be shown from the bottom because it will be a nice wink to such and such a film – and they will accentuate that 'intervisual reference'. There's no greater joy than discovering how much freedom the illustrator has taken with that text you thought you already saw in pictures.

While we're on the subject, let's talk about the relationship between author and illustrator. Many people think that authors and illustrators normally work closely together, phoning each other up all the time to ask about the colour of the buttons of the character on the third spread and sharing sketches. Many people also assume that authors of picturebooks 'choose' 'their' illustrator. This is not usually the case. Especially if you're a first-time picturebook author or a not very well-known one, the editor will usually find an illustrator for your story (but will of course ensure that you can work with the illustrator by asking you to confirm that you like him/her.)

The relationship you have with an illustrator will vary. For one of my picturebooks, I exchanged long emails with the illustrator, mainly because he had new ideas which could have had an impact on the text. For instance, he decided that drawing the ice dove on a stone pedestal, as the text said, would not be very graceful. He asked me if he could instead perch the ice dove on a long wooden stick. I'm very glad I agreed.

© Antoine Déprez

For another picturebook, I had no contact at all with the illustrator until the book was out. I discovered all her wonderful pictures when the book was almost ready to print. I trusted the editor and knew it would be great, and was not disappointed.

Don't expect people to keep you updated all the time about how the pictures are progressing. Illustrators are busy, and editors who receive drawings don't always think of forwarding them to you. Nudge them only if you really can't wait, or they haven't given any sign of life for a rather long time.

It's unlikely that your voice will be heard if, seeing a finished drawing, you complain that it's not at all what you wanted it to be – unless you've got extremely good reasons. One thing on which you might have more of a say, however, is the cover. Do get involved: ask to see sketches and offer suggestions. After all, it will be the face of your picturebook.

Generally speaking, don't expect a thorough and sustained relationship with the illustrator of your picturebooks. Write by thinking of them all the time – even if you don't know who they will be yet – but then, let them work.

Specific types of picturebook

Now that we've been through different picturebook strategies, here's a brief overview of the different types of picturebook to which they could apply:

WORDLESS PICTUREBOOKS

There are picturebooks that don't have any words at all: Quentin Blake's *Clown*, Jan Ormerod's *Moonlight* and *Sunshine*, Raymond Briggs's *The Snowman*. The story functions without words at all – they are, in the strictest sense of the word, *picturebooks*. Does this mean that no one *writes* them?

Of course not. Though they are often written by author-illustrators, sometimes wordless picturebooks have a writer *and* an illustrator. They were written by describing what happens in the pictures, just like your descriptions between square brackets of what happens when no one is talking. If you've got a good idea for a wordless picturebook, don't feel it's silly to write it. Don't think that, because your words aren't literally written down in the finished product, it means they're not there. They are – translated into pictures, just like silent films, which had to be scripted before being shot.

However, unfortunately, wordless picturebooks are not the easiest sell. This is something I find baffling, since they should be by definition the most democratic ones, the easiest to export, and the easiest to leave in the hands of pre-readers. But apparently many adults are perplexed by wordless picturebooks; they don't know how to 'read' them out loud, so they tend to buy them less frequently for their children.

BABY BOOKS AND BOARD BOOKS

Gum-resistant picturebooks for babies and very young children come in many shapes and sizes: inflatable picturebooks for the bath, furry picturebooks to learn about the textures of cacti and cotton wool, musical picturebooks to infuriate everyone on the bus, picturebooks with mirrors to learn narcissism at a young age, picturebooks that clip on to the buggy to occupy the little despot as he is being wheeled around …

These books are often written by people inside the publishing house, or by the illustrators themselves. However, if you have a groundbreaking idea for helping babies learn about shapes, colours, animals, letters and numbers, do try. Such picturebooks can be enormously innovative; look at the work of Hervé Tullet, Leo Lionni and Soledad

Bravi, whose apparently simple geometrical shapes are arranged with staggering intelligence and sensitivity to their audience.

Abecedaries and counting books are always very popular, and publishers love original creations in twenty-six letters or ten numbers. There are amazing examples out there: go to your local bookstore and browse. Borrow a baby from someone if you don't want to look as if you're reading baby books on your own.

COMIC BOOKS

Comic books deserve, of course, their own chapter – even their own book; slotting them in here is a little unfair, but it will have to do. Comic books can sell extremely well and cover all different ages. But they are expensive and take a long time to produce. Writing a storyboard for a comic book is quite different from writing a picturebook text. There will probably be many more pictures and more text than in a picturebook. Decisions regarding angle, colour, orientation and so on developed earlier will need to be adopted for each different panel. Furthermore, comic books have their own vocabulary:

- A **panel** is a unit of the narrative, generally (but not always) framed, in which there tends to be a picture and, often, some text.
- **Speech bubbles**, or **phylacteries**, are the geometrical shapes in which thoughts, speech, onomatopoeic words and various other types of writing (including, sometimes, other pictures) occur.
- The **gutter** defines, in comics, not just the space in the middle of the double spread but also the space between panels.
- **Emanata** are the visual symbols which stand for emotions – surprise, fear, joy. Think of the stars that surround someone who's just bumped their head on something, or the idiosyncratic drops of sweat around Hergé's characters when they're in shock.
- **Motion lines** can be added to indicate movement.

A storyboard for a comic book generally goes into detail as to what the illustrations will represent. Then the illustrator will normally produce *thumbnails* (small, rough drawings) in pencil, which can still be modified. In the last stages – the clean drawings and the inking, then the colour – it's more difficult to accommodate changes.

If you haven't read a comic book since *Tintin* and *Peanuts*, it might be worth having a look at the comics section in a shop. Traditional 'Franco-Belgian' and 'American' comic styles have feverishly cross-fertilized with the Japanese manga and anime traditions, and you might find that comics and graphic novels aren't like the ones you remember. If you feel like writing a graphic novel for teenagers, you'll have to combine thinking in pictures, as described in this chapter, with thinking about adolescence, as we'll soon turn to.

'HYBRID' BOOKS

'A novel in cartoons', says Jeff Kinney of his impossibly successful *Diary of a Wimpy Kid* series. And, indeed, there isn't really a word yet for the cohort of pictorial novellas which have recently taken over children's literature. Hundreds of more or less obvious copycats of Kinney's series now exist.

More generally, many books for first readers increasingly play on illustrations. These books are picturebooks insofar as, according to our definition, they wouldn't function without the pictures; they are not merely illustrated stories. There isn't a huge amount of difference between writing a text like that and writing a picturebook text for much younger readers. Both function by creating interesting interactions between words and pictures, and by relying on the pictures for a good part of the storytelling.

The double audience

One last point about picturebooks that needs to be considered is the double audience. Who are you addressing in a picturebook? Children, of course. But also … their potentially less enthusiastic parents. Picturebooks are one kind of children's book which you can bet will often be read by two people at the same time, and those two people might have very conflicting interests. The adult co-reader, as we call him/her in children's literature criticism jargon, might be principally interested in going back downstairs fairly quickly to curl up on the sofa with the child's other parent, while the child might be much keener to make the bedtime reading last as long as possible.

To put it cynically, adults need to be entertained, too. They will hide your picturebook in the bottom of the cupboard if it fascinates the kid but makes *them* fall asleep. They're not as likely to read it (and recommend it) if they're not getting anything out of the experience. And adults are, often more than children, the people who will talk about your books, share them with other parents, teachers and librarians, and praise them. You don't want to be the person who writes the picturebook that 'my daughter Amelia adores, and I really don't understand why – I can't wait for her to be over it'.

On top of that, it can be good to consider, as you're writing the picturebook, what the 'reading event' (another bit of jargon) will entail. Think of an adult and a child reading the book together. Will they have fun? Will they communicate over it? Is it a matter of the adult reading and the child listening, or will they interact? If you slip a little mouse doing funny things on each page, even if it's never mentioned in the text, you can bet that the child and the adult will soon be looking for it everywhere. It will add to the story. It will add to the event. It will add to the bond between adult and child.

> ## Key idea
>
>
> Anything you can do to trigger a response from child and adult together is good.

You might have noticed, if you've been visiting children's bookstores, that many picturebooks are now highly metafictional – they 'know' they're picturebooks, they address the readers directly, they 'talk' to the child and the adult. An outstanding and famous example is Mo Willems's *Don't Let the Pigeon Drive the Bus!* -the first in his series of pigeon books. These playful, self-referential books play with the reading event: they condition and stage it. Faced with them, the adult and the child readers feel as if they're talking to a third person in the room. And they will try to outsmart one another.

Of course, not all picturebooks need to be like that (thank goodness – we've already got enough smoothie bottles talking to us as if we were best friends and making little jokes). These strategies can get old. But even when writing a more conventional picturebook, do think of the 'double address'. Include details that are likely to be enjoyed by the adult, perhaps even understood *only* by the adult. Some children's literature critics are against in-jokes that speak to the adult over the child's head, but after all children's books are also replete with in-jokes that speak to the child under the adult's nose. Why not make each of them feel a little bit of a VIP in turn?

How to write a picturebook text in ten minutes

This has been a long chapter with a lot going on – it's time for a break before the workshop exercise. Here's a slightly playful take on the 'how to' book – after all we've seen in this chapter, I'll sum it up by giving you the secret to writing a picturebook text in ten minutes, since so many people say it's absolutely possible.

Step 1: Wait for the half-baked ideas you've been collecting and mulling over to coalesce into a Good Idea for a Picturebook. (*Estimated frequency: once or twice a year.*)

Step 2: Develop that Good Idea into a story which would work as a coherent whole formed of interdependent and mutually enhancing words and pictures. Think of the size, shape and orientation of the pages for the story. Think of the style of illustration. (*Estimated time: one week to one month.*)

Step 3: Structure the story into a number of pages divisible by four, making sure that the pacing is right, the story arc has the right balance and there aren't any unnecessary or slow double spreads. (*Estimated time: one week to one month.*)

Step 4: Now work on the text in your mind, picking the right words to express the right things in relation to the right illustrations you're also imagining. Juggle with all that in your mind. Pay attention to rhythm, imagery, vocabulary, grammar. Make sure that you don't repeat in the words what is already visible in the pictures. Imagine the pictures at all times. Say the words out loud to make sure that they sound good. Think of an adult reading the picturebook to a child. Think of a child reading the picturebook to an adult. Tweak the words in your mind until they're all necessary and sufficient. Repeat them to yourself until you know the whole text by heart. Read the picturebook to yourself in your mind (close your eyes to see the pictures). (*Estimated time: one week to six months.*)

Step 5: Open a new Word document. (*Estimated time: 11 seconds.*)

Step 6: Write down the text of the picturebook, as well as explanations between square brackets of what should be shown by the illustrations. (*Estimated time: 10 minutes.*)

Workshop: writing a picturebook text

Grab a couple of sheets of white A4. In this workshop exercise, you're going to write a picture text, along with a storyboard – or at least get as far as possible into the process until you get a good feel for it.

This workshop exercise assumes that you've already got an idea for a picturebook, with a beginning, a middle and an end. We're now going to work on arranging it in picturebook form.

On your A4 pieces of paper, draw 12 (preferably; another number divisible by four is, however, acceptable) rectangles, which will represent your double spreads; split them in half to indicate the gutter. Remember, they can be as narrow or broad as you feel they need to be for your story.

Think of how your story, which exists, at this stage, only in synopsis form, might be calibrated over these 12 double spreads. How much time will you need to introduce the characters and set up the stage before the action can start? (Make this as short as you can.) Over how many double spreads can the main action be deployed? How many will you need to wind down towards the ending?

Think of the 'drama of the turning page' – which surprising, shocking or funny elements can you 'expel' from one double spread to the next to ensure suspense or hilarity?

If you can, draw rough sketches of the composition of each spread: characters can be represented as stick figures, landscapes as lines; it really doesn't matter. Try to get a sense of where the text should go in relation to the pictures. Will it be typed over them or firmly separated from them? Also add descriptions of illustrations, between square brackets, under each double spread.

Read the words out loud: this is a critical stage in the process. Does it flow?

The text is probably too long. No, really, it is probably too long. Edit it down until it's as crisp as it can be – until the pictures do as much of the work as possible.

Review

Let the storyboard sit for a few days without touching it. Then reread it. How well did you achieve the following? Rate yourself from 1 to 10 (some may, of course, not apply) on the following:

- The interaction between words and pictures works well. ① ② ③ ④ ⑤ ⑥ ⑦ ⑧ ⑨ ⑩
- There is repetition between words and pictures. ① ② ③ ④ ⑤ ⑥ ⑦ ⑧ ⑨ ⑩
- The words flow. ① ② ③ ④ ⑤ ⑥ ⑦ ⑧ ⑨ ⑩
- The pacing and rhythm are pleasant; the story is harmoniously distributed over the 12 spreads. ① ② ③ ④ ⑤ ⑥ ⑦ ⑧ ⑨ ⑩
- The reading event is anticipated. ① ② ③ ④ ⑤ ⑥ ⑦ ⑧ ⑨ ⑩

- There are clear explanations for the pictures, with appropriate vocabulary. ⬚1 ⬚2 ⬚3 ⬚4 ⬚5 ⬚6 ⬚7 ⬚8 ⬚9 ⬚10
- The adult reader should be able to enjoy it, too. ⬚1 ⬚2 ⬚3 ⬚4 ⬚5 ⬚6 ⬚7 ⬚8 ⬚9 ⬚10

Tweak it until you think it's as good as it can be. Well done! Writing a picturebook isn't easy at all, so shake your own (right) hand with your own (left) hand, or high-five yourself. If you can write good picturebooks, you will be adored by all publishers.

Where to next?

Let's not suggest that children ever 'grow out' of picturebooks – that's a terrible fabrication by short-sighted educators who want to see children 'progressing' towards verbal language. Picturebooks should be read at all ages, at least twice a week according to recommendations by the World Health Organization (I think). But as children grow and learn to read, they start to encounter other types of writing. And that's what we're looking at next – the difficult art of chapter books, perhaps the least-loved type of children's literature among scholars, and as prone to be terrible as they are to be amazing.

11

Chapter books: action!

'Another chapter! Another chapter! Please, Daddy – pleaaaaase!'

Dad closed the book, stroked Eddie's hair, and stood up.

'We've already read three chapters, darling. We said we'd read just one every evening.'

'But we can't leave it here, with Maggie stuck at the top of that burning building! How's she going to get down?'

'We'll know what happens to her tomorrow evening. Good night.'

Click! The light went off.

'Nooooooo!' screamed Eddie. 'I want to *know*!'

'You need to learn to be patient,' grumbled Dad. 'Sleep well.'

'I won't fall asleep if I don't know! And if I don't sleep I might get scared and I'll come and see you and Mum in your bed and …'

Click! The light went on.

Plop! Dad sat down on the bed again.

'Chapter Six: The Purple Parachute …'

Books for young readers, generally read out loud to them by adults, but not necessarily; divided into manageable chapters, with devilish cliffhangers at the end of each one: chapter books, as I shall call them here – it's a rather unhappy phrase – are a significant slice of the children's publishing cake. The limits of their literary zone are quite blurry; some bookstores will slot them into their under-seven category, others under their under-nine or even under-twelve. Some chapter books might not even have chapters; some books for slightly older children – indeed, even teenagers – might resemble chapter books. Let's say, to simplify, that we're going to talk about books generally targeted at children of primary-school age, from the barely-just-learning-to-read to the more confident young readers.

At first sight, chapter books perhaps appear to you to be the least gratifying type of children's literature. You'd be wrong. This is a readership that is hugely, immensely, staggeringly rewarding to write for. Primary-school kids are, on the whole, pretty great people. They're big enough that they can handle complex ideas and not be worried about big words; they are hugely curious about the world but young enough that they haven't yet acquired that teenage swagger and blasé look typical of adolescent audiences. 'Keen' is the word here: primary-school children are keen. Keen to learn, keen to laugh, keen to empathize, keen to cry, keen to greet you and talk to you at school visits. Keen to read and keen to share their reading. They are a passionate bunch.

Yet, too often, publishers rely on unexciting, old-fashioned or unchallenging chapter books for that age range. Old favourites – Blyton, in particular – are neighbours on the shelves to dull, formulaic books about animals, spaceships, football and more animals. I've got nothing against animals – but I doubt you've bought this *Complete Writing for Children Course* in order to write such books only.

I'm being harsh, though. Many publishers are extremely keen to develop their lists for this age range, and they're looking for quirky, exciting, original, scary chapter books for voracious young readers. It's an amazing playground, so go for it – and don't forget to put on your helmet, because chapter books are, often, all about *action*.

As well as, I hope, your own secret desire to write chapter books and meet the primary-school children who read them …

What should a book for this age range look like?

Chapter books are generally relatively short stories: between 5,000 and 35,000 words. They can be illustrated; in fact, they often are. These illustrations can interact with the words, as in my own *Royal Babysitters* series, or they can be there mostly for decorative purposes, as in, for instance, Marcus Sedgwick's *Raven Mysteries* series. As the double reference to series indicates, they are often (in fact, almost always) part of a series, so a lot of what we're going to talk about here should be read with Chapter 7 in mind.

Such books still have, like picturebooks, a double audience. Granted, a lot of children might read them on their own, but they are also very likely to be read at bedtime by parents to their children, or at school by a teacher. They are divided into chapters of roughly equal length, which slice the stories into manageable chunks. Often, the end of each chapter has a cliffhanger. Scheherazade-like, therefore, they propel the young reader forward until the end of the story.

These books are story-led, full of action, and have strong characters. More often than not, they are expected to be funny or scary, have happy endings, and, on a more cynical note, they are the most policed and politically correct type of children's books. This is partly due to the way they're distributed and sold. Many chapter books don't sell huge amounts in bookstores, but make money through book clubs, school visits, or by being bought by schools and libraries. They also get reviewed less than other types of children's book such as picturebooks and, overwhelmingly, Young Adult literature.

Key idea

Chapter books absolutely need to make it past the adult 'gatekeepers' or 'mediators' by gaining their love and approval, and this love and approval is often conditional on a rather conservative notion of what makes them suitable for children.

Gratuitous violence and sexual innuendo are thus even more difficult to slip into these books than into picturebooks. Editors are very careful that librarians and teachers don't have any cause for complaint, and that they can recommend them whole-heartedly to parents. Don't think I'm exaggerating: a bookseller once told me that a parent had complained to her because my *Sleuth on Skates* (which the bookseller had recommended) had the following sentence in it: 'Maybe a rival chopped her up like aubergine for a ratatouille.'

Similes involving violence against vegetables are thus to be avoided at all costs.

Magic or realism?

Broadly speaking, chapter books are split between stories of magic and fantasy, historical tales, and stories that take place in the contemporary world. On the magical side are stories of witches and wizards – the *Mildred Hubble* series is still a favourite among youngsters, and so is Valerie Thomas's *Winnie the Witch* – of unicorns and fairies and dragons. If you want to know what a good book for that age range entails, you could do much worse than looking at Cressida Cowell's *How to Train Your Dragon* series; that is, if you haven't done so already.

Between magic and realism, quite a few chapter book series take place in Another Historical Period. Stories of prehistoric wanderings, of Roman wars, of medieval knights and princesses, of pirates in the South Seas, of futuristic space adventures on newly colonized planets play upon the supposed appetite of children for the ancient and the exotic. Those often contain magical elements. Such stories can be serious and educational or just seek to delight and entertain. A book like *War Horse*, by Michael

Morpurgo, evidently has didactic purposes: beyond telling a moving story, it also teaches about historical events.

Other writers prefer stories set in realistic or quasi-realistic places and in contemporary times, offsetting the quotidian feel of the scenes with unexpected adventures. Many aspects of young children's lives can be used for these purposes: from school to babysitters through to attraction parks and swimming pools, anything can be a pretext for an adventure. Magical realist stories, where day-to-day reality becomes strangely modified by the arrival of a strange event, are also popular. But be careful with ambiguity; again, though it is by no means a general rule, for this age range publishers tend to be quite conservative. Stories that hover between reality and magic without quite deciding what they are can be of higher aesthetic merit but have lower chances with editors. This is not a very risk-taking area, however much we might deplore that fact.

Whether set in a fantasy land or telling the story of two friends selling lemonade, books for younger primary-age children are generally about discovery, adventure, fun, fear and surprise.

Key idea

Chapter books are often about a world where everything banal can suddenly become extraordinary; where children notice things that adults don't; where objects and animals speak and mysterious doors fling open.

You might want to challenge that, if you find the principle formulaic and derivative, but it might be tricky to convince editors that you'll sell an inordinately sad book to six-to eight-year-olds with success, however gorgeous the language and poignant the illustrations.

The school story

Let's now dive into the most common types of texts for this age range, beginning with the school story. It's difficult to see how these could ever become obsolete: kids go to school; they love it, they hate it; it's the theatre of their terrors, their loves, their hopes, their humiliations. The multiplicity of possible situations makes schools an endless source of inspiration for children's writers.

The school story is eminently hybridizable. You can have a school-story-cum-magic, a school-story-cum-horses, a school-story-cum-dancing … You can have boarding schools, day schools, schools in castles, schools on boats, schools on other planets, schools under water. Teachers also come in all shapes and sizes, from the terrifying Mr Wilkins of the *Jennings* series to the lovely Miss Honey of *Matilda* – not to mention the plethora of magical, extra-terrestrial or otherwise monstrous teachers that recur in children's literature.

School life is so varied (actual children might disagree with that statement!) that it provides a huge number of narrative opportunities. There's day-to-day school life, of course, but even that is pluriform – classes, tests, breaks, sports, lunch, library, assembly, music, being late, having to go to the teachers' common room, bumping into the headmaster when running down a corridor. And then there are the extras: school outings to museums, to cinemas, to theatres; school trips to Lyme Regis, to France, to the Moon (why not!); school projects, from the most serious to the quirkiest; sports days; school plays.

The school can be threatened. It can hold a treasure. It can be haunted. It can be invaded. It's full of funny characters – it's a battlefield between adults (parents, teachers, librarians, assistant teachers, head teachers, cleaning staff, admin staff, caretaker, cook, inspectors); it's a battlefield between children (pupils, and pupils from other schools, and exchange pupils from the other side of the world). A school story can be educational; at school you learn social life, alongside many other things: so stories can teach children not to bully and how to make friends and not alienate people. It can be anti-educational, too – there are many things in school that can be challenged, not least adult domination of children. It's bottomless, really, this well of possibilities that the institution of the school provides, even for us greedy and imaginative writers.

But because of that, it's also a very well-trodden space and you have to be careful not to fall into clichéd patterns. The shy and affable school librarian, the annoying Miss Know-It-All, the cantankerous caretaker … Read widely, and eliminate those stock characters from your writing. There are other aspects of school life which you'll need to be careful about if you're writing about a contemporary school. Everything moves so fast; what do schools look like nowadays? Remember that many schools have smartboards, not blackboards; and that kids are shown videos almost as often as they're given texts to read. Children know everything about school: they spend eight hours a day in there. They will know if you're fondly reminiscing about your childhood – or, worse, that of Enid Blyton: your vocabulary, your descriptions will give it away.

Furthermore, many canonical school stories which have achieved classic status are classist, racist and sexist. Having a boarding school in a story now isn't just a detail, it has class connotations. You have female teachers and a male headteacher? Why, pray? And is there enough diversity in that classroom of yours?

Without becoming completely paranoid about political correctness, it's worth remembering that children's stories carry particular ideologies that strengthen or weaken dominant power structures. And schools, of all places, are microcosms: they're representations of the world in miniature. They're Petri dishes for all the experiments on values, fears and desires that we have regarding children and regarding society.

So they're not innocent spaces: they're eminently political. Everything, from the physical organization of the classroom to the times for assembly, lunch and sports, has social and political significance. Check the hidden values in your fictional schools; unearth what educational thinkers call the 'hidden curriculum', the values transmitted implicitly, outside of the openly educational discourse.

It can sound a bit far-fetched to do a sociological examination of your own representation of school, but naïve classism, racism or sexism might very well be picked up by reviewers and critics.

The adventure story

Most children's stories, for this age range and others, are 'adventure stories' insofar as something happens that's not quite what happens every day. But there's a difference between a story about a school play in which an unexpected girl is picked to play the lead (triggering the mortal jealousy of her peers) and a story about a school play in which the lead actress gradually turns into the character she's supposed to be impersonating (especially if that character is Frankenstein's monster).

Adventure stories for children can be qualified as plots that generally depart so far from the quotidian that, even without the intervention of magical elements, they cannot possibly be qualified as realistic. They generally possess a number of recognizable features, most of which we've talked about already when discussing the 'quest' plot:

- A conflict between two or more people, clans, countries, or planets, with a relatively well-defined goal

- A hero or heroine whose role it is to take charge of a good amount of the quest

- One or more villains

- Stakes that are, if not of life and death, at least higher than whether Cynthia will get to play Ophelia in the school production of *Hamlet*.

The term 'adventure story' is evidently very broad. It encompasses many genres, each of which can be highly successful for the age range we're talking about:

- **Detective stories:** editors would kill to find good detective stories for this age range (young Sherlock has already been done, in case you're wondering).

- **Monster, zombies, vampire and ghost stories:** always a huge hit, and easily marketable (especially around Halloween); for example, see Chris Priestley's (genuinely scary) *Tales of Terror* series.

- **Pirate, knights and world explorer stories:** these are a number of stock characters who can go on quests and fight villains without too much explanation required. Such chapter books often model themselves on *Treasure Island* or *Peter Pan*; be careful that you don't adopt an old-fashioned tone.

- **Science-fiction and space opera stories:** technically speaking, as many a purist will tell you, 'science fiction' refers to a work of art which anticipates the future with imagined scientific discoveries and makes that the centre of the plot. A space opera, more loosely, describes any story set in space or on other planets. So *Star Wars* is a space opera, not science fiction. But there's no need to get too pedantic about it. There doesn't seem to be a huge craze at the moment for stories of space invasions, robots and rockets, but there's still a fairly steady flow of them.

There are, of course, many other types of adventure stories – and many masters to read. Geraldine McCaughrean's take on *Peter Pan*, with her 'sequel', *Peter Pan in Scarlet*, provides a good example of what an old-fashioned adventure story can look like nowadays.

In terms of language, some central characteristics of adventure books targeted at the younger end of primary-age children are:

- fast-paced writing: short chapters, dialogue privileged over description, brief introductions and conclusions, brief transitions
- relatively simple vocabulary: although this is *not*, I emphasize, always the case, adventure stories tend to privilege sophistication of plot over sophistication of language; or at least, to avoid words and sentences that will detract from the plot
- more action verbs than lengthy adverbs, more descriptive adjectives than epithets just there for aesthetic pleasure; dialogues full of exclamation and question marks
- cliffhangers, cliffhangers, cliffhangers.

I can hear you tutt-tutting that you don't want to serve children the same old simplistic soup, thank you very much; *your* adventure story will be gorgeously written as well as entertaining and fast-paced, a kind of *His Dark Materials* for younger readers. Well, thank *you* very much: I warmly encourage you to do so. In fact, I do think there's a place for amazing *literary* adventure fiction for six- to nine-year-olds, and would be curious to read your own take on the matter.

Another central aspect of adventure stories and, in fact, of much children's literature, an aspect which I haven't discussed yet, is getting rid of the parents. For the young adventurers to live their adventurous life to the full, getting rid of the parents remains a very common strategy. Indeed, the lack of parental involvement with their children's lives in Fictionland is properly astonishing. They might be dead, they might be abroad, or they might simply not be aware of what's going on; whatever it is, the kids are blissfully free to roam the premises unsupervised.

There's no reason to be dogmatic about this, but getting rid of the parents is an easy and, frankly, rather clichéd writing strategy. Nowadays, I would argue that it's quite difficult to get away with the 'Oh, I should have said: his parents are dead' old trick. Orphans are hugely rare, and the death of one, let alone two, parents is, thankfully, an infrequent event in the lives of contemporary children. Having it as an 'excuse' for independent adventures can be difficult to defend.

That said, there's a lot of space to play around with the concept of *absent* parents, whether they're dead or lost. Children's literature for a slightly older age range, and for teenagers, often reflects quite thoroughly on the question of the absent parent. Sam Gayton's *The Snow Merchant* is a little girl's quest for her presumed-dead mother. Hilary McKay's acclaimed *Saffy's Angel* similarly follows a group of siblings who want to know the truth about an absent parent. But with chapter books, it is rarer to see such problems explored. Boarding schools, of course, allow for the Parent Puzzle to be immediately solved.

But there is plenty of space for parents in children's books for that age. Parents are a huge part of children's lives. They are authoritative but contestable, funny but serious, boring but playful. In my own *Sesame Seade* series, I've been very careful *not* to get rid of the parents, who have become fully fleshed-out characters in their own right, and comedic characters. I'm not saying it's the right thing to do, but when you're thinking of an adventure, why not think of how the parents could take part in it?

The animal story

The term 'animal story' is generally quite derogatory, at least among laypeople. When my partner leaned over my shoulder earlier to look at what I was writing (a very rude thing to do!), he snorted, '"Animal stories." What are you going to tell them, "Don't write those"?' Of course not. There are many types of animal stories, especially in chapter-book form. The ones he clearly had in mine are so-called 'pony stories' of the *Saddle Club* and *Animal Ark*-type series: stories of talking kittens, of puppies in need of saving, of dressage competitions. But I evidently wouldn't tell you *not* to write those. They might be very commercial, but they can be perfectly good stories, and they certainly have a lot of readers. Within the parameters of their genre, they can also offer a space for creativity. Here are some types of animal stories:

'ANIMAL PROTECTION' STORIES

Such 'animal stories' are generally centred around one main animal character, and one or more child characters who are passionate about this animal. The animal might be threatened (often by adults, sometimes by other animals) and the child(ren)'s role is to protect and save the animal. Another pattern sees the animal escaping or being abandoned away from home, and having to come back. Such stories revolve around the young implied reader's imagined proximity to and affection for animals. They require a strong characterization of the animal character.

'WILD ANIMAL' STORIES

In the case of 'wild animal' stories, there's been a quiet trend for the past 20 years towards environmental tales: stories of children saving baby lions from deforestation, baby elephant from poachers, baby tigers from unprofessional circuses. This 'green' strand of children's literature, which exists more widely, of course, than simply in chapter books, finds itself particularly well crystallized in animal stories.

'PONY STORIES'

The typical 'pony story' revolves around a community of children or teenagers who are passionate about horses. Such stories are as much about the horses as they are about the dramas of friendship, competition and romance in pony clubs or equestrian schools.

'Pony stories' are not to be undertaken lightly: you are talking to an audience that is eminently knowledgeable about the matter. I wrote, pseudonymously, two very commercial 'pony stories' for young readers, and (not being a horse person myself) I had to do long hours of research. Getting the jargon right is indispensable: readers will know immediately if you get the name of a particular brush, grain or saddle wrong.

'Pony stories' emphasize the close relationship between rider and horse. I read countless articles on dressage and jumping, watched countless interviews of professional riders, in order to glean vocabulary and ideas. They talk of a 'connection'; they say that there are days when they 'click' with the horse and days when they don't, and so on. Such research helped me paint (I hope) an honest and vibrant portrayal of the relationship between child and horse.

THE 'LITERARY ANIMAL STORY'

It might seem callous to put it like this, but there's a relatively clear line between very commercial animal stories and the type of animal stories Michael Morpurgo, for instance, is famous for – stories which use animals, often metaphorically, to talk about human existence. *War Horse*, which I've already mentioned, is a good example. Such animal stories can become perennial classics because beyond the adventure they also tackle other themes and questions about existence. They are thus what is often called 'timeless' in their message; E.B. White's *Charlotte's Web*, for instance, is both well written and pertinent: it talks not just about animals, but also about human–animal relations, *and* child–adult relations, *and* friendship, *and* the power of words …

Of course, all animal stories implicitly make a statement about the differences between humans and animals, and often about the callousness and lack of empathy of humans towards animals. But 'literary' animal stories attempt to elucidate such problems and others perhaps more deeply. There's very definitely a space for award-winning, literary animal stories for young children. Michael Morpurgo, despite his prolific output, can't fill it all by himself. I predict, looking into my crystal ball, that the interest in such stories will rise with the growing interest of society and culture in *animality* as an extension of humanity; it's very clear from philosophy and literary studies that we're reaching an age of transition from considering animals as clearly separate from humans to seeing them as simply *differently* human.

The funny story

Funny stories are, and will always be, enormously popular. They aren't, of course, a 'genre' by themselves: any of the types of chapter books discussed above can be a funny story as well. But there are also chapter books for which the main selling point is that they are 'funny stories'. If you're interested in writing that type of book, have a look immediately at the past winners and shortlists of the Roald Dahl Funny Prize, which is a rare award for humorous children's literature.

Writing funny books for children is exhilarating but enormously difficult, because writing a joke is always a leap of faith: will they find it funny? How can I be sure that they'll understand my humour? There are a number of strategies, not all very subtle, which such books rely on. The key is to use not just one, but the whole range, from the most to the least sophisticated. Think of *The Office* or *Blackadder*: alongside intellectual humour, there's a lot of slapstick. It's the balance that counts.

Key idea

Humour questions the authority, legitimacy and status of the power structures in place. For children, this often means adults. Anti-adult humour is rife in children's literature, and liberating.

Let's start, quite literally, from the bottom:

TOILET HUMOUR

It is a truth universally acknowledged (by adults) that a child in possession of a sense of humour must be in want of toilet jokes. Toilet humour is delightful to children, as it is to many adults, principally because it's a taboo subject: proper people don't talk about faeces, vomit, bogeys and dribble – even less about willies and bum holes. And children can sense that adults are very, *very* uncomfortable about these topics. So reading about them in a book is deliciously transgressive, especially if the vomit is 'projectile', the faeces 'steamy', the bogeys 'greenish'.

SLAPSTICK COMEDY

People falling over, beating each other up, running into closed doors, getting drenched or having to move around tied up with rope – all this is a recipe for endless hilarity. Slapstick comedy is actually an ancient and noble form of comedy, which has survived since the ancient Greeks enjoyed the play *The Wasps* to the Italian audience of the *commedia dell'arte* through to *Fawlty Towers*. Be sure to pepper your slapstick with onomatopoeic SPLASHES and POPS and OUCHES, and to direct it against authority figures more often than not.

SITUATIONAL COMEDY

When, for instance, Jennings inadvertently raises his hand at an auction and ends up winning a piglet, much against his will, which he thus has to bring to school – that's situational comedy. Misunderstandings, mismatches and mix-ups provide excellent comedic set-ups.

NONSENSE AND WORDPLAY

The humorous quality of nonsensical and surrealistic tales mostly comes from the liberating impression that things don't need to have an educational purpose, don't even need to have a *significance*. The reader stumbles into a world with new rules. Part of the appeal – and the fun – of *Alice in Wonderland* is the delirious feeling that nothing in here truly matters as much as the authority figures are trying to imply.

Wordplay can range from the obvious to the sophisticated, and in children's literature it can be very sophisticated indeed. Think of the labyrinthine plays on words in Norton Juster's *The Phantom Tollbooth*: some, like 'jumping to conclusions', are on the more facile side while others are more joyfully innovative:

Children, especially at this age, are barely just getting to grips with language; they
notice words that sound funnily similar; they notice the weirdness of metaphors that
we've long learned to forget to notice; they're constantly negotiating their way through
the circumvolutions of language. Puns and wordplay glorify language just as they
temporarily destroy it. They show language as it is: an imperfect tool which contains
more than it seems to say or says more than it seems to contain. Give children good
puns, not the same old ones; make them marvel at the *matter* of language, its little
oddities, its quirky habits. In the process, you'll surely make them laugh, especially
if your ruthless destruction of language is a destruction of *adult* language – parents,
teachers, they sometimes talk nonsense, don't they?

Intertextual humour

Parody, pastiche. We're getting here into a humoristic terrain which assumes from
the reader some previous engagement with other material, which is then parodied,
referred to or mocked in the text. This is, of course, easier to assume when the reader
is an adult; it isn't certain that children will recognize a *Star Wars* reference. It's always
tricky to assume previous knowledge of that type in chapter books. The rule is that the
book should be absolutely understandable – and still funny and witty – without the
knowledge of whatever you're parodying or pastiching. If the reader *does* know, it will
add another level of understanding. It took me 17 years before I could decrypt most
of the jokes in *Asterix in Britain*, but it didn't prevent me from loving the book as a
young child.

SELF-REFERENTIAL AND METAFICTIONAL HUMOUR

You can have a lot of fun with young readers by making them aware of the materiality
and the fictionality of the book they're reading; by having narrators that address them
directly, or stories within stories within stories, or stories that are being written as
they are being read. Such postmodern playfulness is frequent in children's literature.
Again, it assumes a mature engagement with the text as a created object, a work of art,
sometimes self-deprecating and sometimes uncertain about its purpose. Some editors
will say 'yes, please'; others will say children are 'perhaps too young to understand'.
I prefer the former.

Humour comes in so many different and hybrid forms that you shouldn't be ashamed
of using *all* of them. Clever witticisms are great for a while, but there's no need to say
no to a character desiring to slip on dog turd. Humour isn't necessarily more or less
noble; it's only, I think, more or less *original*. The deliriously imaginative slapstick of
many screwball comedies from the 1950s can be worth much more than yet another

Onion article playing on the same tropes. Humour has an enormous role to play in children's literature – not least of which is telling them that not everything needs to be serious and that adults are often wrong – so don't feel that it's belittling your role as a writer to resort to it.

Aspirational stories

Many children's books for this age range could be described as 'aspirational stories': they present the irresistible and unexpected rise of an at-first-quite-unnoticeable child. Ballerina stories and football stories spring to mind. The rags-to-riches pattern is present in most types of chapter book, from pony stories to adventure. The rather clear 'message' is that it is possible for a shy, bookish person to become Someone. And these books being, of course, often read by shy, bookish children, they are bound to strike a chord. Having a children's book labelled 'aspirational' can be a good thing, as adult mediators may be looking for that type of writing to boost a child's waning self-confidence or crippling asociality.

The aspirational dimension of chapter books comes from the need for a happy ending. The tricky question of endings is much debated in children's literature theory, with many scholars arguing that children's literature shouldn't have obligatory happy endings – after all, the argument goes, if we're showing children what life's like, they should know about it with all its flaws. But the opposite predominates in children's publishing: editors aren't keen to take on books, especially for this age range, in which the endings are too sad or too ambiguous. I've had a story for this age group rejected, for instance, on the basis that the little heroine turns into a wolf at the end. That ending was not technically sad or unhappy, but it was considered too ambiguous.

Chapter books are plagued perhaps more than any other type of children's literature by the necessity for clear-cut, happy endings, potentially leading to another book in the series. Picturebooks are, paradoxically, often much darker and much less optimistic than the books given to children who are just learning to read. I think it's fairly safe to say that you can't expect, especially as a first-time author, to be allowed to take too many risks with the endings of your stories for this age range. The rule seems to be that they must not leave the young reader with a sense of despair or inconclusiveness, much as you may deplore it.

Writing for boys and/or girls

We get to a tricky, tricky topic: the relentless *genderedness* of children's books, especially chapter books. Children's literature, in its production, distribution and reading practices, remains a decidedly sexist type of discourse. Children's books are segregated by 'gender' from the very youngest age. They are segregated in bookstores; they are segregated in publishers' catalogues; they are consciously and unconsciously segregated by even the best-willing parents, teachers and librarians.

Children learn very quickly that they shouldn't be reading the 'wrong' books. Especially boys. As many feminist studies of children's literature have shown – and as gender studies scholars have long explained – there's a cultural reflex towards seeing literature 'for boys' as equivalent to literature 'for all'. Little social stigma is attached to girls reading a book clearly marketed primarily at boys. On the other hand, books 'for girls' are very firmly 'for girls only': girlhood, femininity, is 'the Other'. Boys learn very quickly that they should not pick up a Jacqueline Wilson story. Whatever is pink, yellow and red sends clear signals that they should steer away from it.

It gets more perverse than that. Even children's books that are neutral in colour and marketed equally to boys and girls will often fail to land in little boys' hands if they have a female main character. Unconsciously, parents of boys, booksellers advising them and, gradually, boys themselves direct their attention towards books that have male main characters. This is, again, because of the socio-culturally engineered expectation that girls are the Other, the ones that boys won't be interested in and won't understand; while girls are seen as perfectly capable of reading books about boys.

Here is an anecdote to illustrate how far-reaching this assumption can be. A friend of mine, who has two sons, told me she was going to buy one of my *Sesame Seade* books. 'But for me, not for the boys, of course,' she added. 'It's for girls, so they won't read it.'

I immediately opposed this: I know many little boys who have been made to read it and liked it, and we took great care when making the cover of the book and marketing it to make it clear that it was not just intended for girls.

'But the cover is pink!' my friend said. 'You can't say that's gender-neutral.'

I showed her the book, and she was surprised to realize that the cover is not, in fact, pink. It is blue, turquoise and green; the only pink that appears on the cover is a very thin strip at the top. She had to admit that she remembered it as being entirely pink, because she had internalized the 'fact' that it was 'for girls' – simply because of the female heroine.

This social and cultural bias is infuriating and unfair. It deprives boys of fantastic books and forces girls to consider that they will always be the alienated sex. I urge you to please fight it on all possible levels; and this means, among other things, not yielding to the pressure of editors who will often want your chapter books to correspond to one 'gendered' audience over the other. Chapter books are not the only offenders, but they are, it seems to me, perhaps the worst. They arrive into a child's life at a stage when they're learning both to read and to differentiate according to gender. Of course, let's not be naive: by then, they have already been exposed to sexism. But the literature they get at this stage is crucial. If I only have one plea in this book, it's that you don't let people give your gender-neutral books only to girls because you have a main female character, and don't let your books be catalogued according to this arbitrary and oppressive distinction.

Workshop: the perfect chapter

This exercise revolves around crafting a perfect chapter for a chapter book. I'll set it up so you don't have to. This is a pony story (oh, yes) taking place in an equestrian school in Scotland. We're about three-quarters of the way through the book, building up to the climax. The previous chapter left us with a cliffhanger: Masha Banks, eight years old, has just discovered that the school's priceless pure-blood mare, Cézanne, has been stolen by a teacher, whom she always suspected was a horse thief. She's standing, thunderstruck, in the doorway to the stables. The only horse left in there is Pablo, Cézanne's father. He's old and weak, and Masha has never ridden him.

In this chapter you'll have to show me Masha deciding to ride Pablo to follow Cézanne's thief. You'll have to show me how she tames him into letting her on his back, and leaves the stables to run across the fields. You'll close the chapter with another cliffhanger: far away in the distance, they spot a plume of smoke rising above the fields …

The length of the chapter is up to you; two A4 pages are more than enough for the purpose of this exercise, but feel free to write more.

Review

Now reread your work. How well did your chapter sound? Rate yourself on a scale of 1 to 10:

- Think about the introduction. Does it immediately set up the scene and take us into Masha's head as she makes The Decision?   1 2 3 4 5 6 7 8 9 10

- Are there enough setbacks in the treatment of the relationship between Masha and the horse: before she succeeds in taming him? Is there enough suspense?   1 2 3 4 5 6 7 8 9 10

- How well did you describe the horse? Did you manage to communicate a sense of humanity in presenting him?   1 2 3 4 5 6 7 8 9 10

- Is the reader fully engaged in Masha's quest?   1 2 3 4 5 6 7 8 9 10

- Do we get enough of a sense of the difficulty of the task, and of Masha's superior strength of character as she achieves it?   1 2 3 4 5 6 7 8 9 10

- Rate the language used: are your adjectives vibrant, your verbs active and varied, your dialogues lively and realistic?   1 2 3 4 5 6 7 8 9 10

- How eager are we to turn the page to the next chapter?   1 2 3 4 5 6 7 8 9 10

This exhilarating exercise should help you get a sense of how you can draft a chapter from a chapter book – even bang in the middle – with all the 'ingredients', but also with soul and strength. If you have the patience, go back to it and tweak the language. Make it more literary, slow it down; see how far you can go. Or speed it up, cut adverbs and adjectives, make it a short whirlpool of a chapter. Which one do you prefer?

Where to next?

They grow up too fast! Next, we'll be talking about the all-important, but very difficult, transition from primary school to high school; that strange prepubescent era when the little children of yesterday are slowly turning into the teenagers of tomorrow. They still want adventure but they also want romance; they still want comfort but they also want psychological drama ... Turn the page from this chapter to the next, dearest reader, if you want to know what happens to Masha when she's a character in a book for nine- to thirteen-year-olds.

12

Tween and young teenage literature: negotiating the high-school turn

So Goldilocks climbed through the window and into the little bookshop.

'Now,' she said, 'which book shall I choose?'

She tiptoed towards a bookshelf laden with colourful, slim books, and picked up one of an appealing apricot shade. Hardly had she read the first few pages that she knew it would not do; it would not do at all.

'I have read too many books like this,' she decided. 'I'm almost going to high school now; I'm more grown up than that!'

So she tiptoed towards another bookshelf that was curving under the weight of thick, dark books with blood-red titles, and picked up one with an appealing embossed cover. Hardly had she read the first few pages than she knew it would not do; it would not do at all.

'What do I care about moody, spotty old teenagers? I don't want to read hundreds of pages of *emotions.* I still want fun and action!'

She sat down on a spongy purple pouf, discomfited. It was as if no book spoke to her any more. But next to the pouf on a plump wooden table was a little book that looked just the right size and just the right colour. She picked it up, and opened it.

And hardly had she read the first few pages than she knew it would do; it would do very well.

A literature of transition

Age guidelines for children's books are as egregious for authors and readers as they are useful for publishers and booksellers. Right now, we can't do without them. But I'm often baffled by the extent to which publishers insist on fitting your work within a certain age range with an incredible level of precision. In the case of 'mid-grade' literature, which means different things according to who you ask, the boundaries are extremely blurred.

Publishers are, it seems, desperate to buy literature for what could be roughly defined as the nine-to-thirteen age range: those tricky four years straddling the end of primary school and the beginning of high school. These years reflect a gradual evolution, it is assumed by adults, between childhood and adolescence: between a taste for fun and adventure and a preference for darkness and psychology. I'm exaggerating, of course; but this elusive 'literature of transition', ideally, should contain elements of both.

It is within this age range, arguably, that many of what we call 'children's classics' are found, from *The Chronicles of Narnia* to *Harry Potter*. In fact, that age range used to be the one with which children's literature ended. At puberty, it was high time to 'upgrade' to the Brontë sisters. But with the advent of Young Adult literature, which is read earlier and earlier by children who are not, by any stretch of the imagination, 'Young Adults', it is becoming difficult to understand exactly who this type of literature is addressed to. I see it as the literature that bridges the gap between chapter books and fat teenage literature. These are the books which even *Twilight*-addicted teenagers might choose to return to once in a while, to enjoy for a time the comfort and warmth of late childhood. They're also the books which more precocious younger readers might try out while the rest of their peers are still busy deciphering *Mildred Hubble*.

Whatever it is exactly, such literature tends to emphasize initiation, transition and rites of passage. Whether realistic or fantastical, these texts must speak to people who are gradually seeing the cosiness and protection of childhood crumbling away, for better or for worse; people who increasingly desire to assert their independence and to make decisions that matter, not just to them but to others. Their social conscience is developing, like their awareness of politics, and they are realizing that situations are more complex than they once imagined. Parents and authority figures, which it was once merely funny to overturn in the imagination, are now revealed as faulty and imperfect. And romance – indeed even physical contact – isn't a vague happily ever after any more, but a budding reality. Talking about a 'threshold' type of literature in this case isn't far-fetched.

Literature for this age range has a large proportion of high-quality texts. Allying wonderful writing with splendid plot structure, profound reflections on existence and sensitive characterization, such books as those by Katherine Paterson, Philip Pullman, Jacqueline Wilson, Katherine Rundell and Timothée de Fombelle, to name but a tiny few, are diamonds of the children's literature world. Perhaps because it is difficult to write for this age range, or perhaps because it is easier to be aesthetic in doing so, this is arguably the most artistic bookshelf of every bookstore. So if you're up to the challenge, go for it. Between warm action and deep psychology, invade the Goldilocks zone of tween literature.

Social realism

'Social realism' defines fiction that does not shy away from presenting, in the case of children's literature, problematic family situations and children left unprotected or uncared for by adults and the government. The uncontested empress of social realism for this age range is, of course, Jacqueline Wilson, but she isn't alone in representing the realities of children's contemporary situations. Recurrent themes and features in social-realistic children's writing include:

- unconventional family situations (single-parent families, foster families, divorced parents with children from multiple relationships, deceased or absent parents)

- illness, physical or mental, of parents or other children

- law-breaking adults or children

- controversial or taboo adult behaviour (drinking, tattooing, sleeping out, sleeping around)

- an impression of disempowerment on a political scale, or of corruption of the people in charge

- discrimination by gender, race, class or ability

- practices of different cultural, religious and ethnic groups.

Social-realistic novels for children don't need, of course, to be dark and gloomy, but there's generally a balance between the positive and negative aspects of these unconventional situations, especially as they are presented at the tipping point when the growing child can no longer take refuge in his or her imagination. Many social-realistic books for children express exactly this passage from the imaginary to the real, from the latent to the actual.

What is perhaps so poignant about Jacqueline Wilson's novels is the way they stage this loss of illusions, this gradual realization. In *The Lottie Project*, the young protagonist, Charlie, is devastated to realize that her mother is dating someone; in her childish imaginings, they could be 'Jo and Charlie forever', growing old together, with no external intervention. She chooses to imagine her mother as blissfully asexual and entirely focused on her, Charlie, her only child. The arrival of a rival – worse, of a rival's *son* – is sensitively depicted by Wilson as a metaphor for the transition from childhood to adolescence. For this age range, it is important, I think, to be aware of the potential violence of such a revelation, and to unroll it smoothly and kindly rather than in an earth-shattering manner; Wilson's books are beautiful models for this.

Social-realistic novels for pre-adolescents also sow the seeds of political contestation and awareness of social injustice. Elen Caldecott's *The Great Ice-Cream Heist* tenderly but surely highlights matters of racism, classism and social responsibility. Sometimes simply unveiling the conditions of existence of more deprived people than the implied reader – either in their own country or in others' – suffices to create a committed work of children's literature. Sita Brahmachari's *Jasmine Skies*, the vibrant sequel to *Artichoke Hearts*, takes her heroine, Mira, to India, where she's confronted with the extreme poverty of orphaned children. The shock of alterity, the discovery that the world is unfair and that the reader is privileged, blooms in children's literature for pre-adolescents, possibly because authors assume that younger children are still too self-centred to take this fact into account. Hilary McKay is also a major writer of this type of novel: the authority of adults is gently deactivated and children are introduced to perturbing themes, regarding their own birth and family relations.

How do you write social-realistic stories? Firstly by making sure that you understand the social backgrounds and political situations you will be depicting. This includes language, terminology, habits, and historical and cultural circumstances. There's nothing worse than comfortably privileged writers attempting to denounce the plight of the working classes by using hackneyed language and the wrong jargon, and misunderstanding the ways in which these conditions have come to arise. Often, this also leads to sentimentalized visions of 'the poor' and the 'racial other', which groups them into stereotypical social categories and erases individual differences.

Sensitivity is, of course, necessary in all kinds of writing, but when writing about difficult family situations it is all the more important. Humour is, too. Read the unfairly overlooked *Mimi*, by John Newman. In this story, which follows a young girl whose mother has died, he strikes just the right balance between appropriate distance and sadness, and adds a healthy dose of tenderness and fun.

It's tempting to think: 'I'll never be able to write about such situations; I've never experienced them.' But 'Write about what you know' isn't always a helpful motto; it's often reductive, self-centred and overly cautious. However, certainly, *research* what you don't know, and get acquainted with people who do know what you're writing about. You might feel strongly about the fate of illegal immigrants, but even with all the goodwill in the world, reading about it in the papers won't lead to a good story. Many writers do 'real-world research', talking to people who could be representative of the group they're trying to write about. This can be anyone from teenagers who have had abortions to Scout leaders. Such real-world research helps you gain understanding of the variety and complexity of individual situations within what superficially looks like a homogeneous group of people.

You are dealing with literature *for* children and (probably) *about* children. Be careful that you don't assume too much regarding your readers' knowledge of politics, and interest in their own political situation. There's a temptation to stage child protagonists who have always been outraged to be treated badly by 'society', 'because of racism', or of 'stereotypes about being a girl' or 'as the child of parents on benefits', and who try to fight against that. It's a fairly unrealistic representation. Most people take their positions in society for granted unless and until they are 'awakened' to them. Stories of these 'awakenings' can be extraordinary, but be careful not to make them unbelievable; we don't suddenly jump from passive acceptance of our situation to raging rebellion against 'oppressors', with a whole battery of previously unheard vocabulary. This is especially the case when children are the 'awakened' party: would they be fully aware of the rhetoric of the cause they're endorsing? Of the means of shaking things up? Not everything has to imitate the timescale of reality, but social-realistic stories need to be, well, at least a bit realistic.

High fantasy and secondary-world fantasy

At the other end of the spectrum are stories that take place entirely or partly in magical worlds. The former are called 'high fantasy', the latter 'secondary-world fantasy'; the difference might not be huge but it's important to know. High fantasy refers to the type of fiction where the entire world is regulated by some kind of magical force, singular or plural. *Eragon*, by Christopher Paolini, or *The Hobbit*, by J.R.R. Tolkien, are examples of high fantasy. The characters in such stories are not surprised that their world is magical – that dragons exist, for instance – but they might be striving to understand other phenomena. High fantasy is often, though not always, linked to medieval or Renaissance imagery, and/or calls upon mythological and religious creatures and forms of magic.

Philip Pullman's *His Dark Materials*, meanwhile, starts out as high fantasy in the first book (*Northern Lights*) but at the end of the first book and in the following volumes, it appears that Lyra's world is one of an infinity of coexisting worlds, barely brushing against one another. The second world we are introduced to is Will's world, and it is 'our' world: the reader's world. At the beginning of *The Subtle Knife*, Will, by leaving his world and entering another, does something that many children's books for this age range do: have the protagonist leave 'the real world' for a magical one. Think of *The Chronicles of Narnia*, or of *Harry Potter*, of course. Those 'secondary-world' fantasy stories need to account for the threshold between the two worlds, and establish parallels and differences between them. More often than not, the passage from one world to the other will cause surprise, wonder or horror for the young protagonists.

Such stories often map the development of a child into a teenager, using elements of magic and fantasy as metaphors for specific aspects of that development. What are considered to be milestones – the first kiss, the first 'battle' against an authority figure, the discovery of parental weaknesses and so forth – are allegorized, turned into episodes of the quest, embodied. 'Secrets' of eminent importance are revealed or withheld: they symbolize the seemingly cryptic aspects of life which children-turning-into-teenagers are beginning to grasp.

But be careful, with high fantasy and secondary-world fantasy, when trying to stage the woes of the soon-to-be-teenager using magical and fantastical allegories. Many have become hackneyed, overdone, caricatured. For instance, 'elemental' magic – a child discovers he can master fire, and gradually gets close to a girl who can master water, and together they can fight an evil mastermind who is the king of earth, but not without the help of their best friend who controls air – is an extremely common motif. The same applies to dragons, unicorns and other magical animals who will not let themselves be tamed or ridden – unless you have a splendidly original idea on the matter, they're risky. A good example of someone who managed to reinvent the traditional codes of fantasy while preserving the *Bildungsroman* feel of tween literature is Jonathan Stroud, with his *Bartimaeus* trilogy, a highly original story of a young magician who summons an extremely powerful, hilariously camp and very touchy spirit from the past.

Many elements of traditional fantasy are intrinsically sexist or otherwise ideologically problematic. The depiction of magical 'gifts' tends to be essentializing: a people becomes defined (and bound) by their particular magic power; men and women become separated by their different (though often 'complementary') abilities; magical creatures are arranged up and down a qualitative ladder, often in direct subordination to humans or wizards ... In other words, such tales normalize the idea that people are born with certain skills, which they can hone, but which separate them from some groups of people and make them closer to others. Just one look at the vast scholarship literature on classism, racism and sexism in C.S. Lewis, J.R.R. Tolkien and J.K. Rowling makes it clear why you're playing with fire when you work within the fantasy genre. Think of the ideological implications of what you're writing: magic should be handled with care ...

Magical realism

Between realism and fantasy, another type of storytelling has plenty of potential for the nine-to-thirteen age range: magical realism. Originally a creation of South American writers such as Jorge Luis Borges and Gabriel García Márquez, magical realism has now become a fixture of much literature 'for adults', and can be found notably in the works of Salman Rushdie and Angela Carter. Magical realism is defined by the occurrence of magical elements in an otherwise realistic setting, elements which may or may not disturb and distract the dwellers of the 'real world'.

Magical realism has existed for many years in children's literature, with, for instance, the French classic *The Good Little Devil and Other Tales*, by Pierre Gripari, recently issued in English translation but written in the 1960s. In this book of modern tales, the most famous story, 'The Witch of the rue Mouffetard', has a narrator who decides to buy a house in Paris. But it so happens that a witch lives in the broom cupboard ... In an otherwise very realistic 1960s Paris, the occurrence of the magical is unexpected, but to the narrator it is more a source of annoyance than surprise.

Tween literature offers many possibilities for magical-realist stories, or almost magical-realist stories – when the story remains plausible within the framework of the novel, but still appears odd or incongruous in some respects to the reader. Detective or spy stories that rely on such a device include the recent *Knightley and Son*, by Rohan Gavin, which sees a father-and-son sleuthing duo investigating a secret organization, the Combination, with magical ramifications. Anthony Horowitz is also a master of telling stories where it is difficult to prise apart the fantastical elements from the realistic ones. But magical realism can also be used to tell sensitive and poetic stories: Katherine Rundell's *Rooftoppers* is a good example, as well as Sonya Hartnett's books for a young audience, particularly *The Midnight Zoo* – a poetic story of war and loss where Roma children learn to speak to animals.

The advantages of magical realism in relation to this particular age range are quite clear: you will be playing on the notion, described earlier, that the nine-to-thirteens are struggling to distinguish between the real and the imagined. Magical realism eases this transition by slipping into fantasy whenever realism would hurt. It can also present an infinitely nuanced view of the 'truth' or 'reality' of the newly discovered adult world. The child is still able to see through it, to undermine its codes, to find refuge in the healthy notion that it is not as solid as adults may think. The most daring of these stories, such as *When You Reach Me*, by Rebecca Stead, involve a soft playfulness with even the fabric of reality – time and space – which commands respect and captivates young audiences.

Writing a magical-realist story requires sensitivity and subtlety, and, I think, an awareness of the literary heritage within which you are inscribing yourself. Magical realism, in both children's and adult literature, counts among the 'highest' literary modes. It allows for beautiful fine-tuning of emotions, of descriptions, of plot; for ideological nuance and ambiguity. Receptive to barely palpable changes in the characters' minds, in the evolution of setting, in the workings of political situations, it also opens up endless possibilities for feather-light, poetic prose, conveying meaning that is not directly clear. Use it, and introduce children to the beauty of ambiguity.

Action stories

I'm using the term 'action story' quite loosely, to refer to detective, spy and adventure stories, of which there's still a plethora for the nine-to-thirteen age range. Such books – sadly often marketed as 'boys' books' – are exactly what many publishers might be looking for as they attempt to retain their younger male audiences in the difficult transition from childhood to adolescence.

One of the masters of the genre is Anthony Horowitz, whose thrilling spy stories and *Alex Rider* series are immensely popular. Charlie Higson's *Young Bond* series has also found a wide audience. Robert Muchamore takes the genre to a slightly higher age range, but is read by nine- to thirteen-year-olds, too. It is perhaps no surprise that such books are mostly written by men; there's an assumption that spy and detective novels, especially highly technological ones, are by men and for men. Please feel free to challenge the status quo.

These modern action stories must, of course, be fast paced and packed with dialogue and action, with description kept to a bare minimum. Heroes (generally male) tend to be aged from fourteen to seventeen. However, in contrast to Young Adult fiction, there normally isn't any sex in books for this age range, with physical action and political drama privileged over romance. They vary in the level of physical violence inflicted upon antagonists and protagonists, as well as in depictions of the use of weapons. As a common rule, it's better to be careful when describing weapons and their use in children's literature, even for this age range: publishers get squeamish quite easily. As for swear words, they're hugely controversial even for older readers, and action books for tween boys tend to be quite restrained in this respect.

Such books are obsessed with other countries. They take their young heroes to Mexico, to Pacific islands, to Venice, to Russia, to Hong Kong. The exotic settings, which must be thoroughly researched, serve both as backdrops to the stories – as 'playgrounds', one could say, for the protagonists – and as essential plot elements. When writing such action stories, you must make it clear why the action is taking place where it is, and stage the cultural shock encountered by the main character. Of course, this is also risky: it's very easy to fall into parody or caricature of 'local' people, or to become patronizing towards their traditions. Impeccable knowledge of and respect for the places and people described are essential. Julian Sedgwick, when writing his *Mysterium* trilogy, made sure that he set the three books in cities he knew by heart. The first one, *The Black Dragon*, thus takes place in Hong Kong, and the geographical precision of the protagonist's wanderings is astonishing.

But descriptions of the place must be integrated within the story: look at how aptly Sedgwick sneaks an atmosphere into the heart of the action:

> *Danny looks around, assessing their situation. Above and to the left of the buggy and the heated conversation squats a temple. Stylized lions stand guard, weathered and smoothed by the sea winds, and writhing dragons spiral along the length of its ornate roof. Beneath that, vermillion pillars shield a darkened space beyond. The bite of incense on the breeze.*
>
> *No obvious way out, a high wall either side of the temple. Sea to the other side …*
>
> Sedgwick 2013, p. 239

This is what good action books do: make you feel the 'bite of incense on the breeze' as a reminder both of where you are and of the sting of the action.

 ## Key idea

Play on your intended audience's curiosity for places they've never been, objects they've never seen – but link them to the demands of your plot.

Action stories are generally realistic, although some of them include elements of magic, spirituality or technological mystery. Believability isn't at the centre of everyone's concerns when writing or publishing such books; as long as they're internally coherent and, above all, spectacular, the story will work. They are an opportunity to have fun, in the best sense of the term.

Going back to the idea that books for this age range stage the transition between childhood and adolescence, it's worth thinking about how your action story presents its young protagonist. Is s/he going to be fully formed already, a perfect spy, a black-belt in judo, an expert user of firearms? Or is s/he going to be still learning, still in apprenticeship, but gradually getting a taste for independence? The presence of protective or pedagogical adult figures isn't a necessity, but it's a possibility. And you can play with the protagonist's awareness of their flaws as well as of their strengths.

Finally, don't forget to give your protagonist some friends. We've been through this before, but it bears repeating: lone heroes and heroines don't fare well in children's literature. Give them allies, give them best friends, give them siblings, give them sidekicks. They can't be on their mission alone; they need voices to reply to theirs, people to care about, and shoulders on which to lean. It will also make your life easier by allowing for dialogue, which can tell much of the story, instead of resorting all the time to first-person internal monologues.

Workshop: the moment when authority collapses

Tween literature is often characterized by a gradual loss of faith in adult authority – a realization by the child that they will soon be on their own. The magnitude of this realization can be huge: think of Harry's shock when he discovers that Dumbledore is not all-powerful. Or it can be gentler, peppered across a whole novel in the form of small epiphanies. We are witnessing, as readers, a time of transition; of losses and gains, of sadness and liberation. This is the kind of moment I want you to describe in this workshop exercise.

So pick your favourite genre within tween literature – social realism, high fantasy, magical realism, action, or anything else that I haven't discussed, as well, of course, as hybrids – and write a scene where the following events occur:

- A major adult authority figure is shown to have been wrong about something or to have lied.
- This mistake or lie has a huge impact on the plot of the story, and leads the young protagonist to reconsider their future action entirely.
- The young protagonist is in a difficult position not just because of this, but also psychologically upset because the authority figure has been revealed as weak or lying.
- At the end of the scene, the protagonist decides on a new course of action.

Preferably, the scene should include dialogue as well as description; it shouldn't simply be a page of internal monologue. Try to convey the protagonist's emotions in as many ways as possible: not only through direct description, but also, for instance, through dialogue markers ('he stammered', etc.), through physical action, or through description of other people's reactions to the protagonist. Explore different possibilities.

Review

Now reread your scene. As a reader, how well do you think you have achieved the following, on a scale of 1 to 10?

- *Rendering the emotional state of the protagonist:*
  - through a variety of means   1 2 3 4 5 6 7 8 9 10
  - with varied and evocative vocabulary, avoiding corny phrases   1 2 3 4 5 6 7 8 9 10
  - highlighting the fact that the protagonist has suddenly lost a comforting or stabilizing presence   1 2 3 4 5 6 7 8 9 10
- *Moving the action forward:*
  - having registered the necessary changes to the plan   1 2 3 4 5 6 7 8 9 10
  - being aware that, now, the protagonist will need to be acting independently   1 2 3 4 5 6 7 8 9 10

- with a clear new project for what is to come ⎡1⎤⎡2⎤⎡3⎤⎡4⎤⎡5⎤⎡6⎤⎡7⎤⎡8⎤⎡9⎤⎡10⎤
- in a way that is empowering for the protagonist ⎡1⎤⎡2⎤⎡3⎤⎡4⎤⎡5⎤⎡6⎤⎡7⎤⎡8⎤⎡9⎤⎡10⎤

If these elements are present, how well do they brush against one another? Are they fluidly integrated, or detached from one another? Watch for rhetorical questions, which tend to poison descriptions of internal states: 'Why had he done that to Peter? Peter didn't understand.' Are the sentence structures varied?

Now see how you could edit this scene to give it yet more strength. What do you think about using the following?

- Different paragraph indentations and line breaks, to add power to the 'revelation'; and conversely, more tightly packed, longer paragraphs for the protagonist's quick reflections
- A change of focus: instead of telling the scene from your protagonist's perspective, for instance, switch to someone else's eyes
- A jump from the narrative past to the present tense.

Edit and tweak the scene until you think it sounds right.

Where to next?

Next, we shall wade into the dark waters of Young Adult literature, which crystallizes passions, attracts film rights, and leads to bids with many zeros after the first digit. What is Young Adult fiction, and what is a 'young adult' anyway? How do you write a sex scene for that age? And how do you make sure that you're writing in the voice of that elusive creature, a teenager? The next chapter should cover some of these tricky questions.

13

Young Adult literature: the good, the dark and the broody

It's OK.

You have our permission.

These books are from our Young Adult section.

But it's OK to read them even if you are no longer, by any stretch of the imagination, young.

In fact, you'll find that they often have provocative themes and complex characters that are the equal of most of the books you'll find on the 'adult' fiction shelves these days.

So don't sheepishly tell us it's for your kids. We've read them and you can, too.

If you're online as much as I am, and following the right kind of people, you might have seen the viral picture of a sign in a bookstore with the words used as this chapter's title. Funny, yes. But telling, too. Young Adult literature gets a bad press. No, that isn't exactly right; it gets an *excellent* press with bloggers, online reviewers and, above all, Hollywood. But, although it's been shown repeatedly that much of its huge readership is actually above the age of 25, few people admit to reading or listening to books categorized as Young Adult. It's especially incomprehensible to a number of older people, who will often launch into the following argument:

> *Young people nowadays read all kinds of trash! In the old days, we stopped reading children's literature at the age of seven and then put aside childish things and started reading Gaskell, Brontë, Dickens, Austen. None of that* Twilight *nonsense! But now people want childhood to last for ever, and adolescence to last even longer. They can't grow up any more! *grumblegrumble* ageist society *grumble**

That's not the only 'problem' with Young Adult fiction and public opinion. Parents get scared: with all that violence and sex, it's likely that young readers are going to become violent and have sex, too. The Young Adult literature community is particularly passionate and vociferous, and online debates and disputes erupt repeatedly whenever a journalist, author, parent or teacher dares to suggest that it is not 'good' literature, whether from an ethical or an aesthetic perspective. But Young Adult literature also has its defenders, and mighty ones, too: on Twitter, Patrick Ness, John Green and Neil Gaiman, with their cohorts of faithful fans, are always there to dissipate the clouds of anti-Young Adult literature protesters.

Phew. Are you sure you want to enter this battlefield? Yes?

But first, an important question:

What's a young adult?

Yes, what *is* a 'young adult'? How old is a 'young adult'? In this chapter I'm using the term to mean, roughly, anyone from the beginning of adolescence (13) to late adolescence (19 or 20), but others will tell you that a 'young adult' is a person between 18 and 25. Ah, no, sorry – they would have told you so a few years ago, but now this category is called 'New Adult'. But you can bet a new category will appear fairly soon of 'Barely Just Adults' between 25 and 35 …

Adolescence is a social construct: This slice of life, which used to be nondescript, is now multiply labelled; corresponding more or less to high school, it is above all useful as a target for marketers. The birth of adolescence as a concept dates back to the beginning of the twentieth century, but it's only from the 1950s onwards that this time of life started to be seen as a moment for rebellion against parents, spending money that one doesn't have, having premarital sexual experiences, doing drugs, and being obnoxious and incomprehensible.

If you get a chance, read academic work on adolescence and on adolescent literature. You will realize how profound and far-reaching these assumptions about adolescence can be. Is adolescence solely a liberating construct, and is adolescent literature a space for free play, liberating rebellion and glorious contestation? Academic Lydia Kokkola recently published a book on sex in adolescent fiction. She argues that adolescence was invented partly to further separate childhood from adulthood. By using a 'devilish' time of rupture and transition, a hectic 'bumper' between childhood and adulthood, the adult authority behind the book – and behind the very category of 'adolescent literature' – preserves the concept of childhood as innocent, untouched, romantic. And by accentuating teenage 'crisis' – a concept which, in itself, is a construct – the adult stages an authorized and therefore potentially safe rebellion; securely bound, in temporal terms, and therefore controllable.

Another academic, Roberta Seelinger Trites, wrote a landmark book on adolescent fiction where she developed a similar idea. We tend to think that adolescent literature encourages radical dissent and challenges adult authority. In fact, Trites said, such books only allow this 'crisis' to take place for a little while, until the adolescent characters are tucked back into accepting social conventions and preparing for their roles as ruling adults.

Key idea

Adolescence is a social construct, and adolescent literature is still the product of adults. Being a teenager in teenage literature is rarely as liberating and powerful as it looks.

So the 'young adult', or teenager, or adolescent, is a creature, a construct, based on the socio-cultural need to have a discrete time of stormy contestation before duty calls the adult to take his or her place in society. Some other cultures, and most civilizations historically, did not think of the 13–19 age range as particularly distinct from their adult peers. Of course, childhood is in its own way a socio-cultural construct as well. But when writing 'for teenagers', you need to be aware that this category is a recent invention, loaded with political and cultural implications and not as anarchic and liberating as it may seem.

Still, teenagers in reality do enact this 'crisis' of adolescence – arguably because they have a whole literature and film industry devoted to showing them what they're supposed to be doing – and that's what Young Adult literature and film often attempt to emphasize. Again, it's not a new phenomenon. Any would-be author of Young Adult literature would do well to watch *Rebel without a Cause*, which perfectly stages the disempowerment and dismay of adults faced with a rebellious teen. This was already Young Adult 'literature' – in this case, film – but it wasn't called that at the time. *Grease* and *Saturday Night Fever* showed the lighter side of this teenage 'crisis'. And literature 'for adolescents' quite naturally emerged. In the 1970s, Judy Blume wrote her landmark novel, *Forever*, which scandalized parents and teachers but delighted youngsters, and would 'forever' define the freedom of the genre. And then we had Robert Cormier, who wrote sometimes immensely violent novels aimed at teenagers, dissecting all the taboos of contemporary society: read *Fade* for a taster. Melvin Burgess, of course, is the king of 'taboo' Young Adult literature, but his first novels were published before the term existed: *Junk*, which remains the most explicit book for teenagers about hard drug use, is now over 20 years old.

So don't believe people who tell you that Young Adult literature is 'a new phenomenon'. It just hadn't quite been discovered as a phenomenon of such lucrative potential before. It was assumed, perhaps, that bookish teenagers would read few such books, and would prefer to find narratives of early life experiences in books destined for adults but about this particular time of life (hence the emphasis on the Brontë sisters, Austen, Gaskell, Forster, etc.). But now teenagers have been given more sex, violence and questions about the world, and literature has to compete with film and video games. Young Adult literature is now its own, bankable category.

It sounds as if I'm being cynical about Young Adult literature; I'm not. I think it is a tremendous platform for experimental, daring writing. I write books for teenagers which are so full of sex, violence and questions about the world that they are recommended for '14+' in France and are not even publishable in the UK as Young Adult. But authors shouldn't lose sight of the commercial imperatives in this publishing gold mine, and of the fact that it has been engineered as such.

Another question to bear in mind: if, as has been revealed, so many *adults* read Young Adult literature, who exactly are you addressing as a Young Adult author? Nowhere else are age ranges more blurred and reading prescriptions less useful. It's worth remembering the ambiguities of the genre.

 Key idea

A working definition of Young Adult literature could be: books that stage or intensify the imagined torments and discoveries culturally associated with adolescence.

This *staging* can be realistic or fantastical, and the *intensification* can come from their being metaphorically displaced on to, for instance, magical creatures (we'll get back to that); or from their taking place in a situation of general crisis. Young Adult literature has a penchant for political and social commentary, and implicitly discusses the place of teenagers in society – often to highlight their disempowerment, and the necessity for them to exist in the mode of radical contestation.

Young Adult literature can also be much 'quieter' than the portrayal I've given, but I think it is fair to say that most such books are particularly concerned with rebellion and protest of one kind or another, and with social and political taboos. So let's look at how such things can be *written*.

Writing sex, drugs and violence without voyeurism

If you peruse the bookshelves in the Young Adult part of any store, you'll realize that you'd better not be prudish. *Forbidden*, by Tabitha Suzuma, goes into a lot of detail regarding an incestuous sexual relationship between a brother and a sister. I've already mentioned Cormier, who happily jumps from incest to rape to murder, drugs and prostitution. My first book for teenagers revolves around the kidnapping and torture of a young child, and in the second one the main event is the online leakage of a 'selfie' video showing a young girl masturbating. If you're not at ease with themes like that, maybe Young Adult literature isn't for you. It's a literature that wilfully makes its readers uncomfortable, excited, repulsed – a literature of shock.

But shock doesn't need to come from telling. It can come from evoking. This is the crucial difference between showing and alluding to; and this difference is crucial in avoiding cheap voyeurism.

Voyeurism can come from:

- gratuitous presentations of sex, violence and so on that don't reasonably add anything to the plot and are there simply to create a reaction of horror or thrill in the reader
- explicit descriptions of sexual or violent behaviour, which leave the reader with no space for imagination – everything is said
- a desire, whether or not conscious, to elicit actual sexual excitement in the reader, or fascination for the represented violence
- a lack of distance from what is represented; everything is identically focused, and there is no possibility for the reader to detach themselves from what is being shown
- the choice of certain, 'hot' themes – child prostitution, forced marriage, teenage pregnancy and so forth – with little consideration that actual people have experienced them
- an uncritical attitude towards the implications of the episodes represented; an unquestioning narrative voice.

In general, voyeurism is what happens when you're being lazy and want to grab your reader's attention cheaply. It's extremely frequent in Young Adult literature, unfortunately, because of its themes and because of the prominence of sex and violence.

Voyeurism is problematic in many ways. Firstly, voyeuristic literature is rarely aesthetically pleasing – it's a characteristic of low-quality books which want to elicit an easy response from the reader. Secondly, it's worth interrogating the implications in relation to your target audience. Do you want your writing to excite teenage readers sexually? To trigger erotic responses in the under-18s? Do you want your writing to present seductive or fascinating portrayals of violence? There's no need to be moralistic about it: it's not a question of it being good or bad. It's a question raised by a type of literature which speaks across a generational gap.

So how do you avoid voyeurism when writing very racy or violent scenes?

- **Create distance.** Allow your reader the space to observe the scene while still being able to reflect upon it. This can be done in a multiplicity of ways, not least by attracting the reader's attention to details which will trigger reflection. In a scene from my French teenage book *La Pouilleuse*, the young kidnappers are pulling lice out of the kidnapped little girl's hair. This is a scene of psychological torture, of humiliation. While it happens, however, I had the narrator lying on the floor staring at the lice drowning in a glass of vinegar. He isn't fully absorbed in the scene; he is slightly outside of it, and in the drowning lice burnt by the acid there's a sense, too, that the group of young kidnappers are slowly drowning.

- **Create discomfort rather than excitement or fascination.** In other words, don't be a victim of the power of your own words. Make your reader want to see, while at the same time refusing him or her that chance; and make your reader uncomfortable for wanting to see. You can do this by playing up rather than downplaying the voyeuristic tendencies of the book, but making it dissatisfying or unpleasant. My readers often tell me that they feel uneasy when reading my teenage books, because they force them into a voyeuristic position that they actually don't want to assume once they get there. This leads us to the next point:

- **Use voyeurism strategically.** Build up to the moments when it will be actually necessary to shock, to be explicit, to be descriptive. Don't pile them up on top of one another. Make your readers aware that what they are seeing is something the narrative has worked for – something that is justified. It will then only add to it.

- **Be creative and original.** Be absurdly hyperbolic if you need to, be lyrical, be grandiose, or be allusive and euphemistic, but please do something aesthetic and creative with those scenes. Without meaning to belittle Young Adult literature here, literature 'for adults' might give you tips. In *Lolita*, which is, of course, a hugely provocative book, voyeurism is everything it should be: uncomfortable, shocking, distanced, cold and beyond beautiful. Humbert Humbert wants to 'turn [his] Lolita inside out and apply voracious lips to her young matrix, her unknown heart, her nacreous liver, the sea-grapes of her lungs, her comely twin kidneys.' And yes, he also rapes her every night. Use your imagination.

- **Don't be preachy.** Of course, everyone will have a different definition of that; you might already be thinking that everything I've just said is preachy, and that there should be no limits to voyeurism. But if you write those tricky scenes well and carefully, there should be no need for the 'distance' to express itself as moral statements. The narrative voice should render the necessary detachment, a certain aloofness, which will on its own prevent the reader from taking it all at face value.

- **Leave space for the imagination.** Don't tell the reader everything; use allusions, euphemisms, understatements, change focus, suddenly decree that you're not going to say any more about the situation. Create frustration and disappointment as well as contentment and pleasure. In this art of allusion, of distance, resides the difference between a cheap readerly response and a thoughtful, profound response. This is the difference between pornography and eroticism. In one case, the reader will have no space for personal feelings; s/he will be smothered. In the other case, s/he will think about it again and again, and think about why it's affecting her so much. This is the effect you're looking for: *unsettlement*; wanting to see and not to see; seeing and thinking.

 Key idea

To avoid voyeurism, don't subjugate your readers. Make them participate and reflect.

Utopia, dystopia, war, post-apocalypse: the teenager in and against society

Sex and violence aren't all there is to Young Adult literature, of course. The political dimension of this type of book is extremely important. Many of them deal with advanced and complex questions about socio-political organization, the legitimacy of the power structure in place, and teenagers' roles in the world they set up.

In recent years, Young Adult literature has become more explicitly political than ever. This is partly due to the craze for so-called 'dystopian' stories. Dystopia presents a pessimistic future world, generally through a political extrapolation of the world as it is today. It is very much a thought experiment: writing a good dystopia entails asking what the consequences could be of the worst aspects of current society. Climate change, of course, is one; other popular themes include religious extremism, state control, cybersurveillance and terrorism.

'Post-apocalyptic' literature is a branch of dystopia; it defines stories which take place after a disastrous natural or political episode, be it a devastating war, worldwide flooding, a global viral infection or a nuclear bomb.

Dystopia and post-apocalyptic stories used to be fairly rare in children's literature, though Lois Lowry's remarkable *The Giver* – an incredible tender and yet profoundly shocking tale of political manipulation – paved the way in the nineties. Meg Rosoff's *How I Live Now*, another novel of exceptional aesthetic quality, is dystopian and even, at the end, post-apocalyptic. Those two books provide excellent examples of sensitive, non-voyeuristic writing.

The ghost of state control, of governmental manipulation of minds and bodies, is at the core of much dystopia for teenagers. Suzanne Collins's *Hunger Games* series revolves around the institutional cruelty of a centralized government. Lauren Oliver's *Delirium* imagines a situation where teenagers are given treatment against falling in love. In *The Giver*, Jonas is the only citizen to know – apart from the Giver himself – what human beings can really experience (colour, love, hatred and pain, for instance); the rest are 'protected' by the state.

This isn't extremely difficult to theorize: these books address teenagers, people who we imagine are getting to grips with the tricky difference between protection and suffocation, between adult authority and adult authoritarianism. The revelation of a big bad state, intent on reducing young people's abilities to love, fight and ache, mirrors what we imagine teenagers feel like when they think of their parents smothering them, 'the better to protect them', against the world and against themselves. Thus, in Sarah Crossan's *Breathe* duology, teenagers realize that adults have been lying to them – and to the whole of society – about the state of the earth, which is willingly deprived of oxygen so that a multinational company, Breathe, continues to make a profit from selling oxygen tanks. The company here is, of course, both a beneficent and a malevolent entity – both keeping citizens alive and keeping them in captivity.

These tales, therefore, are tales of maturation, and tales of opposition against adults. The state can often be read as a metaphor for adults who don't want to be superseded, who don't want teenagers to become cleverer or more powerful than them. Thinking about your political Young Adult literature in these terms is useful because you can establish quite sophisticated levels of reading: you can have an action-packed dystopian thriller which also articulates a political critique and which also taps into teenagers' impressions of disempowerment and unfairness regarding adults.

Here are a few things that complex political dystopias for teenagers do:

- **World-building:** try to create a solid, structured, internally coherent, complex universe. Importantly, think of the *consequences* of every decision you make about the social, political or natural fabric of this world. For instance, if this is a post-apocalyptic scenario in which the world has been flooded, think of the political ramifications of this flood. Maybe poor people would be vying for dry land, which would be overpopulated and insalubrious, while the richest and most powerful would be able to buy space on giant floating cities. These cities would be all the more powerful as they could drift from dry land to dry land, thus supervising whole areas of the flooded Earth. But they would also be super-protected, in order to prevent immigrants from getting on to them or from attacking them. These floating cities would also be the place of political decisions, and military ones, too; maybe there could be enemy cities in different parts of the globe. And there could be risks from the natural world when roaming the oceans too close to tropical storms. Think of all the implications: you will need to mention where the city-dwellers are getting their water from, how they're producing their electricity, whom they tolerate as servants or assistants.

- **Giving characters a role in this world:** your teenage heroes must have a role to play. They must have a quest, they must be active; they can't just be passive observers of that world. This is a risk with complex world-building: amateurish novels often read like descriptions of dystopia with little characterization, because writers are so in awe of their (sometimes indeed very interesting) worlds that they don't feel their characters need to be fleshed out. But they do. Think of Katniss, in *The Hunger Games*: she has an immensely strong personality, makes decisions, makes judgements about the world she's in; and yet Collins still manages to describe every detail of her complex universe. Think of what you'd like your focus to be in that world. Will s/he be among the powerful or the powerless? Maybe your heroine could be a rich girl on one of these floating cities, unaware that there are poor people living in terrible conditions on isolated islands. Or maybe she could be living on dry land and desperately trying to get on to one of the passing giant floating cities. Whatever you choose, make sure your protagonist *acts*, and doesn't just *react*. Make sure that s/he's critiquing or opposing the system in some way, not just adhering to it passively. Jump into action as soon as you can.

- **Making it clear that their being a teenager is crucial to the plot:** it couldn't have happened to just anyone, to just any old adult. Otherwise it might seem quite unrealistic that teenagers should be in charge. Maybe, as in *The Giver*, adult society is anaesthetized and content; maybe they are all complicit in the political situation; maybe teenagers are, in this world, the only people who are able to sense a particular aspect of the situation, or to practise a certain kind of magic. Make adolescence special, and make this special status count towards the plot. Even better: make adolescence a menace to adulthood.

- **Giving protagonists an aim:** this will keep them active, and searching for solutions, rather than representing them as scared, *re*active and constantly chased. Spell out the object of the quest. Again, even Katniss, who is the victim of the whims of a gigantic TV show, finds small, temporary quests and aims to fulfil. She is never simply floating around waiting for the next danger to get to her. She has a plan.

- **Adding twists, turns and unexpected events:** that clear aim that you're giving your protagonists – make it as difficult to fulfil as possible. Add red herrings, characters who betray your protagonist, twists of fate and twists of luck. And make sure that nothing is as straightforward at the end as it appeared at the beginning. Maybe the government your teenager was fighting for is actually a shadow government – and the real people he should have gone for are people he never thought of as threatening. Of course, many novels rely on final twists of this kind: we find out that the protagonist was being manipulated from the beginning or that her closest ally was an agent of the state. But it's not completely cliché; there can still be excellent stories which play with double, triple and quadruple agents.

All these 'ingredients' will not necessarily yield a perfect political thriller or dystopian novel, but they will set its main ingredients in place: 1. a realistic, internally coherent world where politics, society, culture and nature are closely intertwined, and 2. a character who has a reason to want to oppose, or look further into, the organization of that world. This is the skeleton of most Young Adult literature with strong political content – dystopian, post-apocalyptic or otherwise. It's up to you to flesh it out as you like.

Focalization, language and serialization in Young Adult literature

Focalization, or perspective, in Young Adult literature tends to be looser than in literature for younger readers. Not that first-person narrative isn't the rule – it very much is, and, in fact, probably much more so than anywhere else in children's literature. But Young Adult literature often multiplies narrators, so that several characters tell the story in turn. Sometimes adult voices are heard, too, or the story can jump to an external narrator 'spying on' a group of characters in the absence of the hero/ine. Temporal switches are legion, too: going from past to present and even to the future. Young Adult literature is at ease with flashbacks and flash-forwards, which contribute to complex narratives and are not normally seen as problematic by editors.

Language in Young Adult literature, arguably, isn't typically much more elaborate than in literature for tweens. In fact, many Young Adult books don't display very varied vocabulary, and tend to rely on similar sentence structures. Try to avoid beginning all your sentences with 'I': 'I did that', 'I thought that', 'And then I did another thing'. This is the mark of unsophisticated books. Other hallmarks of Young Adult writing include italicized phrases or sentences – or even whole paragraphs. Finally, Young Adult literature is characterized by a relatively colloquial style, close to spoken language. It isn't normally a literary type of fiction; not that, of course, the writing cannot be beautiful.

Young Adult books are generally big, as a quick browse in any bookshop will tell you. It used to be the case that a 100,000-word book from a first-time author would never even be considered by publishers; now they are legion. Young Adult literature is read voraciously by teenagers and adults who can go through several books a week, and passionately wait for the next instalment. Thus, series – not episodic, but with an overarching storyline – are extremely popular, and publishers are mostly looking for them rather than for stand-alone books. Serialization allows for a build-up of hype and excitement around the books, and it also attracts the attention of film-makers. Popular Young Adult books are indeed frequently auctioned for TV or cinema rights. Thus, series are in demand, and if you have written a stand-alone Young Adult novel with complex world-building and interesting characters, it's very likely that you will be asked for more books by your editor. You might then have to rethink the story so that it can spread over two, three or four books.

The teenage romance

However tough the political climate, however crucial the world-saving, however bloodthirsty the antagonists, you can bet the teenagers will find time and space to flirt, and more. Whether you approve of this or not, romance often isn't just an option: it's increasingly an *expectation* of Young Adult literature. But there are different types of romance in Young Adult literature; here's a quick overview.

- **Romance that isn't at the forefront of the story:** *The Hunger Games*, for instance, has elements of romance, but these are arguably less important than the more pressing matter of having to kill other children.

- **Romance that is essential for the story, but the story has other themes:** this is the case, for instance, in Malorie Blackman's *Noughts and Crosses* series, in which star-crossed lovers, 'underclass' Nought Callum and upper-class Cross Sephy, sustain a tragic love affair. Their romance becomes an allegory for the political situation. Although *Noughts and Crosses* is very much a romance story, other themes are at work: the book is also about racism, politics, society. The two lovers end up separated, and the further volumes substitute their love with yet more loves, making it clear that their romance was central but not conterminous with the story.

- **Romance that is the story:** of course, such books also have other themes, but the fundamental appeal is the romance; *Twilight* is among such stories.

The ingredients of a sizzling romance include motifs such as:

- initial displeasure or dislike on the part of one or both future lovers
- difficulty for both to be together, because of the political climate, because one is currently in a relationship with the other's sibling, or because they belong to different species
- essentially likeable characters: this is something that can be gauged by looking at GoodReads comments. Even what I would consider to be fairly successful romances are disliked by readers when they cannot empathize with, or imagine themselves falling in love with, the lovers. This is particularly strong if the male lead is deemed

'annoying' or 'childish'. The female character is frequently disliked for being 'bitchy' or 'arrogant'. Such reactions, unfortunately, hint at sexist expectations for such romances.

- a relatively long-drawn-out courtship: this appears to be generally more successful among readers than a relationship which develops immediately
- episodes of falling out and reconciliation to pepper the plot
- ellipses and feelings left unsaid in greater quantities than explicit declarations of love: these whet the reader's appetite but don't always satisfy their thirst
- respect on both sides of the equation: Young Adult readers do not seem to enjoy the spectacle of abusive relationships, and have become good at evaluating whether the portrayal of love that is given to them is abusive.

There is no secret recipe for a good romance. Often you will hear readers say, 'It didn't work for me.' Perhaps the male lead was too moody, perhaps he was too cocky; perhaps something about their relationship 'spoke'; perhaps it didn't. The above are not rules, but they're fairly reliable constants.

What I try to think about when writing romance are my own favourite romances. I'm not a huge romantic and tend to prefer doomed relationships: Scarlett O'Hara and Rhett Butler, Doctor Zhivago and Lara. What is it that I like about these particular duos? The woman is unpredictable and hot-tempered, independent and hardworking; the man is strong but sensitive, tormented and taken within events that he cannot control. I try to work these characteristics into whatever I'm writing.

Homosexual or homoerotic relations in children's and Young Adult literature are still relatively rare. But there is a higher and higher demand for such stories, and I have no doubt that in a few years' time they will be extremely common.

Towards 'New Adult' literature?

You've probably seen this label appearing here and there online and in publishers' catalogues: 'New Adult' books are supposedly a category of texts for people who have just left high school but are still either at university or trying to negotiate their place in society; in other words, the 18–25 age range. Having a look at what publishers categorize as 'New Adult', it is striking that such books are almost exclusively, at the moment, romance stories. A lot belong to what we used to call (and still do call) 'chick lit'. At the time of writing, there are few New Adult books targeted at men. Usually sexually explicit, New Adult novels make no secret of their being addressed to plucky and sexually literate young women.

With New Adult books, we are sliding out of children's literature, so I won't say any more on the matter, apart from remarking on the fact that they testify to the lengthening of childhood, and then adolescence, a long way into life – at a time of political instability and economic crisis when 'new adults' are, indeed, attempting to find meaning in life.

Workshop: writing a scene of sex or violence

In this workshop we're at the heart of the 'racier' aspects of Young Adult literature: the tricky scene of sex or violence, preferably, as discussed earlier, without voyeurism (but shocking is allowed!). As a frame, pick either of the two situations:

1 a first sexual encounter between your main characters

2 a rough fight scene.

Write one to two A4 pages of this scene, spending time thinking about focalization, voice, tense and structure.

Review

Now reread your work. How well would you say you have achieved the following, on a scale of 1 to 10?

- The scene has a strong impact on the reader; it does not leave them indifferent.   1 2 3 4 5 6 7 8 9 10
- The reader, however, can distance themselves from the scene.   1 2 3 4 5 6 7 8 9 10
- The vocabulary used is varied, powerful and avoids clichés.   1 2 3 4 5 6 7 8 9 10
- The narrative voice leaves enough unsaid.   1 2 3 4 5 6 7 8 9 10
- The scene is not sexist.   1 2 3 4 5 6 7 8 9 10
- The characters' viewpoints are taken into account, and contrasted.   1 2 3 4 5 6 7 8 9 10

Depending on the success of your endeavour, try to edit the scene until it is to your taste. Then, if you have the courage, pick the type of scene you didn't pick the first time around, and write another scene.

Where to next?

Next, we come to a completely different type of text: poetry. Poetry for children, from zero months to 18 years old, is a discrete genre, not often foregrounded by publishers. And yet it's often the first type of text that one encounters. In the next chapter we'll look at this tricky format and its multiple uses.

14

Poetry for children: rhyme and reason

What sticks in your mind even when everything else is gone? Poetry, songs, nursery rhymes. Will you ever forget the first four lines of 'Twinkle, Twinkle, Little Star'? Unlikely.

Poetry *sticks.*

It's this stickine*ss* of poetry that makes it so precious. It catches you; you think you 'possess' it because you've memorized it, but that's not true – it possesses *you*; it stays in your mind. It's a squatter. And poems you heard as a young child – those squatters won't go away easily.

Poetry, though, is one of the most complex forms of writing – perhaps the most complex form of writing – for children. I might as well be honest: I would never dare to write a line of poetry in English (even though I happily do so in French). Poetry resists your pretend bilingualism. Poetry is what reminds you that this is not, after all, entirely your language.

Poetry glues itself to your mind seemingly easily because it catches on to the asperities of language, the bits that stick out, that command a response. The poetic phrase speaks: it say something you didn't know you wanted to say.

This chapter will be even less about 'teaching you' to 'write for children' than all the others; I wouldn't have the temerity. But let's dive into the subject and see what you can do to illuminate the world for children through poetry, in your own way.

What is children's poetry?

No need to get into a long history of children's poetry – but it's useful to note that there used to be no such thing as 'children's poetry'. Poetry, in the form of rhyming oral tales or nursery rhymes, was an aesthetic and mnemonically useful way of consigning to memory stories, histories, religious texts, fairy and folk tales. In a time before the democratization of reading, voice and ears were all we had to access texts. Children, but also adults, gulped down and remembered thousands of lines.

Later on, poetry became a more elitist art, an aesthetic and philosophical experience first and foremost, and a visual one, too; silent reading of poetry became possible, and even prominent. Contemporary poetry often flatters the eye – sometimes more, at its most conceptual, than the ear. It doesn't need to tell a story; it evokes moments, translating feelings and experiences into language.

But the ancestral, oral dimension of poetry is essential to take into account when writing or reading poetry for children. In the tableau of an adult – a parent, perhaps – reading or reciting poetry to the child, we have a fleeting vision of this ancestral scene when no one could yet read. Poetry for the pre-reading child – in the form of poems, nursery rhymes, songs, picturebooks with rhyming text – must appeal to the ear and stick to the mind. The child must be able to mull over the language long after the poem has ended, long after the last line has erased the penultimate one.

For this child, poetry often offers the first encounters with the alphabet, with numbers, with everyday actions, with animals, and with the sheer beauty and surprises of existence. It articulates, in specific ways, information with a social purpose and also visions that are absolutely unnecessary – and therefore beautifully gratuitous – showcasing the multiplicity and malleability of language.

However, children's poetry, despite this importance of orality, has also always had visual appeal. This is the theory developed by scholar of poetry Debbie Pullinger in her forthcoming book (2015): children's poetry is defined by its being situated on an orality–literacy spectrum. In other words, it calls for the attention of both the ear and the eye. This is why poetry is frequently gloriously illustrated, the words arranged playfully, the letters chiselled like pictures.

 ## Key idea

Children's poetry is a holistic experience, bridging the gap between the heard and the seen.

This is why it is an immensely complex and, if done well, immensely rewarding type of writing for children. Imagine generations of children remembering your lines, holding them in their heads – and being held by them – sometimes for their whole lives, until everything else, including the names of their own children, has gone.

From idea to poem

Because language is the primary ingredient of poetry, poetry for children is somewhat freer of the imperative of story than other types of children's literature. Note that I said *somewhat* freer; it still needs a solid idea at its core. But a good children's poet can write about virtually any fleeting impression, any banal fact of life: Michael Rosen is as brilliant when he evokes the burial of a grandfather as when he versifies about farting.

However, there is a very fine line between that kind of talent and bad poets for children who think that any topic will become suddenly ennobled once they start making their thoughts about it rhyme. Working on the slushpile of children's publishers, you receive a constant flow of insipid verse about trees in the four seasons or red robins in the snow. This kind of 'Hallmark-card' poetry, of which an astonishing quantity still manages to get published, should perhaps be called 'verse' rather than 'poetry': it formally corresponds to what we generally understand by 'poetry' (rhyme, rhythm, metre and line breaks), but it does not have the conceptual loftiness which would qualify it as such.

The best way to learn how to convert an idea into a poem – or rather, to 'grow a poem' around an idea – is to look at what masters of this format are doing. And what they're doing is, often, conveying universal and timeless ideas around a singular, sometimes banal motif. Look at this perfect little gem from Robert Louis Stevenson, 'At the Sea-Side':

> When I was down beside the sea
> A wooden spade they gave to me
> To dig the sandy shore.
>
> My holes were empty like a cup.
> In every hole the sea came up,
> Till it could come no more.

This isn't just a poem about playing in the sand. It chimes with a particularly childlike obsession with the full and the empty, with the transformations operated by time on matter. It evokes eternal concerns: the work of humankind upon nature, and a sense of wonder at one's actions in the world. And, above all, the language is exquisite: it says exactly what it needs to, with no excess and no lack; you can see the water filling in the little cup of sand, you can hear it rustling away; you can almost taste the salt in your mouth. Having read it once or twice, you should already know it by heart. The idea is banal; the execution splendid. There could be no 'pitch' of this (a child looks at the sea filling in a hole in the sand: great); the poem *is* the pitch.

But, of course, there are also poems that tackle difficult themes in the 'real world', that attempt to convey a political message; and they are not necessarily less good. Nowadays, many children's poets – Carol Ann Duffy, Michael Rosen, John Agard, to name a few – use poetry as a vehicle for ideas about society and politics, too. Around these ideas, poems grow, in finely wrought language, and their evocative power does not quite serve so much as constitute the didactic message.

Nursery rhymes and verse picturebooks

Nursery rhymes are now rarely created; they tend to be timeless 'classics', repeated from generation to generation, generally to a musical tune. This doesn't mean that you can't write a book of new nursery rhymes for children or, indeed, with connections in the world of music, attempt nursery-rhyme-like songs for children.

Nursery rhymes often follow the traditional ballad form, mentioned in an earlier chapter, of four beats, four beats, four beats, four beats (or four/three/four/three):

> Twinkle, twinkle, little star,
>
> How I wonder what you are.

This pattern is found in dozens of children's poems and nursery rhymes including those by A.A. Milne, Christina Rossetti and R.L. Stevenson. It is also very common in picturebooks for which the text is written in verse – the most famous, doubtlessly, being *The Gruffalo*, written by Julia Donaldson:

> A **mouse** took a **stroll** through the **deep** dark **wood**.
> A **fox** saw the **mouse**, and the **mouse** looked **good**.
>
> Donaldson and Scheffler 1999

While you are, of course, free to write nursery rhymes, you might find it easier to place a work of poetry with publishers if it is a picturebook text. This might be a good time to say that poetry for children, on its own, unfortunately does not sell well. Rhyming picturebooks, however, are extremely popular. Many of them are of extremely low quality, because the 'poetic' elements serve mostly as a gimmick.

When writing a picturebook text in verse, the added difficulty is that you must juggle with the specific demands of the picturebook format, as detailed in Chapter 10. In other words, the text must remain poetic – namely, find its 'matter' in language itself – while requiring interdependency with pictures. This can appear contradictory, and indeed you will have to find a happy compromise between an entirely self-sufficient text of poetry and a text that can be read only with the help of pictures. Some of the rules of picturebook writing will apply – for instance, the uselessness of describing scenes which are already 'described' by the pictures – and some of the rules of poetry will, too – for instance, evoking feelings and sensations which are not going to be easily conveyed by the pictures.

Many picturebooks in verse are funny. It's not a coincidence: poetry is particularly powerful at caricature, parody, nonsense. Limericks are an obvious example, and so is the nonsense poetry of Carroll, for instance. Part of the humour in many poems for children derives from the surprise created by unexpected rhymes, or by enjambement; within a highly regular metrical and rhyming pattern, you can create a system of suggestions and expectations and betray it at the last minute.

Collections of poems for children

It's worth reiterating that poetry doesn't sell well, and it's unlikely that you'll strike gold with a collection of poems (whether for children or for adults, in fact). Even highly successful poets barely scrape a living from their poetry. And publishing houses rarely put money on debut authors for collected poems. However, exceptions do happen; and after a few 'commercial' books for children you might want to confess to your editor that you've always wanted to write a collection of poems. And they might even agree.

Collections of poems for children can be quite eclectic, but generally they are actually bound by a specific theme, motif, evocation or Ariadne's thread; and they are certainly quite age-specific. A collection of animal poems, especially if you have Ted Hughes's talent, is more likely to sell than a collection of random poems of completely different moods and addressed to different age ranges. The ideal collection of poems has the coherence and the structure of a novel.

This is also because poets, in order to promote their work and to make a living, often have to take an active role, and would be expected, perhaps even more than other children's authors, to put on shows – public readings, poetry workshops, school visits, performances. Poetry thus has to be highly readable, recitable, performable. Books that allow for coherent longish readings, with specific groups of children or teenagers, are more likely to sell in this way. I am sorry, of course, to be bringing back commercial imperatives in what is often considered as the most selfless and disinterested art of all; but such is the publishing world in which we are trying to negotiate a space.

Novels in verse and poetry for teenagers

There is decidedly, however, a much more commercial fringe of poetry for children (save for, as we have seen, picturebooks in verse): novels in verse. Young Adult literature in verse was very much a novelty a few years ago, and it's certainly not common nowadays, but we see more and more novels aimed at teenagers which are integrally written in verse. American writer Lisa Schroeder's novels, for instance, *I Heart You, You Haunt Me*, map the romantic and paranormal adventures of adolescents. Such books seem to be enjoyed by many teenagers, especially young women, for their sensitivity and peculiarity. They perhaps focus more on feelings and on psychology than their prose equivalents. But they also seduce teenagers who usually struggle to read; short and finely chiselled, very different from the thick doorstoppers churned out by the printing presses of Young Adult publishers, they allow for a different experience of reading: briefer, more concentrated, more intense.

Young Adult novels in verse are still a rarity, but they are increasingly well considered in publishing and reviewing circles, especially since Sarah Crossan's stunning debut, *The Weight of Water*. This book is an absolute must-read for anyone who wants to write novels in verse for teenagers. Each chapter is a poem in itself, which contributes to the whole story, laden with subtle political implications, of young Polish immigrant Kasienka and her mother in the UK city of Coventry. The huge success of this short novel confirmed that there is space in Young Adult literature for this kind of work.

How are such books written? Without claim to any expertise, it appears to me that the 'recipe' involves a complex equation of the following:

- Compelling storytelling, following the more traditional 'action-led' or 'character-led' plots of 'normal novels'; characterization, notably, is essential, and goals must be clearly defined.
- Genuine poetic talent, translated as impeccable language peppered with vibrant images, aural effects (assonance, alliteration, rhyme, etc.), which do not just serve the

story but are, more organically, its very fabric. Line breaks are especially important; some online complaints about verse novels are that they are 'just normal text with odd line breaks'. Line breaks must be meaningful, and create surprise, anxiety or emotion.

- A balance of the deep psychological insight afforded by poetry – it's all about allusion rather than assertion – *and* the more prosaic demands of the plot, which sometimes require a loss of ambiguity.
- An understanding of teenage concerns and interests, and an ability to translate those into light, lucid poetry. This is not the domain for obscure or convoluted poetry; it must retain transparency.

Can you find a publisher as a debut author of verse novels? Absolutely, and it does happen, as Crossan's story shows. Do read all you can in the genre, however, and target the agents and publishers who are interested in this type of text. And – wet blanket alert – do remember commercial imperatives. A novel in verse must be pitchable.

Workshop: writing a children's poem

In this workshop, it will be your mission, should you wish to accept it (I certainly wouldn't in English, but would happily do it in French), to write a children's poem – preferably a poem, for now, which could function on its own, read or heard. Adding complications by turning it into a poem for a picturebook text, or a chapter for a verse novel, will make the evaluation more difficult.

1 Pick a situation – it can be an everyday scene or a once-in-a-lifetime event, a day out at Disneyland or a tooth falling out or a child's first-ever goal scored at football.

2 Focus on this situation in order to attempt to extract essential moments, in the form of sensations and thoughts, as you would express a few drops of essential oil from an entire barrel of jasmine flowers. They might be intensely personal but highly relatable episodes – the strange roughness on the tongue when you lift the wobbling tooth and find the hollow space underneath – or they might be entirely banal, singular sights – another child throwing a tantrum near an ice-cream cone that has crashed to the floor. Select no more than three or four of these impressions, instants, intensities.

3 Try to *grow words* for them. There is no other metaphor I can think of for the organic work you have to do here; these feelings and sensations that have no name in your head, pull them out by seizing them with your language, with your words. They are not 'pure ideas', somewhere else in another intelligible world; they exist in an embryonic form which you must reveal. When the right word arrives, ask yourself whether there isn't an even better one. And, when language takes you in an entirely different direction, follow it.

4 Work on effects of rhyme, rhythm, metre, enjambement. Don't feel that you have to adhere to a strict pattern; simply focus on making it ring true. Think of your reader discovering those lines, expecting a word and being happily disappointed that it doesn't come.

5 These scenes may now feel detached from one another, perhaps irremediably. Maybe they don't belong to the same poem any more; maybe they are three

different poems. Maybe, though, you will find a way of moving them around, weaving them together, grafting them on to one another and working on the whole poem again until they are smoothly integrated. If not, it doesn't matter.

Review

Now let your poem sleep a bit, and only get back to it after a little while without thinking about it; it's likely that you know it almost by heart anyway, so there's no point in rereading it until it's cooled down.

When it has, reread it. What do you think? Rate the poem on a scale of 1 to 10 on the following criteria:

- Does it elicit interesting, intriguing,
  powerful sensations? $\boxed{1}\boxed{2}\boxed{3}\boxed{4}\boxed{5}\boxed{6}\boxed{7}\boxed{8}\boxed{9}\boxed{10}$
- Is it quiet enough that you, as reader, can
  dream in its interstices? $\boxed{1}\boxed{2}\boxed{3}\boxed{4}\boxed{5}\boxed{6}\boxed{7}\boxed{8}\boxed{9}\boxed{10}$
- Does it hint at something greater? Does it feel
  lofty enough to accommodate experiences
  beyond the one it attempts to describe? $\boxed{1}\boxed{2}\boxed{3}\boxed{4}\boxed{5}\boxed{6}\boxed{7}\boxed{8}\boxed{9}\boxed{10}$
- Does it *speak*? $\boxed{1}\boxed{2}\boxed{3}\boxed{4}\boxed{5}\boxed{6}\boxed{7}\boxed{8}\boxed{9}\boxed{10}$
- Is it limpid and fresh? Could it speak to a child?
  Or have you taken on a childlike voice to
  enunciate, in fact, grown-up ideas? $\boxed{1}\boxed{2}\boxed{3}\boxed{4}\boxed{5}\boxed{6}\boxed{7}\boxed{8}\boxed{9}\boxed{10}$

Now read it out loud, to yourself or to others. Again, ask yourself the following, rating your answer on a scale of 1 to 10.

- Does it flow? Does it sound fluid, light, does
  it – to put it in a rather clichéd way – trip off
  the tongue? $\boxed{1}\boxed{2}\boxed{3}\boxed{4}\boxed{5}\boxed{6}\boxed{7}\boxed{8}\boxed{9}\boxed{10}$
- Is it catchy, in the best sense of the word – does
  it catch your attention, alert your mind that
  there is something there to wonder about and
  mull over? $\boxed{1}\boxed{2}\boxed{3}\boxed{4}\boxed{5}\boxed{6}\boxed{7}\boxed{8}\boxed{9}\boxed{10}$
- If you aimed at humour, is it funny? If you aimed
  at emotion, is it touching? $\boxed{1}\boxed{2}\boxed{3}\boxed{4}\boxed{5}\boxed{6}\boxed{7}\boxed{8}\boxed{9}\boxed{10}$

Fine-tune it until you are happy that it is as minutely wrought as it could be. The satisfaction in this kind of work is that of an artisan working on a tiny, precious object: it is about perfection in a small box, rather than the grandiose, structured lyricism of a symphonic novel.

Where to next?

Next, we'll be talking about a type of text almost as ancient as poetry: fairy tales. Children's and Young Adult literature has always been strongly inspired by fairy tales, folk tales, legends and mythology. You might be thinking of writing a fairy-tale-inspired story yourself, or even rewriting a tale. The next chapter will do its best to make your manuscript undergo its rags-to-riches story.

15

Fairy tales – between tradition and renewal

Once upon a time, there was a plain, shy teenager with braces and glasses who lived in Slough (or Pittsburgh or …) with her workaholic dad, her alcoholic stepmother and two spotty, bitchy stepsisters. Every day after school, Cindy came home to a dirty mess which it was her duty to clean up.

Once upon a time, there was a young girl of fifteen who was married by force to her cousin. Her cousin lived in a crumbling tower block in North London (or Queens or …), and he was said to have had six wives before her, though they had all disappeared one after the other.

Once upon a time, there was the Queen of Prom and the King of Prom and their loyal clique of subjects at St Ann's Sixth Form. The royal couple had all they wanted, and nothing they didn't want. Until the day the Queen realized she was going to have a baby.

Once upon a time, there was a girl whose father couldn't help but want her because her mum had died, and because she looked too much like her mum, whom he'd loved, not to incite that kind of desire in him all the time.

Once upon a time, there was a boy playing near a lake with a golden football. It was the Adidas World Cup 2018 model. He'd almost cried with joy when his godfather had given it to him. And he was *really* crying now, as the ball had landed bang in the middle of the lake.

Do those ring a bell? I've just made them up, of course, but you all know exactly what they are about. Distorted, modernized, teenage-ized versions of 'Cinderella', 'Bluebeard', 'Snow White'/'Sleeping Beauty', 'Donkey Skin', 'The Princess and the Frog'. Apart from perhaps one or two (you might not be familiar with Perrault's extraordinary 'Donkey Skin', which I strongly encourage you to discover), I could just let you continue the story, and I'd listen to you with that familiar feeling of joyful recognition as well as of delicious surprise, commenting on your creative reinventions and proposing yet another twist on the oft-repeated plot.

Fairy tales, folk tales and mythological and religious stories are hugely popular in children's and Young Adult literature, and not just in their traditional form. They get treated … let's say, quite roughly sometimes, by children's writers. This 'transversal' chapter doesn't focus on a specific age range, but rather looks at different ways in which these tremendously well-known stories can continue to amaze readers from the tiniest toddler to the toughest teen.

'Conservative retellings' of traditional fairy tales and legends

Let's start with, perhaps, the most obvious use of fairy tales and traditional stories in children's literature: 'just' telling them. The 'real' ones, the old ones, the Grimms' and Perrault's and Andersen's, *Arabian Nights* stories, traditional Gaelic or Irish tales, Chinese folk tales, Greek myths, stories from the Torah, the Bible or the Qu'ran. Such stories, on which so much of our culture and literature is based, do need to reach children at some stage in their 'original' form. Countless anthologies of tales and myths are released every year. Of course, apart from the cases when the anthologies genuinely feature the original version of the stories – in the form, for instance, of a new translation of Homer, or of the Grimms' tales – those apparently 'original' tales already qualify as rewritings, as retellings. Because if you, as a children's author, decide that you are going to write a new version of 'Rumpelstiltskin', and even if you rigorously follow the original plot, it will be *your* version: it will be *your* retelling.

I will call these retellings 'conservative retellings', insofar as they do not significantly modify the story structure, character development or general 'message' of the tales, and that they are written in a way that preserves the *feel* of the original tale. This is a bit of an elusive concept, so let's break it down. A 'conservative retelling' of a fairy tale might feature the following elements:

- Clear verbal indicators of the status of the text as a tale, myth, legend, etc. For instance, traditional formulae: 'Once upon a time', 'Open, sesame', 'The better to eat you with'.

- A register of language which also corresponds to – or rather, pastiches – the common perception of the original language in which the story was told. This would lead you to imitate the linguistic idiosyncrasies of the most famous tellers of the tale; giving an 'eighteenth-century feel', for instance, to a retelling of a Grimm story. This also includes using the original terms for objects and characters, even though they might be difficult to pronounce or understand in English.

- A refusal to modernize the tale or to modify it significantly in form or in content.
- Some measure of effacement as the writer of the tale; though this is very difficult to define precisely, it can be qualified as the general impression that you, as the writer, have 'simply' collected the tale from various storytellers and written it down.

'Conservative retellings' are hugely important. We've all read or listened to them. But, let's be honest, publishers aren't dying to take on first-time authors for a 'conservative retelling' of a Perrault fairy tale, an Indian folk tale or a Roman myth. They're more likely to hire an author for that job, after finding an illustrator whom they particularly want for a book like that.

Indeed, illustrations, rather than the writing in itself, are the 'added value' to conservative retellings of tales and legends. *Hansel and Gretel* by Anthony Browne, for instance, is fairly conservative in its language; but it is within the illustrations that his completely new take on the story shines. Similarly, Caldecott-winner *The Lion and the Mouse*, by Jerry Pinkney, retells the traditional Aesop's fable without a word. Publishers might also be interested in hiring very famous authors or poets for that job. So there's not much space on the market for a debut author who would like to launch into this type of work. However, some publishing houses, such as Barefoot Books, publish conservative retellings of fairy tales and might be interested in yours.

Reworkings of traditional tales

What would be more likely to land you a book deal as a first-time author is a retelling of a traditional story with relatively important modifications of content and/or tone.

This is an extremely broad definition, so it's worth going into detail about what it could mean for you to write such a retelling.

EXPUNGED, SIMPLIFIED AND 'CHILDIFIED' RETELLINGS

This is what Disney does with most of the fairy tales and legends it appropriates: gets rid of most of the blood and sex, and makes it, in their view, 'suitable for children'. A 'conservative retelling' of 'Bluebeard' would not eclipse the gory vision of the six dead wives bleeding streams of blood on to the poor princess's key; a bowdlerized version might politely omit this episode, and stain the key in a different way. Similarly, a 'childified' retelling of *The Odyssey* might retain only the episodes considered the most 'child-friendly', and keep mum about Calypso's sex addiction. Again, it is unlikely that as a first-time author you would be asked to do such a retelling, but do keep in mind that, unfortunately, publishers can be quite sensitive about the violent or sexual content of traditional stories and ask you to tone it down – and there will be no hiding behind 'But that's what happens in the *real* version!'

PARODIC RETELLINGS

Parodies and pastiches of fairy tales and traditional stories are by far the most popular type of retelling. It's not a recent phenomenon – of course, *Shrek* contributed to the craze, but parodying popular tales was already Tex Avery's main business plan, and in the 1970s and 1980s there were many books aimed at children that poked fun at traditional tales. If anything, it's become quite difficult now to think of genuinely new, funny ways of parodying fairy tales and legends. But here are some ways of thinking about parodic retellings:

- **Play with the expected tropes of the genre.** Subvert or transgress the expectations of the young reader: Little Red Riding Hood could eat the grandmother, Cinderella could tie her shoelaces better in order to run away from the prince unhindered, the Frog Prince might end up cooked in garlic sauce by the French chef at the castle. Such subverting of expectations, if done well, is not just funny – it also undermines the sanctity of the fairy-tale text, the 'seriousness' of the oral tradition and heritage. It is liberating for the child reader because it pokes fun at an authoritative work they should respect.

- **Play with the antiquated language of the tale.** You can poke fun at archaic phrases, at traditional formulae, at the old-fashioned feel of the tale or legend.

- **Change details to make the tale slightly … different.** What if Snow White had eyes as red as blood, lips as black as ebony and hair as white as snow?

- **Think of how illustrations could subvert traditional representations of the tales and legends.** There's plenty of fun to be had by hiding octopi or flip-flops in those waves that surround Greek myths, or by hiding runaway rats everywhere in a retelling of 'The Pied Piper'. Intervisuality can be hugely interesting and fun – ask yourself how you could include resonances of other works of visual art.

- **Cross tales and legends together for a hybrid experience** – and heighten the joy of recognition in the reader. *The Jolly Postman* and *Each Peach Pear Plum*, by the Ahlbergs, thus marry together many tales and traditional stories, playing with the young reader's familiarity with them and presenting them afresh in their new setting. Many hilarious events can be triggered by the meeting of, let's say, all the nasty witches and stepmothers of fairy tales, or all the marine monsters of *The Odyssey* …

- **Breathe a new, fresh spirit into an old tale, trying to find an interesting 'spin' on it.** The remarkable *True Story of the Three Little Pigs*, by Sczieska and Smith, thus begins with the amazing premise that the Wolf needs to explain himself: he definitely didn't do anything bad, his intentions were misunderstood – it's the *pigs* who were the true culprits. And then the hilarity begins … as well as a profound, fascinating reflection on the truth value of fictional characters, and the status of the (highly unreliable) narrator.

POLITICAL RETELLINGS

Many retellings of fairy tales for children have a political edge, if only because a large quantity of them consists of feminist retellings. This is the case, for instance, with *Princess Smartypants*, by Babette Cole, which subverts expectations by presenting a princess who absolutely doesn't want to get married. Such stories are now quite common, so be careful that you don't fall into the trap of making yours clichéd and expected. In France, feminist retellings of fairy tales are so numerous I can't even keep track.

Some contemporary adaptations and retellings of tales and legends are profoundly politically committed, anticapitalist or communist, for instance. I can cite the (again, French) book *Le Petit Chapubron rouge*, by Alain Serres, which retells 'Little Red Riding Hood' but keeps interrupting the story with ... adverts! In this highly postmodern picturebook, the 'message' is that the child should be made aware of the incongruity and flashiness of advertising. But readers might actually end up liking the adverts more than the story ...

MODERNIZED RETELLINGS

Often, political retellings and parodic retellings belong to what could be called a modernized retelling of a fairy tale, legend or myth: a displacement of that story into a contemporary setting. What would a modern little girl do, faced with a wolf in the middle of the woods? Why, perhaps Instagram it instantly and post it on Twitter (think of what the birds on the trees could do with that) – leaving the wolf more than enough time to eat her in the process ...

But modernized retellings can also be apolitical and/or not meant to be funny at all. Roberto Innocenti's version of 'Little Red Riding Hood' is thus a poignant and meticulous story of a child in a city. Generally speaking, modernized retellings rely on the following strategies:

- Adapting context, setting and backdrop to make it correspond to the experiences of a child now: this may involve turning a rural setting into an urban one

- Adapting language to turn it into natural, contemporary speech

- Adapting portrayals of family situations, relationships between adult and children, and so on, to make them more contemporary: divorced parents, not-so-old grandparents, children who have to go to school, and 'fairy godmothers' who might be social workers ...

- Adapting endings or the 'moral' of the story to make it suitable for an audience of future citizens now – erasing, for instance, as mentioned above, the sexist connotations of a given tale, or deleting all trace of racism from traditional stories

- Making the story into a new format, using postmodern strategies, or playing with the aesthetics and poetics of the book to make it decidedly contemporary.

If you're writing a modernized version of a tale, myth or legend, it's quite likely that you will depart sufficiently from the original story that it won't be immediately obvious which one you picked; and you'll have a large amount of freedom in the process. In fact, this retelling might end up falling into the following category: modern tales.

'Imitations' of fairy tales and legends: the modern literary fairy tale

Andersen's tales are not the same as Perrault's or the Grimms': they are literary fairy tales. This means that Andersen made them up entirely, whereas Perrault and the Grimms collected their tales from oral storytellers and wrote them down. Hundreds of literary fairy tales and legends are still being invented. Generally linked to a particular tradition or genre, but sometimes not quite so easily pinpointed, these 'imitations' of tales aspire to become 'classics' like Andersen's, Perrault's and the

Grimms'. Publishers might be interested in this 'classic' feel, as it ensures perhaps not spectacular but enduring sales. And, indeed, some do: Oscar Wilde's *The Happy Prince* and *The Selfish Giant* are now considered tales in their own right. And look at Roald Dahl's *The Enormous Crocodile*, for instance, or, to a lesser degree perhaps, J.K. Rowling's *The Tales of Beedle the Bard*.

What are such works characterized by?

- **A fairy-tale or legendary 'feel':** this is extremely difficult to define, of course, but when reading these stories you can generally sense that they are modelled on traditional tales, even if they don't retell a particular one. There is a feeling of universality, even in the telling of a singular event, and a general impression of an enclosed, autarchic world.

- **The appearance of traditional themes (topoi) or characters of fairy tales, legends or myths:** there might be a castle, a quest, a prince, a golden ball, a sleeping princess. There might be a prophecy at the birth of a much-wanted child. Those details might be woven into a much larger structure, but they signal the tale-ish nature of the story.

- **A structure which recalls that of traditional stories, tales and legends;** or characters that are quite flat, or at least archetypal-sounding rather than highly psychologized.

A good example of a modern literary tale is Anthony Browne's *The Tunnel*, which has a distinctive fairy-tale feel, the structure of a traditional story, characters that recall Hansel and Gretel, elements of many different fairy tales – from 'Little Red Riding Hood' to 'The Snow Queen' – but which tells an entirely new story. There are many others, some of which are also parodic or political. We can cite Jeannette Winterson's *King of Capri*, a deliciously Marxist modern fairy tale where the rich become poor and the poor become rich.

Writing a new tale can be a very interesting and very rewarding endeavour, as I discovered when writing one of my French books, *La Louve*, which follows a young girl turning into a wolf. You can count on an immediate feeling of warm familiarity and recognition on the part of the young reader, while ensuring that you will also (you hope) surprise or amuse them. You will be situating yourself within a long tradition of storytelling, thus strengthening your own legitimacy but also offering something new, timely and relevant. Much can be achieved with this kind of story, and I encourage you to think of all its possibilities.

Fairy-tale or legend-inspired texts for older readers and Young Adult literature

I have only, so far, tacitly tackled picturebooks or tales for quite young readers. But, of course, texts for older readers and Young Adult literature are not devoid of fairy-tale or legendary ancestry. In fact, such stories positively pullulate in the literature for tweens and teens. Again, they play on both the joy of recognition and the pleasures of defamiliarization. There's no reason why those timeless stories might cease to 'speak' to teenagers.

Go to your local bookstore, and head for the 9–13 and 13+ aisles. In the more girly section, you don't need to look very far to find 'Cinderella' everywhere, from Meg Cabot's *The*

Princess Diaries onwards. 'Theseus and the Minotaur'? No problem, head for *The Hunger Games*. Or Percy Jackson, which, of course, spans the whole of Greek mythology. David Walliams's latest and, as usual, hilarious book, *Demon Dentist*, plays with 'Hansel and Gretel', but also with 'Snow White'. *Twilight*? That's just 'Beauty and the Beast' revisited. If you need it to be even clearer, head for *A Tale Dark and Grimm* by Adam Gidwitz. Or try the incredibly dark, profound and beautiful *Tender Morsels* by Margo Lanagan, loosely based on the relatively little-known tale 'Snow White and Rose Red'. Yes, from social realism to chick lit to adventure stories, humorous tales and teenage paranormal romance, there are fairy tales, legends and myths everywhere. Add your own, if you dare.

Why do such patterns function so well in Young Adult literature? And how can you make them function in *your* Young Adult take on fairy tales? I have already mentioned the fact that they play on recognition and defamiliarization. Here are a few more answers:

- **Tales and legends articulate deceptively simple value systems.** I say 'deceptively simple', because of course there's nothing actually simple about jealousy, cowardice, parental affection, anger, love. But fairy tales and legends make such feelings and values easier to handle. Young Adult stories loosely based on tales or legends tend to replicate this apparent simplicity: they present clear-cut systems of good and evil, and apparently indisputable values and personality traits. Of course, the most interesting Young Adult books then subvert this order and dissolve it into a haze of ambiguity.

- **Characters in tales and legends are archetypal, predictable and embody specific qualities or flaws.** Again, Young Adult literature – especially fantasy – borrows from this neat characterization. Characters can appear excessive, or simply slightly flat, because they are made of extreme, solid feeling. But many Young Adult books make them progress into increasingly sophisticated beings, mimicking on a narrative level the passage from an 'infancy' of feeling towards other people to a more adult, nuanced vision of the world. Do all characters need to lose their archetypal simplicity? Your choice. *Harry Potter* preserves, almost until the end, the stereotypical character of the evil-stepparents-Dursleys.

- **Tales and legends confer a sense of universality, of timelessness, to a Young Adult book.** They mythify what could otherwise be taken as an 'anecdote' in the life of a teenage protagonist. In other words, they make teenage stories 'resonate' with the sound of an ancient and universal voice. Troubles, desires and aspirations are taken to be meaningful beyond singular experiences. Try to see how your own work can communicate this sense of importance, this feeling that there is a universal experience behind the event you are narrating.

- **They play upon the fears and hopes associated with growth.** This would be Bettelheim's interpretation: the fairy tale eases the passage from childhood to adulthood. But Bettelheim wouldn't necessarily have said that teenagers still needed them. Well, they clearly do. Tales and myths 'speak' to them because they map the experiences of a young consciousness emerging into the world, clashing against other people, and trying to be initiated into a society, into a role. Heighten those aspects of your story to give it a sense of wider purpose, of a rite of passage.

- **They are full of sex, blood, magic and passion.** Of course! Play up the sexual tension in a rewriting of 'Rapunzel', and you end up with a steamy love affair at the top of a tower. Add some extra gory details to a retelling of 'Snow White', and you've got yourself a Gothic tale of deer hearts in wooden boxes … I'm making it sound easy; it isn't. But a good guideline could be: look at what's left unsaid in traditional tales and legends, and spice up those unsaid bits before serving them to your young audience. Don't make anything explicit, or you'll lose the power: just spice it up.

- **They cultivate an unrealistic fantasy of what life is like.** This is the problematic aspect, of course, of the previous point. A lot of the Young Adult literature based on tales or legends is hugely escapist, narcissistic and complacent: it presents the world as a pliable place which will always bring about what is wished for by the young protagonists. It lulls the reader into the comforting conviction that his or her existence is controlled by benevolent fate. If you want to avoid this (which indeed, I think you should), think about how realistic your story would sound without the intervention of some kind of divine (or narrative) help. Are you being wishful? Are you lying to 14-year-old ugly ducklings by telling them they can all become Queen of Prom? Should we even still care about this popularity-contest cardboard royalty? Alongside these concerns about narcissistic wishes, there are also, of course, concerns about the inherent sexism in most fairy tales, folk tales, myths and legends.

Should you choose to write Young Adult fiction based on tales or legends, you'd be in good company: almost all major children's writers have yielded to the irresistible pull of traditional storytelling. In fact, almost all major writers for adults have, too – and this is my cue to tell you to have a look, if you haven't already, at Angela Carter's fairy tales.

Workshop: inventing a new fairy tale

For this workshop, I'd like you to either synopsize a tween or teen story, or write a short modern fairy tale (for instance a picturebook text or a short story), by inventing the rest of one of the five 'Once upon a time' beginnings I sketched out at the start of this chapter. I hinted at the fact that I could just ask you to continue the story … Well, now I want you to do just that.

Review

Now reread your work carefully, and let's try to evaluate how successful it is as a modern 'retelling' or reinvention of a traditional tale. Try to give yourself a mark from 1 to 10 on the following criteria:

- The balance of tale or legend topoi and
  reinventions   `1` `2` `3` `4` `5` `6` `7` `8` `9` `10`
- A modern take married with a traditional feel   `1` `2` `3` `4` `5` `6` `7` `8` `9` `10`
- A story that is relevant now, but feels timeless `1` `2` `3` `4` `5` `6` `7` `8` `9` `10`
- Characters who are complex, but with
  archetypal traits   `1` `2` `3` `4` `5` `6` `7` `8` `9` `10`
- Successful chosen tone – humorous, political,
  scary …   `1` `2` `3` `4` `5` `6` `7` `8` `9` `10`

Of course, nothing prevents you from writing a modern tale that doesn't strike this balance, and that instead chooses to privilege one aspect – the contemporary story, for instance – over another – the fairy-tale 'feel'. It's up to you to decide which way you would like to tweak it.

Well, well, well, we're almost done with the writing and ready to take it one step closer to its happily-ever-after: the publishing stage. But first, like Cinderella getting ready for the ball, it's time to turn that rushed, raw, rags-wearing manuscript into a beautiful princess. The next chapter gives you the not-so-magical formula for this transformation to occur.

16

Drama-free editing and polishing

If one day you knock on my door just to say hi, and the door opens and I'm standing there in my pyjamas, looking inordinately grumpy, with dark bags under my eyes, a cup of strong coffee and all fingernails bitten down to the quick, it probably means you've decided to pay me a visit while I'm editing.

I *hate* editing.

Ten books later, it doesn't get better. Writing can be fun, it can also be difficult, it can be frustrating, it can be exhilarating, but writing is *life*; writing is *existence*; writing is what I would still do if I wasn't paid to be doing it.

Editing, in contrast, is the constraint that comes with being paid to do it. With it getting published. With it getting read. It is, quite simply, an extremely painful process; at least it is for me. Other people love it. But I won't lie to you in this chapter, and pretend that you should really be excited about editing. You don't need to be excited or enthusiastic about edits; you need to be pushed by a strong sense of duty, of urgency and of purpose.

In this chapter I'll be talking about self-editing, or at least editing *before* you submit your work to publishers. This is, perhaps, the most difficult and also the most crucial moment of your whole career. If there's one thing you should remember about this process, it's that you shouldn't waste the hours you've spent writing your book by not editing it, or editing it sloppily.

Because then, quite simply, it will *fail* to find a publisher.

Putting the manuscript away

The first temptation when emerging, dizzy-eyed and warm-cheeked, from a large piece of writing – let's say a long-winded Young Adult novel – is to reread it all instantly. It might be two in the morning; your partner might be snoring peacefully in the bed next to you, undisturbed by the fervent typing while you whooshed through the climactic scene of the book; now it's done, you've finished it! Let's reread it all, *now*!

By all means, do that. If that's what you want, do it. Reread the whole book, until eight or nine in the morning, if you can afford to pull an all-nighter. And do congratulate yourself: you've done it. You've finished the book. That's an amazing achievement.

Rereading the whole book in one go, in the feverish aftermath of its completion, you might be overcomed by either of the following feelings:

• This is a work of genius: the next Carnegie, the next Branford Boase, the next – screw that – the next Man Booker Prize.

• What the hell is going on here? Gosh, I can't believe I've spent so much time working on this heap of rubbish.

The former is more likely if you've been editing as you go along, or if you've followed a synopsis, simply because the story and language are more likely to feel already polished and in place. The latter will likely happen on 30 November, the last day of NaNoWriMo, when you haven't even reread anything of what you've been writing for the past month.

In both cases, just don't trust yourself:

1 Close the document.

2 Don't reopen it the next day.

3 Don't reopen it the day after, nor the day after.

4 Don't reopen the next week. Resist temptation.

5 Wait two or three weeks. Yes, two or three.

'But I want to send it to agents!' Agents will not take on an unedited manuscript. Want a cautionary tale? Every year, hundreds of people 'finish' novels, in the sense that there's a final full stop to the work. Then these people enthusiastically send those 'finished' novels to all the agents they can think of. Then they wait. Then all the agents say no. The agents say no because they receive hundreds of novels every month, and normally they only pick the novels that they know won't require too much work before they're sent to publishers, because they know publishers want novels that won't require too much work before they're published.

These hundreds of people see their work rejected entirely, and they have no other choice but to confine the 'finished' (read: unfinished) novel to a drawer. No agent will look for a second time at a novel they've rejected, unless they specifically encourage the writer to edit it some more before sending it again. These manuscripts are entirely wasted.

Among them, a non-negligible number, with the right amount of editing, might have attracted the attention of an agent. *It's too late now.*

But what do you do while you're waiting to cleanse your brain from the accumulated excitement, fear, despair and emotions that you felt while writing? You look back, and you proceed methodically. You prepare the next stage: editing.

Here are some tips. Without looking at your manuscript again, try to answer the following questions (it's worth writing your answers down):

- What was I trying to achieve in that novel?
- What was the *theme*, and what was the *thesis*? (Look back at Chapter 2.)
- How was the character development supposed to work? How was the main character, in particular, meant to evolve?
- Which scenes do I remember as particularly difficult to write? Why?
- Which scenes do I recall blitzing through? Why?
- Where would my book fit, commercially speaking? Which books is it comparable to? Why is it different?
- What is particularly distinctive about this story? Why did I fall in love with it, again?
- How did I want it to sound? Which aspects of the language did I want to privilege?
- If I deviated from the original synopsis in significant ways, why did this happen?
- Did writing the ending modify the way I thought about the rest of the book?

While you're still not looking at the manuscript, try to answer these questions and think up more questions, specific to the work. You might already be able to formulate editorial wishes if there are problematic aspects of the work that you are already lucid about. *Write them down.* This can be in the form of: 'Thinking back, I'd probably like Clara's evolution from shyness to assertiveness to really come through. She's a secondary character, but I felt towards the end that she was becoming more important.'

New ideas might come to you. *Write them down.* Don't consider the book as finished: new threads, new thoughts, new events can still be integrated. 'Maybe Clara's path could be more believable and more interesting if I added a backstory explaining that she used to be a very precocious child, very fragile … Maybe I could have a flashback scene where she narrates her experiences at school.'

Think about the manuscript when you're washing the dishes, doing lengths at the swimming pool or going down the interminable escalators of the London Underground. Don't reread it yet; it's likely that whatever's on your mind, whatever you're remembering and mulling over, are either the most problematic or the most interesting aspects of the manuscript. The glorious and the ugly. If you reread it too soon, your mind will be clogged by all the elements in the book, leaving no space to think about what's particularly tough or particularly good about those tricky and exceptional moments.

Do try to write as much down as possible, and to organize your notes so that your rereadings of the manuscript will be as methodical and rigorous as possible. For instance, your notes could look like this:

> 1 *Theme - does it really come through that it's about mourning & leaving the past behind?? Maybe taken over by more trivial quests (e.g. candy shop)*
>
> 2 *Clara's path - add background story? See where it could go in bits and pieces. Strengthen bond w/ Ludovico. Long dialogue with him was difficult to write - does it sound good? Prepare it more?*
>
> 3 *Check foreshadowing works re: Tessa's mother losing her job.*
>
> 4 *Symbolic thread of the <u>theatre</u>, of people giving <u>performances</u> - not sure it carries through, remember it getting abandoned towards the middle.*

If these elements are important to you, if they are what's left in your mind, it probably means they will be crucial in the editing process. And having them in front of you when rereading will give your editing the all-important sense of *purpose*. Of course, you will also discover much more when you finally click 'Open' and get that manuscript back in front of you on the white screen.

Rediscovering the writing with fresh eyes

Your first rereading will be partly for 'pleasure' – you will, I hope, be delighted to find details you'd forgotten about, little turns of phrase you didn't think yourself capable of, and fascinating resonances from chapter to chapter. It may also be cringe-worthy: typically, at least two or three scenes, especially the most passionate or intense, will have been written in a frenzy, and you may find them mawkish, sensationalist or simply very sloppy.

Don't start editing too much, though (apart from correcting obvious typos or small errors). Reread it fast, a pen in hand (or with Track Changes activated). This is your first opportunity to mark your manuscript whenever something attracts your eye as worthy of attention:

> Clara wasn't sure she could remember a time when she hadn't been the dorky girl at school, with bottle-thick glasses and incapacitating blushes. Her mum had told her she used to be a lively, assertive little girl, and she sometimes felt she could remember that time, but maybe it was all in her head; maybe she'd created those memories to fit her mum's faulty ones.

Pay particular attention to the points you raised on your own without having reread the manuscript: colour-code them, if necessary, to make it clear where and when issues arise. And don't forget to comment on the manuscript when you feel you're doing something right. There's nothing wrong with a 'YES! More of that!', or a 'Perfect action scene. Don't touch', or 'Interesting detail here. Mention it again in Chap. 5'. In fact, being objective about where you're good is an indispensable corollary to being objective about where you're bad. Identifying those moments will give you clues to how to address the problems that you've raised.

Once you've reread the work once or twice and annotated it, you will need to zoom out again and ask yourself the truly difficult question: are the issues you've noted relatively straightforward to address, or will they require … some serious restructuring?

Restructuring and shuffling text around

Of course, you're thinking: 'Oh, it will be straightforward; no restructuring required.'

Go beyond this first reaction. Once again, proceed methodically. The following questions could help:

- Of all the issues you raised, could some be addressed by moving scenes or chapters around? For instance, you might have unearthed the problem with Clara's wobbly characterization: the reader doesn't know enough about her childhood and only learns about it towards the end. Could you move that scene towards the beginning?

- Is the reader given some aspects of the plot too soon, or too late? Could this be addressed by breaking up 'revelation scenes' and scattering the different elements across the story more harmoniously?

- Are there plot holes or inconsistencies? Can you resolve them by adding or removing elements of the plot and tightening the structure?

- Are some parts disproportionately long, or short? Look specifically, in a 'traditional' plot structure, at the exposition scene(s) (generally too long), the 'first failure' (generally too long), the climax (generally too short), the ending (generally too short).

These might look like colossal changes, but actually they remain relatively easy. Once you've shuffled scenes around, write memos to yourself: 'So-and-so is now being mentioned in Chapter 2 for the first time, so don't forget to move up the description that's given of him in Chapter 6.' This will be relatively quick.

More major changes

However, sometimes, more major changes are needed. You'll know it, not just from patiently rereading and annotating the work, but also from a gut feeling, a sense that it's just not right. These major changes could include the following, which are quite common:

- **Getting rid of a character,** even an important one, who doesn't add much to the plot. That could mean redistributing whatever s/he does across other characters.

- **Changing the age of one or several characters.** This could be because you've realized that your book functions better in another age range, with commercial considerations in mind. Of course, it's not just a matter of changing two numbers in the book. Everything needs to be rethought.

- **Changing the narrative voice** – from 'I' to 'he', for instance. This might happen if the narrative feels too claustrophobic, or too self-obsessed, or on the contrary too detached. Again, that goes above and beyond modifying pronouns. The entire feel of the narrative will need to be transformed.
- **Changing the tense of the narrative.** This could emerge if you feel the writing is too slow and would benefit from being written in the present instead of the past; or, by contrast, if you realize that you want your book to have a more 'classic' feel, and move to the past tense. Quite a tricky change.
- **Eliminating secondary plotlines.** This is often necessary when they don't add much to the general storyline, and/or clog up and slow down the general pace of the story. The problem is that deleting them will often cascade into deletion of secondary characters, and might also require rethinking the moments when this secondary plotline is used to 'connect' to the main storyline.

These are the changes that are a real pain in the neck. They will make you sweat and swear that you'll never do it again. They're painful because they're another leap into the unknown. How do you know it will truly make the story better? Well, you don't. You do it, and you see what happens. However, do save versions of the work in progress, so that you can go back to earlier edits.

Another problem, of course, is that after doing major edits your brain will be full again of the manuscript and you'll have to let it breathe some more, take more time over it, repeat the previous process *again*. It may feel long and unrewarding. But please remember: *it's in your best interest.*

 Key idea

If agents reject your work once, they won't look at it again. And editing does make your work better. *Always.* It's not just wishful thinking; it works.

Editing down

The last stage of this first (yes, first …) bout of editing will be editing down. It is 100 per cent likely that your book is too long. Yes, I promise. It will need to lose weight. It will need to lose words. It will need to lose (ouch!) scenes.

When we write, and especially when we write fast, we write too much. We aren't careful to say just enough; we write in a splurge, an unbound stream of consciousness. And thanks to it the manuscript grows. But then the manuscript must shrink again.

Editing down must occur on both micro and macro levels; both at the level of the sentence and the level of the whole book. Take your manuscript. Here are a few things that are probably (nay, certainly) too long:

- **The exposition is too long.** Look at it winding and unwinding into endless presentations of what is there and what is to come. Cut it down.

- **Descriptions are too long,** particularly physical descriptions of characters. Look at how much they slow down your story. Cut them down.

- **Dialogues are too long.** And, within them, individual sentences are too long. Look: they are too close to what a real dialogue would be like, that is to say, unstructured, convoluted and fat. Dialogues must convey a message, give a direction to the story, or reveal important elements of characterization. Cut them down.

- **Internal monologues and descriptions of psychological states are too long.** Look, look – they're complacent and narcissistic. They're repetitive, too – look, it's the second time you've alluded to her loneliness; it doesn't add anything to call it 'solitude' there. Cut them down.

- **Action scenes are too long.** There's only so much fighting, running and drowning a reader can take in before their eyes start glazing over. Look, that one is almost a page and a half of swords clinking. Cut it down.

- **Your sentences are too long.** Yes, I promise. Look at that one – did you ever plan to put a full stop at the end of it, or – must I conclude – perhaps you added yet another clause, and then another, and then (with brackets for good measure) yet another one, in the hope that – perhaps – using dashes would distract the reader from the fact that it absolutely doesn't end logically, but rather with a question mark, when in fact this was grammatically completely incoherent?

I can't take the time here to talk about micro-editing, but thankfully there are some books which will help you much better than I could. The classic *Elements of Style*, by E.B. White, will teach you how to achieve crisp, necessary and sufficient language. My favourite remains William Zinsser's *On Writing Well*, which, although it is about non-fiction, is applicable to any type of writing. Such writers will show you how to squeeze the essence out of impossibly long sentences. This is all you need.

Oh, just one last trick: 'Ctrl+F editing'. Have you noticed that you overuse the terms 'then', 'maybe', 'really'? The solution is at your fingertips: Ctrl+F: Search for these terms and replace or delete them. This works, too, for entire phrases – 'What he didn't know was', 'He jumped to his feet' and so on.

Spending time on editing will teach you to know your own writing. If you're just beginning to write, you probably don't actually know what you're capable of, what you're struggling with, and what your writing style is like. You can't really get to know that by writing. It's the editing process that will make it shine, and gradually your 'internal editor', that nasty but knowledgeable little demon, will be able to help you as you go along. 'No, not another "really", can't you see you've already used it twice on this page?' So take the editing process seriously, and tease out of the text enough information about yourself to summon that peculiar little guest.

Beta readers

However, you might also want to summon other guests. By now, you're probably getting bored with being alone with yourself. You want *readers* – *real* readers – people who will get to know and even enjoy the world you've been so painstakingly building. And those readers, at this stage, will also be useful to you. So choose them well.

The people who read your work at the editing stage are often called, in the creative writing community, 'beta readers', as opposed to 'alpha readers', who will read your work at an even earlier stage – pre-editing, or even as you go along. Most writers keep beta readers preciously, treat them well and regularly feed them text (and cookies). You can have one, two or ten beta readers. But choose them well and keep them happy. They are rare and important assets to your work.

Where do you find beta readers? Sometimes, in your own home: Stephen King and Michael Morpurgo entrust their wives with this difficult task. My own preferred beta reader, at least for my work in French, is my mother. But careful, this isn't about kisses and congratulations. Your beta readers must, ideally, fulfil the following requirements:

- They must be highly cultured, voracious and discerning readers, preferably knowledgeable in the genre you write in, but also in other literary genres from 'low' to 'high' fiction. And other art forms, why not? They must be able to compare your work to other similar (and dissimilar) pieces.

- They must be constructive and sincere. They have to be kind in their honesty if there's something wrong with your work, and you need to be able to trust them if they tell you you're getting it right.

- They must be good at pinpointing exact places where your text doesn't work, whether at the level of a sentence, of characterization or of the whole plotline. The more precise their comments, the easier these problems are to address.

- As an optional extra, they must be imaginative and creative, and therefore able to suggest potential ways of addressing the issues that they've raised.

You must be firm when selecting beta readers, and make sure that they are the right people for the job, in your best interest and in theirs. You're going to ask them for a huge investment in terms of time and energy. You must be able to trust that you will make the most of that investment – it's only fair – and that you will *both* get something out of it. So when some writers do use their mothers, wives, husbands and sisters as beta readers, it means they're lucky enough to be close to people who can help them so well. Most people, especially 'closet writers' in families where no one ever opens a book, don't benefit from asking their mum to read their work and comment.

So, to get back to my earlier question, how do you find beta readers? Where do they lurk? How do you catch them?

- Look for people around you who love to read and who read widely. This is the first sign that the person might be willing to spend time looking at your work. Those people may be friends, extended family, colleagues and so on.

- For children's literature and Young Adult literature in particular, target people in the educational system, in school libraries, or quite simply parents. Enquire around; maybe one of your acquaintances knows someone who is a school librarian, a school teacher, a bookish parent.

- Join a book club or an online community of readers such as GoodReads or Shelfari – which you should do anyway – and once you've become acquainted with a number of people and have identified some who might have the right profile, begin to ask (politely and personally) if they would be willing to help.

- Join a writing group or an online community of aspiring writers such as SCBWI (we'll get to that in a next chapter), and again, once you've become integrated, begin to look for potential beta readers. You can also offer to beta-read for them, too.
- Get acquainted with already-published writers in a similar genre, and ask them (as politely and humbly as you can possibly manage) if they will have a look at your work.

All these types of beta readers have advantages and disadvantages:

- The disinterested reader, the 'passionate' member of a book club, might be completely incapable of advising you as to the commercial viability of the book: they might 'love it' without realizing that it could never sell in its current form.

- The school librarian, teacher or parent might be tempted to ask you to make it more educational or more 'suitable' for the children they know so well. They might also test-drive the work on the children, which isn't something you should do quite yet, for reasons we'll get to in a minute.

- The beta reader who is a member of an active community of readers might be the best option: knowledgeable about the market, highly involved, and passionate. But of course they might prefer to read published rather than unpublished work.

- Aspiring writers can be superb beta readers, but let's not get too idealistic: it's not a jealousy-free choice. If you're unlucky, you might end up giving good work to a superficially very kind aspiring writer who will advise you to delete everything that was good about your text. Less cynically, it's also quite frequent for young or aspiring writers to find fault with texts simply because they don't correspond to what *they* would write.

- The last option is the riskiest and, frankly, the least likely to work. Writers, especially famous writers, are assailed with such requests every day. Many specify on their website that they won't read any unpublished work; *by all means respect that*. Should one of them agree to read it, you cannot expect them to look at it again in the future.

Let's be honest, finding beta readers becomes much easier once you're already published – as often, it's a virtuous circle. By then, your agent might introduce you to other of her writers writing in a similar genre, or your publisher might put you in touch with their own home-grown writers. You will also gain insightful, passionate readers who would be delighted to read your work and comment before anyone else has seen it.

WHAT DO YOU ASK BETA READERS?

A relationship with a beta reader is built over time. You can't expect them to be on the same wavelength immediately. It's your responsibility to guide them; to help them to help you: you must be very clear about what kind of feedback you're expecting. Of course, this feedback is also going to depend on the different beta readers, if you're lucky enough to have accumulated a nice little army of experts in different domains. Nina might be the best person to ask whether your dystopia stands out in a crowded market. Leo might be the intellectual, the art lover, who can help you with style and language. As for whether the plot works, always ask Ophelia – she's got an eye for inconsistencies and wobbly structures … All of this, of course, you can't know until you begin to work with them. The relationship will develop on both sides, and you will have to be shrewd when receiving their criticism for the first time, to identify where they can be useful to you.

For each piece of work that you give beta readers, you must tell them *exactly* what you want from them. You're asking them for purposeful reading, reading that will lead to potential modifications, reading that will help the work progress. These guidelines are better given in writing. Here's an example of what they might look like:

To	Louise
Subject	Manic Manor

Hi Louise!

Thanks so much for agreeing to read *Manic Manor*. I hope you like it … I'm pretty happy with it, I think, but there are a few things here and there that bother me. I'd be particularly interested in your opinion on the following:

- The first few pages. I feel like the description of the trees drags on. Then again, it's important for foreshadowing …
- The character development of Lila. In particular, is her relationship with Thomas believable, given how much she seems to have moved away from her family since the beginning of the story?

The risk, of course, is to influence your beta reader's first impressions of the text. But, firstly, it's the price to pay for a reading that pays specific attention to what's bothering *you*. Secondly, don't worry, beta readers will *always* find other problems that you hadn't noticed, and relieve you of anxiety about what you thought was a huge issue. Thirdly, if you really don't want to influence your beta readers, leave your questions open, as exemplified above.

 Key idea

Don't forget to ask your beta readers whether they genuinely enjoyed the book, but make their reading as purposeful as possible.

Reward beta readers. It's not always a fun job, and it's a huge undertaking. Thank them for their time. Give them free books if and when your work is published, with acknowledgements in said books and on your website, and with offers of equivalent work for them. Many writers engage in mutual beta reading, though it's not always a perfect option, especially if they work within exactly the same genre – jealousy again, unconscious or conscious … Other things you can offer your beta readers are hours of baby-sitting, car-washing, going to the post office for them, or simply a nice big dinner. They're worth it.

'But, but, but! Wait a minute! Why not *children*?' I hear you ask. Surely they should be the best beta readers for children's literature!

Well, of course if you can give your work to children or teenagers who are exactly the right target audience, why not? But be careful – children, it's understandable, don't want to be mean to their beloved godfather or to their parents' friend, and they might just tell you they love it even if they never finished it. And even if they did love it, you might find it very difficult to extract precise knowledge about what they loved. They might be too shy, or quite simply they might not have reflected upon what they particularly like. And if you try to extract an answer from them, they might obligingly respond by pointing at a completely random bit of the text just to get rid of you and your annoying questions.

The other risk with asking children if they like the text is that you may then be tempted to write, in your cover letter to agents, 'I gave it to children I know, and they loved the book!' which might as well be a huge neon sign with an arrow towards your name flashing with the word AMATEUR.

REACTING TO BETA READER FEEDBACK

Beta reader feedback is essential, but it will probably hurt. That depends, of course, on how prepared you are to take in the fact that people might not adhere entirely to the world you created. You think you are ready – most people think they are – and then when the actual feedback comes in we all crumble. There's no need to say that it's not personal; of course it is. It is your writing, so it's *personal*; no need to pretend otherwise. The first effort will therefore be to overcome the feeling of disappointment ('I thought it was perfect!' – it never is), the feeling of guilt ('I gave her something to read that wasn't perfect!' – that's why she agreed to be your beta reader), and the feeling of fear ('What will I do now?' – just read what she says and think about it). Not to mention the possible anger.

Something we need to remember, before we even look at it: we will pay much more attention, and be much more affected by, the negative comments than the positive ones. Even if there are ten positive comments and one negative comment, we will solely focus on this one. Now that's said, let's dive into their feedback and see how to respond to different critiques.

When looking at beta-reader feedback, take each piece of feedback individually at first rather than looking at the whole lot, because some comments might be right and others might not be. For each comment, ask yourself questions along these lines:

- Had I noticed the issue that s/he raises? Did I even have an inkling of it?
- How convincing are her/his reasons for pointing this out as an issue? Is s/he influenced by her/his own preferences?
- Do I have to address the issue?
- How do I address the issue?
- What would be the impact of addressing this issue on the rest of the work?

And, optionally, if you had the luxury of having several beta readers:

- Did anyone else think it was an issue? Did anyone actually like that particular aspect of the work?

The idea isn't to find fault with your beta reader or to find a convenient excuse not to do the editing work, but rather to evaluate whether his or her judgement stems from personal preference or points at a truly problematic aspect of the work.

Be particularly attentive to beta-reader feedback about general structure, believability and character development. Those are the aspects, I think, that are the most difficult to evaluate on your own. If a reader tells you a passage is too long, it probably is. If they tell you the ending needs to be better foreshadowed, it probably does. If they tell you a character isn't credible, then you'd better get to work on that.

So back to square one, then … editing, editing and editing again. And then comes the time when it's *almost* done.

Proofreading, polishing and formatting

Proofreading, by now, should be almost done, but if you have problems with spelling, go through it again. Check those things that spellcheckers can't always pick up on:

- **Punctuation problems:** using double (" ") and single (") quotation marks inconsistently (just pick one!); inconsistencies with spaces before and after commas and full stops; inconsistent use of the capital letter after colons (:) (don't use them at all in the UK); inconsistent use of hyphens, em-dashes and en-dashes.
- **Mistakes which horripilate editors:** 'were' and 'we're'; 'they're' and 'their' and 'there'; 'you're' and 'your'; 'its' and 'it's'; and apostrophe + s instead of plurals.

Polishing the text will require taking a last, long look at it and making sure that there's nothing else you can squeeze out, clarify, intensify or condense. It means paying specific attention to potential repetitions. It means making sure that everything is in place, solid and consistent, and that any glitches that may have appeared in the last round of edits are smoothed out.

Finally, look at the formatting. I'm here assuming that you will be formatting the text to submit it to agents and/or publishers. Keep it extremely simple:

- Times New Roman, 12 point, double-spaced
- Not justified (though I personally prefer to justify text, many agents and editors don't; do check their specific guidelines if there are some)
- Wide margins
- Pages numbered
- File name: yourname-nameofwork
- Saved as PDF and as Word document.

Done?

Well then … let's send it!

Oh, wait. There's still the workshop exercise to go. Because I know you haven't been editing while I was talking. You've just been reading and thinking about editing. Now let's do it …

Workshop: editing a book chapter

For this exercise you need a chapter, or a few pages, of a work in progress, if possible from a piece of work nearly finished by now. I'd like you to go through the different rounds of edits as described in this chapter, and even, if you can, to do a 'pilot' beta-reading (which, I guess, makes it an alpha reading) with the help of a benevolent friend or family member. The point is to achieve, on a smaller scale, what would be necessary on a larger scale of the entire work, but keeping it manageable.

Importantly, *please keep the original version of the work.*

Let's sum up the different stages:

1 Let the piece of work rest for a while; meanwhile, write down aspects you remember as problematic or interesting.
2 Discover the work with fresh eyes: first round of edits (annotations).
3 Second round of edits: modifications.
4 Ask beta reader for feedback.
5 Another round of edits.
6 Proofreading and polishing.

Review

Now reread the new passage, and compare it with the original version. As objectively as possible, how would you rate, on a scale of 1 to 10, the improvements in terms of:

- Structure?   1 2 3 4 5 6 7 8 9 10
- Language?   1 2 3 4 5 6 7 8 9 10
- Characterization?   1 2 3 4 5 6 7 8 9 10
- Depth?   1 2 3 4 5 6 7 8 9 10
- General feel?   1 2 3 4 5 6 7 8 9 10

Ask your beta reader, if they still have some patience, to rate this improvement as well. Hopefully, it should be significantly improved, if not exponentially better. If not … well then, maybe, you're a genius who benefits from having your work entirely untouched.

But probably not.

Where to next?

Well, it looks like we're ready to send off your children's text to the publishing world … Again, congratulations. So few people make it this far, and so few people take so much care to get it right. The next chapter will take through the last hurdle – making your proposal absolutely watertight. Once more, it's important to take time over this step because it can be a determining factor as to whether or not your work will be picked up.

PART THREE
Finding a publisher

17

Almost there! Proposal, pitch and planning the next stage

SUBJECT: GOOD MORNING MOON!

From: author@gmail.co.uk

To: info@thelondonliteraryagency.co.uk ; submissions@agentsforchildrensbooks. co.uk; enquiries@danielbrownliteraryagent.co.uk ; susannajones@thesohoagency. co.uk ; (…+14)

Dear Sir/Madam,

Having always wanted to write for children since the birth of my own children, I now propose to you a picturebook text entitled *Good Morning, Moon*, illustrated by my friend's daughter Cassie. Cassie loves *Good Morning, Moon* and took it to her school where her teacher read it to the rest of the class. They were transfixed! I think *Good Morning, Moon* has potential to become a true classic, and the characters could be turned into plush toys or video games. It is a genuinely fresh and beautiful story which has an educational purpose, too, as it teaches children to say hello to nature and respect the environment.

I am also sending you a 100,000-word adventure story for children between 8 and 15. It is called *Barnaby Barnes's Big Blue Balloon* and it follows young Barnaby (12 years old) and his faithful dog on a tour of the world in a giant balloon.

I hope you will be happy to represent me and say 'Good Morning, Moon!' with me soon around a glass of bubbly.

Yours sincerely, etc.

How many Fatal Mistakes can you circle in this agent proposal? Don't laugh – this is not an exaggeration at all. People send in proposals like this all the time. You won't, of course, and that's why you can afford to titter a little bit. But it's still a crucial stage of your becoming a published author, and it shouldn't be taken lightly.

This is your entry into the difficult world of rejections, almost-acceptances, acceptances and professional writing. Good luck!

Agent or no agent?

For the purposes of this chapter, I'm going to assume that you will actually be looking for an agent to represent your work. In the UK and the United States, it is by far the most common process for would-be writers. It isn't the case in many other countries, including France, where agents are non-existent and authors pitch directly to publishers. But in English-speaking countries, many publishers (especially big ones) do not accept unsolicited manuscripts. Your path to publication must therefore be in two stages: 1. you convince an agent to represent your work, and 2. that agent is successful in placing your work.

However, there are exceptional cases:

- A few publishers do accept unsolicited manuscripts. Small presses, in particular, are generally open to unsolicited submissions. This is something you can check on publishers' websites. If a publisher expressly says that they don't accept unsolicited manuscripts (or 'not at the moment'), then don't send anything. Of course, we've all heard stories of writers landing six-book deals by being plucky enough to send their unsolicited manuscript directly to the head of Penguin UK, but I'm not sure that there's an actual person behind any of those rumours. Don't annoy editors.

- A publisher might find you (lucky you!), for instance, through your blog, or by looking through your work in an anthology or zine, or by visiting your class at the end of an MA in Creative Writing. This happens relatively frequently. In this case, technically, you don't need to go through an agent. However, most people in this case choose to look for an agent before they start dealing with the publisher. Of course, you should make it clear that a publisher is already interested in your work, and agents will doubtless bite.

- You might know an editor in a publishing house, and you can therefore ask her/ him directly to read your work. Generally, editors receive such requests all the time, so they would have to be your close friend to agree. But if they do pick your work, again, you might not need an agent unless you want one.

The important question is – why should you want an agent?

Internet forums are rife with passionate debates about whether or not authors should 'represent themselves'. Here's a summary of the pros and cons of having an agent:

	PROS	CONS
Financial	An agent will negotiate the conditions of your contract, trying to get the most money out of the editor (or the most advantageous conditions in the long term).	An agent takes (on average) 15 per cent of all your book earnings (royalties, advance).
Editorial	Most literary agents are able to work with you on your text even before it is submitted to publishers, to give it the greatest chance of success.	Agents might be looking for, or more comfortable with, a specific style or genre, and ask you to modify your work to fit it.
Career development	An agent will always be on your side, talking to editors strategically about your choices. Their interest in your career is important, so they will be able to advise you on what to write next.	Your agent might refuse to represent some of your work if it doesn't fit with their strategy for you. They could also fail to address your concerns about being pigeonholed, for instance.
Psychological support	Your agent is the person you can vent your anger to and ask for comfort, and who will always be nice to you.	You can become emotionally dependent on the relationship.
Professional relationships	Agents communicate with editors, the finance team, the marketing team, etc., for all matters that are sensitive (e.g. money), so your relationship to the same people can be entirely 'innocent' of such matters.	This also means that you are not directly debating matters which might affect you enormously, and which perhaps you would do differently.
Legal advice	Agents can read book contracts, understand all the clauses and elaborate a plan to get you the most out of them.	You might not have the same priorities as your agent regarding book contracts.

Personally, I fall decidedly within the 'Pros' column. I know writers who don't have agents, but they aren't first-time writers: they're hugely experienced, strong, no-nonsense and, yes, relatively old writers who've understood enough about the system through the years and are able to fend for themselves. In France, I'm always confronted by the 'not having an agent' situation, and it's hell: earnings are meagre, incomprehensible clauses are sneakily added to contracts, and it makes the author–editor relationship unhealthy.

Key idea

Having an agent doesn't mean you should just relax, lean back and not pay attention to anything regarding the legal and financial sides of your job. It just means that you can discuss them with someone who is an expert.

So, in this chapter, I'll assume that you're looking for an agent; if not, just skip it.

Looking for an agent

Finding a good agent entails looking for a good agent. A good agent means someone who is good for your work: someone who represents the type of texts that you're trying to produce, which means they can give you editorial advice, target the right people for your work, and negotiate your contracts according to their thorough knowledge of the market for that type of text.

Where do you find this *rara avis*, then?

- The best advice is to look for books similar to the one you're pitching. You should already be doing this anyway, to assess what's on offer in your chosen genre and format, but it also has another advantage. Most authors acknowledge their agent in their books – and if they don't, you can generally find who they're represented by on their website. This means that you can garner a list of agents who represent the kind of work you're doing. Of course, there's no need to target an agent who already has a client doing *exactly* the same thing: an agent who represents someone writing zombie school fiction might not want to take on your own zombie school fiction. But someone who seems good at representing funny, paranormal children's books might be interested.

- Follow agents on Twitter (we'll get to that in more depth soon) and follow their blogs if they have one. Watch out for announcements that they've chosen to represent someone, and look at what type of text that person writes. You will soon be able to spot patterns in the people they're choosing to represent *now*. Because, of course, whatever you read that is published has already been years in the making, so maybe the agent for the books you've read in your genre has moved on and is looking for something different. On Twitter, you can gauge what they're interested in, in real time.

- For more general searches, the *Children's Writers' & Artists' Yearbook* is a precious source of agent addresses, with clear guidelines. And, of course, online there are countless lists of literary agents.

- Should you try to find an agent in the United States if you're in the UK, or vice versa? Probably not; at least at the beginning, stay in your country, as it will be more convenient for everyone involved.

What you *don't* want is a scam agent, an agent who will ask you for money and/or try to place you with vanity publishers. Such 'agents' unfortunately exist, and they might try to reach out to you if you make it clear on Twitter or Facebook that you're unagented and looking for someone. Of course, real agents might do that, too. So how can you tell? A few guidelines:

- Real agents, if they reach out to you, will make it clear why they're interested in your work, and show that they have read it (they might have seen, for instance, extracts you posted on your website). They will also *never* offer representation immediately, or any kind of contract. They will offer to talk to you on the phone first and/or read more of your work.

- A quick Internet search should help you establish the following: the agent is easily found on the Internet; already has clients; these clients *exist* and are published by established publishers thanks to the agent. These clients are in the same kind of area as you: they form a coherent whole.

- Real agents will *not ask you for money at any stage of the representation process.* That is, they will not ask you for money to read your work; they will not ask you for money to photocopy your work or send it to publishers; they will not ask you for money for phone calls; they will not ask you for money in exchange for editorial suggestions. Agents never ask you for money – whatever money they earn is taken from your earnings, which means they don't earn anything as long as you don't.
- If, after searching, reading their email, and talking to them, you're still not sure if the agent you've found is a real one, it probably means they aren't a real one. Real agents are impeccably professional about what they do, and they will not sound ambiguous.

Book proposal 101: dos and don'ts

What should your book proposal to agents consist of? Here are some dos and don'ts:

- ✓ DO check guidelines on each agent's or agency's website, and follow these guidelines over anything that the following dos and don'ts might state.
- ✓ DO personalize your query, explaining why you picked this particular agent/agency and why you think it's a good fit for your work.
- ✓ DO send a pitch and a full summary of the work.
- ✓ DO state what genre your work belongs to, which age range it targets (not 'all ages', please), and what other works it compares with.
- ✓ DO send your work to a 'batch' of several agents at the same time (although, of course, not as a group email!), unless one of them specifies they want exclusivity on the manuscript.
- ✓ DO wait for the first few to reply before sending to another batch, so that if you get personalized feedback you have the chance to edit your manuscript between sends.
- ✗ DON'T begin your email with a generic 'Dear Sir/Madam' or 'Dear Agent'. Find the agent's name.
- ✗ DON'T send a bulk email to ten agencies! Send emails one by one.
- ✗ DON'T send the whole book if it's a novel. Generally, the first three chapters or equivalent will be requested. There is no point in sending the whole book.
- ✗ DON'T mention that 'children have loved the book', or that 'a teacher you know recommended it to the school', even if it's true.
- ✗ DON'T send an unfinished project. Seriously, *don't.* I know, I know, such-and-such got an agent and then a book deal for an unfinished project. If you pitch a project and the agent wants more, and that 'more' isn't ready, it's quite likely that the agent will be disappointed. They need to know that you can finish a book brilliantly, not just start it brilliantly. Do you want to make things more difficult for yourself at pitching stage? Then finish the book before pitching it.

Let's go through the different sections in detail.

The pitch: hooking a professional reader in a few lines

Your query will have to contain a pitch of the work you want to be represented for. A pitch is a short, preferably snazzy description of the work, giving a sense of:

- what the story is about
- who the main character is
- why it's original and new
- whom it will sell to.

The agent wants to see this pitch because they'll use it, too, when trying to sell to editors. And editors want to see it because they'll use it, too, when trying to sell to the marketing team. And the marketing team need this pitch because they'll want to sell the book to libraries and schools, and to bookshops, who will need a pitch to sell your book to customers. In other words, it's not just about grabbing the attention of the agent. It's about showing the commercial viability of your work all the way down the line.

What if your work isn't 'pitchable'? Well, that's an issue. It's often an issue for me, and I've had countless books rejected because the pitch wasn't strong enough. Many classic children's books have poor pitches, partly because they're too complex to be easily pitched. But sometimes it's just a matter of teasing out the pitch from your story. Ask yourself the questions that you should have considered ever since the beginning of this course book:

- What's my main character's quest and why has s/he been chosen for it?
- What makes the story exciting or interesting?
- What makes it original and new?

A common way of formatting a pitch is the following:

> As soon as 11-year-old Zoe Zaster meets Caspar Flynn, they become best friends. But no one else seems particularly interested in the new boy in the school – in fact, it seems that no one else actually notices him. No one apart from the Headmaster, and he doesn't look too pleased about it … Where does Caspar come from, and what old school secret is he threatening to unveil? A spooky ghost and murder-mystery story for plucky 8- to 11-year-olds.

This format can be broken down as follows:

> When [name and age of protagonist] does [first important episode in the book], s/he [conclusion of the episode]. But [problem raised or start of quest] – and on top of that [tension heightened]. Will/ does [quite general question meant to whet reader's appetite]? A [genre/ format/ type of story] for [age range].

This is a very basic format and it does sound corny, so tweak it as much as you want, but the basic ingredients are there. Another common way to pitch a book is to include direct addresses to the reader: 'What would you do if your mother accused you of murder?', 'Imagine opening the door and finding that a flying saucer has landed on your freshly mown lawn.' Effects of surprise or humour are always welcome: 'Rabbits, mice, kittens, chicks: Jacquie Quirk loves cute and cuddly animals. Especially every Sunday, when she turns into a snake.'

Many agents on Twitter organize 'pitch contests' from time to time, and/or post successful pitches on their websites. You can also find inspiration from looking at blurbs on back covers of books, or at pitches on authors' websites: it is essentially the same exercise.

Summarizing your book

You will need to provide a summary of your book (unless the guidelines on the agent's website specifically *don't* ask for one). This is because the agent hooked by your three or four lines of intriguing pitch will want to see what happens next, and what happens at the end, before they bother to ask for a full manuscript. Yes, it may feel a bit artificial.

This summary doesn't need to be incredibly exciting (though all the better if you can make it so); it needs to be factual and informative. Explain what happens in the story; go through all the major events, and all the way to the end. The length of these summaries will vary depending on the length of the book, but one to two pages is an acceptable format.

Author bio

Your author biography ('bio') should contain useful, relevant and, if possible, exciting information about yourself. No need to list all your qualifications unless they are relevant. Do mention any creative writing courses you've been on, and any previous experience of publication. If you are young, mention your age; agents and publishers are always looking for young authors. If you have a quirky hobby or if you have done any bizarre jobs, mention that as a funny sign-off. This is your opportunity to make the agent want to meet you and, as I will repeatedly say in the next few chapters, *you* are an important aspect of your work in modern-day publishing. So whip up a nice, intriguing biography that makes you sound as interesting as your books:

> *I'm a twenty-three-year-old accidental accountant who's always wanted to be a writer, and I can't wait to be able to trade Ernst & Young for Simon and Schuster on my LinkedIn page. Last summer, I was voted 'best picturebook writer' by my classmates at the Cambridge Institute of Continuing Education Creative Writing Course (6 weeks), though maybe this was influenced by how hard they laughed at my terrible drawings. This is why I am proposing to you only the text of a picturebook, and hoping that a more suitable illustrator will be found. When I am not crunching numbers or doodling unrecognizable animals, I play ice hockey and walk my ridiculous, enormous dog, Zozo.*

As you can see, there's nothing particularly exciting about this aspiring author's life, but s/he still manages to make herself sound personable and endearing, as well as conveying important information (age, experience of creative writing, current activity, ambition and hobbies).

Recap: the letter and proposal

Unless otherwise specified on agents' websites, this is the form that your query should take:

Letter/email:

> Dear Name of Agent,
>
> [Pitch of the book]
>
> [Author bio]
>
> [Extras: reasons for choosing this particular agent or agency, suggestions for publishers who might be interested in the work, comparison with other works.]
>
> [Sign off]
>
> [If you have a website, Twitter account or any other social media presence, indicate it here.]

Attachments:

- One or two pages of summary
- First three chapters of a novel (or equivalent), or full text of picturebook.

Ready! Check once more that you're not sending it to the wrong agent … All good? Press send!

…

Now wait.

Wait.

…

Wait.

How to deal with the wait and rejection

You will doubtlessly have to wait, and you will doubtlessly be rejected. This is fact: even if your work is wonderful and your pitch impeccable, it is extremely likely that your work will be rejected by a number of agents. And that you will have to wait a long time for these rejection letters to arrive.

How long is a long time? Any length of time. Some agents don't reply at all if it's a no. Others do, after a couple of months. The golden rule: don't nudge before at least two months. Not even to 'acknowledge receipt'. If your email is in your Sent box, there's a 99.9-per-cent chance that it's been received and is just waiting calmly in the agent's crowded inbox, and only a 0.1-per-cent chance that it got lost in the ether of the Internet. Don't make them annoyed at you before they've had a chance to look at your work. If and when you really need to nudge them, email them rather than phoning.

While you are waiting, don't complain on Twitter that you're waiting. Don't complain on your blog. Don't complain on Facebook. Don't complain at all. Don't post passive-aggressive statuses saying that it's been too long. Don't Tweet agents directly to ask them (even with smileys and *x*s) whether they've seen your work. Don't sound desperate and amateurish; social media and blogs are a public arena.

And however tempting it might be to follow every single tweet and blog post by the literary agents you've submitted to (and to try to work out whether they're secretly talking about your work when they mention 'a great read over a cup of tea'), it's healthier to stop yourself from doing so. You won't gain anything; it will simply prevent you from being productive and writing more. (Oh yes, did I not mention that? You should be writing something else already. We'll get back to that.)

The first rejection emails and letters will soon begin to arrive. This might be a very difficult time, and again it's necessary to keep away from the 'Refresh' button on your inbox. It's likely that sometimes you'll get several 'No' emails in a day; try not to let them upset you. I personally think it's not incredibly useful to think about 'writers who had lots of rejections before they were finally taken on', because these tales all suffer from survivorship bias (see Chapter 9). It's also very damaging to spend your time on Twitter looking at who got a book deal lately, especially if 'six agents wanted the book, which was then auctioned at seven publishers for an undisclosed six-figure sum'.

> ## Key idea
>
>
>
> Take what's happening to you as *your story*. This is the story of how *you* will be getting a book deal; not someone else. All these stories are different.

And there are, also, different types of rejection letters. Though there's no need to spend too long analysing them, it's worth noting the difference between:

- **standard rejection letters:** 'Thank you for your manuscript. Unfortunately, it does not quite correspond to what we are looking for at the moment.'

- **personalized rejection letters:** these vary hugely. An agent might say, for instance, 'I thought the story was very good, but I've stopped representing this type of work. Why don't you try Caroline Smith at the South London Agency?' Or they might say, 'There is potential, but at this stage the work is not quite developed enough.' This should *not* be interpreted as 'Please resubmit an edited version to me': only 'Please resubmit an edited version to me' should be interpreted as such.

- **almost-acceptances:** this is when, as mentioned above, the agent isn't committing yet to your manuscript, but asking you 1. to resubmit the work with significant rewrites, or 2. whether you have any other work they could look at.

Standard rejection letters can be demoralizing, but they don't necessarily mean that your work was rejected after a brief perusal by the agent's gum-chewing nineteen-year-old summer intern. It could be, in fact, that the intern was impressed and passed it on, but that the agent simply didn't *love the* book. That's the hard truth: agents need to fall in love with your book and your style (or, failing that, feel that it's such a bankable idea that they'll sell it for hundreds of thousands of pounds). Sometimes, manuscripts are good, well written, well structured, and … they just don't have this mysterious extra thing that makes the agent go, 'I'll take it.' And because they can't articulate that easily, they just send you a standard rejection letter.

Personalized letters are a good sign, as they show that the agent was willing to spend some time on your work. In the best cases, they will explain exactly what didn't work with the manuscript.

Under no circumstances should you write back to the agent asking for more details as to why they rejected your manuscript. A brief thank-you email is enough. But as far as they're concerned, their job is done regarding your work. Agents' first priorities are to find their own clients work and to supervise their careers: you will appreciate that when you find an agent. Getting other clients is an important aspect of their job, but they can't spend all their work days emailing back and forth to explain to unsuccessful candidates why they weren't successful. They don't have the time, and it will annoy them. Just acknowledge receipt of their rejection, thank them if they've written to you personally, and move on.

When the wait lengthens

Sometimes rejections accumulate, weeks of waiting stretch into months, months into a year, and you start running out of agents to send your work to, and you start being frankly disheartened about the whole process.

This is a very painful stage, and you need to ask yourself a number of questions:

WHAT KIND OF FEEDBACK DID I GET?

Did you receive only standard rejection letters or personalized feedback? How many times were you asked for the full manuscript? Did you get encouraging feedback or was it mostly non-committal?

The type of feedback you received should help you gauge whether your manuscript ever got close to be picked for representation. Frustratingly, it does happen that a manuscript gets plenty of attention at pitching stage, and you're asked for the full manuscript, and then it's 'No thanks'. If this is the case, you will probably get some feedback as to what didn't work in the full manuscript, and you should take it into account.

Some more difficult questions might emerge:

SHOULD I GET A FREELANCE EDITOR?

This is a very tricky question, and if you're just getting started you're probably not even thinking about it. But after a year of rejections, and having carefully analysed the reasons why your work has been rejected, you might conclude that the manuscript isn't quite solid enough – but that it just needs a push in the right direction to get it to a publishable state.

Freelance editors vary in quality, service and fee, but they are not cheap. A full manuscript critique might cost you upwards of £600, and a query critique £70–80. They might charge you per hour of work (including phone conversations), or per page, or have a standard fee. Unfortunately, it's quite difficult to tell who will be a good editor and who won't, especially as excellent Young Adult editors might be less good middle-grade editors and vice versa, and the profession isn't registered – so anyone can claim to be a freelance editor. The best way of finding a freelance editor is to ask fellow aspiring writers, for instance on SCBWI forums. Look at the editor's qualifications: have they taught creative writing courses? If so, where? Are they also professional editors for a publishing house? Which one? Are they writers? Of what kind of books? They should have some legitimacy, traceable clients and feedback. Feel free to email the people they say they have helped, to obtain honest advice and comments on their practices.

SHOULD I SPEND LESS TIME PITCHING THIS MANUSCRIPT AND MORE TIME WRITING THE NEW ONE?

Yes. You *should* be starting on a new project already. This is for several reasons:

- If you get picked by an agent, they will want to know what else you're working on.
- If you get picked by an agent but they fail to shop your first manuscript, they know they will have something else to pitch quite soon.
- If you get picked by an agent and then an editor, having another project in the pipeline will drive up the demand for your current work.
- Having a new project is necessary for your sanity.

The last point is arguably the most essential. You need to feel that the manuscript you are currently pitching isn't the be-all and end-all of your writing career. I know you might be thinking that it's the best thing you could ever write, and dreaming that it will become an instant success. But the truth is, very few first-time novelists manage to place their work. Most people send a stream of work again and again and again until one manuscript is finally picked. This is completely normal: why should anyone expect you'd get it right on your first try? Well, because the media make you think so. They are wrong.

> ## Key idea
>
>
>
> Start a new project, and you'll see how much better it will be, and how little the first project defined you. You need to detach yourself from this first project.

SHOULD I GIVE UP ON THIS ONE?

This is the trickiest question of all. When should you give up pitching a project? There's no easy answer to that, only guidelines. You should give up …

- when you've used up all the agents who might potentially be interested
- when you don't honestly believe in the project any more
- when you never got anything better than lukewarm feedback
- when you are becoming engrossed in a new project that seems better
- when it's making you feel depressed, ashamed and guilty.

Then it's time to move on. Shelve the manuscript – there will be others. Don't despair – one day it might make an unexpected comeback. Start anew – this early 'failure' won't define your career. Talk to others – most authors had just the same experience.

Get started, seriously, earnestly, on the next project.

Acceptance

But in the midst of all these rejections, an email might pop up that says: 'Thank you for this very interesting pitch and the first three chapters which I very much enjoyed. Could I please ask you for the full draft?'

Breathe!

Then send the full draft (making sure you've got the latest version …) and a professional-sounding email: no 'OH MY GOD thank you sooooo much here is the full draft – I sooooo hope you like it.' None of that. Show your appreciation, but keep calm. They don't know that someone else isn't looking at it just at the same time, and you want to cultivate that ambiguity. 'Dear X, Thank you very much for your interest. Please find attached the full draft of [TITLE]; I look forward to hearing from you in due course.'

They might then get back to you to say that it's actually not for them. But they might say that actually, it *is* for them. If an agent likes a manuscript, they will tell you so quite forcefully, because it is in their interest to snap you up before another agent does. They will say they 'love' the manuscript, they are 'very excited' to meet you and talk, that they 'can't wait' to know you better, etc. Again, stay calm. This is their professional self talking; don't read too much into it. It's great that they want your manuscript. But now that they want you, you also need to ascertain that you want *them*.

First things first: did this agent contact you very quickly after you sent the first batch of manuscripts? Then it might be that you've written something quite hot. In this case, it's worth sending a quick email to all the other agents (separately!) who have got your work, indicating that you have already received interest in the manuscript (don't brag), and that you would be curious to hear their opinion on the matter. This is particularly important if you have a Dream Agent and s/he's *not* the one who contacted you first; email him or her a personalized email, saying that you have received interest from another agent but that you were particularly keen to hear his or her feedback.

If you're not in this situation (for instance, if this is the first agent to show genuine interest in your work after several weeks or months of pitching), reply – again, professionally – that you are delighted that they like your work and would be happy to talk to them, probably on the phone (unless you happen to live a few streets away).

First contact with the agent

Your first contact with the agent will allow you to assess whether you would like them to be *your* agent. You might feel that you haven't really got a choice, but don't let them sense that. In this conversation, you'll see whether your two personalities 'click', and you will check whether you both have the same vision for the book.

- You will hear why the agent is particularly interested in your work. Ask him/her whether s/he thinks it would require some more editorial work before sending it to publishers, and, if so, what kind of work.

- S/he will probably try to 'sell' his or her work to you, as well as the agency. Ask, politely, who s/he has worked with recently.

- Ask which publishers s/he has in mind for this particular work, and whether s/he already has contacts within these publishers. If there's one publisher in particular that you feel is a good fit, suggest it and see what s/he says.

- Talk to him or her about your career plans: are you intending to quit your day job and become a writer, or are you a busy bee with many other commitments? Both are fine, but the agent might like to know.

- Ask him or her what the next step is. Does s/he want to meet you in person? Will s/he work on the publisher proposal with you? Will s/he want to see an edited version?

- Make small talk; see how you get on.

The agent may want to ensure that they are 'officially' representing you by asking you to sign a contract of representation. This is quite common and is not extremely binding: it generally states that you should not simultaneously ask another agent to sell your work, and that, should the agent find a publisher, you agree that a percentage of your earnings will be pocketed by the agent. This percentage, by the way, is generally 10–15 per cent.

If, at the end of your conversation, you feel that you are both on the same wavelength and that you like where this is going, then go for it. *And celebrate!* Getting an agent is an amazing feat. You've gone through yet another hoop. It's likely that, once it's all official, the agent will tweet 'Welcome to @mynewauthor !' and that his or her other current clients will greet you and welcome you into their circle. Get in touch with them; enjoy the few hours of Twitter fame. You might be asked to provide an author bio for the agency's website. Getting an agent is something you should announce widely and post about on your blog (more about that later).

And then rest back for a little while, and … wait again.

Workshop: Writing a pitch and agent letter

This workshop will focus on writing a perfect query for your manuscript. It can be, of course, for a novel, a picturebook, a series, a collection of poems – it doesn't matter. But make it as appealing and catchy as you possibly can. Write a letter, based on the model described above, and a summary of the work. Step by step:

1 Write a pitch for the work, designed to hook the reader. What happens? To whom? Why is it exciting? Who is the work for?

2 Write a personable, informative author bio: who are you? What parts of your life are relevant to this piece of work? What other parts are just quirky or interesting?

3 Provide some desirable extras. Why did you pick this agent? Which other children's books does yours compare with? Is there anything else you'd like to add?

4 Write a summary of the work.

Review

Leave the letter and summary aside for a little while, then go back to it with fresh eyes. How successful are the following on a scale of 1 to 10?

- The reader understands what the work is about. ⬛1 2 3 4 5 6 7 8 9 10
- The reader understands who it is targeted at. 1 2 3 4 5 6 7 8 9 10
- It sounds like an exciting work. 1 2 3 4 5 6 7 8 9 10
- You sound like a professional, interesting person. 1 2 3 4 5 6 7 8 9 10
- The summary gives a clear idea of the work. 1 2 3 4 5 6 7 8 9 10
- There are no typos or grammar mistakes. 1 2 3 4 5 6 7 8 9 10

A few tweaks until it squeaks, and you're ready to send it off.

Where to next?

Next is another wait: the wait for your manuscript to seduce yet another professional reader, the editor. And ... another few professional readers, too – the marketing, finance and foreign-rights teams. This is the true Dragons' Den of publishing. What's your role in all this, and what are you supposed to be doing in the meantime? The next chapter will help you wait without twiddling your thumbs or biting your nails.

18

Shopping time: from agent to editor

This is how I remember the year that my agent shopped my first manuscript to editors.

From: clementineanxious@stress.com to Agent

Hey, hi, how's it going? Any news on the manuscript? x

From: Agent to clementineanxious@stress.com

Hi Clem – no news yet from BigPublisher, but GreatPublisher just said they're not looking for this type of text at the moment x

From clementinesad@tears.com to Agent

Ah well! onwards! Let me know when you hear x

[*Ten minutes later*] From clementineangst@impossiblerelaxation.com to Agent

Have you heard yet? x

From Agent to clementinedesperate@suchalongwait.com

Not yet x

From Agent to clementineedgeofchair@freakingout.com

Sorry, Clem – BigPublisher says no (see below) and I just got a phone call from OtherHugePublisher, they like the style but they don't think it's appropriate for the age range x

From clementinedesperate@devastated.com to Agent

Ah well! Onwards! Ha-ha. Hopefully LovelyPublisher will take it x

From Agent to clementinehitsbottom@horriblysad.com

Hi Clem – I'm afraid it's a no from LovelyPublisher, they've already got a similar book lined up for next year x

[*Repeat ad infinitum*]

Yes, I'm one of those stories that aren't the 'usual' path: picked up immediately by an agent (the day I sent the manuscript), and then … a whole year of unsuccessful shopping. This was the hardest time by far, and it's not discussed very often – there's this conception that you've got nothing to do with the process – when, in fact, you very much do.

Coping with the wait

A few of the rules that applied to 'Waiting for an Agent to Reply' also apply to 'Waiting for an Editor to Reply': among others, *not complaining* on social media, *not stalking* the editors you know are currently reading your manuscript, and *not nudging* them to give you a reply. Remember – at this stage *everything* should go through your agent.

Your agent will probably give you, if you request it, the full list of people they are sending your manuscript to. They won't be sending it indiscriminately to everyone, and there's a reason why they will settle on a particular order. Some of these reasons you might not ever know about, but they're in your best interest. Maybe your agent has just struck a very successful deal for another author with Amanda Smith of Publisher A, and that's why they're keen to present your book to her first rather than to Laura Marley of Publisher B, who did something not very decent to another author. That said, feel free to ask questions about their choices.

Generally, agents will try to sell your books to more prestigious publishers first, and then go 'down' the list. However, they might feel that your book would fit particularly well with a small press they know well. Again, it's up to you to say whether or not you're comfortable with that.

What should you be doing in the meantime? Keep your eyes peeled for books coming out that are similar to your own. Scour children's bookshops. It can always be useful to shoot a brief email to your agent, saying 'I've seen that Bloomsbury has just published a book about an expedition to the North Pole, edited by Zara Lautmann. Maybe you could send it to her and show the similarities with mine, though mine takes place in the Sahara.' Like agents, editors are sensitive to personalized submissions and such details can help.

Feel free to email your agent to check on the progress of the submissions. Your agent will always tell you when your manuscript has been rejected, but if your sanity depends on her updating you more often (to say who's got it at the moment, etc.), then by all means ask. Agents have treasures of patience to give to their clients, and they are generally good at soothing and reassuring them.

 Key idea

Try to stay calm, detached and professional. What you should be doing beyond fretting and refreshing email is polish your online presence, as we'll discuss very soon, connecting with other aspiring authors and 'real' authors, and, most important of all, *working on the next project.*

What if the book doesn't sell?

Sad fact: some books picked up by agents don't sell. Let's return to my own story: my first manuscript never sold. My agent shopped it tirelessly for a year, and though it went to a few editorial committees and received some praise, no one picked it up. As you can imagine, this is quite a crushing process. When you think you're doing things right – landing an agent in the blink of an eye – not landing a publishing contract feels unfair and incomprehensible.

The effects of this long, long, long wait with no success could be:

• you losing faith in your own book: by seeing all the criticism piled up by various editors, you start to see it as a failed manuscript

• the agent losing faith in your book, for the same reasons

• the agent losing faith in you as a writer and client

• you becoming demoralized and not wanting to write another line.

This is why it is imperative that you start working on another project. If this one doesn't sell, you need to be distanced enough from it that neither you nor your agent will think about it as a failure. You need to be ready to move on; you need to have fallen in love with another story.

I finished the manuscript for the first *Sesame Seade* book a year or so after we started shopping the previous manuscript, which was a Young Adult novel. My agent was enthusiastic about *Sesame*, and began to shop it immediately. She never fully gave up on the previous manuscript, but *Sesame* naturally took over and sold relatively quickly. This goes to show that you might not have any idea, when you get an agent, what the next year and a half are going to be like. Maybe your agent chose to represent you on the basis of a Young Adult series and will eventually sell your picturebooks. Again, it is your responsibility, both to yourself and to your agent, to be working on something else while s/he is shopping your first work. Do discuss it with him or her, so that you know you're on the right track, but *work*.

When the book sells

And then one day something amazing might happen: a phone call from your agent telling you …

• that an editor is interested, and would like to take your book to acquisitions, where s/he thinks it has a good chance of being accepted

• that an editor is interested, has no worries that the book won't be accepted, and would like to meet you to discuss a few changes

• that an editor definitely wants the book and is ready to sign the contract now.

All of these are absolutely fantastic news and you should by now be jumping up and down with bliss, trying to spare your agent's eardrums on the other end of the line. I'll leave you to do this for a few seconds …

…

Here we are. Now, you might be surprised to hear your agent's reaction: 'Yes, this is brilliant news. Now let's tell the other publishers who have your manuscript that we've received interest, and ask them to get back to us asap if they're interested, too.'

This might sound very callous to you: who cares about the others? *One publisher* wants me – that's all that matters! But, of course, it's in your and your agent's best interests to play up the competition between different publishers, in order to get the best deal, and not just in terms of money.

So your agent will politely reply on your behalf to the interested editor and say that they will leave another week to other publishers, should they decide to show interest too. Editors are used to that, though I know it sounds extremely scary to first-time authors; I remember thinking the first editor would be so offended not to be immediately picked by us that she'd declare she wasn't interested after all. Of course, that didn't happen.

Your agent will then call up other editors who currently have the manuscript, and who probably haven't opened it yet. S/he will tell them: 'We've got a potential offer. Please take a few days / a week to read the manuscript and tell us if you would be interested, too.' It's incredible how much value a manuscript gains in the eyes of an editor as soon as they hear another editor has their eyes on it. Suddenly, the pile of paper languishing on the corner of their desk becomes A Wanted Manuscript, and they'll be reading it with a positive prejudice, thinking, 'Hmm, I wonder what that other editor saw in it … I guess *that's* interesting …'

If no other editor shows interest in the book, it doesn't mean they all think it's rubbish and are rubbing their hands imagining their colleague wasting money on this pile of junk; it could simply mean that they like it, but don't feel they can afford the time and money it would take to organize an auction. If, however, one or more editors do declare interest, then your agent will organize an auction for the manuscript.

If not, s/he will get back to the first editor and say that they would be interested to discuss conditions. Whether or not an auction happens, you will meet the prospective editor(s), and this will probably happen in person rather than on the phone, unless you live very far away.

Meeting editors

If all goes well, meeting your (potential) editor(s) should become one of your most treasured memories of the Story of How You Became a Published Author; even more so, I think, than meeting your agent, because this time you're *this* close to sealing the book deal. And editors sure know how to make you feel wanted.

If you wrote a love story about two sugar mice meeting in a sweet shop and eloping together, expect to find a small plate of sugar mice on your potential editor's desk. If the heroine of your Young Adult novel is called Daisy, it's likely that a vase full of the eponymous flowers will be in full view when you walk in. If neither applies, you will still be greeted with quite a lot of chocolate, cake and smiles. Your editor will make you feel special. And it's not disinterested, of course: they want to publish your book, and they want you to want them to publish your book.

Normally, your agent will be accompanying you to this first meeting, and you will both be able to ask and answer questions. Here are a few that you can expect to be asked and should have an answer for:

- Do you see this book as the first in a series or as a stand-alone? If the former, do you have ideas for further books?
- What are your next projects?
- How do you see your career developing?
- Would you be willing to do school visits?
- How Internet-savvy are you, and how much time are you willing to devote to marketing and promoting your book online?
- Would you be open to talking to journalists and blogs?
- Would you be open to editorial changes on this manuscript?

Of course, they will be asking those questions much less bluntly than I'm putting them here. Everyone in publishing is eerily cheerful and polite, and it will sound much less threatening than that. But don't be fooled: they like your book, but they are assessing whether you are a good asset *as a writer* for the company. That means someone who is ready to promote their book, to talk to readers about it, to write more, and to edit their work.

This is your chance to be enthusiastic and say that, yes, you will happily set up a Twitter account if you haven't done so already, go to schools, and rewrite your manuscript entirely if they so desire. I'm being, of course, sarcastic. This is your chance to be honest. If you don't want to do school visits, if you're too busy to be much invested in marketing your own book, or worried you might be, you must voice these concerns now, rather than keeping them secret until the book comes out and the marketing team realizes that they can't count on you.

It's also your opportunity to see whether this is truly the right publisher for your book (though you might feel that you don't have a choice). Think about asking the following questions:

- What kind of editorial changes would you like me to make? Ask the editor to be precise: are they planning to make it much more commercial?
- How many foreign sales would you expect to get with this book? What does the foreign-rights team think of it?
- What would be your marketing plan for the book?
- Would I be able to have a say regarding the cover, the choice of illustrator, the back cover blurb, etc.?
- How well connected is the publisher with journalists, blogs, etc.? What exposure will my book receive?
- Might there be plans to turn the book into an app / video game / electronic resource / other?

I trust that you, too, will find polite ways of putting these important questions. Don't ask about advances and royalties, though; this is your agent's job, and this is a nice and cheerful meeting where money is generally not mentioned. No offer, at this stage, has been made, so it's better to keep it all in the conditional.

If you are seeing several editors that day (or over several days), that's great; just don't mention the other editors, and certainly don't ask questions by saying 'BigPublisher told me they expected to sell foreign rights easily – what do you think?' Generally, editors don't know which other publishers are eyeing the manuscript, and it's in your interest to keep it that way.

You will then discuss it all with your agent, to make sure s/he and you are on the same wavelength regarding editors. Much of your discussion will be factual, and the agent will bring in knowledge from previous deals. But you must also acknowledge the more mysterious side of these meetings, which is the *human* aspect. Some editors, however enthusiastic and full of interesting plans, will not 'click' with you as much as others might. This is something you should definitely pay attention to, because you will be working with this person over a chunk of your career, and a non-negligible one at that (your first book!) and such professional relationships are always partly influenced by personal chemistry.

The book deal

At some point that day or the next, one or more editors should make a proposal for a book deal. This is the moment you and your agent have been waiting for, and your agent will take over then – s/he will be receiving emails from the editors and letting you know what they're offering.

At this stage, there will be quite a few things to be taken into account to either decide which offer to take (in the case of an auction), or which way to negotiate (in the case of a single offer). Whatever happens, *your agent will negotiate.* You need to be ready for him/her to say to you that s/he won't accept the offer as is, even if you are jumping up and down begging him/her to just take it. Negotiating is part of the deal, and the publisher will be expecting the agent to haggle.

The following are just some of the parameters that the agent and your will be taking into account (not in order of importance!):

- the size of the advance
- the rate of the royalties for print (hardback and paperback)
- the rate of the royalties for ebooks
- which rights are being waived regarding translation
- which rights are being waived regarding adaptation (film and otherwise)
- how many books you are being contracted for
- the deadlines you are being set.

These are elements within the contract. But there are also other things that are not technically in the contract but will influence your decision. For instance:

- how well you 'clicked' with the potential editor
- the prestige of the publishing house
- the quality of the books they publish
- the style of illustrators they generally employ
- their openness to future changes in your career path with them.

In the case of multiple offers, you might end up with tricky choices to make. For instance:

- Publisher A is a very powerful, very prestigious publisher that would sell foreign rights easily and perhaps adaptation rights. It has a huge marketing and publicity machine. However, it is also very commercial and will want to make sure that your book fits its list by making it what you think is 'less literary'. It might also be keener to keep you as 'the writer of animal stories' that you are now. The advance is very good.

- Publisher B is an up-and-coming, very dynamic medium-sized publisher. It is very well reviewed and has been getting lots of awards lately. The editor is lovely and very keen and she will surely help you polish your manuscript until it sparkles. The advance is small, and they're less likely than Publisher A to sell foreign rights easily – but the book might just strike gold with all the personalized effort it will put into promoting it. It doesn't like niches and is open to your changing your career plan next time and publishing a comic book after your YA romance.

- Publisher C is an established, quite high-quality children's publisher. It gets good reviews, many awards and many foreign rights sales. It is a bit more old fashioned in its style than Publisher A, and it's not as edgy as Publisher B. It is offering a good advance. It will doubtlessly promote the book well and it is particularly good at getting Book Club deals. Publisher C is quite literary, specializing in sophisticated children's fiction, and will push you in that direction.

Tricky, huh? Try adding some extra complications:

- The editor who picked your manuscript at Publisher A is actually covering the maternity leave of another editor, but she assures you that the other editor also loves the book, of course (of course) ...

- Your agent has just struck an amazing deal with Publisher B for another client and has managed to triple the size of the advance. She's confident that she might do just the same this time.

- There are rumours that Publisher C might soon be bought out by Publisher D. And then what would happen to your book? We can never quite predict what individual authors might experience, especially new ones, in such situations ...

Your head's probably buzzing by now, if you thought an auction just meant: 'We'll take the highest bidder.'

Key idea

If there's an auction, you and your agent will have a long, difficult and probably stressful discussion about which publisher to pick. When there's only one offer, your agent will still try to negotiate to get more money and better conditions.

Money matters: frequently asked questions about advances and royalties

I don't want this section to sound like a Writing Salary 101, but it might be helpful to go through a number of myths and questions to do with advance and royalties, as these seem to crystallize writers' anxieties and media hype.

WHAT'S AN ADVANCE?

An advance is a fixed sum of money that is given to you by your publisher in exchange for your book. This money is yours, and you can do anything you like with it (but don't forget that you'll have to pay tax on it …). It will reach you, generally, in three chunks: one when you sign the contract; another one when you submit the final version of the manuscript; and a third on the day the book is actually published. This money goes through your agent, who deducts his or her fees (generally 15 per cent).

No publisher will ever ask you to repay your advance. The only reason this could happen would be if you failed to submit your manuscript on time. Even if your book doesn't sell enough to pay back the advance, this will never be money you 'owe' the publisher. They made a bet on you; it's their fault that they miscalculated it. However, you will not earn any extra money on the book sales until the advance has been earned out.

WHAT ARE ROYALTIES?

Royalties are the money you earn every time one of your books is sold. It is a percentage of the price of the book. This percentage varies according to the type of book (paperback, hardback, ebook) and whether you are the sole author of it (illustrators might earn royalties, too).

WHAT DOES IT MEAN TO 'EARN OUT' YOUR ADVANCE?

'Earning out' an advance refers to the moment when the amount of royalties you have received equals or surpasses the amount of the advance.

To take a (very simplified with unrealistically round numbers) example:

Imagine you earned a £1,000 advance for a picturebook text.

Your picturebook retails for £10; for each sale you earn 10 per cent, namely £1.

In order to earn out your advance, your book will have to sell 1,000 copies. Until then, you are not earning any extra money on top of your advance.

An alternative would be, of course, that your publisher sells your picturebook to a foreign publisher, for, say, £1,000. A good proportion of that (the rate varies) will go into your pocket, that is to say, towards paying back your advance. This is why foreign sales are very important: they can allow you to earn out your advance very quickly.

WHAT IF I DON'T EARN OUT MY ADVANCE?

If you had quite a small advance and you don't earn it out over a long period of time, it's not great; it might mean the book isn't doing very well, as generally advances are commensurate to how many books the publisher expects to sell.

I said *generally*, because we live in a strange capitalist world whose logic is sometimes a bit difficult to follow. In certain circumstances, the publisher could actually expect that you *won't* earn out your advance.

This is the case, particularly, with extremely 'hot' books acquired at auction. Let's say you struck gold with your manuscript: five, six, seven editors want it, it's the Next Big Thing. This could be because of its intrinsic literary merit, but it's more likely to be because they can smell that it will sell. So they need to buy it. And they might make you an advance offer, say, upwards of £100,000.

This is great news for you, as it means you've got that money and no one apart from the taxman will take any of it away from you. But it's also great news for the publisher, because thanks to this advance it has already created excitement around your book. The deal will be announced as 'an undisclosed six-figure sum', and you and your book will be hyped up. The very existence of this advance, in other words, will be part of the publicity plan of the publisher for this book. To put it simply: part of this advance is publicity money.

Now, to earn out this advance, your book, which, let's say, retails at £10 and on which you earn £1 per book sold will have to sell 100,000 copies before your advance is earned out (with or without the help of foreign sales). It's quite a big number, but it's likely that it will happen, since, after all, hype generally works well and people will be curious.

However, for your publisher, it might not matter so much whether you earn out your advance or not. Your publisher earns a larger percentage on each sale than you. Of course, that percentage represents gross profit; it still has to pay bills, and deduct money it's spent on your promotion and marketing, before your book is profitable for it. But even if its net profit is only 10.5 per cent of the book, then whenever you earn out your advance, it will *already* have made a net profit on your book.

So, to put it bluntly, the publisher doesn't need you to earn out your advance in order for it to make a net profit on your book. The publisher might not even believe that your book will ever earn out its advance, because it knows it will make a net profit on it anyway. It might sound callous and cynical, but many books now function on this business model.

Of course, it's *always* better if you can earn out your advance, whether you're a fairly anonymous beginning author or a hyped-up exciting newcomer. Earning out your advance notably means that your publisher is more likely to commission books from you in the future.

I GOT A TINY ADVANCE! WHAT DOES THAT MEAN?

It can mean many things and they're not necessarily bad for you. Firstly, a small advance means that it will be earned out more quickly, which is great. It probably also means, however, that your editor isn't willing to bet too much on your book. This isn't because your book is bad. It's because you're a new author, and the book might be a bit niche, or they know the book won't sell to supermarkets, or that it won't sell abroad. *Ergo*, you're not a good candidate for huge amounts of money. But they still love your book, or else they wouldn't have taken it.

Having a huge advance sounds like a better position, and it's likely that the publisher will be making more effort to sell your book now that it has put so much money into it, but it can put more pressure on your shoulders and lead to more eye-rolling when it turns out Germany and Korea don't want to buy it.

 Key idea

The size of your advance really isn't as clear-cut a matter as you might think. Don't fret too much about it.

Once the agent and editor have talked it through at length, the book deal will be made. It should be said, by the way, that at no point during this process should you be talking about it on social media. You should absolutely wait until the contract is signed before making it public. In fact, do consult your editor about that, as they might want to reveal it at a different time.

So relax, celebrate and wait for the contract to arrive. In this book I won't go into detail about what the contract should contain; but should you have any doubts, join and contact the Society of Authors, which offers a free contract-reading service to all members.

Quitting your day job ... or not: children's writing and money

Yes, I know. All this while I've been saying 'small advance', 'huge advance', without actually mentioning any numbers. And I know you're wondering how much you can reasonably (or indeed unreasonably) hope to earn thanks to your long-nurtured *Wunderkind* of a manuscript. The truth is – there really aren't any 'typical' numbers. I would be lying if I gave you a list of 'approximate' figures for children's books of different genres and different lengths or for different age groups. There are no averages to speak of.

But that's not *really* what you want to know anyway; what you want to know is – can I make a living out of writing for children? Some people (myself included) wouldn't wish to do so for all the money in the world: I love my job as an academic and wouldn't want to be a full-time writer. Even so, though, my earnings from children's writing are a considerable part of my income, so it is important to discuss money matters even if you are not intending to quit your day job.

You will probably have read dozens of articles on the Internet about how dire the situation is for authors at the moment. Though they may vary in dramatic intent, the general message, which is quite true, is the following:

- A handful of authors are hugely successful, and make enormous amounts of money.
- A certain number of authors make a comfortable living out of children's writing, though not much more than the average salary.
- The vast majority of authors make less than minimum wage per annum.

This is true in most countries, which is why what we typically see are people writing 'on the side' of a full-time job, or of a part-time job. But your earnings from writing might be much more substantial than just 'pocket money'. Someone who earns £10,000 a year thanks to their children's writing but also has a full-time job paying £30,000 sees a quarter of their income coming from their books, which is a very welcome addition.

On the other hand, (most) full-time writers will necessarily earn more from their writing than (most) part-timers, because, among other things:

- they will have more time to write more books (= more money)
- they will have more time to promote those books (= more money)
- they will have more time to do school visits (= more money).

Full-time writers will earn more from their writing than part-time writers, but overall they might still earn much less. Furthermore, people who have a permanent job have at least a part of their income that is stable, so it's easier for them to save up, plan for the future, get a mortgage and not worry about where the next contract is going to come from.

You can tell that I'm leaning towards one side more than the other: I do think that it is, financially, a much more advantageous situation to have a full- or part-time job outside of writing, especially for first-time writers. Unless you happen to strike gold with your first manuscript, it's unlikely that you will make a comfortable living out of writing, at least in the first few years.

However, this is only the pragmatic reply. Ideologically, of course, I don't support a system which perennially puts authors in the difficult situation of having to choose between an impoverished career running after contracts in a domain they like, and a life spent 'writing on the side' of a not necessarily beloved full- or part-time job. We should absolutely be supporting the notion that writing in general, and writing for children in our case, is a worthwhile activity which deserves to be paid more, and more consistently. This is why many authors decide to self-publish, or become 'hybrid authors' (authors who are both self-published and traditionally published): they feel that, in doing so, they can recover some power and independence over their earnings, and avoid being in the precarious situation of a 'wait' between two book contracts.

So no, I wouldn't advise you quit your day job just because your first book series sold for £25,000 and that happens to be equal to your yearly salary. Next year isn't guaranteed to bring you the same amount of money. But at the same time, I encourage you to vocally support writers' rights to be paid more, to be paid on time, and to consider their activity not just as a hobby bringing in pocket money, but as a career producing highly valued goods.

Key idea

In a few years, you'll see whether you can reasonably make a living out of your earnings, should you wish to take the leap. It is possible that you might be able to do so.

Where to next?

Well, now that you're 'in' (did I mention you should be celebrating right now? What are you doing reading this book? Go brag to your friends and family!), you might want to know what it's going to be like to work with a team of people who are keen to make your book as beautiful and successful as possible. And it might create some interesting tensions … The next chapter discusses your relationship with your publisher.

19

You're in! Working with an editor and a publishing house

Dear Authorial Agony Aunt,

Help me!

After three years of passion, I have suddenly discovered that my editor is cheating on me with another author. I found out because he accidentally sent me an email addressed to the other author. I immediately knew they'd done it; the email had an attachment: the third version of a manuscript with suggestions for edits.

Since then, I've looked at my publisher's winter catalogue, and I suspect that my editor might well have been having other affairs. Apparently, he's responsible for 'the 8-12 range', which would mean that it isn't the first time he's been seeing other authors. When I think I believed him when he said I had a unique voice…

Also, I read the first few pages of the other author's manuscript, and I really, really don't understand what he sees in it!

I haven't told my editor yet that I found all this out; I just can't. Something's broken inside me and I feel lost and betrayed. What can I do?

Painfully yours,

Speechless Author.

Ah, the joys and pains of working with an editor! The jealousy, the pride, the passion! The worry when you're not getting any awards or foreign sales, and the relief when it turns out s/he loves your next book! It's not an ordinary professional relationship, and editors know it. They will make you feel extremely special – and extremely stressed. But they don't hold *all* the power, and you shouldn't let them take over; an editor will respect you all the more if you keep them on their toes.

Though many self-published authors would argue that they left the 'traditional' publishing system because they were fed up with depending on a whole army of other people who mostly upheld opposite values to them, an author's relationship with his or her editor can be one of the best parts of being a professional writer. So enjoy it.

What does an editor do?

Your editor, especially if s/he acquired your book, is responsible for it from the beginning to the end. This doesn't mean s/he's the only one working on it, of course, but s/he will be supervising it and, ultimately, many of the important decisions made on the book will be his or hers. Of course, the editor will consult (and sometimes be pressed to change things by) the foreign-rights team, the marketing and publicity department, the finance department, and other editors. The design team will have a huge influence on what your book looks like. And many decisions will have to be approved by other people in the publishing house, especially if it's a big publisher: the choice of an illustrator, for instance, might have to be validated by the marketing and publicity department. In smaller publishing houses, editors tend to have more power.

But a lot of your editor's work that *you* are going to see will focus on the following aspects of your book:

- The story itself: plot, characterization, language and so on. This is what we generally understand when we talk about an editor's role: s/he will help you work on your book until it's better quality and corresponds to the age range s/he wants to target

- The overall appearance of the book, including the cover and blurb

- S/he will be your first port of call for most matters related to your book (for instance, s/he will inform you of foreign sales, award nominations and sometimes reviews). You will also be assigned a publicist who will be in charge of marketing-related and school-related news and requests

- Your career development: it is generally in your editor's interest to assist you in birthing new works, from pitch stage to fully fledged book.

There will be moments when you won't see eye to eye with your editor. Frequently, this occurs over such issues as:

- you wanting to be more 'literary' and your editor wanting you to be more 'commercial'

- you wanting your books to be less 'gendered' and your editor insisting on marketing them 'for girls'

- you wanting your books to be for a different age range.

In these circumstances, it's worth remembering that your editor is often equally torn. Most editors are literature lovers; most children's editors have true faith in children's ability to understand complicated books, and not to be put off by convoluted sentences and 'difficult' vocabulary. Most editors would love to publish edgy, interesting, contentious books. However, editors have to negotiate with the marketing, finance and foreign-rights teams, and with their own bosses. There are company policies that also impede them.

> ## Key idea
>
>
> Whatever you may hear from your editor might not be exactly their own wishes, but rather a calculated equation between what they wish they could do and what they know they'll be able to get away with.

The first editorial meeting

In the first editorial meeting, which might be in person, over the phone or as a conference call, you and your editor will probably go over:

- the finalizing of urgent details: the book's title; the title of the series (if applicable); the targeted age range; the genre(s) of the book
- corrections and edits to the manuscript
- if applicable, synopsis and/or partial draft of the second book in the series
- what you should be thinking of doing to promote your book when it comes out (and until then)
- who's who in the publishing house; you might meet your publicist and be taken on a tour of the offices.

This is an exciting time and an opportunity to get to know your editor better, but important information will be exchanged.

Make sure that you voice all concerns that might arise. It's essential to be honest and direct with your editor from the beginning, because you must retain power in this relationship. If, in this first editorial meeting, your editor tells you they're thinking of a sparkly pink cover for your series and you just nod and say it sounds amazing but are actually crying inside, you're already losing. Stand up to your editor; state, politely but firmly, that you don't want to be put in a niche with this first series and ask whether there could be another marketing strategy; offer one.

My warning particularly concerns *niches*, because UK/US publishing is terrible for pigeonholing authors. In other countries, it doesn't matter so much how many different types of fiction you write; in fact, it can look better if you're an all-rounder, churning out picturebooks, YA novels, tween series and funny comics. But in the UK and the United States, it's all too easy to end up being characterized as 'the funny writer', or 'the girly writer' or 'the dark broody YA writer'. This is because it's convenient for publishers to build a brand around an author; to give him or her a recognizable identity.

Often, your books will look the same, even when they have no characters or storylines in common, and they will be expected to have a similar 'feel'.

There's not *much* you can do about this, but there's a *little bit*. It might not seem like a very real threat to you at the minute, but believe me, at some stage you will find it frustrating to be not just pigeonholed as a children's author, but as a 'children's author of funny ghost stories for 6- to 8-year-olds'. Spare your future self the annoyance of thinking that you didn't do enough in the early stages of your career to prevent that. Editorial meetings are your opportunity to state that you will be interested in doing other types of work, that you will draw the line at some stage (e.g. yes to girly school stories, no to pony stories), and that, though aware of the necessity to construct a brand identity, you don't want to close any doors. If you feel they're beginning to pigeonhole you or your work, offer constructive suggestions for how they could pitch your books to a wider audience. If assertiveness is something you truly find difficult, defer to your agent.

You will need plenty of assertiveness, though, to tackle the next stage: edits. Again.

Do I have to accept all the editorial changes? Negotiation and conciliation

But your editor loved the book! Where do all these changes come from? This is the perplexed reaction you might have when the editor discloses to you the vast quantity of edits s/he is asking you to consider for the manuscript. Some may include destroying entire secondary plotlines, moving chapters around, developing a character; things you don't do in five minutes. Normally, you should have seen it coming: the editor, before they acquired your book, should have told you what s/he intended to do. Still, it always comes as a shock when you're presented with the tightly pencilled-over manuscript.

Honestly: after edits, your manuscript will be ten times better. I've never looked at a book of mine and thought, 'It was so much better before.' I don't think many people feel that. Most editors have years of experience, a true literary sense, an eye for detail, and it's in their best interest to spare you unnecessary changes and keep you happy. In other words, what you're seeing here on the manuscript is only what the editor sees as the necessary changes.

Well, *necessary* … We'll see about that. A brief anecdote here: a friend of mine, when he went to his first editorial meeting, was met by his editor with a pencil and a pencilled-over manuscript. The editor said: 'I've annotated your manuscript and edited it. We'll go through it together right now. We'll leave in the annotations and amendments we agree on, and erase the ones that you manage to convince me are not needed.' He then added, 'I've been an editor for 20 years. I've used up a lot of pencils, but I've only ever had one rubber.' And he produced a pristine rubber, clearly never used.

It was, by the way, a joke.

There's a slightly scary but very true motivational statement which applies to edits: 'Edit the hell out of it so that your readers don't criticize the hell out of you.' Editors want to protect you (and, of course, themselves!) against accusations of wobbly plot structure, weak characterization, poor language and so on. You don't want to be that author attacked on GoodReads for resorting to 'InstaLove', flat dialogue and clichéd expressions. Especially now that everyone's opinion on your own work is so readily available on the Internet, edits are crucial.

It doesn't mean that you should always agree to all the edits. Your editor will expect you to challenge some of them and s/he will have factored in that part for negotiation. In fact, you will often be able to tell when edits are entirely negotiable, or even simply suggestions. But sometimes it might sound as if an edit is entirely necessary: your editor might ask you to delete an entire secondary plotline with its associated characters, for instance. S/he will argue that it doesn't add anything to the main plot, that it distracts from it, and that it's not fully resolved at the end: the only solution is to get rid of it.

What if you don't agree? Well, you first have to admit she's got a point. That secondary storyline isn't fully integrated into the overall plot, and it's true that you've had a bit too much fun with these four characters that don't bring anything other than their own story. But you might think that this secondary storyline still provides welcome breaks in an otherwise very busy, very intense plot. Maybe you put it there for comic relief. Maybe the associated characters are interesting and endearing. Try to present all this to your editor – factually and courteously. Then, as it's unlikely to make him/her change his/her mind, you'll have to make constructive suggestions for how you could keep that secondary storyline while making it relevant and interesting. This might include tying it more strongly to the main plot, involving the secondary characters more in the overall resolution, and making sure that, if this secondary plotline functions as comic relief, it's actually funny.

Your editor might still be inflexible, or s/he might tell you to have a go at it and get back to him/her. Then you'll probably realize that it would take much less time and energy to delete that secondary storyline in the first place, but if you really intend to keep it, work on it. Convince your editor that the book can't function without it; that it would be a lesser book. And if you can do so, you will have achieved a rare feat: making an editor recognize that his/her edits weren't actually necessary.

For more minor edits, it's all a question of conciliation and negotiation, and you'll get better at it over the years. Your editor might have linguistic pet hates: s/he might disapprove of your use of the comma, of your Americanisms, of your flowery resort to imagery. This is something you'll quickly learn to joke about, and which can generally be accommodated.

Again, I generally put more in my first draft than I think I can get away with. For instance, as I know that not all of my 'sophisticated terminology' (i.e. difficult words) will be accepted, I put in a third more than I actually feel the manuscript 'needs'. That way, my editor can delete a few and I can accept it with grace and magnanimity, outwardly sounding extremely generous but inwardly grinning a Mephistophelian grin as I recall all the ones that got away. So, if your editor doesn't like one little language tick that you have, but that *you* love, definitely don't self-censor; on the contrary, use and abuse the privilege of putting it in your first draft.

Cover art, blurb, endpapers, flaps: your (non-)influence on them

While edits are quite 'intimate', in the sense that they take place between you and your editor (although, as I've said, some of the edits might be motivated by external forces), everything else to do with your book is shared between different departments. The design team is responsible for producing a book cover, endpapers, potentially flaps. The publicity team creates promotional material. The foreign-rights team integrates your book to their catalogue. As a general rule, the further away from your story this material is, the lesser will be your influence on them.

In decreasing order, here are the things you can expect to have some influence (or not) upon:

THE CHOICE OF ILLUSTRATOR

This choice is often a choice between different illustrators, already picked by the editor. In other cases, editors will already have picked a preferred illustrator and will simply ask you whether you like him/her, by sending you a link to their website. The illustrator will then be asked to produce sketches, which you are more than welcome to comment on. At this stage, it is still possible for you to give constructive feedback: the style is 'too cute' and should be messier; the characters are a bit stilted; maybe we could vary the angles of the different pictures. As long as they're not unreasonable, these requests are likely to be heard. But after the sketches have been approved, there's little you can do in terms of radical changes. Illustrators are paid for their time, of course, and editors won't appreciate you asking them to change everything in the definitive version.

COVER ART AND DESIGN

You will have a minimal amount of influence on the choice of cover. It is possible that you will be asked for your opinion at different stages, but generally your opinion matters less than that of the publicity department, which will probably give the cover art to a bunch of children and ask them which one they prefer. Tough, but fair: you might not like the cover, but if all the children begin to salivate when they see it, then you must bow to their superior taste.

That said, there is some leeway. I'm very particular with colour – I hate garish colours or colours that clash – and though I appreciate that many children's books these days have to look as if they've just come out of a paintball field, I couldn't cope with what the cover of my second *Sesame* book was supposed to look like. I loved the drawing, but the colours jarred – they were was gaudy and loud.

Instead of sending an annoyed email wondering what had happened to their sense of taste, I spent 20 minutes devising a very polite, very positive email, explaining factually why I thought it wasn't quite right at the minute but how easy it would be to make it better. I noted that the conjunction of Sesame's apple-green trainers on a turquoise background was not a very happy one. I noted that it was unclear from the light-purple sky whether it was night time or day time. I remarked upon the incorrect colouring of the Cambridge buildings, which are not that tinge of brownish-green. I suggested that they made the sky darker to show it was night-time, and surrounded Sesame with a white halo to replicate an episode from the book. I made precise suggestions which made it clear that I knew something about colour arrangement (which I do, and it helps if you do know what you're talking about). My editor thanked me and forwarded my email to the designer.

The revised version arrived and it was *perfect*.

This kind of small victory comes at the cost of remaining extremely professional, proactive and positive-sounding. If you sound angry, negative or derisive, no one will listen to you, and you will be known as 'that author who is difficult to deal with'. If you truly feel you can't send an email while staying polite, go through your agent. They will soften the edges of your righteous anger.

BACK COVER BLURB, AUTHOR BIOGRAPHY

These are written either by the author or by someone at the publishing house (with, of course, some negotiation between the two). If you can write good, appealing blurbs and fun, endearing author bios, they will love you.

PROMOTIONAL MATERIAL

You will have very little say regarding promotional material created for your book. In fact, you might not even see it all. The publicity team might send you the press release and the dossier they'll send to journalists, libraries and schools, but it's for information, not for feedback; it will all be printed out already. The influence you can have on this promotional material, ahead of its creation, is solely 'positive': you can only add to it. Suggest, for instance, particular people who might be especially interested in buying the book. Offer to write the blurb yourself. If they ask you for a biography, take this opportunity to make your voice heard. Save for that, there's not much you can do. One type of promotional material you might have more influence on is the website they might create for your book (if your book is a big deal).

FOREIGN-RIGHTS MATERIAL

You will have pretty much zero influence on this. If you ask, you might be shown the Frankfurt or Bologna catalogue with your book in it, and that's all. They know better than you how to attract foreign publishers to your book.

Key idea

In most situations, your editor, publicist and designer probably know best. You might disagree for personal reasons, but it's their job. It can help to think of how annoyed you would be, in your own day job, if someone who's never worked in your profession came to give you advice and contest your decisions. Of course, there are exceptions, and you'll learn to spot them over the years.

Fast-forward into the future: writing a book proposal

This isn't something you need to think about right now, but soon enough – *very* soon, in fact, if the book you sold is a stand-alone – you'll have to strengthen your position within the publishing house by proposing new ideas. In fact, you should already be thinking of the next thing and discussing it with your agent. And at some stage, when the ideas have sufficiently taken shape, you will present them to your editor in the form of a book proposal.

So what should a book proposal consist of?

There's a common misconception about publishing, which is that once you're in the place, that's it – pretty much anything you write will be accepted, and your editor will be extremely open to your new ideas. In my experience, that's not true. That second contract is extremely difficult to get, and it can be heart-breaking to see proposal after proposal being rejected by the editor who adored your first work so much. You'll feel that you've lost your power over the editor; that the first manuscript was a fluke, a lucky strike, and that you're now completely stripped of all your genius.

It's not exactly what's happening, of course. There might be a hundred reasons why it's so difficult to win over your editor a second time with your new book proposal:

- **It's too different from your first work.** Your editor is trying to build you as a brand; therefore they want a homogeneous corpus of texts from you. This is the problem I explained earlier: pigeonholing is extremely frequent. Publishers don't much like to have a debut author spread-eagled on their list between picturebooks and urban fantasy.

- **It's too close to the first work.** This is the exact opposite of the situation outlined above: your editor has a sense of déjà-vu when reading your new proposal. There would be no point in contracting you, for instance, for two series aimed at the same age range, covering the same kind of ground, and in the same genre: you would be competing with yourself.

- **They're waiting to see how well the first book does.** Until they know for sure that you are universally adored by school librarians and passed from hand to hand in the playground, they might not want to commit yet to a second work.

- **Contracting a book from a book proposal is just *that* difficult.**

This last point is important. The huge difference between a fully written draft and a book proposal is, I feel, that the former is exciting and the second is not (or, at least, not usually). With a full book, even knowing the pitch and maybe the ending, an editor can have, for a few hours, the wonder and marvels that are allowed to first-time readers. Book proposals, on the other hand, are quite clinical: though pitches can be exciting, it's difficult to elicit enthusiasm from a summary. Elements that might appear completely uninteresting or convoluted in summary form suddenly take shape when they are integrated within a plot. Book proposals are therefore both a blessing and a curse: a blessing because they allow your editor to tell you not to get dragged into a bad story, but a curse, too, because that story could actually have been a good one. Book proposals allow editors and authors to be conservative and safe.

But now that you're in, it's all part of the game and you will have to abide by the rules … as far as your conscience allows, at least.

Where to next?

Next is what could happen if you don't want to abide by the rules. If this chapter elicited only annoyance in you, if you don't believe you should constantly resort to diplomacy and negotiation over the book you want to write, or quite simply if you think you'd like there to be another way to get your book out there – you might want to self-publish. While this book is traditional publishing oriented, the next chapter will briefly cover the basics of self-publishing, and of hybrid publishing, as a perfectly viable career option.

20

Self-publishing

Good reasons to self-publish (*not*):

• *Fifty Shades of Grey* started out as self-published, and it was then picked up by a traditional publisher and made millions, so it's definitely the way to go.

• The world isn't ready for my genius and that's why it keeps rejecting my book.

• Editors are useless – they don't know anything about literature; publishers in general are out to get your money and won't let you have any of it.

• I don't need anyone to tell me what to do. I can do it all on my own.

• It's the future. In the future there will be no publishers or agents any more. I'm in the future already. The future looks so great when you're in it.

• It'll be easy to fit into my heavy work schedule, and I won't have to work to deadlines. I'll be my own boss!

• I have all the skills I need. I can design, promote, do the layout … It's easy when you know how to do it.

• Children's literature is the perfect type of literature for self-publishing.

Do you believe any of the above? If so, read on – in this chapter we will look at and to some degree challenge some of these ideas.

But first, let's start with the obvious, basic question.

What is self-publishing?

Self-publishing refers to ways you can get a book 'out there' without involving a publishing house. It is distinct from 'vanity publishing':

- **Vanity publishing** refers to a specific type of publishing, through a publishing house, but for which the author has to pay. So not only do you not sell your work (you give money to the publisher 'in exchange' for your work), but you also still have to share your profits from potential sales with the publisher. The supposed advantages of the 'deal' are that the publisher will promote your book. *They won't.* Vanity publishers will take your money, that's all. They might send your books to a couple of journalists and organize one or two events, but that's it. Avoid them at all costs.

- **Self-publishing,** on the other hand, is when you publish your books through your own means, and promote and sell them on your own. In the olden days, that meant paying (an extortionate amount) for your books to be printed, and then roaming the country in your car with copies, hand-selling them to bookshops, to schools or directly to customers. Nowadays, however, with the Internet, self-publishing is *theoretically* free (we'll see that, in practice, it isn't).

When you self-publish, you should be the sole or the majority earner. Of course, many online platforms take a commission on each book sold, but it's not the same thing as a vanity publisher.

Self-publishing is now much more mainstream than it used to be because the Internet and the advent of e-readers have simplified and cheapened the process greatly. Not only is self-publishing cheap but buying self-published books is cheap, too. This means that demand *and* supply have grown – exponentially. There are thousands of self-published books being uploaded daily, from non-fiction treatises on boats to alterglobalist short stories. Self-publishing allows for very niche books to be published; books that would never have found a traditional publisher. It also allows for authors to reap the rewards of extremely commercial books. But the torrent of self-published works has, in many respects, become a kind of alternative slush pile. And, as in every slush pile, there will be treasures. Sometimes.

Self-published works of Young Adult and New Adult literature are legion, and can be enormously popular. They are targeted at an Internet-savvy, story-hungry population in their late teens to early forties. But what of self-publishing in *children's literature* – for instance, books for tweens, or even picturebooks? It's growing, but more slowly. Not all children have an e-reader or a tablet, and even if they do, it might not yet be easy enough for them or their parents to find self-published books for them.

The extra issue, of course, with children's literature, is that publishers are seen to act as gatekeepers. The 'Bloomsbury', 'Hachette', 'Walker' stamps guarantee that the book is indeed suitable for that age range, or else publishers would be held accountable. Parents who could buy self-published works for younger children might be worried that they cannot ensure that the book is of good quality and appropriate without reading it all first. While teenagers will happily seek and download books that certainly do *not* have the approval of mainstream publishers, younger children are still at the mercy of their parents' decisions and debit cards. This doesn't mean that you shouldn't think about self-publishing if you're writing for pre-teens, but simply that you will have to think quite hard about your communication plan.

But first, do you both *need* and *want to* self-publish?

Why and when self-publish?

I went through the wrong reasons to self-publish, but there are some very good ones:

- **Your work targets one particular group of people.** You might be writing, say, stories intended for children who are diabetic, with a diabetic main character. No traditional publisher will look at something so specific; you might have more luck with a diabetes charity but, if not, you could consider self-publishing such works. Many children are affected, after all – not enough to seduce a traditional publisher but enough to ensure that you will be selling quite a few. Plus, it will be easy to target charities, associations and specialized blogs and magazines to promote your book.

- **Your work is too edgy or niche for traditional publishing.** As I've said repeatedly, the UK/US children's literature market isn't open to risk-taking, ideologically controversial works, or books deemed 'too scary' or with 'too much ambiguity'. Your book could be splendid, but too audacious for this market. If it is of very high quality, it could gain quite a following by being self-published on the Internet.

- **You already have a few traditionally published books,** but your editor has rejected the last one you produced; or they don't want you to branch out into a different style or genre. We'll tackle that later: hybrid publishing is a perfectly valid venture.

- **You have a captive audience** and you know for sure that they will be interested in your work, whether self- or traditionally published. For instance, you might be an influential blogger or podcaster of free children's stories you make up, and over the years parents have told you they would love to buy their children a book by you.

- Whether traditionally published already or not, **you want some of your books to be available quickly** or in conjunction with specific events such as a Christmas special or an Olympics special, for example; the timetable depends only on you.

Another two possibilities, perhaps less straightforward and more 'experimental':

- **You've never managed to get traditionally published,** and you want to see whether it's really because your works can't find an echo with anyone, or whether it's because the publishing industry just isn't responding.

- **You know of a small group of people who enjoy your stories,** and you want them to have access to them for a small fee. If it sells beyond that group, great – but if not, it's not the end of the world.

Key idea

Self-publishing shouldn't be what you opt for out of bitterness towards the traditional publishing system; it shouldn't be something you decide to do on a whim.

The most wrong reason for self-publishing is that it would make easy money and won't need much attention. There's nothing further from the truth. Success does not come easily at all, and self-published authors who manage to make a living out of it are extremely hardworking, committed, business-savvy extroverts who produce enormous amounts of writing and tirelessly engage with their readers.

A couple more questions to ponder:

SHOULD YOU SELF-PUBLISH IN THE HOPE OF GETTING TRADITIONALLY PUBLISHED LATER?

This is contentious. Many successful self-published authors assert that they would not give into the traditional publishing industry even if they were asked: they want to earn their own money, be in control, and communicate directly with retailers, customers and schools. But quite a few self-published authors *do* end up being courted, and bought out, by traditional publishers. This is because, of course, traditional publishers have the machinery to take their book to the next level; possibly to obtain film rights, for instance. You don't have to think about that right now, though; when Random House comes knocking on your door sheepishly apologizing that they rejected your manuscript which is now the most successful self-published series for 8- to 11-year-olds, you can take your time and think about it.

CAN SELF-PUBLISHING ACTIVELY HARM YOUR CHANCES OF GETTING TRADITIONALLY PUBLISHED LATER?

There's no easy answer to this question. It depends on what you've self-published, on how well that self-published work was received, and on your potential editors' views about self-publishing. Now that self-publishing is getting increasingly mainstream, the stigma attached to it is gradually dissolving. Still, publishers quite like their 'debut authors' to be as *debut* as possible: they enjoy the virginal blankness of a Google search for their name (apart from a blog, a Twitter account, etc.).

But can it actively discourage publishers from publishing you? It's all a question of quality and branding. If Googling your name brings up a hundred images of badly designed, gaudy covers of self-published books, accompanied by terrible reviews or by an aggressive marketing campaign, and/or if your self-published books are erotic science fiction and you're trying to get traditionally published for a series of pony picturebooks, you might have a problem. If your self-published books are badly edited, sloppy and clichéd, your editor might give your manuscript a pass. On the other hand, if your self-published books have won awards, gained recognition, have good reviews, and are not directly opposed to what you're attempting to publish traditionally, it should be fine. Think about your 'brand' on the Internet when you begin self-publishing, and all will be well.

Hybrid publishing

Hybrid publishing is a rising phenomenon, and recent studies have shown that 'hybrid authors' tend to earn more than entirely self-published authors *and* entirely traditionally published authors. Hybrid publishing refers to the practice of self-publishing some of your works while other works are published by a traditional publisher. So, for instance, you might have a successful tween series with a big publisher, and also some self-published Young Adult books online which sell to a different audience.

There are many advantages to hybrid publishing, on top of the unique advantages of self-publishing and traditional publishing. For one, you don't lose touch with the world of traditional publishing and all the useful contacts in it, and it even brings you readers whom you can talk to about your self-published books. You can also always fall back on one type of publishing if the other doesn't work out. Self-published books can serve to 'pad out' a year of less active traditional publishing.

They can also support one another, if your self-published works are spin-offs from your traditionally published books. You absolutely need to consult your publisher about this, of course, but they might be happy with you releasing side-stories, Christmas specials, novellas or other kinds of creative work linked to your traditionally published book or series – but for your own benefit. An encyclopedia of your own fantasy world, sold for £5 online to an army of fans … Yes, it can be quite lucrative. But, of course, your publisher must agree to it.

Hybrid publishing is something that many traditionally published authors are now turning to, after years, sometimes decades of their writing career. With their experience, contacts and captive readership, such writers can turn to more experimental forms or try new types of storytelling, and they know that there will be someone to buy their self-published works. For debut authors, it is a much more difficult task because you won't have the readership, the experience of a strong editing process or the necessary contacts to help you design, edit and lay out the work.

Online self-publishing: the basics

I'm going to assume here that you will want to self-publish online, as opposed to getting books printed and hand-selling them. That said, getting books printed can be a nice addition to your e-published books, for contests, special editions, anniversaries and so forth. Websites such as Lulu.com allow you to get books printed for a reasonable fee.

There are several platforms for self-published works, but the most famous and the most popular one is Amazon (whether you should encourage it is another matter). Through Amazon, you can package your work for Kindle, and readers from the entire world can look up your book, buy it and review it. Amazon retains a small percentage of the sale.

You can also sell your work through your website, as PDF files: e-readers will have no problem with those. This will involve adding (typically) a Shop section to your website, with a PayPal account.

You can also self-publish for free: giving out freebie stories through your website, or through an application like Wattpad, allows you to build a readership for future (more lucrative) ventures, and to get feedback on your work.

Whichever way you choose, there are a number of important things to consider, which all boil down to one overarching principle: don't be stingy. Self-publishing might appear free, but it shouldn't be. If you're not willing to pay people to help you, then you're unlikely to end up with a good product. You will need to pay for:

- **The book cover.** Even though such works are entirely dematerialized, you will still need a book cover to attract readers. And nothing screams 'self-published amateur' more than a sloppily designed book cover. If you were planning on doing your own, I would strongly encourage you not to, unless you are a designer by profession. Hire a designer. There are websites, such as 99 designs.com, which will even allow you to ask designers to propose a number of possible designs to you before you opt for one. It can be expensive (£200 on average), but it is a one-off cost and you will be sure to have something professional-looking.

- **Illustrations.** They don't come cheap, and if you need illustrations you will, again, need to hire an illustrator – and not your nephew's friend 'who draws really well'. Only professional illustrators 'draw well enough' for a book to look professional. And such people will not draw for free; don't even ask them: it is hugely insulting. Don't suggest that you will share royalties with them to compensate for the lack of advance. Give them a flat fee. With beginning illustrators, you should expect at least £30 per small illustration, more for colour. Established illustrators are unlikely to agree to illustrate your self-published book but, if they do, the cost might be triple, quadruple or ten times that.

- **Editing.** Again, I would very strongly encourage you to hire a freelance editor so that your work is as strong and as polished as it can be. Yes, it will be another £500 or more, but your book will end up being so much better than it is at present – and readers will recognize that.

- **Web design.** We'll get into that in the next chapter, but if you decide to set up a professional website, you will need to pay a web designer.

- **Marketing and promoting.** This will include, potentially, buying advertising space on Facebook or Twitter, getting postcards or bookmarks printed, and of course the running costs of your website. And you will need a professional photo if you want to look good on your website.

Self-publishing a book could – and, indeed, probably *should* – end up costing you at least £1,000. This may sound like a lot, but you have to think of it as an investment: if you are serious about self-publishing, if it is something you are hoping will make you money, you need to be ready to put money into it. No entrepreneur can begin work from nothing. And, frankly, it is still one of the cheapest business ventures you can think of. Just don't be stingy at the start.

Keeping the child reader in mind when self-publishing

This is a tricky one: how do you keep the child reader in mind while self-publishing? Self-publishing is still very much an adult-to-adult business: as mentioned earlier – children don't generally scour Amazon looking for awesome new book series. Teenagers are easier to reach, but if your book is a series for younger readers, you will have to use your imagination. Here are a few tips:

- Illustrations, again, are vital when writing any book for young readers, and so you should make sure that you have found a good illustrator. Try to think as a children's editor would: what would be the most attractive cover for your target audience? Resist the urge to think about your book as 'a book for all ages': focus. If you're not sure, send different designs to parents of children who are in the age range you are targeting, and ask them for feedback.

- Also try to find guinea-pig children on whom to test-drive your (already-edited!) book. Not only will that give you a clearer idea of exactly whom you're targeting, but it might also give you a number of nice quotations to put on your website or in the book.

- Don't forget parents, teachers and librarians, who, as I mentioned earlier, might be the ones who will not be too keen to let their children read self-published works. Try to gain their trust and validation. This will be helpful when thinking about how and where to market and promote your book – having a few contacts in schools and children's bookshops will be useful.

- Polish your pitch: looking at traditionally published books which are similar to yours, make the summary and the pitch as captivating as you can, and as age-appropriate as possible. Make it clear to what genre the book belongs, and which readers are likely to enjoy it. The easier you make it for people to understand what it's about, the better.

- Allow web users to download or read extracts from the book: the first chapter, for instance. This will give them a perspective on the work and could lead them to ask their children if they'd be interested in reading more.

Above all, remember that it will be harder to get your book into the hands of children than it would be if it were a printed book with the stamp of a traditional publisher. You need to be ready for people being suspicious about it, and you need to have the confidence to tell them about it and convince them that it is, in fact, just as good as traditionally published children's books.

You are not alone – counting on others when self-publishing

Despite the 'self' in the word, you are not alone in this enterprise; or, rather, you *shouldn't* be alone. Lean on a strong team: a designer, an illustrator, an editor, a web designer, maybe a publicist. These professionals will help you make your work professional. Also lean on friends and family: give them material that will help you spread the work about your book: business cards, postcards, flyers. Don't turn them into an army of obnoxious marketers but, if they like your book, ask them courteously to help you sell it. Encourage readers to leave reviews on various platforms. Make friends with bloggers and get them to review your book. You will gradually develop a base of fans, interested readers and professional readers – as well as teachers, librarians, parents and, of course, children – who will be willing to tell other people about your work.

It will be difficult, tiring and sometimes cringe-worthy to have to market your book – and yourself – so much. But that's the choice you're making if you decide to self-publish.

Where to next?

The next chapter will be, precisely, focused on promoting and marketing your book, which is as important if you're self-published as it is if you're traditionally published. These days, publishers are very reliant on authors to market their own book and, although you will be assigned a publicist, they will expect you to do a lot of the outreach work.

PART FOUR
Finding readers

21

Promoting your book: the basics

When my first book was published in 2010 in France, I waited until the day it came out before writing a Facebook status. Along with a link to the publisher's website, it went something like this: 'Hey, everyone … how's it going? Just a little thing, I've got a book out, and, like, no pressure because I hate that kind of self-promotion thing, but if you want to check it out … Anyway, bye.' Needless to say, everyone was fairly surprised, apart from the two or three people I'd dared to warn in advance that I had a book coming out. Perhaps unsurprisingly, that book sold a small number of copies and then vanished from all bookstores.

In the UK or the United States, this would *never* have happened: your publisher will corner you, early on, to ask you about your strategy regarding promotion and marketing. The publisher will have a Twitter account and a Facebook page, and will build up anticipation before your book comes out. Still, on your side it will be about more than just planning a promotion plan for your book. It will be about *doing* it. And unless you're, by nature, über-confident to the point of arrogance, it might feel extremely difficult to gather the strength to actually tell people about your book – and tell them in a way that will make them want to buy it.

This chapter will show you the basics of how to do this. And, hopefully, how not to sound like a pretentious prat or a shy wimp in the process.

Don't be ashamed of calling yourself a writer!

Writers are, generally, introverts. Apart from very few specimens, the writers you see giving countless interviews, presenting to hundreds of people, signing books tirelessly and wittily, and mingling with other writers at launch parties had to teach themselves to become extroverts. They had to practise giving talks; they had to practise interview techniques; they had to practise small talk, they had to practise acting like people who enjoy being around people. After a while, you might end up convincing yourself that you were always an extrovert at heart, but I don't think that's true. I think you just learn to become better and better at acting like an author.

And a crucial point of this performance is to assert yourself as a writer, namely, to say, 'Hi, I'm X and I'm an author.' Weirdly enough, this simple sentence is extremely hard to utter for many debut authors. You might find yourself suffering from impostor syndrome – particularly if you think your first book is a fluke, if not many publishers wanted it until some tiny press became enthusiastic about it, or if you don't know any other authors and are quite awed by the circles of chatty literati you're suddenly entering.

You might also think that your £5,000 advance, although a very welcome chunk of money for your ISA this year, doesn't qualify you as 'a writer', and certainly won't allow you to quit your day job any time soon. That doesn't matter. You deserve to be called a writer just as much as Lemony Snicket or Michael Rosen; you are no different.

 ## Key idea

Calling yourself a published author has nothing to do with the size of your advance, or your day-to-day job, or the publisher who publishes you, or how long you've been writing.

The first step in promoting your book is therefore to practise saying to people, when they ask you what you do, that you're a writer. Or, if you prefer, that you're 'a teacher and a writer', or 'a consultant and a writer', or 'a plastic surgeon and a writer'. Don't tell them you 'also write on the side', or that you 'write as a hobby'. Your books are available for everyone to buy; they are making you and your publisher money. *You are a writer.* Tell people, not arrogantly, but informatively; there's no need to make a big deal of it but, if they ask you more about it, you need to be ready to talk about your work.

Don't hesitate to say, in addition, that you are a *children's* writer. You will find that being a children's author makes people particularly curious about your work (some people, of course, will also be immediately derisive, in which case you can just move to talk to someone else). Most people have children or grandchildren, or know people who have children and grandchildren, and I have found that people who are vaguely connected to small humans are often desperate to find good children's books for them.

They generally have quite a narrow view of what children's literature consists of. They'll ask you: 'Are your books appropriate for seven-year-old girls?' as if all individuals of that description had exactly the same tastes.

That doesn't matter so much; a surprising number of people will be extremely keen, once they hear you're a children's writer, to buy your books, get you to sign them, and gift them to their niece/son/goddaughter/neighbour's children. This can happen anywhere and at any time, and it is all part of good book promotion – so don't shy away from telling people you're a children's writer. It could lead to easy and friendly sales. This is especially the case if the people you meet have never encountered 'a real writer'; the novelty wears off if all your acquaintances are already equipped with plenty of writerly friends.

Again, try to motivate your friends and family to tell people they meet about your newly published books. There's no need to turn your family home into the *MadMen* headquarters, but if they inform their child-friendly acquaintances about your children's books, it will multiply their chances of being bought. Word of mouth is extraordinarily powerful – the *Harry Potter* series was not pushed by its publisher very much until it became apparent that hundreds of children and parents were talking about it in playgrounds and at the school gate.

People who count: booksellers, librarians, teachers

That was the nice(ish) aspect of book promotion. By far the most cringe-worthy aspect of having a book published is going to meet people who are professional readers of children's books. They, on the contrary, will be used to children's writers. They will look at you and your work with the trained eye of an expert reader, and they will have their own expectations. You will need to convince them because they are the people who really count.

BOOKSELLERS

Booksellers are crucial. In the few weeks leading up to your book coming out, go on a tour of various booksellers in your neighbourhood or town, and ask to see the managers to discuss potential collaboration. This is excruciatingly difficult to do if you're shy, but it is indispensable and your publisher will doubtless insist on it. Keep it professional: explain what your book is about, say that you are a local author, that you would be interested in doing events (if you are!), and give the bookshop owner a copy of your book as well as, if possible, a promotion pack from your publisher. Ask them if they will stock your book, hinting at the fact that several people around the area will be interested in buying it. Don't be pushy or pretentious, but be confident: make it clear that it is in their interest to stock the book.

A note on bookstores: there are very few bookstore chains still in existence in the UK, and Waterstones does not stock *all* books that come out, even from very big publishers.

The decision is made centrally, for all the Waterstones branches in the UK. You may be disappointed to find out that your book is not being sold in Waterstones shops. However, individual Waterstones outlets do have the option of ordering books that have not been ordered centrally, so it is worth paying them a visit, introducing yourself as a local author, and getting them to order a few copies of your book. If they see that the book does well, they will order more.

Independent bookshops are typically receptive to local authors' requests, and they will probably order your book if you pay them a visit. However, they often function on a sale-or-return basis. So it's crucial for you to get sales in brick-and-mortar bookshops if you want to increase the visibility of your book and the faith of local booksellers. Tell people you know to buy your books in shops rather than online.

Booksellers who love your book will be of phenomenal help. They will promote it to schoolteachers and parents, hand-sell it, put it on display. Some authors who are particularly good at arts and crafts offer to create special displays for their books at their local bookshop, often tied in with an event or a launch. This is the kind of relationship you want to develop with the booksellers near you, and it will be helpful throughout your career.

SCHOOLTEACHERS AND SCHOOL LIBRARIANS

These are people who will be able to spread the word about your book to parents and children. They may also invite you to do school visits, buy your books for the library, and perhaps even study them in school.

If you have no contacts with local schools, it may be difficult at first to get in touch with teachers and librarians; ask your publisher for help. Schools are busy and rarely reply to speculative emails from writers offering school visits. To increase your chances, insist that you are a local author, and highlight – however hypocritical it may sound to you – the educational potential of your books. Professional readers in schools are always cautious about what to recommend to parents and children, and they will be more likely to spread the word about your books if they deem them to be age-appropriate, not offensive, and of educational value.

Again, giving out free copies of books can help, though this can go only so far; you won't be receiving many author copies, and you can't just give them all away with no guarantee that they will actually be read. Trade a copy in exchange for it being the book chosen for the school's next book club or in exchange for a (paid) school visit, or as a prize in a school-wide writing competition revolving around your books.

Key idea

Professional readers of children's books should be your main target in the months and weeks coming up to your book being published, and this will probably be the most tiring and difficult task for you.

Getting in touch with reviewers

Depending on the age range your book is targeting, and on the type of book, it will be more or less easy to get in touch with reviewers. Generally speaking, reviewers are book bloggers: don't count too much on journalists, unless you are already in contact with some. The status of children's literature in the media in the UK is appalling. *The Times*'s firing of their only children's book reviewer, much-decried among children's literature people, went unnoticed in the general press. It is online that parents and teachers now go to find reviews of children's books and keep informed about what's being published. Schoolteachers and librarians also get their knowledge from professional magazines such as *Carousel*, which it is your publisher's responsibility to target.

Unfortunately, not all children's books are reviewed equally online. Young Adult literature dominates the book blogging world, with hundreds of hugely committed young (and slightly older) reviewers who are also GoodReads- and Twitter-savvy. If your book is YA, it will automatically attract attention in those circles. Your publisher will be sending proofs to dozens of selected bloggers, and you can count on quite a few reviews. It is a good idea to 'make friends' on Twitter or Facebook with YA book bloggers long before your book is out, and to build anticipation for it over a period of several months.

For picturebooks, there are also a good number of specialized websites and blogs, and they will also find their way into parenting forums. Again, contacting these people on Twitter, Facebook or through their blogs can be a useful strategy.

However, between picturebooks and Young Adult literature, the cyberspace is desperately silent. Your book for seven- to nine-year-olds is unlikely to be reviewed very much, unless it is an astonishing success. For this age range, publishers count much more on professional journals and magazines or on direct contacts with schools. This could be different, of course, if your book has a particularly 'hot' or controversial topic, or if you're a celebrity; but if your book is 'just' a nice, mainstream, funny ghost story, it might sell by the thousands without getting more than a handful of reviews.

How do you contact book bloggers without sounding obnoxious? The most subtle strategy is to get in touch on Twitter, making friends with them long before asking them to do anything for you. Follow them, and join the conversation: reply to their tweets, retweet their reviews, get to know them personally. Don't think of it in an instrumental way. Chances are they will notice your website and see that a book of yours is coming out soon. Ask them politely if they would like to be added to the list of advance reading copies (ARCs) sent by your publisher. If so, tell your publicist. Remember that nothing compels any book blogger to write a review for books they receive, and of course nothing compels them to write a *good* review. Be canny here – if you see that blogger X detests David Walliams, and your book is a funny and quirky old-fashioned story in the style of Roald Dahl … don't tempt fate.

Keep tabs on who is currently reviewing your books or has reviewed them in the past; use an Excel spreadsheet if necessary. This information will be precious to you in the future: for the next book, you will be able to tell your publicist the names of people who have warmed to your work. Don't send books to, or don't ask for reviews from, people who make it clear that they want to remain independent: many book bloggers explicitly refuse to be given books in order to be impartial in their reviews.

Contacting professional reviewers isn't something you just do in the build-up to the book release; it will go on and on through the years. You may be surprised to find that a book that garners almost no reviews and is almost unnoticed at the beginning of its lifetime will finally begin to be reviewed months, even years later. If you're a debut author in a not-very-hot genre that isn't often reviewed, be patient. Don't think that the absence of reviews means that the book isn't actually being read; remember that your target audience – children – don't often bother to post reviews of the books they like, or have the opportunity through their school blog to review books they enjoyed. Kids might be talking about your book right now in playgrounds all over the country, and none of it will be visible on the Internet until a blogging-savvy parent, teacher or librarian happens to pass by them.

To launch or not to launch?

When your first book comes out, it's a good idea to hold a launch party. Don't expect there to be a launch for each of your books, especially if you're writing a series; but the first one is always worth celebrating. Discuss it with your publisher well in advance. You will need to establish:

• how much the publisher is willing to pay for food and drink
• where the book launch could take place
• how many people you can invite
• who can come from the publishing house.

The loveliest launches are the ones that take place in independent or intimate bookshops where people deeply care about you and your work. Tell your friends and family, as subtly as you can, that they will be expected to buy the book there – it's hugely impolite for your friends to turn up with Amazon-bought copies for you to sign, and then drink three glasses of wine and eat all the food (it unfortunately happens). The bookshop will put your books on display, sometimes throughout the whole day, and for them it is an easy way of selling 30, 40 or 50 copies of your book in just one evening – not to mention other books that your guests might also find themselves drawn to when the alcohol rises to their heads.

Book launches are great parties, and you can make them even better by doing the following:

• **Make decorations** that play on the theme of your book: a cardboard castle for your medieval mystery story, plastic spiders for your Halloween-y picturebook …
• Ask your publicist if s/he will provide you with **bookmarks, stickers or postcards** with your book on them.
• **Provide special cakes and treats.** I had, of course, a ton of sesame snaps for my *Sesame Seade* launch.
• **Include speeches from different people:** yourself, the illustrator, your editor, your publicist … Keep them brief and funny. Do think about what you are going to say

beforehand. I improvised mine and ended up suggesting that all my friends who didn't know one another before that evening might hook up during the course of it. Not hugely child-friendly.

- **Give a reading:** again, keep it short, and if you're a bad reader, don't do it.
- If there are children there, prepare **child-friendly activities** for them in relation to your book. It might be a good idea to use them as a pilot study to rehearse, in miniature, your presentation to schools – why not?
- A **book signing** is a necessary part of your book launch, and you might find it surprisingly exhausting – partly because you will know everyone there and will have to talk to them while thinking of witty things to say (ah, the life of the artist!).
- **Take pictures with a good camera.** They will be useful for your memory shoebox, but also for blog posts.

Invite as many people as the bookshop will let you: friends, colleagues, family, Twitter and Facebook acquaintances. Make it clear that people can come with their children and with friends (though they will have to RSVP). The more people that are there, the more likely you are to sell many books on the day and, of course, the more animated your party will be.

Radio, TV, printed press, blogs: ten interview tips

Finally, in the run-up to the release of your book and shortly after, you will be asked by all kinds of different people for interviews, descriptions of your book, author biographies, and to reply to various questions. Those are fun at the beginning, but they are very time-consuming and can become a real source of anguish, because they are, of course, your opportunity to make your book sound eminently buyable. You will probably spend much more time on them than you should, and make common mistakes: long answers, a very earnest tone, and descriptive rather than entertaining replies.

Furthermore, the style of interview will depend on the medium. If you're replying by email, you have plenty of time and can even run your answers past your publicist or agent if you're really insecure. If you're on the radio or on TV, nerves will have to be factored in. If you're being interviewed by a journalist who will then write up the interview, you have little control over what s/he will keep: do everything you can to have the right to read the interview before it's printed.

Here are ten tips to make these first few interviews as compelling as possible:

1 **Before the interview, make a list of the things you really want to say.** This list shouldn't be longer than three or four items, but consider these as crucial points to make in answer to the questions you're asked. These points, of course, should be 'hot' enough that they will increase interest for your book. For instance, your book might be: about autism; drawn from your experience as a carer for autistic children; and already auctioned for film rights. Those things are exciting: you need to talk about them. To you they might be much less important than the fact that the book is a rewriting of the myth of Theseus, or that you agonized over the gender

of the protagonist. But these should in fact be supplementary items on the list, only tackled if you get the time and the opportunity.

2   **Twist your answers so that you can place the items on your list.** This is a well-known trick of interviews, and politicians are very good at it. If you're asked where you get your inspiration from (as you certainly will), go straight to the point: 'Well, in this particular case, I was inspired by my own experience as a carer for autistic children …' Don't waste time talking about the fact that you don't know where ideas come from and so forth. Use it as an opportunity.

3   **Keep all answers brief.** For blog interviews, people won't read long blocks of text: paragraphs should be four lines or fewer. For radio or TV interviews, unless they're live, you will be edited down if you don't keep it short. And if it's live, you will be interrupted – sometimes in quite a humiliating fashion – if you go on and on.

4   **Keep important matters at the beginning and at the end of each answer.** In the middle, you can afford to waffle on a little bit about your writing life, about the more literary aspects of the work, etc. But if you have important points to make, make them first or last.

5   **Pre-empt the questions that will be asked.** Some of them will recur: 'When did you start writing?' 'What's your favourite book/author?' 'Where do your ideas come from?' 'Do you have a working routine?' Others will be specific to your book: 'How easy was it to think like an autistic child?' The more you rehearse these questions, the crisper your answers will sound.

6   **Be funny and witty.** This is very hard for many authors, whether or not they are introverts, and especially for authors of 'funny' books: it doesn't follow that you can be funny in person when you manage to be funny on the page. But people must warm to you, and humour is the best way of ensuring that they will in such a short amount of time. Self-deprecating humour, in particular, can be very effective, but don't say that your book is rubbish …

7   **Don't come across as arrogant or proud.** Insecurity often translates as an excess of confidence in interviews, and it can be very grating, particularly with young authors who've got everything to prove. Watch your vocabulary, watch your attitude. Be gracious to other authors; acknowledge sources of inspiration, show respect to your peers, offer reading suggestions in similar genres to your own. Be nice.

8   **Narrate personal stories or anecdotes if they are relevant.** People will be drawn to your work much more if they can see in the interview that you are an empathetic person with an interesting and complex life story. Don't reveal things that you might then regret, but if something in your private life is relevant to your book, do mention it.

9   **Don't express bitterness towards anyone, especially not the publishing industry or readers.** I once heard a catastrophic interview with a debut author who ranted on about how difficult it is to get published, and how frustrating it is that readers can't seem to be able to tell the difference between a first-person narrative and an autobiography.

10 **Keep the book in focus at all times.** Ultimately, this isn't about you: it's about selling your book to people who will like it. Prepare for interviews by gathering anecdotes

surrounding the book and reorient every question towards the book: make the book the star of the interview.

You've done all this? Great! But what if the interview, when it comes out, is unrecognizable?

That's unfortunately something that happens very frequently. You might have said that your favourite book was C.S. Lewis's *Narnia* series but that you grew to dislike them because of their sexism, and go! The interview title will read: 'Get rid of *Narnia*, debut children's author recommends.' You can bet that no one will pay any attention to your book, but that you will gain a flurry of Tweets alternatively supporting and insulting you. Don't waste too much time and energy apologizing, saying that your words have been cut or simplified, and don't reply in anger or in agony. Write a brief blog post, to the point, to defend your position, and let it be ancient history. Everyone will have forgotten your existence tomorrow anyway.

Where to next?

Well, that's a cheerful way to end a chapter! Let's not be too pessimistic – not everyone will have forgotten. And especially not if you are present online. In the next chapter we'll get to something I've been hinting at for quite a while now – the necessity to have a website, an online presence, and the advantages and disadvantages of being an author in this permanently connected world.

22

Building an Internet presence

'Good evening, darling! How was your day?'

'Not great. I tweeted 12 times and no one replied.'

'Ah. Did you make progress on your manuscript?'

'Oh, yes, I wrote a couple of hundred words. But then I decided I'd write a blog post instead on procrastination and how difficult it is for authors to focus.'

'And … did that go well?'

'Yeah, I shared my blog post on Facebook and it got 25 likes. Oh, 26!'

'Hmm. What else have you been up to?'

'On Pinterest, you mean?'

'…'

The life of a full-time or even part-time author these days is very much taken up by technology. Unless you're a practising Luddite … No, sorry – *even if* you're a practising Luddite, you'll be politely asked to become the 2.0. author and socio-technological being that everyone expects you to become if your books are going to encounter even a tiny bit of echo among readers. Your publisher will want you to promote your book online and develop a *platform*, that is to say a corner of the Internet that is yours and that people are willing to visit.

This is, of course, free work. Does it ever make any money? Well, certainly sometimes. It's not uncommon to get emails from people you don't know telling you that they stumbled across your blog, liked your style and bought your book. You often see people tweeting to one another – 'Which book should I read next?' – and actually following recommendations. Good books that started out relatively unnoticed can gather momentum online.

Yes, *but*. While you're on the Internet doing all this free work, you're not writing your next manuscript. Many authors get sucked into online promotion and marketing, partly because they feel they ought to, and partly because it's fun, but it can also be a waste of time; especially if it is done without method, without warmth and without limits.

Let's start with some thoughts on 'virtual' versus 'real' interactions. However you may feel about online 'life' and relationships, don't let anyone convince you that they're not 'real'. There's nothing 'virtual' about being online, apart from the less tangible mode of exchange with people. If you use the Internet well, if you become comfortable with it, you will make very real friendships, acquaintances and work contacts. You will very really promote your book, and it might turn into very real sales. You will encounter very real readers. It will be very really gratifying, exhilarating and fun.

But, of course, the Twittersphere, Facebook and blogs are also, by nature, extreme. You encounter all kinds of people, who behave online differently than they would in 'real' life. They might be excessively enthusiastic, or excessively awful and critical. Some reviews on GoodReads might knock you out for several days. Some comments on your blog might take your breath away. And if by some sad twist of events one of your offhand tweets is misinterpreted, you could be exposed to a torrent of hatred. It's a strange world, constantly changing, where the most felicitous and happy things can occur, but also a crowded, ferocious world, where everyone is attempting to grab everyone else's attention and to feed off the successes or misfortunes of others.

So, in the words of Albus Dumbledore: 'Use it well.' It's probably more dangerous than an Invisibility Cloak.

Social media: how much do you need?

It's a matter of compromise. There are many books I don't like – even some I hate – by people I know, personally or online, and by publishers I know – some of which publish me. I just don't say it. If I were a reviewer or a blogger, or even solely a children's book academic, I could afford to publish bad comments about other people's books. As a children's author, you can't. You would gain a terrible reputation, and your reputation matters to your publisher. You have to be reconciled to the idea that your actions involve the responsibility of your publisher to a large extent, especially if you are tweeting and Facebooking explicitly about children's literature, publishing and writing.

A lesser 'risk' of social media is making friends only with other authors. When you start noticing that your timeline is full of complaints about writing, of '#amwriting' (the either most oxymoronic or most pleonastic hashtag in existence) and of book (self-) promotion, it means that most of your contacts are writers. And though that's great – you'll probably make friends with people with whom you have a lot in common – it also means that you're not truly reaching out to your potential readers. Sure, some of these writers might pick up your book, especially if they are genuinely interested in children's literature or if they themselves have children – but they're not your target audience.

Finally, don't set up an account for *all* the social media websites in existence. There's absolutely no point in being everywhere; pick two or three, maximum, and invest your efforts and time into updating them.

Key idea

Only use social media you *enjoy*. If you're doing it reluctantly and grumpily, your 'online persona' will be that of a reluctant and grumpy author.

With those caveats in mind, here's a quick overview of the main social media websites you might want to use:

Facebook and Twitter

FACEBOOK

To me, Facebook remains the friendliest and the most useful social medium. To use it at its fullest, create 'lists' of friends. Your closest friends will have access to all your statuses and pictures, your acquaintances to a few less, and your 'professional' list to even fewer. Juggling with these isn't difficult at all.

I would advise against creating an author fan page when you're just getting started. Many people have stopped 'liking' pages because there are too many. And Facebook is now configured so that pages don't reach out to everyone who subscribes – this is in an effort to get people to pay to enhance the visibility of their posts. Additionally, updating an author page as well as your personal profile can get tiring. And, finally, your author page might end up sounding like a torrent of self-promotion, and put readers off.

Instead, enable 'following' on your normal Facebook profile. People you don't know can now have access to your 'public' updates. You can then strategically choose which statuses and pictures to publish as 'public'. You can also decide whether your followers can like or comment your posts.

Facebook is particularly multifarious: you can have short, fun updates, but also long statuses; you can link to your blog posts, share reviews, share pictures, share articles. These shares have a longer lifespan than a tweet, and can trigger interesting and useful conversations.

TWITTER

Twitter, it seems, is *the* social network for writers, illustrators, bloggers, editors and agents. It is extremely likely that your editor and agent will be on it, as well as most writers you will meet. Twitter can be, at first sight, quite daunting and unfriendly. You will need time to build up your follower count, and to understand exactly what on earth you're supposed to be talking about.

This is because arriving on Twitter is very much like stumbling into a room full of people who aren't interested in talking to you. You will need to signal to them that you exist, by following them – think of it as politely cough near them. If they like the sound of your bio, and visit your website and like it, they might follow you in return.

Another way of gaining people's attention is by responding to their tweets – don't feel that it's rude or weird: that's what Twitter is for. In fact, you won't be using Twitter fruitfully if you just take it as your personal broadcasting station, screaming at the top of your voice and not engaging in conversation. Participate, and people will start paying attention.

Twitter can be tiring, because many tweets are very silly; this seems to be endemic to the network and, unfortunately, the children's literature contingent on Twitter is no exception. For one or two interesting tweets, links to fascinating blog posts or insightful reviews, you might have to wade through dozens of very silly statements. You have to accept some of the silliness, but it can get draining.

Twitter also has the flaws of its qualities: it is instantaneous and brief, but therefore it is also extremely ephemeral. Your tweets will be immediately sucked into everyone's crowded timelines, and unless they get immediately picked up and retweeted, 90 per cent of them will fall into immediate oblivion. Do feel free to tweet several times about 'important' news at different moments of the day, since people drop in and out.

GENERAL TIPS FOR BOTH FACEBOOK AND TWITTER

For both Facebook and Twitter, here are a few general tips:

- Share links, especially to articles or blog posts that are relevant to your activity but that aren't directly concerned with you and your work. If people identify you as an interesting 'sharer', they will follow and like you.
- Try to be yourself: natural, witty and conversational. Don't try to impress and don't be snotty. If you let yourself go a little bit, people will warm to you.
- Share pictures and impressions about events you're going to, books you're reading, people you're meeting.
- Share your blog posts and big news.
- Be careful about posts that might indicate to people (i.e. *everyone*) where you are at any given time. Especially if there's no one home. I know it sounds paranoid, but it's increasingly common for people to have their house burgled when they've made it clear on Twitter that they were at a concert all evening.

Other social media

Twitter and Facebook are the kings of social media for writers, but there are many other websites out there, including:

GOODREADS

This network of readers (note: *readers*) allows you to mark books as 'to-read', 'reading', 'read', and to give them reviews as well as stars. GoodReads is primarily a tool for sharing reading suggestions, reading one another's reviews, and talking about books. Self-promotion isn't actively discouraged, and you can create an Author Page, but it's not the main aim of GoodReads and you must respect the fact that the website is a community of readers.

GoodReads reviewers can be very harsh, and, as discussed below, you really shouldn't respond to reviews of your own books. However, it can be helpful, even if you're not on GoodReads, to have a look at reviews once in a while to gauge the reactions of your readership to your book.

The issue with being an author on GoodReads is that it becomes difficult to be honest with your reviews. Personally, I'm not on GoodReads; I picked another, lesser-known reading network. When all your writer friends are on GoodReads, it means that you can't leave frank comments about their books if you didn't like them. And maybe you should, indeed, refrain from leaving bad comments, even within 'measured' reviews. It's not seen as good form in the profession to disparage the work of colleagues, and you never know who might hit back when your next book comes out. Petty and hypocritical, I know – but that's how it works.

On GoodReads you can easily identify and target bloggers and readers who might be likely to enjoy your books, and get in touch with them to discuss giveaways, for instance.

PINTEREST

Pinterest is a very, well, *interesting* social network. It allows you to 'pin' to a virtual corkboard pictures, articles or blog posts pinched from various websites, with added comments. You can 'repin' items pinned by your friends, and they have access to your boards as well. Using Pinterest can be useful for writers on many different levels:

- You could provide readers with a 'visual track' to your novel, by creating an album of photographs, with, for instance, one picture per chapter. This 'bonus material' can be linked to from your website or your blog.

- You can show your research and your work in progress by pinning pictures or blog posts which will be useful to you during the writing process. For instance, what does a mountain gorilla actually look like? Oh, and here's an interesting blog post on what they eat … Pinterest can help you gather all this information in one convenient, reader-friendly place.

- You might build and tweak the structure of your books by creating private albums and turning them into corkboards on to which to pin and unpin different chapters.

- You could showcase and share with readers your various interests beyond writing – baking, travelling, owls, coats of mail – anything that you find fun and intriguing. Readers will learn more about you, and people with similar interests who aren't yet your readers might pick up your books after visiting your Pinterest profile.

TUMBLR

Between Facebook and Twitter, there's Tumblr, the trendy younger brother, with generally shorter posts, easily customizable designs and appealing pictures. Tumblr is just another blogging device, but it is very popular among youngsters, which could help you find readers directly. However, beware … don't be the creepy person on Tumblr who tries to make friends with the teens. This should go without saying, but on the Internet you have to be extra careful when people under 18 are talking to you. They might email you, tweet you, even ask you to be their friend on Facebook. Remember to keep a distance – they're kids.

YOUTUBE

Having a YouTube channel will enable you to post short or long videos about yourself and your work, as well as book trailers, interviews and anything else you might like to vlog (understand: *video blog*) rather than write down. YouTube pages are easily customizable and getting high numbers of views (OK, *very* high numbers of views) could even make you money.

INSTAGRAM

There's not an extraordinarily huge amount of things you can do on Instagram for the purposes of your writing career, but showing your fun, photo-taking, life-loving side is always a plus, of course.

LINKEDIN

LinkedIn does not appear to be a hugely helpful social and professional network for a writer. At least, it's not a tool for communicating with readers. It can help you establish professional connections, of course, but few people in the industry are very active on LinkedIn, or so it seems.

Increasing your online presence

Beyond social networks, there are a few things that you could do to increase your online presence. There are some that you should *not* do, as well.

- **An Amazon author page.** Although the writing and publishing community is at best very ambivalent about Amazon, Amazon sales and reviews do count, and having an Amazon author page is a way of ensuring that people who would like to buy your book via this platform have the possibility of checking out who you are, what fun things you have to say, and of clicking a link to your website. Your author page will gather all this information. They are easy to create and to personalize, and you should definitely get one as soon as your books are beginning to come out.

- **Profiles on the websites of your publisher and your agency.** Normally, you should be asked to fill in something for these by your publisher and your agent, but if not, do ask. Don't let them write a flat, unexciting biography; if that's the case, ask politely whether you may contribute to it.
- **A Wikipedia page.** *Don't write your own.* Wikipedia will delete any page they suspect was written by the person in question or their friends. The golden rule with Wikipedia is that you shouldn't have anything to do with it. Someone, somewhere, at some point, might create a Wikipedia page for you and/or for one of your books. Wikipedia is not a promotional tool and shouldn't be used as one.

Again – pick just a couple of these social networking tools or online platforms. Don't feel as if you have to be everywhere; better to focus your efforts on just a few that you really enjoy. If you're a very private person, Pinterest and GoodReads might help you: you can 'hide' behind your interests. If you're chatty, warm and fun, go for Twitter and Tumblr. If you're outgoing, professional-sounding and personable, Facebook is ideal. Try several, but keep only a few.

Most importantly, all these scattered social networks and platforms need to be united somewhere. That somewhere will be your author website, an indispensable place, entirely controlled by you, where your readers will find out more about you and know where else to find you.

Setting up an author website

This is not the place to talk about the practicalities regarding website set-ups; there are plenty of good books on the subject, as well as online tutorials. But here are a few things you will have to decide regarding your author website:

- **Buying your domain name versus going for a free website.** The advantages of the former are that it looks much more professional, you can move your website more easily, and no one else will pinch your domain name. The disadvantage is that it costs money (approximately £10 to £20 a year). The advantages and disadvantages of the free website are exactly the opposite. I would recommend buying your own domain name. It will look sleeker and more professional.
- **What should your domain name be?**
  - http://www.firstnamesurname.co.uk (or .com) is ideal if it's available and if your name is quite rare.
  - http://www.firstnamesurname-author.co.uk is good if you have a few namesakes around who are busy blogging about pottery or flamingos.
  - http://www.firstnamesurname-nameofyourbook.co.uk is typically a bad idea: you will, of course, write more books.
- **Choice of host.** It can get quite tricky to decide who the best host is going to be. My recommendation would be to compare prices, and then take advantage of current discounts. Most hosts will cost you roughly the same amount, so you might as well move in with the one that's currently offering you one free year if you subscribe for three. Again, books on website building will help you with this question.

- **Building your own website from scratch versus going for website packages** (versus hiring a website designer). If you know nothing about programming and coding (test: do you know what an FTP client is? No?), building your own website from scratch will be tricky. Not impossible, but tricky. I taught myself a few years ago from online tutorials, and it gets quite addictive and fun, but after a few handmade websites that I never updated properly (they're not very convenient to update), I gave up. The only website I still have that I built myself is the *Sesame Seade* series (http://sesameseade. com), which I built by tweaking a free template, and which I don't update often as it's meant to be quite static.

  What you'll probably prefer is a platform that allows you to write in WYSIWYG (What you see is what you get): no need to worry about HTML language, it's all in a box with handy buttons for font, layout and so on. The most popular ways of doing this are through WordPress and Blogger. WordPress is more customizable and more flexible, and it is possible to create an entirely static website, while Blogger is more blog-oriented. Blogger is more user-friendly. Have a look at both and at other platforms, and remember that you can always move your website from one to the other if you have bought your domain name and have an independent host.

Once all these practicalities have been sorted out, here's the really important question: what should an author website contain?

Your author website *must* have:

- **An About page, with an author biography and a photograph.** After your catchy, fun biography, you could include several biographies of different lengths, to help potential bloggers/journalists to talk about you in just a few lines, in a paragraph, or in more. Author photographs are always very awkward (at least for some people) and it's probably better to pay a professional photographer to take 20 good pictures of you and be done with it. I have not done so, and thus look silly in my author photograph. Bonus points for including personable, quirky elements of your private life in your biography. And pets are always a highly valuable extra, especially in photographs …
- **A Books page,** possibly subdivided into several pages (one for each of your books). On each page, have:
  - a picture of the front cover of the book
  - an indication of the genre and the age range
  - the pitch
  - a slightly longer summary
  - if it is an illustrated book, further pictures from inside
  - links towards online and brick-and-mortar retailers – this is a tricky one. Many of your potential readers will want to buy the book from Amazon, but don't just put an Amazon link: it signals that you're not interested in supporting independent and chain bookstores. Link to as many retailers as possible, and encourage readers to purchase the book from an independent bookstore.
  - snippets of reviews, with links pointing towards them
  - nice things people have said about the book (a bonus).

- **A blog.** This can be on the website itself (easy if you're on WordPress or Blogger), and could even be the first page people land on. Or you can point to a blog external to your author website. We'll get to that soon.

- **An Extras page.** This is a space for you to have fun and tell readers things they can't have known just from reading the books. For instance, you could have a book soundtrack, a visual track made of pictures, deleted scenes, character backstories and writing anecdotes. Make it exciting and a treat for the people who have enjoyed the book.

- **A Contact page,** which gathers your email address, your telephone number if you're comfortable giving it online, and links to everywhere else you might want people to find you on the Internet: social media, other blogs and so on. Mention your agent here and the email addresses of your editor and publicist.

- **A School Visit/Events page.** Here you will state what your school visit and event fee is, who to contact (your publicist, generally) in order to have you in a school, and where your next events will be. You can also have testimonies from people who've had you at their school, together with pictures.

These rubrics are the bare necessities of your author website. But you could consider adding the following:

- **A Writing Tips page.**

- **A Frequently Asked Questions page.** This might quickly become a necessity. FAQs are very helpful because you can politely point people towards them when you get emails from readers asking you similar-ish questions. Try to send personal replies but, to avoid spending your days writing emails, explain that there's a lot in your FAQs that they might like to have a look at.

- **A 'Selected Posts' page.** I keep one of these to make my most important blog posts (on writing and on academia) more visible. Blog posts are ephemeral; they get swallowed into the depths of a blog. Write the titles and link to them on a special page and people will be able to browse more easily.

- **A Guest Book.** If you don't want people to be able to leave comments anywhere else on your website (apart from your blog), you can have a Guest Book to encourage them to tell you everything about how much they like you, your books and your blog.

- **Widgets from Twitter, GoodReads, Facebook or equivalent.** Those convenient boxes will tell your visitors what you've recently been tweeting about or reviewing.

- **An Awards page,** when and if you start collecting trophies and medals for your books.

This list doesn't include pages you might need but which aren't necessary for everyone: a page for your self-published work (which will therefore have to be or link to an online shop), for instance. If your book is 'about' something quite specific, such as the plight of a family faced with the mother's multiple sclerosis, you might want a page dedicated to multiple sclerosis and how you came to write about it, and what people can do to help cure it.

In general, an author website should be:

- **informative:** it should be the first port of call for anyone who is genuinely interested in gaining information on you and your books.

- **clear and concise:** keep everything clean, neat, not flashy or fiddly. Snazzy design really isn't the key to attracting visitors: it's ease of use and quality of content that matter.
- **promoting your books:** without sounding pushy, an ideal author website should firmly orient visitors towards retailers.
- **friendly and interesting:** the readers who already like your books must find the same spirit on your website, and people who discover your website must feel attracted to the books, thanks to your tone and wit.

For children's writers, of course, this audience will be mainly one of adults. But once in a while the odd child might end up on your website. Hence the question: Should a children's author website be child-friendly?

Sometimes, you don't have a choice: you just *can't* make your website child-friendly. This is my case. I write blog posts about academia as well as children's literature, and sometimes these posts have 'adult humour'. They're also about things that children aren't interested in. My author website isn't for children, and I indicate it clearly on the main page. Similarly, if you're also a journalist, or an author for adults, or a politician, you might be using your website for other purposes and not be able to make it child-friendly or appropriate for younger audiences.

So where do child readers go in this case? Well, you can always create another website (yes, another one!) for your *books* only.

Getting a website for your books only

This is particularly useful in the following cases:

- As mentioned before: you want to be free to write any kind of content on your main author website.
- You write for many different age ranges and in different genres which are inappropriate to have on just one author page (picturebooks with pink ponies on the left-hand side, YA cover with hand grenade on the right hand side: I don't think so).
- You have one or several book series.

Creating a separate website for your books on their own will allow you to make sure that the content is completely appropriate for child and teenage readers and that you won't be in trouble with teachers and parents. A few things you might want there, alongside the necessary About and Contact pages, are:

- a Reviews page listing all the press your book has had
- material for use by schoolteachers, librarians or parents
- more bonus material, even more – and some more!
- pages for fan art and fan fiction
- A News page, or even another blog specifically for this book's (or book series') news.

As always, link to your main author website from your book website, and vice versa. Yes, it can be a bit of a pain updating both, but that's the price of freedom.

Let's now talk about one part of this 'online presence' business which is still very important, despite common claims that it's gradually disappearing: blogging.

An author's blog

Blogging is a divisive topic. Some people hate blogging, others love it; some people do it every week, others hardly ever; some people think it brings in readers, some think that it's only authors talking to other authors. Some authors do a very minimal amount of blogging: they blog only when they have news (a book coming out, a new book deal, a trailer, some reviews, a festival, etc.). Others are much more committed bloggers, whether by choice or by obligation.

I'm not one of those people who believe that there is one 'best' way for authors to blog, but I do think that your author blog should give its readers content that is not just about promoting your books. Or at least ... not directly. In fact, the best blogs are the ones that promote their writer's books indirectly, by providing really exciting content that keeps readers coming and eventually getting curious about your books.

What kind of content is that? Here are a few examples:

- **Informative generalist blog posts about writing and getting published.** Very much the kind of stuff this very book offers: I could have posted it in instalments on my blog instead of delivering it whole to my publisher. I have always read – and still do – author blogs which give that kind of content because I think it's very interesting to get other people's insight and knowledge on those topics. Aspiring writers find such blog posts invaluable. Of course, with such posts you are talking to authors and aspiring authors mostly. Keep them pedagogical, brief and informative.

- **Blog posts about your way of writing, researching, editing and so on.** Slightly more self-centred, such blog posts tell your readers about, for instance, what type of music you like to listen to when you write, how you researched your latest novel and so forth. To keep them interesting, you must make sure that there is a universal dimension to them despite the fact that this is *your* technique.

- **Blog posts about one of your books.** These can be, just like 'extra' material, pathways into your latest book: explaining the inspiration behind it, clarifying a point, picking up on a frequently asked question, and generally adding to the conversation around your book.

- **Blog posts about your life.** Interesting things might happen to you that have nothing to do with writing. Travelling, cooking, working two jobs, any anecdotes that you might find funny or touching – they can sometimes make good blog posts. Readers will discover a more personal aspect of your life.

- **Any other interests you may have.** Maybe you play the saxophone, maybe you make home-made ice cream, maybe you paint and draw. Write about that, too. Share recipes, share videos of yourself playing, share pictures of your paintings.

- **Reviews of books.** Again, however hypocritical it may sound, don't give bad reviews to living writers (at least not in your field). If you're going to review other books, pick the ones you truly loved.

- **Interviews of other people.** Interview your agent, your best writer friend, your editor, or anyone you feel might be interesting to have on your blog.

These are just a few possibilities for different types of blog posts which might all, in their own way, attract readers, make them engage in conversation with you, and eventually, perhaps, buy your books. But don't *push* the books on to them. Often, people will buy your books when you least expect it. For instance, I once wrote a funny blog post bemoaning the trend of book soundtracks; I'd had to write one in my latest YA novel. I explained that my taste in music was abysmal and that now everyone would know about it. That blog post was shared an astonishing number of times, and several people told me they'd buy the book simply because they were so curious to see how shameful my playlist was!

Beyond such blog posts, of course, you will have to write ones that are purely there for purposes of self-promotion. These include the following:

- **Announcements:** of new books coming out, of new book deals; 'cover reveals' to (build up anticipation), revelation of the illustrator's name; of film deals; of foreign-rights sales.
- **Round-ups of reviews:** if you're getting many reviews (well done!), gather them in one blog post once a week or once a fortnight rather than blogging every day about them.
- **Book giveaways:** these can be hugely popular. Organize a book giveaway on your blog for every book that's just come out, asking people to take part by leaving a comment or by sharing the link.

The important thing about blogging is to have varied, informative and useful content. It can't just be a platform for you, yourself and your books. People aren't interested in you enough to subscribe to your blog simply to hear news about you. But if you can be useful to them, and funny and warm, and touching and interesting, and thought-provoking, they'll come back.

Now here are a few strategies to make your blog posts attractive. They are difficult to follow, but they are the characteristics of many popular blogs:

- **Illustrate** your blog posts with pictures (from legal sources).
- Use **bullet points** or **numbered lists** to organize your blog posts; it makes them more easily navigable.
- Highlight particularly important sentences by making them **bold**.
- Use **short paragraphs** rather than big blocks of text.
- Make blog posts as **brief** as possible.
- **Ask questions** throughout: 'How about you – how do you write about touchy topics?', 'What do you think of this strategy?' 'It sounds crazy, doesn't it?' It will encourage people to leave comments.
- Have **'share' buttons** underneath each blog post, making it easy for readers to spread your post on Twitter, Facebook and all other networks.
- Link to **past blog posts** as much as possible using hyperlinks ('I've already talked about researching books *here*, but today I'm going to talk about a specific aspect of research'). This will increase the visibility of your blog posts over time.
- **Reply to comments.** There's nothing more irksome than godlike bloggers who drop a post on their blog and then serenely retreat to their higher spheres again, never bothering to acknowledge that someone took the time to comment.

Blog comments, by the way, are getting rarer and rarer in the age of social media. You'll doubtlessly find that your blog posts get more comments on Twitter and Facebook than on the blog. Twenty people might be sharing ideas under your Facebook post, and no one on the blog. This is a sad fact, but there's nothing you can do about it. Do reply to each comment to encourage readers to share their thoughts again at another time.

Extras

Let's now focus on some ways of spicing up your blog and your website by adding extras. These, which should be both informative and promotional, are meant to interest potential readers in buying your book as well as to thank current readers for having bought it. Here are a few examples:

- **Games for child readers.** If your book is for young readers, you could have a special part of your website to get them to play around your book. Print-outs of characters they can colour in, labyrinth games, word games – there are countless possibilities and, of course, they depend on what your book is about. You could post activity sheets or recipes; tutorials for fancy-dress-making in the style of your characters; suggestions for parties and party games around the theme of your books … anything that your little fans may be excited about doing.

- **Exclusive material.** Discarded scenes, Christmas or Halloween specials, bonus chapters, character descriptions, letters from one character to another: this is proper writing, but for free, and it enhances the experience of reading your books.

- **Book trailers.** This is not the place to get into the art of book trailers, but they are very popular and they can be particularly exciting, especially for children's writers. Hire someone or do it yourself: you can read extracts from the book, film real places that refer to the book, or create an animated version of it if it's a picturebook. Bribe a child or teenager you know to act in it. Some book trailers can look quite kitsch and shabby, so be careful that you don't do something too pitiful, but they can certainly enhance awareness of your book and titillate potential readers.

- **Book soundtracks.** However icy I may feel towards the concept, many readers are interested in the type of music you, as an author, would associate to your book.

- **Pedagogical sheets or book group questions.** More on the educational side, these are meant to encourage teachers to share your book with a classroom, or students to read your book with their book club. This is particularly useful if your book has a clear pedagogical edge; it might be, for instance, about the Civil Rights Movement, and your website is a good place for extra, non-fictional material about it.

Are you overdosing on advice for self-promotion yet? I thought so. Don't worry – reacting to this by gritting your teeth is a healthy reaction, I think. Self-promotion is cringe-worthy; it's not fun. It never happens without a lingering sense of guilt. And maybe it should be so. Try not to fall into 'humble-bragging' ('Wish I had time to reply to all the emails I'm getting from readers [sad face]'; 'With this book tour I'm finding it so hard to begin writing the next book properly!' 'So happy for my friend XY for her award nomination! Her book is so great. And this is such a nice award – got it last year and it looks great on my mantelpiece.') You will soon recognize people like that – people who fall into …

The perils of self-promotion

When 70 per cent of all tweets, Facebook statuses and blog posts from your fellow writers and illustrators are about A New Review of Their Book, A New Interview of Them, A New Article about Them and A New Award They're Nominated For, you quickly lose your own inhibitions and start doing exactly the same thing.

And you do it partly because we have to – because publishers these days see writers as prodigious multitaskers. We're expected to sell our books, not just write them. We're expected to get people excited about them, we're expected to talk about them and we're expected to be as visible as possible. It's not just a question of money: if your books don't sell, if you're not *visible*, your future books might not even ever find a publisher. So get promoting.

But for goodness' sake, *within reason*. I'm generally fine with the ocean of more or less humble-bragging which I wade through everyday on my Twitter and Facebook accounts. But there should be a special part of that ocean in which to drown those authors who out-brag everyone else in the most ludicrous ways imaginable.

1 THOSE WHO RETWEET EVERY SINGLE SNIPPET OF PRAISE THEY GET

> Aww thanks! <3 <3 RT@randomreader hey i liked ur book

> I'm so glad you did ☺ RT@somereader your book is funny! I loled

> So sweet thank you!! RT@readeranonymous looking forward to your next book

That is the equivalent of having dinner in crowded restaurant and sporadically shouting out at the top of your voice:

> "So adorable!! Laura's just told me, 'That's a lovely dress you're wearing!'"

> "Ohhh thank you very much, Sam, for telling me 'You chose exactly the right wine!'"

> "I'm so so so SO touched by what Fiona's just said! She said, "You've always been a good friend to me"!'

People would look at you as though you're completely insane. OK: someone praised you in a public space where other people might overhear. But that is not the equivalent of saying: 'Please take my praise and broadcast it to your 800 followers.' What even is the point? If I follow you, I probably like you already or think I might do in the future. Why would @purplegothreader1995's cryptic and frankly quite uninteresting praise of your book make me like you more?

But there's worse …

2 THOSE WHO SHARE FAN MAIL AND EMAILS

You get an email or letter from little Zoe, nine years old, whom you met a few months ago on a school visit. She says thank you for coming to visit, it was great to meet you, here's a drawing, please come back … Huge ego boost, mood enhanced for the rest of the day. But it's not enough. Some people have to post it, the whole letter or email, to Facebook, Twitter and their blog.

Don't do it. It's an email, right? A letter, right? You had to type in your password to access it, or open your post box with a key, right? I know little Zoe didn't technically say: 'Please, Mrs Author, don't use this private communication for means of self-promotion', but doing so is *not* OK. She wrote it to *you*, not to your followers and Facebook friends.

3 THOSE WHO TWEET AND FACEBOOK ABOUT EVERY SINGLE LITTLE THING

12.31. Invitation to do a school visit! yay!

12.34. Fun to open email from editor and get new illustrations. Happy!

12.40. New blog post already has 12 comments ☺

12.42. 13 comments now! ☺ ☺

12.48. Email from agent – discussing next book series! exciting lol

12.52. Oh new review of my book here!

Every single day in the life of a writer has several cool *little* things happening in it. *Little* things. Not all of them tweetworthy. And all of them, put together, tweedious in the extreme. Save them up for a weekly blog post; select the best ones. Or at least be clever and spread them out between non-self-promoting tweets.

It is scarily easy to become that kind of writer, and frankly quite distressing when you used to be a shy, introspective, humble person, and all of a sudden you find yourself tempted to post to Twitter the contents of a private email you just got.

> ## Key idea
>
>
>
> People aren't going to love you *less* if you don't post everything; they just *won't know about that particular thing*. It's OK; they don't need it to love you. In theory. If they do, you have bigger things to worry about.

Battling Internet addiction

One of the reasons why crazy and disproportionate self-promotion happens is that you might simply be an Internet addict. That's when it becomes impossible *not* to check social media and email every few minutes; when every finished page of prose means a 'reward' of five or ten minutes (or more) online, and a tweet about the number of words you wrote; and when googling your own name becomes more important than writing the book.

Then you've got a problem, and here's how to solve it:

- Download an **Internet-blocking software.** Free ones include Self Control for Mac and Cold Turkey for PC. These pieces of software will allow you to tick websites you don't want to be able to go to – Facebook, Twitter, email, etc. – and still be able to use the Internet, for research purposes, for instance. Interestingly, after three or four hours of blocked Internet, you won't actually want to go back online when the little icon starts sparkling again to tell you that you can now check email and social media. You're generally so deep into your work that you've reached a comfortable, galvanizing zone – and you don't want to open up to all that noise again.

- Set **clear targets** before you're 'allowed' online again. This can be a number of words, or a specific amount of time spent writing.

- For a day or two, **time yourself** every time you go on social media. Just set a stopwatch running, and clock in and out every time. You might be surprised – indeed, even scared – to see how long you've spent on there.

- After that, set a **time limit,** per day, on your use of social media. Whether it be 30 minutes or an hour, force yourself to leave when time's up.

- When you're stuck for words or can't find inspiration, make yourself **leave the house:** walk the dog, go for a swim, go shopping. If you stay at home, you will be drawn to the computer, tablet or smartphone and idly check email, Facebook, Pinterest and Google News.

Another type of addiction is self-googling. Especially if you've just had a book come out, you might be checking every few minutes to see whether there's been a new review on a blog, on Amazon or on GoodReads. To avoid this, set a Google alert with your name and the name of the book: once a day, you will receive everything you need to know that's been published in the past 24 hours about yourself and your precious new little book.

However, I would recommend *not* checking such things too often. Reviews, in particular. Good ones will make you happy for a short time, while bad ones will make you absolutely miserable for a very long time. It's probably better to delegate this task to your partner, parents, agents and editor; they will tactfully spare you the painful stuff, and send you the complimentary words. In any case, should you happen to stumble upon a bad review online, the absolutely unbending and general rule is: *don't respond.*

How not to respond to reviews

It bears repeating: *never respond to reviews.* It's very tempting, when you see a bad or mediocre review of your work, especially when it contains factually incorrect information, or typos, to respond to it. It's never, ever a good idea: you will appear weak, hot-tempered and grumpy. Remember that reviews are for readers. They are not for you to see. They are not meant to make you angry. They are meant to communicate to other readers informationi about your book. The blogger or commenter isn't expecting a response from you, even if they say things like 'Ms Jones, you can't write!' or 'I want to ask the author, how could you possibly think this was a good idea???' Just tell yourself they don't really want to ask you. It's a rhetorically convenient way of putting their thoughts into words.

People on the Internet can be very nasty. And they don't care that you can see their nastiness. They can also be wrong about many things. The best attitude you can adopt is pretending you've never seen their review. Even if it keeps you awake at night, don't respond. Even if they're incorrect or dishonest, don't respond. Even if you suspect they might be giving you a bad review out of spite or jealousy, don't respond. Even if they clearly haven't read the book, don't respond. Even if they are trying to give you a bad reputation, or writing false accusations, don't respond.

It doesn't mean that you shouldn't defend yourself, but you can do it in your own time, on your own website, where you are fully in control of everything. If you have been repeatedly accused of historical inaccuracies in your latest YA book, for instance, and you really think that it's an unwarranted attack, it could be worth writing a blog post about where you found your sources and why you were actually correct. Don't link to the bad reviews or the people who accused you! No need to give them extra publicity.

As always, it's essential to think twice or thrice about everything you post online, especially if it's publicly visible. Responding to bad reviews, especially in the heat of the moment, could cost you and your publisher dearly. Try to distance yourself from these reviews; everyone gets them. The more interesting, popular and controversial your writing, the more you will get. It's tough, but you must focus on your work and attempt to ease the pain by writing more. And if you suspect that some of the severe reviews might in fact be right, then take them into account as constructive criticism. And write more, and better.

Where to next?

Now that you're equipped with a flashy website, a regularly updated, interesting blog, and lots of ideas for extra material, it's time to … meet your readers. In the real world. Your young readers – sometimes very young readers … In the next chapter we'll talk about that most exciting, most daunting, most amazing of times: encountering the young people who are reading your books.

23

Talking to kids: the real child readers and you

'There, that's brilliant,' said Gary. 'Are you ready to face your fans now?'

He escorted me down to the ground floor. As soon as people caught sight of me, there was an amazing squeal and stir and flash of cameras. I was led to a chair almost like a throne with a canopy above it, declaring I was Rosalind Hartlepool, Child Wonder Writer. I sat down on my grand chair, selected a pen from a handful waiting on the table and smiled at the girl first in the queue. Gary beckoned her over and helped her get her *Four Children and It* open at the title page.

'Hello, what's your name?' I asked.

'I'm Rebecca, probably your biggest fan,' she whispered shyly. She was shy of *me*!

I wrote *To Rebecca, with love from Rosalind Hartlepool* on her book in my best handwriting and she thanked me as if I'd given her a wonderful present. She walked off clutching her book to her chest, saying, 'I've met Rosalind Hartlepool!' over and over to her mother.

If there's one person you'd expect to be quite familiar with meeting child readers by now, it's Dame Jacqueline Wilson, former Children's Laureate and internationally adored godmother of children's literature. Yet, as the above extract shows (from her recent novel *Four Children and It*, 2012, pp. 92–3), Jacqueline Wilson isn't against romanticising the moments when writers meet their readers and fans. In fact, she does it several times throughout her works – most touchingly perhaps in *The Lottie Project*, when Charlie's until-then secret school project is read out loud to – and loved by – her whole classroom.

There's something mythical, something hallowed, about meeting your young readers. It's life-changing, humbling, terrifying, and immensely stressful. You might entertain fantasies of it right now – maybe it's even your ultimate aim. And perhaps it should be – because the affection you'll receive when you meet child readers will be enough to make you happy for several days.

But it's hard work, too – very hard work. It's not just love, home-made cupcakes and cute drawings, it's also a part of your new job – more precisely, a part of the 'salesperson' side of your new job. And like everything else, it's not innate – it has to be learned.

But above all, how to make the most of those frankly quite extraordinary moments, and bask in the joy of being a children's writer and not one of those boring adults writing for boring adults and facing all kind of boring criticism.

Sorry, what's that you're muttering? I can't hear you. It's OK, there's no such thing as a stupid question – just speak up … You don't what? You don't … What? *You don't actually like children?*

Do children's writers have to like children?

Every time I do school visits or go to a book fair, there's always a grumpy paedophobic author somewhere. S/he's been writing for longer that I've been alive and s/he's seen it all. S/he's sipping coffee in the teachers' common room and ranting about those damned kids and their unimaginative questions. S/he's in here for the money, not the experience. S/he's going on and on and on about 'that annoying kid who always asks how long it takes to write a book and where I get my ideas from.'

And me, meanwhile, young, enthusiastic and naive and rather a fan of younger humans, I'm all like 'Oh my! Goodness me! How can you possibly say that, you monster, you ogre? Surely it is the greatest happiness in the world to talk to little readers, however dumb the questions! Surely the marvellous feeling of profound and inexplicable bliss that fills one when one is faced with children is universally shared!' and I put my hand on my heart and I think of the cute freckles, dimples and missing teeth, and I swallow back tears of shock and fear and I wonder if this clearly deranged author should really be allowed to roam the school premises.

Slight exaggerations may have found their way into the previous two paragraphs, but the question's not a stupid one. Should children's authors actually like children? I don't mean just tolerate, but actually *like* them? Should they feel increased levels of happiness, a certain special sense of connection, when in the presence of the *kawaii* beings? After all, there are dozens of misanthropic adult authors who don't give a damn about their readers. And no adult author will ever be asked to confirm that they like adults.

'Oh yes, I love adults – I just love them. I love their happy faces when I sign their books, and they always come up with things that I find just wonderfully unexpected and marvellous … How can I explain it? It's so mysterious. I can't say why, but I've always been at ease with adults. Maybe it's because I haven't forgotten what it feels like to be an adult. I get on with them really well. They're great, basically, and that's why I write for them.'

We'd think them crazy. What if some authors actually like writing for children because they think it's a great experimental platform – which it is – but don't really have anything to say to *real* kids outside of what they tell them through their art? How much of it is about the *idea of childness*, the ability to play with concepts, art forms, narratives that are particular to children's literature – and how much of it actually has to be about real children?

That's the crux of the matter, really. You can love the idea of children just as you love the idea of backpacking up and down the Andes, but you might suddenly find yourself a little bit less keen if you actually ended up parachuted into the mountainous jungle. I think I love real children. I think I love talking to them. I think they make me laugh, they surprise me and amaze me, and I think being around them makes me happy, but rationally there's no way this sweeping generalization is possible without a pre-existing idea of kids as a cool bunch of people, without a pre-existing idea of 'childness' as a special property for a human to have.

Because it's a bit like saying 'I love cats'. You might love cats. But in fact you don't. You don't love *all* cats. You don't like the ones that scratch and bite, bizarrely enough; you prefer the cuddly ones that purr. Similarly, when you go into a primary classroom, you will probably tend to prefer the enthusiastic little Hermione whose hand shoots up into the air all the time to the sexually precocious duo of boys who ogle you and snigger and scribble down things to each other on pieces of paper.

So we have to grant one thing to the paedophobic writer: at least they're seeing the kids as humans. As fallible, annoying, boring and silly, but as humans. The blissful, all-loving writer who 'just adores kids in general' might as well be saying that they love cats. Or old people. Or gays. Or Tories. Or dyslexics. You get the idea.

There are people who just love writing and, for them, going into schools to talk to real kids is one of those things you have to do in your day job but that you don't particularly like, such as brainstorming the name of a new guava-and-tapioca shampoo or filling in an Excel spreadsheet with the office's stationery budget for the year or whatever people who have real jobs do.

And then there are the ones bumbling around like a flotilla of fairy godmothers, hopelessly endeared to the little readers, envisaging their work as a sort of whole project of life and mission for and with children, and unable to understand that some writers may tailor every single one of their books for people whom, in reality, they don't care about very much.

What if you're one of them? Well, your publisher should be told, and in fact should have been told ages ago (I did mention it when discussing the First Meeting). They'll just have to accept it. Best-case scenario, you'll still be fine with doing *some* visits, *sometimes*. If not, well, you just won't do school visits. You won't do festivals. That's OK – I know a few authors who don't do them at all. You have to know that your publisher will probably find it quite problematic, because such events sell books and enhance your profile. But they won't force you.

If you're one of those authors who 'adores children', there's something to take away from this, too. Try to think of child readers more as individuals, rather than as an undefined collective. Some will enjoy your books and some won't. They'll all have their favourite moments. You won't like them all. That's OK. You're writing for a whole group of different humans beings, not just a category.

With that in mind, let's go to schools.

Doing school visits

Your publisher will (or rather should) set up some school visits for you, or at least put you in touch with a local bookstore to get you started on doing school visits. But you'll also have to find your own. It's much more difficult than it sounds; sending unsolicited emails to schools in your area won't yield many replies, because teachers are extremely busy and they don't know you. You'll have more luck if you approach schools directly. If you have children of the right age, or know the parents of such people, take advantage of it. After a while, when you become better known, it's likely that schools will begin to contact you to ask you to come.

But what do school visits actually consist of? Here are the main things to know, and to tell the school teachers if they don't already know:

- **School visits typically consist of a one-hour talk to a large part of the school, if not the whole school.** Of course, you are free to say that you would prefer to see fewer children, but normally you will be speaking to any number of children from 80 to 300. In primary school, if your book is suitable for roughly seven to eleven-year-olds, you will probably have the whole school there. In secondary school, you might have fewer year groups, but they are generally larger schools than primary schools so this might still represent a lot of teenagers.

- *Make sure* that you ask the school how many children will be there, and how old they will be.

- **School visits are generally organized in partnership with a bookshop.** Someone from the bookshop will set up a small stall in the room where you'll be giving the talk. After the talk, children can buy the books and there will generally be a book signing. The children's parents should have been told in advance by the school that an author is coming. That way, children will come on the day, should they wish to, with money or a cheque to buy your books.

- *Make sure* that you tell the person in charge, a few times if necessary, to inform the children's parents that you will be coming.

- **Generally, children will not know you or your books on the day of the school visit.** Particularly if you are a debut author, it is extremely unlikely that the school will have taken the time to introduce you to the children in advance, and asked them to read your books. Therefore, you will be unknown to them. They might not even have looked up your books on the Internet.

- *Make sure* that you present your books and explain what they are about, in an exciting and enticing way, during your talk.

Having gone through these general aspects of school visits, let's get a bit more into detail.

Different authors do things differently, and it's very important that you only do things you're comfortable with. I panicked when I first heard I'd have to do talks in front of whole schools that weren't familiar with my books; in France, school visits are very different – you visit only those schools which have worked on your books, and there's not much to do apart from stay there, answer questions, smile and watch the plays/ drawings/projects they've done around your books. But in the UK, *you* have to convince *them*, and your talk might have to turn into a bit of a one-wo/man show.

You'll always hear about authors who do amazing things on school visits. So many of them play the guitar (damn those people who master bar chords!). Julian Sedgwick juggles with knives and spits fire. How do you compete with that? The disgustingly talented Katherine Rundell does tightrope-walking. Maybe you also have a secret or not-so-secret talent that could come in handy. Can you sing? Can you doodle?

But for the more common people like me and perhaps you, all is not lost. There are still ways of doing a brilliant author talk without taming wild tigers while playing the ocarina with your nostrils. A few pictures (most authors use PowerPoint), some good activities and jokes, and you're in. Here are some suggestions for a good author talk:

- **A fun hook, linked to your book.** Marcus Sedgwick's talk on his Young Adult novel *She Is Not Invisible* begins with a bunch of really fascinating *coincidences*, because one of the themes of the book is coincidences.

- **A presentation of the book or series.** This doesn't need to be boring and descriptive (it shouldn't be). Dilute this presentation throughout the talk, adding fun facts, anecdotes, linking it to other books or films, working through it with the audience.

- **A presentation of yourself.** Again, don't turn this into a self-centred autobiography. Children love the quirky details; they absolutely don't care about your MA in Creative Writing at Bath Spa – it definitely won't add to their desire to read your books. But they will love to see pictures of your pet lizard, like author Robin Stevens's, especially if she was the inspiration for a character in your book. They also like seeing pictures of yourself as a child (especially around their age). They love anecdotes.

- **An activity of some kind.** These differ greatly according to age range and theme of the book. I do a theft mystery, inviting volunteers on stage to be the suspects and the sleuth. If your book is about Japan and you're Japanese, you could get the children to write or read Japanese characters. If your book is a spy mystery, get them to solve special secret codes or riddles. If it's a serious, psychological YA book, you can get more intimate and ask the teenagers to share experiences around a theme (as long as it's not inappropriate). Whatever you do, try to get the audience engaged. They will be extremely keen to contribute, especially in primary schools.

- **A reading.** I don't like reading out loud, and don't do it particularly well, but it's good to give the children a taste of your books. Pick a passage that is particularly representative of the book, and full of fun, tension or horror.

- **Questions to the audience.** And listen to their answers! Ask them for their opinions on what you're showing. After a while, you'll get more and more comfortable with responding to their comments, bouncing back at them with more questions, and getting into a conversation. Good questions to ask include: 'Which books do you like?' It's useful, too, to get an idea of what children and teenagers are reading *now*. 'Does anyone here write?' Then ask them questions about *what* they write.
- **Jokes!** Try to be witty and funny. Primary-school children love anything that attacks the authority of their teachers (not too violently, though …), so have fun with that. Don't laugh at them; laugh with them.

You might want to leave time at the end for the audience to ask you questions. These can be extremely interesting and fun. Often, you will find that children are interested in when you started to write, how a book is made and so on. I once got asked by a tiny six-year-old: 'How do you stick all the pages together?'

You might want to have extra slides at the end of your presentation, where you show pictures of the cover in development, book proofs, the printing process, character sketches – anything that can give them an idea of the book in progress. This could be part of your general presentation, of course, but in my experience the younger children can find it a bit difficult to keep up with terms such as 'publisher', 'printer', 'designer' and so forth; and you don't want to lose them because of technical details. For an audience of secondary-school children, such presentations are perfectly appropriate, but they can sound a bit teacherly.

 Key idea

> Your primary aim in doing school visits is to get children and teenagers excited about your book.

Primary schools versus secondary schools

As a short side note, there are very notable differences, as you probably know if you're a parent, between primary- and secondary-school children. The atmosphere just isn't the same, and your talks should not be pitched similarly for these two different audiences. You will notice that primary-school children are extremely – sometimes deliriously – enthusiastic; you'll hardly need to win them over at the start. They will all want to answer your questions, they'll be very keen to participate in whatever activity you suggest, and they will not be inhibited by the presence of their peers. They are curious, passionate and always like to learn more. Talking to primary-school children is therefore relatively easy if you're cool, easy-going and fun, and have interesting things to show them.

In secondary school, a mysterious shift happens; within the first few weeks the last remnants of joyous insouciance are gone. You might find audiences of teenagers more difficult to relate to at first (unless you're a secondary-school teacher, in which case you might think that primary-school children look as if they're on speed all the time). Teenagers will look at you differently. They will be very wary of the way you talk to them, and will not express their feelings or opinions very readily. They might seem, at first, closed or uninterested. Don't take it personally. They are more inhibited than their younger peers, and they might actually be loving every single minute of your talk. Ask them questions, joke with them, get them engaged. Never talk down to them (this is, of course, also valid for younger children, but for teenagers it's an immediate turn-off). Make it clear that you value their opinions. After a while they'll relax, appear more confident and less hermetic. You will then be able to have profound, fascinating conversations, and they'll remember you for a long time. It's always a joy to receive emails from teenagers after school visits, telling you, in all confidentiality, that they loved the talk. They very rarely ever say that to your face.

Key idea

Pitch your talk appropriately: that might be the take-away message here. Be sensitive to the difference in atmosphere between primary and secondary school. It helps, I guess, if you're regularly around children or teenagers; if not, your first visits might be a baptism of fire.

And what about the very young children?

Depending on the type of books you write, you could end up giving talks in Reception years of primary schools, or even in nursery schools. Children under six are fascinating and fun, but they are hard work. They will not be interested in you as an author – they barely understand what that means – but they will be interested in your books and in your telling them stories. Read your picturebook to them; get them to draw in response, or to sing or recite passages, or to organize little play scenes from the book. Ask them plenty of questions. They need to be kept entertained.

All kinds of questions ... and all sorts of answers

Part of the fun of doing school visits (and meeting readers in general) is answering their questions. And their questions might be ... very unexpected. Be ready for the worst, including indirect comments on your personal appearance ('How much do you weigh?' 'Why are you old?', or, as I more flatteringly (?) got once, 'Are you a teenager or an adult?'). Be ready to answer some of the most typical questions you'll be asked, not all wacky, of course:

- **'Where do you get your ideas from?'** This is a typical 'journalist' question as well as a common one from children. It gets a bit boring, answering this question all the time, so you could do what Marcus Sedgwick does and answer it at the very beginning of your talk.

- **'When did you start writing?'** This is your opportunity to explain the genesis of your oeuvre.

- **'What's your favourite book?' 'Who's your favourite author?'** Try to find authors and books that they know about. You might be surprised: in many schools I go to, children haven't heard of Philip Pullman, for instance, though they might recognize the title *His Dark Materials*. If you've asked them, as I suggested earlier, what their favourite books were, you could pick from those. David Walliams and Jeff Kinney, at the time of writing, are all the rage in primary schools, and I happen to love their books, which makes it easy to get into an excited conversation with the children. Don't cite authors for adults to primary-school children; they don't care.

- **'How long does it take to write a book?'** The typical answer includes explaining that it depends on the type of book, on how you got the idea, and of going from synopsis to full book.

- **'How much do you earn?'** A very common and tricky question. You can jokingly say, 'Nothing until you buy the book!' but it's a bit dishonest. With secondary-school children, you can go far into the intricacies of author advances and royalties. If you feel comfortable doing so, give them actual numbers: they're interested, and I personally think we shouldn't hide these things from readers, even young ones. With primary-school children, explain it honestly too, but don't go into as much detail and be careful with vocabulary: they might not have heard yet of 'percentages', 'fractions' and so on.

- **'Have you met any famous authors?'** Ouch! That question is slightly painful to the ego. It means, 'You're OK, but have you met, like, really famous authors?' Don't get all miffed and wounded; just answer sincerely. With the younger ones, you might be surprised to discover that when you tell them 'Yes, I've met Anthony Browne', or 'Jacqueline Wilson', or 'Suzanne Collins', they might look completely blank. (I once got asked again, 'OK, but have you met, like, really really famous authors, like Jules Verne?'). Often, they don't actually know author names (which makes one wonder why they asked the question in the first place). Name titles that those 'famous authors' wrote, and their faces will suddenly light up. And if you don't know anyone famous, that's fine; just joke that you haven't been able to get past their bodyguards.

- **'Is this book about your life?'** I get asked this quite often, but more worryingly about a YA book that includes kidnapping and torture. Of course, your presentation should mention it if the book is largely autobiographical; if not, talk a bit about real-life events behind your work, or lack thereof.

- **'Can you give us writing tips?'** I'll let you deal with that one.

These are all perfectly reasonable. But there are other, rather more bizarre questions which you might be faced with, for instance: 'Do you have a mummy?' (Me: 'Yes'); 'Is she going to pick you up after this?'; 'Who's your best friend?' and 'Where are your boob straps?' (I was wearing a strapless dress that day) …

Oh yes, there are also questions that are … not quite questions: 'My mum's got the same T-shirt as you'; 'I have a cat' (extremely common, that one, and generally completely unrelated to the general conversation); 'I was watching *Scooby-Doo* the other day … and then … like … it was … there was a snake … and …' (stream-of-consciousness 'questions' by the tiny ones); and of course the usual, blushing, 'I forgot what I was going to ask', to which you should gracefully reply, of course, that it happens to the best of us and it's not a problem at all.

Other ways of meeting young readers

School visits aren't the only way of getting in touch with potential and actual readers.

- You will probably be invited to do **events at bookshops,** which can be very hit-and-miss. If there's no one in the shop, it's cringe-worthy. The booksellers will lasso in everyone of the right age, but it can be difficult to retain their attention. If you're very famous, then you just turn up and do the signing; if not, you will have to give an abbreviated version of your school talk, possibly using a clipboard with pictures instead of a PowerPoint.

- **Book festivals** might invite you to talk to large audiences of children, and they will generally be made up of school classes with their teachers. Apart from the fact that these physically don't take place in schools, they are very similar to school visits.

- You might negotiate with schools to come and do **writing workshops.** Try to tie in these workshops with the type of book you're writing: a detective novel workshop, a picturebook or comic workshop, a pirate adventure story workshop …

- **Skype school visits** are increasingly common, and it's up to you to decide whether you want to run them as normal school visits, or have something shorter and more interactive.

- **Award ceremonies** present another opportunity to meet readers and talk about your work.

Whenever such opportunities arise, do make sure that there is a bookshop at the event, and/or that you get suitably paid for your time.

Paid?

Money matters

Yes, authors (most often) get paid to do school visits, workshops and festivals. It comes as such a surprise to most people (including, sometimes, debut authors themselves!) that it's worth reiterating. When you're doing a school visit, you're *working*. This is not just for your own amusement or to nurse your superiority complex. While you're there talking to the children, you're not writing your next book. This isn't just a hobby. You travelled all the way to be here and give a talk that is a proper show. And you will go home exhausted (school visits are intensely tiring). It's absolutely normal that you should be paid for your time.

You should charge for school visits for all these reasons and even more. The whole profession depends on our being rigorous about what our requests are. If you don't charge, schools will tell other authors they invite that they don't want to pay them either.

> ## Key idea
>
> You cheapen the work of all authors if you cheapen yours.

That said, there are a few exceptions. When a bookshop organizes the visits, they generally won't be able to pay you; but they should cover travel expenses, and you will sell a lot of books. Furthermore, at the very beginning of your career, you might want to give away some local school visits for free, if only to get some practice and to make friends with schools in your area. Some authors, however, would argue even then you shouldn't accept visits that are not paid.

How much to charge? This is a tricky question. The Society of Authors suggests a standard rate, but everyone can set their own fee. Schools know this, and they know it's more expensive to get the most popular authors. You might want to have different fees according to where the visit takes place; if it's in your home town or city, charge a hundred pounds per visit, but if you have to travel for several hours, double that. You can have a half-day fee and a full-day fee. Remember that school visits are very tiring and that you might not be able to do more than two a day; don't sell yourself cheap, and don't accept inappropriate offers from schools – packing four visits into one day, for instance, or getting you to see the whole school from Reception to Sixth Form at the same time. Be strict and very clear with schools about what you will and won't do.

You will need to invoice schools or festivals to be paid for your visits. Here is a standard model of an invoice for an author visit:

Cambridge, 07/20XX.

Clémentine Beauvais

Address

UTR number

National Insurance Number

Kindly requests the payment of a fee of   £XXX

And of travel expenses

Train tickets   £XX

Taxi to venue   £XX

(Please find receipts attached.)

Total to pay: £XXX

For the author event   'Supersleuthing with Clémentine Beauvais'

at   Super Amazing Literary Festival

on   30/09/20XX

Bank details for the transfer.

With thanks,

[signature]

You might want to give each invoice a number to make it easier for you to track payment and to do your taxes later.

Responding to fan (e)mail

Of course, there are other ways in which readers will get in touch with you, and one of them is by letter or (more probably) by email. You will also get tweets, and probably Facebook requests, which you'll have to decide whether to accept or not (remember that children under 11 aren't supposed to be on Facebook, and I wouldn't recommend accepting friend requests from anyone under the age of 18).

The way you reply to emails and letters is, of course, entirely up to you, but do bear in mind, if the senders are children, that there are a number of things you might want to be careful about when responding. Don't offer to meet up. If they would like to meet you, mention the next time you'll be doing a book signing, or make up a polite excuse. This is to protect yourself.

Similarly, you'll have to decide on a policy as to whether you agree to look at children's and teenagers' writing. When you're an author, you'll soon be inundated with requests to have a look at people's work. It's easy(ish) to say no to adults, because they understand that you don't have the time, but it might be difficult to have the same discipline with younger readers, who on top of that will tell you that they, of course, adore your book. They would also genuinely benefit from your insights. Remember that anything you take on will have to go on top of all your other work.

Additionally, young readers may ask you, naively and with the best of intentions, to do things that you shouldn't really do, such as giving them or their school free books, or coming to their school fair. They don't realize that we should be getting paid for this, and it's very awkward to explain this to young people. If it's something that really matters to them, ask them if you can get in touch with their teachers.

A final warning: there are scammers out there who send very convincing 'fan' emails, saying that they love your books, that they run a charity, and could you please send free signed copies of your books to the charity for a competition? Don't yield. While the request may be legitimate, most often it will be a scam and your free, signed books will end up on eBay, for the benefit of the scammer.

Signing books in style

Seriously, do we need to talk about signing books? Well, maybe I'm socially inept, but when I got my first books, I was a bit lost. How am I supposed to sign those? *Where* do I sign? (Answer: the title page, not the blank page that comes first). What do I say? I started with a boring, boring 'To X, with best wishes, Clémentine Beauvais.' At the beginning I didn't even write the date or the place.

Well, now I know better! Because, dearest writers, being a children's author means you can have awesome fun extras when you sign books:

• Play around with paratext: is there an illustration on the title page? Use it! If it's a character, draw a speech bubble and write your message in it – 'Thanks for coming!' 'Enjoy!' 'Keep reading!' 'Have fun!'.

- Get a personalized stamp – I have a clementine-shaped one – into which you can write the date.
- Get stickers, multicoloured pens, anything that might make your book signing really special. Let the kids pick which colour they'd like.
- If the child has the name of a fruit, flower or anything else that can be doodled, and that you can doodle, then doodle away …
- If the child played a part in the activity during your talk, show that you remember it by mentioning it in your comments.

One last piece of advice: get the child to spell out his or her name. Really, do. Even if she says 'My name's Emma' – just check. There are so many alternative spellings for certain names. If the child is too young to be able to spell their name, ask the nearest adult.

And above all – enjoy. Meeting readers will make you ridiculously happy, proud and giggly. It will also be exhausting and stressful. But hopefully this chapter should have prepared you for the most common questions and problems.

Where to next?

In the final (yes, final!) chapter, we'll talk about meeting other authors, and networking to get your career going, feel less lonely, and have fun with colleagues. Others will make you stronger … so find them out, and find out how, by turning the page now.

24

Networking and getting stronger

Talking shop is authors' favourite thing. And authors talking shop sounds a bit like this:

'Hey, did you know Awesome Editor also writes *The Spiderweb Mysteries* under a pseudonym?'

'No way! I was wondering who that was. She rejected my latest proposal.'

'Did she? What was it about?'

'A love story between the tooth fairy and Rumpelstiltskin.'

'Ah, it must be because she recently contracted Miracle Debut Author on a romance story between Tinkerbell and Jack (of Beanstalk fame). Do you know Miracle Debut Author?'

'No, who is she?'

'You haven't heard? She's only 21! They've bought three books from her for something like £25K a book. Indiscreet Agent told me about it the other night at Big Publisher's Christmas party.'

'Well, let's hope Miracle Debut Author does better than Last Year's Miracle Debut Author – her saga didn't sell at all as expected.'

'Really? I thought it did well!'

'No. Indiscreet Salesperson told me it was a huge flop, but Stressed-Out Publicist is trying to cover up for it by talking about the film rights all the time.'

'Is there going to be a film?'

'There *isn't*. Film rights have been sold, but there isn't going to be a film.'

'I didn't even like that book. Have you filled in your tax return yet?'

'Oh God, *tax return* … My accountant says …'

You get the gist. Authors love to talk shop, and they also love to be just a little bit in awe of some people, and just a little bit snarky about others. But it's all a big family of course, lots of people smiling and laughing and making hearts with their hands … There's a lot of humble or not-so-humble bragging, some back-stabbing, and a healthy dose of competition in publishing. I would lie if I told you that the writerly world is infinitely stretchable, that every newcomer is welcomed with beaming grins and that there is never any jealousy at all.

But when you meet the right people, it just clicks. With some writers, there's no need to pretend you're always working on a masterpiece, always on top of things, always delighted with how your books are doing. With some writers you can talk about your doubts, your problems, your frustrations, and also your little joys and achievements.

As in all jobs, you don't choose your colleagues, but at least with this one you have a choice about who you decide to hang around with. Make the most of that freedom.

Meeting your writerly 'siblings'

One of the best ways of beginning to meet other authors is by asking your agent and editor to introduce you (via Twitter, email or otherwise) to your 'writerly siblings'. That is to say, your agent's other clients, and your editor's other writers, whom they think you'll get on with, or who do a similar sort of literature. It might sound wishful, but you have a good chance of getting on with these writers – because if your agent and/or editor picked them, they might have quite a few things in common with you. And they're easy to get in touch with, because your status relative to theirs is already a little bit 'special': you're not just another debut author, you're their agent's new recruit and your book will be next to theirs in next year's catalogue of their publishing house. Get in touch with them.

This is how I met someone who would become one of my dearest friends-and-colleagues, Julian Sedgwick – who signed with the same agent as mine, and whose trilogy sold to the same publisher at mine, precisely at the same time. Both debut authors, we met up for the first time in a café in Cambridge, and it immediately worked: we were on the same wavelength. Over the years, we've been talking about writing, editing, writing the next book, writing the next book proposal. And also about life beyond writing, of course.

Such friendships are immensely precious. Not only are they what friendship should be like – valuing the person for what they are – but they are also a welcome source of comfort in what can sometimes feel like a very lonely world. Authors, especially children's authors, don't like to admit that things sometimes go wrong, that our careers don't look like what we expected, that we are disappointed in how our books are doing, that we don't feel quite happy. Partners and non-writerly friends, however adorable and supportive, don't always understand; they'll say, 'Well, write something else, then!' if you say you're not happy with what you're writing – not realizing that your editor precisely doesn't *want* you to write anything else. This is the kind of conversation you can have with other writers.

Of course, as always, beware – you can't tell other writers *everything*. If you've got a secret book deal that hasn't been announced yet, don't tell other writers – even 'unofficially' or 'confidentially'. If you know something embarrassing or problematic about another author, keep it to yourself. It's not great to broadcast to other authors that Carnegie Winner has now got depression and can't deliver her next manuscript – even if your agent or editor very unprofessionally let it slip. And if you yourself are having issues and aren't sure that you can deliver your next manuscript on time, your agent should be told, not your writer friend. It's a very small world and in the industry, things get around – you'd be surprised how fast.

> ## Key idea
>
>
> Don't gossip about others, and don't give your colleagues, albeit friendly, good reasons to gossip about you.

Writers' networks and associations

To meet more authors, Twitter and Facebook are always good ideas, as well as blog networking. But you might also want to have more sustained conversations (and some real-life ones!) with other children's authors. For that purpose, it can be very helpful to be part of a group or society of authors. Don't forget to claim the membership fee against tax.

- **SCBWI,** which you can join even as an unpublished author, has subgroups everywhere in the UK and beyond, and local groups regularly organize events – from drinks at a pub to weekend retreats. Get in touch with the closest SCBWI group and you'll meet plenty of people – unpublished as well as published.

- Joining **the Society of Authors** is always a good idea. It can provide legal advice, augment your visibility, and you will be in touch with authors of all kinds of literature (including non-fiction), all around the country. You will also be kept aware of opportunities for bursaries, retreats, competitions, and other useful information.

- There are many **children's literature-specific author associations and societies,** some more 'secret' than others. Author Allsorts may or may not invite you to join them. The Scattered Authors' Society, as it says, 'doesn't advertise; but word gets around'. Some groups are even more specific: writers of children's historical fiction, YA groups (those are becoming increasingly important, especially since the reign of Children's Laureate Malorie Blackman), picturebook writers and illustrators ... you will discover them as you hop from blog to blog and website to website.

- Some of these more or less informal societies have their own **blog,** and getting a slot on these often-visited platforms can be a great opportunity for you to get in touch with more authors and potential readers, and have your voice heard. An Awfully Big Blog Adventure (ABBA) is the Scattered Authors' Society's blog, The History Girls publishes blog posts on historical fiction for children, and Author Allsorts also has a daily blog.

- Another solution is, of course, to create **your own informal gathering of local authors**. Ask your local bookstore, spread the word on Twitter and Facebook, and send an email around to other authors, offering to meet up. A nice, quiet pub in the evening is probably the best option. These meetings could grow into monthly or bi-monthly meet-ups. You could organize a 'Christmas lunch' – after all, not working in an office shouldn't mean you don't get a Christmas lunch! Be creative, generous and open. Make things easier for everyone by setting up Doodle polls or Facebook events.

Writing retreats and residencies

Within such groups and societies, and sometimes through other means, it's possible to go on writing retreats with other authors. These retreats can consist of many things:

- **Actual monk-like life:** you and the other authors, eating together but working on your manuscripts the rest of the time. Where? A lighthouse in Cornwall, a farmyard on the Isle of Skye, with no Internet connection, for a week.
- **A career-energizing weekend:** you and other authors, listening to invited speakers, exchanging ideas, working on potential collaborations.
- **Just good fun:** you and other authors eating cake, talking shop, dancing until three in the morning and nursing your hangover the next day over your manuscripts.

Retreats can be a welcome break from an otherwise quite lonely time with your writing.

The first type I described is closer to a residency, and indeed becoming a writer-in-residence somewhere can be something you might aspire to. Some universities, such as Bath Spa, have writers-in-residence to support their creative writing courses – though you may have to wait until you're a bit more famous before they take you on. More modest writer residencies might offer you money and accommodation for a day or two a week in exchange for your writing and giving talks or seminars to local schools or to local aspiring writers. Very prestigious residencies, such as the McDowell Colony in the United States, offer significant amounts of money and a monastery-like isolation in the middle of the woods. They are not always very children's writer friendly, but you might as well apply – you never know. Obtaining residencies, especially prestigious ones, is a good way to increase your productivity and your reputation. If you are free enough that you can leave your city, county or country for two weeks to six months, by all means look for residencies.

Collaboration with other authors

One of the most amazing things to come out of meeting other writers and illustrators is collaboration. You might find yourself stuck on a train with a random author from a book festival. You might talk about something that you're vaguely thinking about writing, and the other writer might go, 'Hey, that's funny – I was thinking about something similar … but also different …' 'What if we wrote it together?'

Or, in the case of an illustrator, that other person might start doodling some funny things on a napkin while you talk about your ideas …

Works written in collaboration with other authors can take several forms:

- stories written 'with four hands', but with no clear indication of who wrote what: a blended narrator
- stories with two narrators, each of which we might suspect 'belongs' to each author
- books of short stories around the same theme, or where each chapter is written by a different author.

One of my French novels is a political tale written with six other authors. It all started with an email from one of them: 'Hey, girls – how about we did something in common? I have no idea what, but let's talk.' So we talked. By email – sometimes a hundred a day! – on a special forum we'd created, and by chatting about it, too. A few weeks later, we'd had an idea: seven stories, about seven families (one chapter per family and per author), taking place over a week after the rise to power of a despotic government. We each wrote a chapter, and then each edited another person's chapter. Selling the book was not easy – some publishers didn't like all the chapters – but we eventually did and the book was very successful. Of course, it isn't completely coincidental, since having seven people promoting it at the same time can only help sales …

Talk to your agent and editor if you're considering collaborating with another author. They might also suggest that you take part in, for instance, a volume of short stories or tales for children. Highly successful books, such as *Losing It*, are collections of short stories by famous authors, and there are equivalents by less famous ones. Generally around one theme (Halloween or Christmas stories, teenage romance, travels …), these books can be a very good way of becoming better known, and of trying your hand at a different genre or format.

Dealing with jealousy (yours and other people's)

Whatever you do, from the moment you get in touch with other authors – aspiring, published and established – you're exposing yourself to jealousy. Not necessarily your own. If you're confident, kind and happy, there's no reason why you should be particularly jealous of others. But even the toughest, most generous writer can feel down at times when they're not managing to write, or to get a next contract, or to be nominated for an award, and they see torrents of tweets about other people's film rights, multiple-book deals, and book prizes for frankly quite rubbish stories. There's nothing wrong with that, it's only natural.

Here are a few ways of dealing with your own jealousy towards other people's work:

- Remember that social networks emphasize successes and never talk about failures. While you're busy wondering why your book seems to be the only one that never gets nominated, a hundred other authors are doing so, too. But they're not tweeting about it, of course. The only people tweeting about awards are people who are nominated for them, and their editors and agents. And those tweets get retweeted. You are seeing only the small percentage of writers who are temporarily having all the fun.

- Similarly, these days, you hear about many, many, many people's good news. Without the Internet, you would never have heard about this unknown 25-year-old from Dakota getting a four-book deal with Simon & Schuster. It probably wouldn't have reached your ears until her books became actually impossible to ignore. And this might never even have happened; you quickly forget about people whose good news you agonized over, when it turns out that the book just doesn't do well or does just reasonably.

- The life of a published writer is exhausting, because it's an alternation of little joys ('Hurrah! Good review!') and little sadnesses ('Oh no, YA book project rejected again'). Sometimes there are bigger joys ('Amazing! US rights sold!') and bigger sadnesses ('Oh damn, book series discontinued'). Again, you're getting only a deformed image of that if you follow people on Twitter or Facebook. The little joys will be blown up out of proportion, and every review will look like The. Best. Thing. Ever. And the bigger joys are going to be Just Oh My God You Guys I Have to Tell You Something But First I Must Make You Wait For It. There will be BIG REVEALS of information that really isn't quite so important ('In three days you will hear something HUGE' and it's film rights; OK, good news, but there will probably never be a film, and if there is, it will be in three years' time). Authors are told to make announcements, to broadcast their news in the most lyrical way possible. Everything is blown out of proportion. Don't fall into the trap of believing that it's always as extraordinary as people say.

- Everyone writes different things. It's helpful to remember that, because it can be tempting to think that someone else is a 'better writer' because they're getting more deals, more foreign rights and more reviews. Actually, it could simply be that their book is striking a chord at the moment because it's in a genre that sells and with a timely theme. Not that you shouldn't strive to do that, too, but you wouldn't have written that book in the first place. Try to be happy for them.

- Only compare what's comparable. Of course your picturebook series isn't going to get Hollywood film rights. Of course your action-packed spy story isn't going to be nominated for the Carnegie. You have made a number of choices which aren't compatible with a large number of award bodies, foreign-rights sales, bloggers and so on. And everyone knows that. Your editor will not be expecting as many reviews for your chapter book as they would be for a YA novel, because yours just isn't the kind of book that gets reviewed online.

- Train yourself to ignore all of this and de-dramatize. Practise positive thinking. This isn't just about jealousy, but about all the negative thoughts which will doubtlessly begin to nag you after a few weeks as a published author. Stop looking compulsively at Twitter all the time; go for a walk. Distance yourself from other people's good news; learn to congratulate them and move on. Work, work, work. Focus on your own work.

But you have to expect that your own successes will be the object of other people's jealousy, too, and that can be a terrifying realization. Especially if you're young, if you already work in publishing, or if you can be in any way suspected of nepotism, you might encounter some coldness on the part of other authors. You might be a target of their insecurities. And unpublished authors might now start to gossip about how you got your book deal, and disparage your work. What can you do to deflate *their* jealousy?

- Remain extremely humble at all times, especially on social networks. Don't humble-brag, and don't brag. Share your good news, sure; but also share many other things, and don't wax lyrical about minor things. Don't ardently retweet every piece of praise that comes your way. Don't be egocentric: not everyone's interested in you. Don't talk about your books all the time when you meet people in real life, even if they seem interested: they might just be acting polite. In short, don't have a bad attitude.

- Share other people's good news, too, and your excitement and interest in their work. Do it sincerely, not automatically; do it only when you truly believe that they've written a great book, or when you're genuinely excited about their next book. Congratulate people, and encourage aspiring writers. Be generous with your time and attention, and don't patronize anyone. Ask people questions about how their work is going, and show them that this matters to you; remember what they're currently writing and follow it up with them.

- Share your doubts and fears as well as your joys and pride. Be the sincere, heartfelt voice on Twitter, honest about the difficulties of this writing life, and capable of articulating them without subtly turning it into hidden bragging. If you've failed, and the failure makes a good story or a cautionary tale, tell it.

Where to next?

What next, indeed, now that we've reached the end of this book's many chapters? A conclusion, of course, with some last snippets of advice and a few more tips for the rest of your career. And some good wishes for luck, and joy, and passion, and for favourable auguries for your work. Or at least, may you have enough to counterbalance the inevitable twists of fate and unlucky strikes – and to be able to incorporate everything you've learned into your work even more effectively.

Conclusion

I would like this conclusion to be upbeat and fun – hurrah, you're a published writer! Children are reading your book as we speak! But it would be unfair not to mention the inevitable baby-blues you'll get, at some point, when your darling book is out there, being read, skim-read, reviewed. Forgotten. You'll sometimes wonder – is that really what I wanted? Why didn't *more things* happen? You *will* feel disappointed. You will sometimes also feel like an impostor. Both of these things might happen at the same time. When people say they like your book, you'll wonder whether they're telling the truth; when people say they don't like your book, you'll feel that they're doing so out of spite. You'll love your books and hate them; you'll feel protective towards them and also strangely distanced.

You'll become a schizophrenic writer, which is, really, the only kind of writer there ever is.

Sometimes all will be well – sunny afternoons of whooping word counts, typing under the walnut tree in your friend's garden; sometimes all will be rubbish – there will be a three-star review on GoodReads, a 'terrible' other book getting a film deal, or simply a child's polite nod when their parent asks him, in front of you, if he liked your book – he *clearly* didn't. Those afternoons will be dark and sad.

Yes, you'll become a bit of a diva.

But in the middle of all this melodrama of being a published writer, here are a few things you shouldn't forget:

DON'T FORGET YOUR NEXT DEADLINE

You will always have a deadline from now on. Deadline for your next book proposal, deadline for your next manuscript, deadline for your next edits. You can't let yourself be sidetracked by gloomy thoughts or moments of elation; keep calm and carry on. You are responsible for your work and career. Your editor now relies on you to do the job properly, your agent now relies on you to deliver your manuscript on time, your readers rely on you to tell them the next story. It's not about you and your feelings any more: it's about your career.

DON'T FORGET TO BE ADVENTUROUS

Diversify, update, rebrand – and keep going. If one series doesn't work out, if you have to change editor, publishing house or agent, if you suddenly decide you want to write erotica for the third age … think. Dare. Challenge yourself. Write under a pseudonym.

Try new things: a screenwriting summer course, a drama workshop, a writing trip to Denmark. Read new books: scientific non-fiction, autobiographies of intellectual women, graphic novels about war. Write differently – impose new rules on yourself. Write every day, in secret, 500 words of a Completely Different Project. Write short stories. Write a picturebook. Pick a chapter at random in the second part of this book and commit to writing in the format that it advocates.

DON'T FORGET REALITY CHECKS

The hashtag 'first-world problems' has become hackneyed (and supposedly 'funny') now, but there's a lot of truth in it. When you catch yourself thinking your world has collapsed because of a hateful tweet, a poor review or because your book failed to win an award, it's time for a reality check. You're earning money doing something you love doing. You're sitting at a desk, cats wrapped around your ankles, warm tea at your side, making up stories for other people to read. Your situation is ludicrously comfortable. Stop whimpering – work. You are more privileged than the vast majority of people in the world.

DON'T FORGET TO HELP BUDDING WRITERS

You were once there; you know what it feels like. Whenever possible, help budding writers. Help them with their writing, help them find an agent, help them read the right things. Recommend books to them (*cough* … like this one … *cough*), recommend blogs and websites. Offer to read their writing. Give them honest and kind advice. Don't shy away from telling them that being a published writer is hard work; don't break their dreams, but help them be more rational.

> ## Key idea
>
>
> Celebrate the diversity and strengths of new people coming into this career. If you like their work, encourage them and help them achieve what they would like to achieve.

DON'T FORGET TO HAVE FUN

That one speaks for itself, but it's surprisingly easy to forget when there are suddenly contracts and deadlines to negotiate …

DON'T FORGET THE PRIDE AND JOY OF WRITING FOR CHILDREN

Be proud of your work and the work of others. But be tough, too – don't tolerate low-quality stuff, don't praise mediocre pieces because you feel it would help your career. Extol the pleasures and the beauty of children's literature; become a champion of children's books. Make people understand that we need high-quality literature for children. Defend your work. Don't smile demurely when people make sarcastic remarks about children's books. Fight for our cause!

Whenever possible, oppose the type of literature for children that considers children to be brainless consumers. Oppose publishing practices that dumb down children's literature, and that make it sexist, racist and classist. Celebrate publishers and writers who have the intelligence not to talk down to children, and who are committed to giving children an unforgettable childhood.

Give your own child readers that unforgettable childhood, too. You have a power that very few other authors enjoy: that of leaving your imprint on their imaginations, however discreet, so that even in 70 years' time, when your book has all but fallen into oblivion, there will remain something of it in the actions and thoughts of a venerable old pensioner.

Bibliography

CHILDREN'S AND YOUNG ADULT BOOKS MENTIONED

CLASSICS

Alcott, Louisa May. 2012/1868. *Little Women*. London: Vintage.

Blume, Judy. 2005/1975. *Forever*. London: Pan Macmillan.

Briggs, Raymond. 2013/1978. *The Snowman*. London: Puffin.

de Brunhoff, Jean. 2008/1933. *The Story of Babar*, and others. Translated by M.S. Haas. London: Egmont.

Buckeridge, Anthony. 2001/1953. *Jennings Goes to School*, and others. Kelly Bray: Stratus.

Dahl, Roald. 2008/1978. *The Enormous Crocodile*. London: Puffin.

Galbraith, Frank and Ernestine. 1994/1948. *Cheaper by the Dozen*. New York: HarperCollins.

Grimm, Jakob and Wilhelm. 2007/1812. *The Complete Fairy Tales*. Translated by J. Zipes. London: Vintage.

Gripari, Pierre. 2013/1967. *The Good Little Devil, and Other Tales*. London: Pushkin.

Hergé. 1975/1963. *The Castafiore Emerald*. Translated by L. Lonsdale-Cooper and M. Turner. London: Egmont.

Juster, Norton. 2008/1961. *The Phantom Tollbooth*. London: HarperCollins.

L'Engle, Madeleine. 2007/1963. *A Wrinkle in Time*. London: Puffin.

Lindgren, Astrid. 2012/1945. *Pippi Longstocking*, and others. Oxford: Oxford University Press.

Lionni, Leo. 1996/1959. *Little Blue and Little Yellow*. New York: William Morrow.

Milne, A.A. 1989. *Winnie-the-Pooh*. London: Mammoth.

Murphy, Jill. 2013/1974. *The Worst Witch*, and others. London: Puffin.

Nesbit, E. 2009/1899. *The Story of the Treasure-Seekers*. London: Hesperus.

de Saint-Exupéry, Antoine. 2009/1945. *The Little Prince*. Translated by K. Woods. London: Egmont.

Pearce, Philippa. 2008/1956. *Tom's Midnight Garden*. Oxford: Oxford University Press.

Pienkowski, Jan. 2005/1970. *The Haunted House*. London: Walker.

Sendak, Maurice. 2012/ 1963. *Where the Wild Things Are*. London: HarperCollins.

Sewell, Anna. 1998/1877. *Black Beauty*. London: Wordsworth.

Tolkien, J.R.R. 1987/1937. *The Hobbit*. London: Unwin Hyman.

Verne, Jules. 2011/1865. *From the Earth to the Moon*. Ware: Wordsworth.

White, E.B. 1986/1952. *Charlotte's Web*. Bath: Chivers.

Williams, Margery. 2007/1922. *The Velveteen Rabbit*. London: Egmont.

CONTEMPORARY CHILDREN'S AND YOUNG ADULT FICTION

Beauvais, Clémentine. 2013. *Sleuth on Skates*, and others. London: Hodder.

Beauvais, Clémentine. 2014. *The Royal Baby-sitters*, and others. London: Bloomsbury.

Blackman, Malorie. 2001. *Noughts and Crosses*, and others. London: Corgi.

Brahmachari, Sita. 2011. *Artichoke Hearts*. London: Macmillan.

Brahmachari, Sita. 2012. *Jasmine Skies*. London: Macmillan.

Brahmachari, Sita. 2013. *Kite Spirit*. London: Macmillan.

Burgess, Melvin. 1997. *Junk*. London: Puffin.

Caldecott, Elen. 2013. *The Great Ice-Cream Heist*. London: Bloomsbury.

Christopher, Lucy. 2009. *Stolen*. Frome: Chickenhouse.

Collins, Suzanne. 2008. *The Hunger Games*, and others. New York: Scholastic.

Cormier, Robert. 1988. *Fade*. New York: Delacorte.

Cowell, Cressida. 2003. *How to Train Your Dragon*, and others. London: Hodder.

Crossan, Sarah. 2012. *The Weight of Water*. London: Bloomsbury.

Crossan, Sarah. 2013. *Breathe*. London: Bloomsbury.

Earl, Esther. 2014. *This Star Won't Go Out*. London: Penguin.

Fine, Anne. 1999. *Madame Doubtfire*. London: Penguin.

Gaiman, Neil. 2002. *Coraline*. London: Bloomsbury.

Gavin, Rohan. 2014. *Knightley and Son*. London: Bloomsbury.

Gayton, Sam. 2012. *The Snow Merchant*. London: Andersen.

Gidwitz, Adam. 2011. *A Tale Dark and Grimm*. London: Andersen.

Green, John. 2012. *The Fault in Our Stars*. London: Penguin.

Haddon, Mark. 2004. *The Curious Incident of the Dog in the Night-time*. London: Vintage.

Hartnett, Sonya. 2013. *The Midnight Zoo*. London: Walker.

Higson, Charlie. 2005. *Silverfin*, and others (*Young Bond*). London: Puffin.

Horowitz, Anthony. 2003. *Stormbreakers*, and others (*Alex Rider*). London: Walker.

Kinney, Jeff. 2007. *Diary of a Wimpy Kid*, and others. London: Puffin.

Lowry, Lois. 1994. *The Giver*. London: HarperCollins.

McCaughrean, Geraldine. *Peter Pan in Scarlet*. Oxford: Oxford University Press.

McGowan, Anthony. 2006. *Henry Tumour*. London: Doubleday.

McKay, Hilary. 2001. *Saffy's Angel*. London: Hodder.

Meyer, Stephenie. 2011. *Twilight*, and others. London: Little, Brown.

Morpurgo, Michael. 1982. *War Horse*. London: Egmont.

Muchamore, Robert. 2004. *The Recruit*, and others (*CHERUB*). London: Hodder.

Ness, Patrick. 2009. *The Knife of Never Letting Go*, and others. London: Walker.

Ness, Patrick. 2013. *A Monster Calls*. London: Walker.

Newman, John. 2010. *Mimi*. London: Bloomsbury.

Oliver, Lauren. 2011. *Delirium*, and others. London: Hodder and Stoughton.

Palacio, R.J. 2013. *Wonder*. London: Random.

Paolini, Christopher. 2005. *Eragon*, and others. London: Corgi.

Pass, Emma. 2013. *ACID*. London: Corgi.

Priestley, Chris. 2007. *Uncle Montague's Tales of Terror*, and others. London: Bloomsbury.

Pullman, Philip. 1995–2000. *His Dark Materials* trilogy. London: Everyman.

Rennison, Louise. 2001. *Angus, Thongs and Full-frontal Snogging*, and others. London: Scholastic.

Rosoff, Meg. 2004. *How I Live Now*. London: Penguin.

Rowling, J.K. 1997–2007. *Harry Potter and the Philosopher's Stone*, and others. London: Bloomsbury.

Rowling, J.K. 2008. *The Tales of Beedle the Bard*. London: Bloomsbury.

Schroeder, Lisa. 2008. *I Heart You, You Haunt Me*. New York: Simon & Schuster.

Sedgwick, Julian. 2013. *The Black Dragon*, and others (*Mysterium*). London: Hodder.

Sedgwick, Marcus. 2009. *Flood and Fang*, and others (*Raven Mysteries*). London: Orion.

Sedgwick, Marcus. 2013. *She Is Not Invisible*. London: Orion.

Shannon, Samantha. 2013. *The Bone Season*. London: Bloomsbury.

Shelton, David. 2012. *A Boy and a Bear in a Boat*. London: David Fickling.

Snicket, Lemony. 1999. *The Bad Beginning*, and others (*A Series of Unfortunate Events*). New York: HarperCollins.

Stead, Rebecca. 2011. *When You Reach Me*. London: Andersen.

Stine, R.L. 1994. *Night of the Living Dummy*, and others (*Goosebumps*). London: Scholastic.

Stroud, Jonathan. 2005. *The Amulet of Samarkand*, and others (*Bartimaeus Sequence*). London: Doubleday.

Suzuma, Tabitha. 2010. *Forbidden*. London: Random.

Terry, Teri. 2012. *Slated*, and others. London: Orchard.

Thomas, Valerie and Paul Korky. 1986. *Winnie the Witch*, and others. Oxford: Oxford University Press.

Walliams, David. 2013. *Demon Dentist*. London: HarperCollins.

Wilson, Jacqueline. 1998. *Double Act/Bad Girls*. London: Corgi.

Wilson, Jacqueline. 1998. *The Lottie Project*. London: Corgi.

Wilson, Jacqueline. 2012. *Four Children and It*. London: Puffin.

PICTUREBOOKS AND COMICS

Ahlberg, Janet and Allan. 1999. *The Jolly Postman*. London: Puffin.

Ahlberg, Janet and Allan. 1999. *Each Peach Pear Plum*. London: Puffin.

Child, Lauren. 2005. *I Am Too Absolutely Small for School*, and others. London: Candlewick.

Cole, Babette. 1986. *Princess Smartypants*. London: Hamish Hamilton.

Corentin, Philippe. 2003. *Plouf!* Paris: L'école des loisirs.

Cronin, Doreen and Betsy Lewin. 2002. *Click, Clack, Moo! Cows That Type*. London: Simon & Schuster.

Blake, Quentin. 1995. *Clown*. London: Cape.

Bravi, Soledad. 2010. *The Noise Book*. London: Gecko.

Browne, Anthony. 1983. *Gorilla*. London: McRae.

Browne, Anthony. 1986. *Piggybook*. London: McRae.

Browne, Anthony. 1989. *The Tunnel*. London: MacRae.

Browne, Anthony. 1994. *Zoo*. London: Red Fox.

Browne, Anthony. 1998. *Voices in the Park*. London: Corgi.

Burningham, John. 1984. *Granpa*. London: Cape.

Donaldson, Julia and Alex Scheffler. 1999. *The Gruffalo*. London: Macmillan.

Erlbruch, Wolf. 2008. *Duck, Death and the Tulip*. Translated by C. Chidgey. London: Gecko.

Frisch, Aaron and Roberto Innocenti. 2012. *The Girl in Red*. North Mankato: Creative Editions.

Ormerod, Jan. 1981. *Sunshine*. London: Frances Lincoln.

Ormerod, Jan. 1982. *Moonlight*. London: Frances Lincoln.

Pinkney, Jerry. 2009. *The Lion and the Mouse*. New York: Little Brown.

Rosen, Michael and Quentin Blake. 2005. *Michael Rosen's Sad Book*. London: Candlewick.

Scieszka, Jon and Lane Smith. 1989. *The True Story of the Three Little Pigs*. London: Puffin.

Smith, Alex T. 2011. *Claude in the City*, and others. London: Hodder.

Tan, Shaun. 2010. *The Red Tree*. Melbourne: Lothian.

Tullet, Hervé. 2011. *Press Here*. London: Chronicle.

Willems, Mo. 2004. *Don't Let the Pigeon Drive the Bus!*, and others. London: Walker.

Winterson, Jeanette and Jane Ray. 2004. *The King of Capri*. London: Bloomsbury.

POETRY

Milne, A.A. 1989/1924. *When We Were Very Young*. London: Egmont.

Michael Rosen's A to Z: The Best Children's Poetry. London: Puffin.

Stevenson, Robert Louis. 2008/1885. *A Child's Garden of Verses*. London: Puffin.

Accessible academic texts on literature, children's literature and picturebooks

Arizpe, Evelyn and Styles, Morag. 2003. *Children Reading Pictures: Interpreting Visual Texts*. London: RoutledgeFalmer.

Bader, Barbara. 1976. *American Picturebooks from Noah's Ark to The Beast Within*. New York: Macmillan.

Booker, Christopher. 2004. *The Seven Basic Plots*. London: Continuum.

Campbell, Joseph. 2008/1949. *The Hero with a Thousand Faces*. Novato: New World Library.

Grenby, Matthew O. and Immel, Andrea (eds). 2009. *The Cambridge Companion to Children's Literature*. Cambridge: Cambridge University Press.

Hollindale, Peter. 1988. *Ideology and the Children's Book*. Stroud: Thimble Press.

Hollindale, Peter. 1997. *Signs of Childness in Children's Books*. Stroud: Thimble Press.

Kokkola, Lydia. 2013. *Fictions of Adolescent Carnality: Sexy Sinners and Delinquent Deviants*. Amsterdam: John Benjamins.

McCloud, Scott. 1994. *Understanding Comics: The Invisible Art*. New York: HarperPerennial.

Mickenberg, Julia and Nel, Philip. 2008. *Tales for Little Rebels: A Collection of Radical Children's Literature*. New York: New York University Press.

Nikolajeva, Maria and Scott, Carole. 2001. *How Picturebooks Work*. New York: Garland.

Nikolajeva, Maria. 2005. *Aesthetic Approaches to Children's Literature: An Introduction*. Oxford: Scarecrow.

Nodelman, Perry. 1988. *Words about Pictures: The Narrative Art of Children's Picturebooks*. Athens, GA: University of Georgia Press.

Nodelman, Perry. 2008. *The Hidden Adult: Defining Children's Literature*. Baltimore: Johns Hopkins University Press.

Tatar, Maria. 2009. *Enchanted Hunters: The Power of Stories in Childhood*. New York: W.W. Norton.

Trites, Roberta Seelinger. 2000. *Disturbing the Universe: Power and Repression in Adolescent Literature*. Iowa City: University of Iowa Press.

Reynolds, Kimberley. 2011. *Children's Literature: A Very Short Introduction*. Oxford: Oxford University Press.

Rose, Jacqueline. 1984. *The Case of Peter Pan. Or, the Impossibility of Children's Fiction*. London: Macmillan.

Stephens, John. 1992. *Language and Ideology in Children's Fiction*. London: Pearson.

Watson, Victor. 2000. *Reading Series Fiction*. London: RoutledgeFalmer.

Zipes, Jack. 2001. *Sticks and Stones: The Troublesome Success of Children's Literature from Slovenly Peter to Harry Potter*. London: Routledge.

Resources on creative writing, project-managing and publishing

An Awfully Big Blog Adventure: http://awfullybigblogadventure.blogspot.co.uk/

Authors Allsorts: http://authorallsorts.wordpress.com/

King, Stephen. 2012. *On Writing: A Memoir of the Craft*. London: Hodder.

Perry, John. 2012. *The Art of Procrastination: A Guide to Effective Dawdling*. New York: Workman Publishing.

Publisher Weekly: http://www.publishersweekly.com/

Preditors and Editors: http://pred-ed.com/

Society of Authors: http://www.societyofauthors.org/

Society of Children's Book Writers and Illustrators: http://www.scbwi.org/

Strunk, William and E.B. White. 2000/1935. *The Elements of Style*. London: Longman.

The Children's Writers' & Artists' Yearbook. London: Bloomsbury.

Writer Unboxed: http://writerunboxed.com/

Zinsser, William. 2006/1976. *On Writing Well*. New York: HarperCollins.

Index